Wissenschaftliche Untersuchungen
zum Neuen Testament · 2. Reihe

Herausgeber / Editor
Jörg Frey (München)

Mitherausgeber / Associate Editors
Friedrich Avemarie (Marburg)
Markus Bockmuehl (Oxford)
Hans-Josef Klauck (Chicago, IL)

270

Jeremy W. Barrier

The Acts of Paul and Thecla

A Critical Introduction and Commentary

Mohr Siebeck

JEREMY W. BARRIER, born 1979; BA in Mathematics and Natural Science; MA in New Testament from Freed-Hardeman University; 2008 PhD from Brite Divinity School, Texas Christian University; Assistant Professor in Biblical Literature at Heritage Christian University, Florence, AL.

BS
2880
.P4
B27
2009

ISBN 978-3-16-149998-2

ISSN 0340-9570 (Wissenschaftliche Untersuchungen zum Neuen Testament, 2. Reihe)

Die Deutsche Nationalbibliothek lists this publication in the Deutsche Nationalbibliographie; detailed bibliographic data is available in the Internet at *http://dnb.d-nb.de.*

The book was printed by Gulde Druck in Tübingen on non-aging paper and bound by Buchbinderei Held in Rottenburg.

Printed in Germany.

For my mother, Mary Janet Barrier

Acknowledgements

This project has been an incredible journey for me up to this point. It has taken me through my doctoral studies at Brite Divinity School, libraries across North America and Europe, Turkey, Greece, and Italy for research, various national and international SBL conferences, an AELAC (Association pour l'étude de la littérature apocryphe chrétienne) meeting in Bex, Switzerland, and the 2nd International Summer School in Coptic Papyrology in Leipzig, Germany (thanks to the encouragement of Carl R. Holladay and the assistance of the Christian Scholarship Foundation, Inc.). So much of the research has been dependent upon so many people through their assistance, generosity, and willingness to offer some charitable gesture toward me.

There are so many people who have been a source of encouragement to me, I am afraid that I will forget everyone. So, first and foremost, I want to thank my family; my spouse Robin, and also my children, Samuel and Sophia, who have been a constant stress relief to me with their smiles. Robin has been incredibly patient with me, as I often found myself heading back over to the office late in the evening to work on the book. In addition, I am also extremely grateful to my parents, Wayne and Janet Barrier, who have been so instrumental in encouraging me to dream, think, work hard, and finally complete my doctoral education. I am also thankful to brothers and sister and their families; Jenny, Harvey (especially for the ribs), Lan, Jamie, Katie, Joey, Anna, Gracie, and Noah. One of the greatest counterweights to my research has been the wonderful luxury of leaving my studies for a few days and spending time with my family, so that we can discuss the Pine Hill Haints, Tanner, the most recent Barcelona win, and everything else that has nothing to do with Paul and Thecla! I am also thankful for the support offered by Robin's parents, Larry and Delba Samuels, for the many times that they allowed Robin and I to come with the kids, so that I could fly out to Texas, as I was completing my dissertation at Brite Divinity School. Everyone has been very encouraging and helpful.

As I also mentioned in my dissertation, there have also been many people who have been instrumental in helping me to complete my dissertation, and then to develop it into this tome. For five years I traveled back and forth to Fort Worth, Texas, and numerous people helped me in many ways to accomplish this task, so, thanks go to everyone at Jacks Creek for much encouragement and financial help, Wade and Julie Osburn for books and burritos, Rachel Steele and Laura Sanders-Wilson for helping Robin with the kids, for the workers at DFW, who fast-tracked me through security checks and held airplanes for me (more than once or twice), Charles and Ruth Webb, Clay and Katie Chapman, Sheila Owens at HUGSR, Bill, Peggy, Sunshine, and Liberty, Joey and Kay Delay, Joe and Ramay Noles, David Warren (many prayers), A-J Levine for advising and encouragement, Heritage Christian University, Larry Welborn (thanks for encouraging me to dream), Nathan Guy (my best friend), Michael Jackson at HCU (thanks for all of the tech help), Terry Edwards, North Carolina, Thomas and June Barrier, and many others that I am failing to remember by name.

I have also been greatly encouraged by the assistance of David Balch, Warren Carter, and Lyn Osiek. I am so thankful that Lyn had the insight to be able to help me narrow down a topic, and then guide me through the process with many edits and revisions. Peter Dunn has been especially encouraging, precise as an editor, and an indispensible colleague as he has welcomed me as a friend and scholar into the many discussions surrounding the *Acts of Paul and Thecla*. I am very grateful. I am also grateful for his willingness to introduce me to his friend and mentor, Willy Rordorf, who was also helpful to me in this project. I assume full credit for my inability to catch every error and mistake. Those who have read and edited have been wonderful, but I fear there is still much that could be redone or reconsidered. Last, but not least, this effort is part of my devotion and service to God, whom I honor and revere above all else.

July 2009   Jeremy Wade Barrier

Table of Contents

Part I
Introduction

Part II
Commenatry on the *Acts of Paul* 3–4

Abbreviations

3 Cor	*3 Corinthians*
AA	*Acts of Andrew*
AAA	Richard Adelbert Lipsius and Maximillian Bonnet, *Acta apostolorum apocrypha* (Leipzig: Hermann Mendelssohn, 1891–1903; Reprint, Hildenscheim: G. Olms Verlagsbuchhandlung, 1959).
AAApos	*Apocryphal Acts of the Apostles*
AJ	*Acts of John*
ANT	Elliot, J. K, *The Apocryphal New Testament: A Collection of Apocryphal Christian Literature in an English Translation* (Oxford: Clarendon Press, 1993).
AP	*Acts of Paul*
APt	*Acts of Peter*
APTh	*Acts of Paul and Thecla*
ATh	*Acts of Thomas*
ATit	*Acts of Titus*
ÉAC	*Écrits apocryphes chrétiens.* Edited by François Bovon and Pierre Geoltrain with an Index by J. Voicu. Bibliothèque de la Pléiade. Saint Herblain: Gallimard, 1997.
MPl	*Martyrdom of Paul*
NTApoc	*New Testament Apocrypha* (eds. Edgar Hennecke, Wilhelm Schneemelcher, and Robert McLachlan Wilson; trans. R. McL. Wilson; 2 vols.; Rev. ed.; James Clarke & Co.: Cambridge; Philadelphia: Westminster/John Knox Press, 1992).
ΠΠ	Carl Schmidt, *ΠΡΑΞΕΙΣ ΠΑΥΛΟΥ: Acta Pauli: Nach dem Papyrus der Hamburger Staats und Universitäts-Bibliothek* (Glüchstadt und Hamburg: J.J. Augustin, 1936).
PPM	Ida Baldassarre, ed., *Pompei: Pitture e Mosaici* (10 vols.; Roma: Instituto della Enciclopedia Italiana, 1994).

Textual Witnesses[1]

Abbreviation/Name/Location/Date/Publication

Greek Manuscripts and Papyrus Fragments

$\mathfrak{P}^1$ — Hamburg Papyrus (BHG 1451*), Hamburger Staats und Universitäts-Bibliothek, Hamburg; III–IV CE; Carl Schmidt and Wilhelm Schubart. *ΠΡΑΞΕΙΣ ΠΑΥΛΟΥ: Acta Pauli nach dem Papyrus der Hamburger Staats und Universitäts-Bibliothek.* Glückstadt and Hamburg: J. J. Augustin, 1936.

$\mathfrak{P}^2$ — Michigan Papyri 1317 and 3788/Berlin Papyrus 13893
– Michigan Papyri 1317, University of Michigan, Ann Arbor, Michigan; III–IV CE; H. A. Sanders. "A Fragment of the *Acta Pauli* in the Michigan Collection." *HTR* 31 (1938): 70–90;
– Michigan Papyri 3788, University of Michigan, Ann Arbor, Michigan; III–IV CE; H. A. Sanders. "Three Theological Fragments." *HTR* 36 (1943): 165–67; Colin H. Roberts. "A Fragment of an Uncanonical Gospel." *JTS* 47 (1946): 56–7; Colin H. Roberts. "The Acta Pauli: A New Fragment." *JTS* 47 (1946) 196–99; W. D. McHardy. "A Papyrus Fragment of the *Acta Pauli.*" *ET* 58 (1947): 279.

---

[1] See Mauritii Geerard, ed., "Acta Pauli," *Clavis Apocryphum Novi Testamenti* (Corpus Christianorum. Turnhout: Brepols, 1992) 117–26 for a more complete listing of manuscripts and papyri of the *AP*. The only publication lacking in his work is the more recent *editio princeps* of Bodmer XLI (Cop^B) completed by Rodolphe Kasser and Philippe Luisier, "Le Bodmer XLI en Édition Princeps l'Épisode d'Èphèse des *Acta Pauli* en Copte et en Traduction," *Mus* 117 (2004): 281–384. Also, the abbreviations follow those found in (1) Peter W. Dunn, "The *Acts of Paul* and the Pauline Legacy in the Second Century," (Ph.D. diss., University of Cambridge, 1996) x; (2) the Prolegomena on pages XCIV–CVI in Richard Adelbert Lipsius and Maximillian Bonnet, *Acta apostolorum apocrypha* (Leipzig: Hermann Mendelssohn, 1891–1903; Reprint, Hildenscheim: G. Olms Verlagsbuchhandlung, 1959); (3) the improvements made to the Latin versions by Oscar von Gebhardt, ed., *Passio S. Theclae virginis: Die lateinischen Übersetzungen der Acta Pauli et Theclae nebst Fragmenten, Auszügen und Beilagen,* (TUGAL 7 [Neuen Folge]; Leipzig: J. C. Hinrichs, 1902); (4) Carl Schmidt, *ΠΡΑΞΕΙΣ ΠΑΥΛΟΥ: Acta Pauli: Nach dem Papyrus der Hamburger Staats und Universitäts-Bibliothek* (Glüchstadt und Hamburg: J.J. Augustin, 1936), in reference to the usage of Syrian and Armenian versions, and (5) the edition of Carl Schmidt. "Ein neues Fragment der Heidelberger Acta Pauli." *SPAW* (4 Feb. 1909): 216–20 (Cop^{1frag}); which I added in order to clarify my sources within the commentary.

            – Berlin Papyrus 13893, Berlin, Germany; III–IV CE; Carl Schmidt. "Ein Berliner Fragment der alten Πράξεις Παύλου." *SPAW* (19 Feb. 1931): 37–40.

𝔓³   𝔓^Oxy 1602 (=Gent, Bibliotheek van de Rijksunviersiteit, inv. 62); Ghent, Netherlands; IV–V CE; Bernard P. Grenfell and Arthur S. Hunt, eds. and trans. "1602. Homily to Monks." Pages 23–25 in *The Oxyrhynchus Papyri Part 13*. London: Egypt Exploration Fund, 1919.

𝔓⁷   Bodmer Papyrus X; Bibliotheca Bodmeriana, Cologny-Genève; III CE; Testuz, M. *Papyrus Bodmer X–XI. X: Correspondance apocryphe des Corinthiens et de l'apôtre Paul. XI: Onzième Odes Salomon. XII: Fragment d'un Hymne liturgique.* Cologny and Genève: Bibliotheca Bodmeriana, 1959.

A   Codex Parisinum Graecus 520; Paris; XI CE; collated by Thilo and Tischendorf; *AAA*.

B   Codex Parisinum Graecus 1454; Paris; X CE; *AAA*.

C   Codex Parisinum Graecus 1468; Paris; X CE; *AAA*.

E   Codex Vaticanus Graecus 797; Rome; XI CE; *AAA*.

F   Codex Vaticanus Graecus 866; Rome; XI CE; *AAA*.

G   Codex Barocciano Graecus 180/*Codex Grabe/Recension G*; Bodleian Library, Oxford; XII CE; Johann Ernest Grabe. *Spicilegium SS. Patrum ut et Hæreticorum: Seculi post Christum natum I. II. & III. quorum vel integra monumenta, vel fragmenta, partim ex aliorum patrum libris jam impressis collegit, & cum codicibus manuscriptis contulit, partim ex MSS. nunc primum edidit, ac singula tam præfatione, quàm notis subjunctis illustravit : tomus I. sive seculum I.* 2d ed. Oxford: E Theatro Sheldoniano, 1700; *AAA*.

H   Codex Oxoniensis Miscell. Graecus 77 (=Oxoniensis Huntingdonis); Oxford; XII CE; *AAA*.

K   Codex Parisinus Graecus 769; Paris; XIII CE; *AAA*.

L   Codex Palatinus Vaticanus 68; Rome; XIII CE; *AAA*.

M   Codex Vaticanus 1190; Rome; XIV CE; *AAA*.

Coptic Manuscripts and Papyri Fragments

Cop¹   Heidelberg Papyrus (BHO 882); Heidelberg; VI CE; Carl Schmidt. *Acta Pauli aus der Heidelberger koptischen Papyrushandschrift.* Mit Tafelband. Leipzig: J. C. Hinrichs, 1904.

Cop^1frag   Cop¹ Papyrus fragment; see Cop¹ above; Carl Schmidt. "Ein neues Fragment der Heidelberger Acta Pauli." *SPAW* (4 Feb. 1909): 216–20.

Cop^B   Bodmer Papyrus XLI; Bibliotheca Bodmeriana, Cologny-Genève; IV CE; Rodolphe Kasser and Philippe Luisier. "Le Bodmer XLI en Édition Princeps l'Épisode d'Èphèse des *Acta Pauli* en Copte et en Traduction." *Mus* 117 (2004): 281–384.

Cop^M   Unpublished Bodmer Papyrus (trans.W. E. Crum, "New Coptic Manuscripts in the John Rylands Library." *BJRL* 5 (1918–20): 501.

Latin Manuscripts and Papyrus Fragments[2]

ℭ	Codex Casinensis 142 (*c* in *AAA* and part of the C$_c$ recension according to von Gebhardt); Monte Cassino, Italy; XI CE; *AAA*.
A	Recension A is represented by two manuscripts (Codex Latinus 5306; Paris; XIV CE; and Codex 479; Toulouse; XIV CE). See von Gebhardt, *Passio*, VII–X).
B$_{a,b, \text{ or } c}$	Recension B is represented by three versions (B$_a$, B$_b$, and B$_c$) entailing a total of 24 manuscripts of which von Gebhardt used 7 of them for his translation. See von Gebhardt, *Passio*, X–XXIII.
C$_{a, b, c, \text{ or } d}$	Recension C is represented by four versions (C$_a$, C$_b$, and C$_c$, and C$_d$) entailing a total of 21 manuscripts of which von Gebhardt used 12 of them for his translation. See von Gebhardt, *Passio*, XXIII–XXXIV.
d	Codex Digbaeno 39 (part of the C$_d$ recension according to von Gebhardt); Bodleian Library, Oxford; XII CE; Johann Ernest Grabe. *Spicilegium SS. Patrum ut et Hæreticorum: Seculi post Christum natum I. II. & III. quorum vel integra monumenta, vel fragmenta, partim ex aliorum patrum libris jam impressis collegit, & cum codicibus manuscriptis contulit, partim ex MSS. nunc pr mum edidit, ac singula tam præfatione, quàm notis subjunctis illustravit : tomus I. sive seculum I.* 2d ed. Oxford: E Theatro Sheldoniano, 1700; *AAA*.
s	Boninus Mombritius (or Bonino Mombrizio), *Sanctuarium seu Vitae sanctorum* (Milan, 1476 [Lipsius, *AAA*, C] or 1477); a book (actually surpassed in textual significance by von Gebhardt's Latin edition) that collated 10 Latin manuscripts. See *AAA*, C–CI for more details.

Other Manuscript Translations

Syr.	Syriac versions (BHO 1152–1154). There are four syriac versions (s^a, s^b, s^c, and s^d,) referred to by *AAA*, CII, but this level of distinction is not necessary in this commentary. I follow Schmidt, who typically refers to them as "Syr." in *ΠΠ*. See Wright, William. *Apocryphal Acts of the Apostles: Edited from Syriac Manuscripts in the British Museum and Other Libraries.* 1871. Repr., Amsterdam: Philo Press, 1968;
Arm	Armenian versions. See Conybeare, Frederick Cornwallis, ed. Pages 49–88 in *The Apology and Acts of Apollonius and other Monuments of Early Christianity.* London: Swan Sonnenschein; New York: MacMillan, 1894; or Conybeare. *The Armenian Apology and the Acts of Apollonius and Other Monuments of Early Christianity.* 2d ed with an Appendix. London: Swan Sonnenschein; New York: MacMillan. 1896.

---

[2] See von Gebhardt, *Passio*, for the Latin critical text of the *APTh*.

Key to Numeration of the *Acts of Paul*[1]

ÉAC[2]	Thompson[3]	Schneemelcher[4]
AP 1 Damascus		*AP* 1
AP 2 Antioch₁		*AP* 2
AP 3–4 *Acts of Paul and Thecla* (*APTh* 1–43)		*AP* 3.1–43
3.1–26 Iconium	4.1–26	*AP* 3.1–26a
4.1–18 Antioch₂	4.26–43	*AP* 3.26–43
4.1	4.26	*AP* 3.26b

---

[1] Consult the key to the numeration of the *AP* in Peter W. Dunn, "*Acts of* Paul," xii–xiii also. Several small variations and amendations have been included in this key to numeration. For instance, J. David Thompson's *Concordance* (see footnote 6 below) has been added in order to align it with other texts; the designation of *3 Cor* has been removed; and several corrections to misidentified lines have been corrected (e.g. *3 Cor* 1=*NTApoc* 2:254.1–11 has been corrected to 10.1 (not *3 Cor* 1) = 254.3–13 (not 254.1–11). In this case, Dunn mistakenly begins the numbering of lines with one at the beginning of new chapters. So, when he identifies 254.1–11, he is correct that one is dealing with lines 1 to 11 in *AP* 10.1, but this is erroneous due to the fact that lines 1–11 of chapter 10 is actually lines 3–13 on page 254 of Schneemelcher's *NTApoc*.

[2] Willy Rordorf in collaboration with Pierre Cherix and Rudophe Kasser, trans., "Actes de Paul," *ÉAC* (ed. François Bovon and Pierre Geoltrain; Index by J. Voicu; Bibliothèque de la Pléiade; Saint Herblain: Gallimard, 1997), 1127–77.

[3] J. David Thompson, *A Critical Concordance to the New Testament Acts: Acts of Paul* (eds. Watson E. Mills and David Noel Freedman; The Computer Bible; vol. 44, book 1 and 2 of *The Computer Bible*; Lewiston: Edwin Mellen, 2001). The Key to the numeration of Thompson is as follows:

1.1–5=$\mathfrak{P}^1$, pages 1–5; 2.1–2= $\mathfrak{P}^1$, pages 6–7.1–9 (lines 1–9);

2.7–11= $\mathfrak{P}^1$, pages 7.10–11 (page 7, line 10 through page 11);

3.1–7=Lipsius–Bonnet *MPl* 1–7;

3.50–57=$\mathfrak{P}^7$ that has been published in M. Testuz, *Papyrus X–XI, X: Correspondence apocryphe des Corinthiens et de l'apôtre Paul. XI. Onzième Odes Salomon. XII. Fragment d'un Hymne liturgique.* (Colony and Genève: Bibliotheca Bodmeriana, 1959), pages 50–57; 4.1–45=*AAA*, *APTh* 1–45.

[4] Wilhelm Schneemelcher, "The Acts of Paul," *NTApoc* (eds. Edgar Hennecke and Wilhelm Schneemelcher; ed. and trans. Robert McLachlan Wilson; Rev. ed.; James Clarke & Co.: Cambridge; Philadelphia: Westminster/John Knox Press, 1992) 2:213–70. I am only including lines of the actual text in my referencing. For instance, 263.1–4a is page 263, lines 1 through the sentence ending on page 4 (called part a). Summaries and discussions that are supplemental to the text do not factor into the numeration.

ÉAC	Thompson	Schneemelcher
4.2	4.27	*AP* 3.27
AP 3–4 (cont.)		
4.3	4.28	*AP* 3.28
4.4	4.29	*AP* 3.29
4.5	4.30	*AP* 3.30
4.6	4.31	*AP* 3.31
4.7	4.32	*AP* 3.32
4.8	4.33	*AP* 3.33
4.9	4.34	*AP* 3.34
4.10	4.35	*AP* 3.35
4.11	4.36	*AP* 3.36
4.12	4.37	*AP* 3.37
4.13	4.38	*AP* 3.38
4.14	4.39	*AP* 3.39
4.15	4.40	*AP* 3.40
4.16	4.41	*AP* 3.41
4.17	4.42	*AP* 3.42
4.18	4.43	*AP* 3.43
Codex *A*, *B*, and *C*[5]	4.44	
Codex *A*, *B*, and *C*	4.45	
Recension G		
AP 5 Myra		*AP* 4
AP 6 Sidon		*AP* 5
AP 7 Tyre		*AP* 6
AP 8 Jerusalem to Smyrna		
AP 9 Ephesus		
9.1–13 (Cop[B])		*AP* appendix
9.1		263.1–4a
9.2		263.4b–10a
9.3		263.10b–264.2
9.4		264.3–6a
9.5		264.6b–12
9.6		264.13–17
9.7		264.18–27
9.8		264.28–38
9.9		264.39–265.2
9.10		265.3–4
9.11		265.5–12
9.12		265.13–19
9.13a		265.20
9.14–28 (Cop[1])		*AP* 7
9.13b	1.1	251.1–14a
9.14	1.1 (cont.)	251.14b–21a
9.15	1.1 (cont.)	251.21b–25
9.16	1.2	251.26–252.3a

---

[5] *AP* 44, 45 and *Recension G* are not included in *ÉAC*, but I have placed them here, considering that I refer to them as *APTh* 44, 45, and *G* throughout the commentary. The numeration of 43, 44, and *G* follows the identification system as proposed by the *AAA*.

ÉAC	Thompson	Schneemelcher
		AP 7 (cont.)
9.14–28 (Cop[1]) (cont.)		
9.17	1.2 (cont.)	252.3b–17
9.18	1.3	252.18–24a
9.19	1.3 (cont.)	252.24b–33a
9.20	1.3 (cont.)	252.33b–34
9.21	1.4	252.35–253.2
9.22	1.4 (cont.)	253.3–253.13a
9.23	1.4 (cont.)	253.13b–15
9.24	1.5	253.16–21a
9.25	1.5 (cont.)	253.21b–28a
9.26	1.5 (cont.)	253.28b–33
9.27	1.5 (cont.)	253.34–36
9.28	1.5 (cont.)	254.1–2
AP 10 Philippi₁[6]	3.50–57	*AP* 8
10.1		254.3–13
10.1-3 Letter of the Corinthians (to Paul)		
10.2	3.50–51	8.1.1–16
10.3	3.51 (cont.)	8.2.1–5
10.4-6 Letter of Paul (to the Corinthians)		
10.4.1–21[7]	3.52–54	8.3.1–21
10.5.24–32	3.54 (cont.)–56	8.3.24–32
10.6.34–40	3.56 (cont.)–57	8.3.34–40
AP 11 Philippi₂		256.27–257.10
AP 12 Corinth		*AP* 9
12.1	2.1	257.11–22a
12.2	2.1 (cont.)	257.22b–29a
12.3	2.1 (cont.)	257.29b–
		258.6a
12.4	2.1 (cont.)	258.6b–7
12.5	2.2, 2.7 (begins)	258.8–15a
12.6	2.7	258.15b–21
AP 13 Voyage to Italy		*AP* 10
13.1	2.8 (cont.)	258.22–28a
13.2	2.8 (cont.)	258.28b–
259.3a		
13.3	2.8 (cont.)	259.3b–9a
13.4	2.8 (cont.)	259.9b–12a
13.5	2.8 (cont.)	259.12b–19a
13.6	2.8 (cont.)	259.19b–23a
13.7	2.8 (cont.)	259.23b–33
13.8	2.8 (cont.)	259.33–37
13.9		260.1–9a
13.10		260.9b–12a
13.11		260.12b–22
AP 14 Rome: The Martyrdom[8]		*AP* 11

---

[6] Also known as *3 Corinthians* (1) due to the probability that *3 Cor* predates the *AP*, and (2) a complete separate textual transmission with overlap between the *AP* and *3 Cor* being evidenced in Cop[1].

[7] Verses 14, 22, 23, and 33 have been cut out of the *ÉAC* text as being Latin additions, following the shorter recension of *3 Cor*.

ÉAC	Thompson	Schneemelcher
14.1	3.1	11.1
14.2	3.2	11.2
14.3	3.3 and 2.9 (begins)	11.3
14.4	3.4 and 2.9–10	11.4
14.5	3.5 and 2.10–11	11.5
14.6	3.6	11.6
14.7	3.7	11.7

I will be using the numbering system proposed by *ÉAC* for several reasons. One, the translation of the *Actes de Paul* for *ÉAC* is the work of the text critical team that is producing the most current critical edition of the *AP* that includes all available manuscripts and papyri of the *AP*. Two, *ÉAC* makes a distinction between the accounts of Iconium and Antioch, which follows the text of Cop[1], therefore representing the earliest known account of the chapter divisions in the *AP*. In addition to using the numeration as suggested by *ÉAC*, I have also included the addition of *APTh* 44, 45, and *Recension G*, which are found within the critical edition of the *AAA*, and have not been preserved in the edition of *ÉAC*.

---

[8] *The Martyrdom of Paul (MPl)* or *Martyrium Pauli* 1–7.

Part I

Introduction

Chapter 1: The Ancient Novel

1.1 The Ancient Novel and the Early Christian Novel

The early Christian novel has traditionally been separated from the ancient novels, but within this introduction, I will argue that it is more accurate to locate the early Christian novel as a special type of the ancient novel. Also, I intend to argue that the *APTh* (and the *AP* as a larger corpus) can be interpreted more appropriately if one reads these documents with the genre of the ancient novel in mind. Before making my case, I will consider first some background information that is important for understanding Greco-Roman novels and the Christian novels of antiquity.

In 858 CE, Photius, patriarch of Constantinople, stated that sometime around the year 400 CE, Leucius Charinus, a Manichaean in Egypt, collected the five major acts of early Christian literature (excluding the Acts of the Apostles now included in the Christian canon), known today as the *Apocryphal Acts of the Apostles (AAApos)*.[1] These five major acts are the *Acts of John, Acts of Paul, Acts of Peter, Acts of Andrew,* and the *Acts of Thomas*. One finds these documents so intriguing because they began to appear in the latter part of the second century, and the early Christians seem to be reading them and enjoying them alongside what are now considered "canonical texts" that reflect the orthodox positions of the early church. Classicists and New Testament scholars alike have had difficulty in identifying the genre of these ancient documents. This has caused the *AAApos* to fall somewhere between Christian studies and Classical studies,

---

[1] See Photius, *Biblotheca* 114, Ἀνεγνώσθη βιβλίον, αἱ λεγόμεναι τῶν ἀποστόλων περίοδοι, ἐν αἷς περιείχοντο πράξεις Πέτρου, Ἰωάννου, Ἀνδρέου, Θωμᾶ, Παύλου. Γράφει δὲ αὐτάς, ὡς δηλοῖ τὸ αὐτὸ βιβλίον, Λεύκιος Χαρῖνος (quoted from *TLG*). Mentioned in Constantin von Tischendorf and Theodor Zahn's *Acta Joannis* (Erlangen: Deichert, 1880), 215; Bernhard Pick found it through Zahn, *The Apocryphal Acts of Paul, Peter, John, Andrew, and Thomas* (Chicago: The Open Court Publishing; London: Kegan Paul, Trench, Trübner & Co., 1909), x; and again in Bremmer, Jan N., "The Five Major Apocryphal Acts: Authors, Place, Time, and Readership," *The Apocryphal Acts of Thomas,* (ed. Bremmer; Leuven: Peeters, 2001), 156.

while not always gaining the attention they deserve, because neither classicists nor biblical scholars have attempted to claim them.[2] Classicists reject
them due primarily to the fact that they fall under the rubric of "Early
Christian Literature," and biblical scholars reject them, because the content
of the material has been considered unorthodox and "false" as a record to
early Christianity.[3]

In 1983, Tomas Hägg published his work, *The Novel in Antiquity*, as the
English counterpart to his Swedish edition, *Den Antika Romanen* (Uppsala:
Bokförlaget Carmina, 1980) and for the most part continued this division
for recent discussions, by accident (or not), for how discussions were carried out on the ancient novel. In both the preface[4] and "CHAPTER I, The
Novel in Antiquity – a Contradiction in Terms?" Hägg discusses the fact
that what his book is addressing is a newly emerging genre in the Hellenistic period that is nameless, and the reconstruction is primarily the part of
the classical historian.[5] The key quote in this discussion is that of Julian
the Apostate who, in the year 363 CE, wrote in a letter "All made-up stories of the type published by writers of earlier ages in the shape of historical accounts – love stories and all that kind of narrative – are to be rejected."[6]

Interestingly enough, Niklas Holzberg offers a bit more information for
the delineation of the ancient novel. Holzberg bases his definition on references made to the subject as recorded in Greek from the Byzantine period,

---

[2] The history of research on the ancient novel precedes Hägg, but for current discussions, they begin here. See also Erwin Rohde, *Der griechische Roman und seine Vorläufer* (2d ed.; Leipzig: Breitkopf und Härtel, 1900) and Rosa Söder, *Die apokryphen
Apostelgeschichten und die romanhafte Literatur der Antike* (Würzburger Studien zur
Altertumswissenschaft 3; Stuttgart: W. Kohlhammer, 1932). Tomas Hägg published his
work, *The Novel in Antiquity* in 1983 "creating" the rubrics of discussion. In particular,
look at chapter one, "The Novel in Antiquity – a Contradiction of Terms?" See also the
advancement of these ideas as presented in Niklas Holzberg, *The Ancient Novel: An Introduction* (London; New York: Routledge, 1995), 8–27.

[3] See Éric Junod, "Actes Apocryphes et Hérésie: Le Judement de Photius," *Les Actes
apocryphes des Apôtres. Christianisme et monde païen* (François Bovon, et. al.; Publication de la faculté de théologie de l'Université de Genève; Geneva: Labor et Fides, 1981),
11–24. See also Hans Conzelmann, *Acts of the Apostles*, (ed. Eldon Jap Epp with Christopher R. Matthews; trans. James Limburg, A. Thomas Kraabel, and Donald H. Juel;
Hermeneia; Philadelphia: Fortress, 1987), xlii, where the *AP* are quickly dismissed as
relevant literature due to several reasons. One reason in particular is the "senseless"
miracles that are found throughout the text.

[4] Hägg, *The Novel*, vii–viii.

[5] Ibid., 2–3.

[6] Ibid., 3; Holzberg, Niklas, "The Genre: Novels Proper and the Fringe," *The Novel in
the Ancient World* (ed. Gareth Schmeling; rev. ed.; Leiden/Boston: Brill, 2003), 17. See
Flavius Claudius Julianus (Julian the Apostate, 331–363 CE), *Epistulae* 89b, line 347,
...ὅσα δέ ἐστιν ἐν ἱστορίας εἴδει παρὰ τοῖς ἔμπροσθεν ἀπηγγελμένα πλάσματα παραιτητέον,
ἐρωτικὰς ὑποθέσεις καὶ πάντα ἁπλῶς τὰ τοιαῦτα (quoted from *TLG*).

and in Latin from late antiquity that refer to the "ancient novel" texts as "*drama, (suntagma) dramatikon* ('dramatic narrative') or *komodia* in Greek and *fabula* or *mimus* in Latin."[7] These two categories basically address a group of writings that would have been "fictional reproductions of everyday life in the ancient world"[8] in the form of either a tale of two lovers "happily joined together only at the end of the work" or as a "comedy."[9] Holzberg argues that by late antiquity there was already an isolated definition of the genre that the ancients would have thought of when discussing the ancient novel. Then Holzberg discusses the characteristics of the "idealistic and comic-realistic novel" and proceeds by suggesting which novels fit within this framework.[10] Following this section, Holzberg addresses a large group of texts that fit into the category of "fringe novels." It is within this section that he deals with the early Christian novel as a fringe novel, thus designating it as outside of the parameters of the ancient novel.

Before looking more closely at his assessment of the early Christian novel, for the purpose of clarity and understanding the territory better something should be said about what one expects to see when looking at the "ideal" ancient novel. Hägg does very little in terms of defining the characteristics of the ideal novel, but on the contrary expects the reader to notice the characteristics rising to the top after reading through *The Novel in Antiquity*.[11] On the other hand, Holzberg is somewhat more explicit about definitions by dividing the characteristics of the ancient romance into two areas: *Motifs* and *Narrative technique*.[12] Put quite simply, this section highlights the stock details of the ancient novel. The ancient novel typically begins with a young man and a young woman of exceptional beauty who fall in love, make vows to one another and then face incredible obstacles. The young lovers – sometimes newly wed – after betrothal, usually are separated for various reasons, pledge fidelity, and then face numerous perils. These perils usually come in the shape of pirates, shipwrecks, journeys to far off, exotic lands such as Alexandria or Ethiopia. At different points, the gods intervene in the situation, sometimes for the good of the couple and sometimes for the worse (very much the case as first set forth by Homer). After a series of events, following the two lovers' adventures being told in parallel accounts, they finally reunite at the end for the

---

[7] *Ancient Novel*, 8.

[8] Ibid., 9.

[9] Ibid., 8.

[10] Ibid., 9–11.

[11] For Instance, Hägg begins on page 5 of *The Novel in Antiquity* with "Chariton: Chaereas and Callirhoe" and immediately begins discussing the first line of the text without prefacing it with any discussion of the ideal characteristics, quite in irony to the title of the chapter, "The Ideal Greek Novel."

[12] Holzberg, *Ancient Novel*, 9–10.

happily ever after ending. These factors will resurface again once I return
to look at the *APTh* more closely.

After overviewing some of the stock elements of the ancient novel, let
us now return to the reasons given by Holzberg for the exclusion of the
early Christian novel. It must first be noted that I believe Holzberg's reasons for the exclusion of the "Early Christian novel-like literature" to be
tenuous and dubious. While I admit that there are "thematic parallels" that
"resemble situations typical for the novel," he nonetheless excludes them.[13]
Holzberg is willing to concede a "new type of fictional prose narrative,"
entitled the "early Christian novel," but is unwilling to go any further.[14]
Holzberg argues that the early Christian novels are essentially a second-
tier production or Christianized variation of the ancient novel, while
falsely assuming that novels must be pagan in order to represent the novel
accurately. Secondly, Holzberg seeks to exclude the early Christian novel
as a "fringe" novel based upon the reception of the novel in the sixteenth
and seventeenth centuries. He notes that, during the birth of the modern
novel in the sixteenth and seventeenth centuries, "authors looked to ancient
novels for inspiration, influenced solely by the pagan idealistic type (in
particular by Helidorus' *Aethiopica*) and its comic-realistic counterpart
(especially the Greek and Latin *Ass* novels)."[15] Therefore, the implications
of Holzberg's reasoning is, if the early Christian novels were rejected as
second class novels within the birth of the modern novel, then we will continue to reject them. First, this assessment fails to factor in the effects of
Christendom upon the perception and reading of early Christian novels
during the sixteenth and seventeenth centuries.[16] Second, the concern for
orthodox and heretical writings would clearly have located the ancient
novels within the realm of heretical documents, while at the same time
have limited the possibility for people to view them as documents of literature or entertainment due to their Christian[17] nature.[18]

---

[13] Ibid., 22.

[14] Ibid., 23.

[15] Ibid., 23–24. This reference to the "*Ass* novels" is in reference to the Latin text by
Apuleius entitled *Metamorphoses* (also called *The Golden Ass* as entitled by Augustine of
Hippo) and the Greek text *Ass Romance*, or also entitled *Lucian or the Ass* (or *Asinus*).

[16] In particular, I am referring to the apocryphal/heretical nature in which they were
received which limited the reading this literature for fear of heresy. See Junod, "Actes
Apocryphes et Hérésie," 24; and Gérard Poupon, "Les Actes apocryphes des Apôtres de
Lefèvre a Fabricius," *Les Actes apocryphes des Apôtres,* 25–47.

[17] I chose to say "Christian nature" rather than "religious nature" due to the irony that
the stock ancient novels are all religious in nature, albeit pagan.

[18] Again see Junod, "Actes Apocryphes et Hérésie," 24; and Gérard Poupon, "Les
Actes apocryphes des Apôtres de Lefèvre a Fabricius," *Les Actes apocryphes des Apôtres,* 25–47.

In all fairness, since the publication of *The Ancient Novel*, Holzberg has responded to some criticism in Gareth Schmeling's 1996 work (revised in 2003), *The Novel in the Ancient World*, by attempting to step back in a small way from some of his previous assertions. Namely, he first of all admits to the anachronistic nature of the discussion, but apologetically asks for leeway, considering that there simply are no ancient names to describe the genre.[19] But on the whole, there is surprisingly little change that takes place in his use of definitions.

In an attempt to answer these reasons for rejecting the early Christian novel as an ancient novel, I will attempt to answer each of these problems with plausible reasons to argue in return as well as provide an overview of the *APTh* as a test case for *AAApos* as legitimate examples of an ancient novel. First, in reply to the early Christian novel being a variation and by-product of the ancient novel, one might note the following. It seems inconsistent to suggest that the early Christian novel only describes the reception of the genre due to the fact that according to Holzberg's own timeline, the ancient novel was still in development. Take for instance, the production of Apuleius' *Metamorphoses*, where a second century document coincides with the production of part of the *AAApos*.[20] Also, the time of production of the *AAApos* falls during the midst of Holzberg's unfolding of the development and history of the "ideal novel" as it continues on into the third century as part of the "Second Sophistic."[21] It hardly seems plausible to describe the development of the early Christian novel as simply a glimpse of how the ancient novel was received, considering that it was developing at the same time as the "ideal novel."

Regarding the reception in the sixteenth and seventeenth centuries, it hardly seems a plausible reason, considering the religious climate of these centuries. There were a number of socio-political factors that would have influenced the selection of materials as much as anything else. One cannot forget that once the *AAApos* were considered unorthodox, this labeling diminished the importance and influence of these documents significantly, even up to the present. The religious and social environment is still not in such a position that masses of people will be exposed to or see any need to consider reading the *AAApos*.

One also finds it interesting for Holzberg to make a statement that "no readers or critics are likely even to have considered counting Iambulus' 'travelogue,' the *Life of Aesop*, the collected pseudepigraphic letters of Hippocrates, the *Ephemeris* of Dictys and the *Historia Apollonii Regis Tyri* together with Chariton's *Callirhoe* and Petronius' *Satyricon* as variations

---

[19] Holzberg, "The Genre," 11.

[20] Ibid., 77.

[21] Ibid., 84–105.

of one and the same literary genre."[22] It hardly seems possible that one could argue with Holzberg considering that modern critics have, for the most part, created the literary genre that he is discussing. This statement says more about the contemporary reader than about the ancient reader. This ultimately is something that must be answered by identifying the ancient readers and the reception history of the documents that is defined, ironically, as a very diverse and broad group of readers by Holzberg.[23] Pervo, quite the opposite of Holzberg, suggests:

> It is doubtful that a librarian, ca. 175, faced with the Greek *Metamorphoses* attributed to Lucius of Patrae, *Leucippe, An Ephesian Tale,* and the *Acts of Paul* would unhesitatingly place the first three on one shelf, so to speak, and the last elsewhere. The two last items have much in common.[24]

I also find it difficult to call the early Christian novel a fringe novel, especially if Hägg is correct that "the people who needed and welcomed the novel are the same as those who were attracted by the mystery religions and Christianity: the people of Alexandria and other big cities round the Eastern Mediterranean."[25] This hardly sounds like the fringes, but rather represents the majority of the masses as the mystery religions and ultimately Christianity swept through the Mediterranean region and eventually dominated even the political sphere of the Empire. In fact, as recent studies have concluded, there is a general agreement that the readership of the ancient novel (whether one is looking at the "Sophistic" novels or the "early" novels) is going to be rather diverse, crossing both educated/uneducated and wealthy/poor categories as they seemed to have had a far reaching impact.[26] To add to this, within a recent study on readership and the ancient Christian novel, Bremmer approaches the question by reflecting upon the readership of the *AAApos*.[27] While there is quite unanimous agreement that most upper class Greek and Roman males could read, Bremmer takes the

---

[22] Ibid., 26.

[23] Ibid., 33–35.

[24] Pervo, Richard, "The Ancient Novel Becomes Christian," *Novel in the Ancient World*, 694.

[25] *The Novel*, 90.

[26] Ewen Bowie, "4. The Ancient Readers of the Greek Novel," *The Novel in the Ancient World*, 92–96.

[27] Ewen Bowie, "Les lecteurs du roman grec," *Le monde du roman grec* (M.-F. Baslez, et. al.; Paris, 1992) 55–61; Bowie, "The Readership of Greek Novels in the Ancient World," *The Search for the Ancient Novel*; Bowie, "The Ancient Readers of the Greek Novel," *The Novel in the Ancient World*, 87–106; Tomas Hägg, "Orality, Literacy, and the "readership" of the early Greek Novel," *Contexts of Pre-Novel Narrative* (ed. R. Eriksen; Berlin and New York, 1994) 47–81; Susan Stephens, "Who Read Ancient Novels?," *The Search*, 405–18; J. Morgan, "The Greek Novel. Towards a Sociology of Production and Reception," *The Greek World* (ed. A. Powell; London, 1995) 134–39; and Bremmer, "The Apocryphal Acts," 160–70.

argument the next step by demonstrating that quite a number of women would have been readers of the *AAApos*.[28] In fact, there is physical evidence that the written form of the *APTh* was even so popular with people that small codices have been found containing them, thus suggesting a very widespread and general use of the literature in both the reading of the materials and also in the oral presentation of the materials.[29] For these reasons as mentioned above, it appears that a reconsideration of the *AAApos* as an example of the ancient novel is in order.

1.2 The Ancient Novel and the Acts of Paul and Thecla

As will be noted in the commentary, there are extensive points of contact in the similarities of motif, language, themes, choice of words, expressions, etc. between the *APTh* and other ancient novels. In particular I have referred to Apuleius' *The Golden Ass*[30] (or *Metamorphoses of Lucius Apuleius*), Heliodorus' *Aethiopica*, Achilles Tatius' *Leucippe and Clitophon*, Chariton's *Callirhoe*, Longus' *Daphne and Chloe, Joseph and Aseneth*, and finally the summation of Parthenius, *The Story of Pallene*.[31] For the purpose of summarizing some of these touchpoints between the *APTh* and the ancient novel, consider the following parallels. At the beginning of the *APTh*, one is introduced to the major figures in the tale, primarily Paul and Thecla. At the beginning, Paul is introduced in terms pointing primarily to Paul's inward beauty, but not leaving the outward beauty unaddressed.[32] The author immediately parallels Paul to the immortal in the statement that "for some times he appeared as a man, but at other times he had the face of an angel."[33] Paul's counterpart is Thecla, a young virgin betrothed to one of the leading men of the city, named Thamyris, who hears Paul's preaching in Iconium. As Thecla becomes more mesmerized by Paul's teachings

---

[28] "Apocryphal Acts," 164–67.

[29] Harry Y. Gamble, *Books and Readers in the Early Church: A History of Early Christian Texts* (New Haven and London: Yale UP, 1995), 236. Books were not simply for the purpose of reading, but also for the purpose of presenting and speaking the contents to those who could not read.

[30] See footnote 26 above.

[31] For example, see the *3.8.1 Textual Notes*, notes 3, 8, 9, 10; *3.18.1 Textual Notes*, notes 4, 6, 10; *3.18.2 General Comment*; *3.22.1 Textual Notes*, note 9; *3.25.1 Textual Notes*, notes 8, 10, 12; *4.1.1 Textual Notes*, notes 2, 6, 7, 10; *4.2.1 Textual Notes*, notes 1 and 7 for examples. This is not a comprehensive listing of the notes that I have offered as possible connections between the *APTh* and other ancient novels.

[32] For more discussion on the authenticity of Paul's description, see János Bollók, "The Description of Paul," *The Apocryphal Acts of Paul and Thecla*, 1–15; Robert M. Grant, "The Description of Paul in the Acts of Paul and Thecla," *VC* 36 (1982), 1–4; Abraham J. Malherbe, "A Physical Description of Paul," *HTR* 79 (1986): 170–75.

[33] *AP* 3.3. This is my translation.

on chastity and such, Thecla's mother, Theocleia becomes concerned and tells Thamyris that:

For three days and three nights, Thecla has not risen from the door, neither to eat nor to drink, but she is gazing intently as though enraptured, thus she is closely attached to a foreign man who is teaching deceptive and divisive words, so that I marvel how one of such modesty as of the virgin is being burdened (so) painfully.[34]

On another occasion, once the "love affair" has intensified, Paul is thrown into prison as one who has brought social disorder, and Thecla proceeds to come to his prison cell, where she "kisses his bonds" (καταφιλούσης τὰ δεσμὰ αὐτοῦ) and she is described as "chained to him by affection" (συνδεδεμένην τῇ στοργῇ).[35] The sexual overtones can hardly be missed. They are by all means intentional. In fact, this is precisely where much of the controversy has fallen over the *APTh*. Holzberg takes notice of the anomaly as grounds for exclusion as a "fringe"document.[36] On the other hand, Pervo questions the judgment of modern critics who adjudicate the ancient novel based on such flimsy grounds of whether it promotes hetero-sexual marriage.[37] It is also this same text that leads Melissa Aubin, based on the work of Kate Cooper[38] and Judith Perkins,[39] to conclude that the *APTh* are purposefully trying to confound "differences between the sexes" as Aubin sees the ancient romance as the primary teacher of this.[40] How-ever one eventually defines the relationship between the two characters, the text clearly seeks to set Paul and Thecla in the leading roles of the young lovers, but with a twist. Interestingly, in the case of the *APTh*, the "social backbone" of the ancient novel, marriage, is somehow being rein-terpreted.[41] This is carried out to the fullest extent by (1) Thecla's ability to avoid marriage,[42] (2) actually to be a heroine to the full extent and capably get through a number of adventures without the rescue of her lover, and then (3) finally come to the end of her life "happily ever after" unwed. All of the specifics are quite similar to the typical heroine in the novel.[43]

---

[34] *AP* 3.8.

[35] Ibid., 3.18–19.

[36] Holzberg, *Ancient*, 23.

[37] Pervo, "The Ancient Novel becomes Christian," 685.

[38] *The Virgin and the Bride: Idealized Womanhood in Late Antiquity* (Cambridge, Mass.: Harvard UP, 1996).

[39] *The Suffering Self: Pain and Narrative Representation in the Early Christian Era* (London: Routledge, 1995).

[40] Melissa Aubin, "Reversing Romance? The *Acts of Thecla* and the Ancient Novel," *Ancient Fiction and Early Christian Narrative* (ed. Ronald F. Hock, J. Bradley Chance, and Judith Perkins; Atlanta: Scholars Press, 1998), 257–72.

[41] Brigitte Eggers, "Women and Marriage in the Greek Novel: The Boundaries of Romance," *The Novel in the Ancient World*, 260.

[42] *AP* 3.21–22, and 4.8.

[43] Eggers, "Women and Marriage," 273–74. Compare also *AP* 3.22 to Parthenius, *The*

Another example of the overlap between the *APTh* and the stock ancient novel is the "adventure" theme. Paul and Thecla (mainly Thecla) consistently find themselves trying to overcome various trials and exploits of the young couple (mainly Thecla).[44] First, there is the prison experience already mentioned above, then Thecla is threatened to be burned alive (3.21–22), and in Antioch Thecla is stripped and thrown to die fighting lions in the arena (4.7–8).[45] Throughout these adventures, the erotic is subtly but consistently mixed with the life-threatening ordeals that Thecla must overcome. The presentation of these events runs in a chronological fashion with the appearance of the historical narrative in the same fashion as the ancient novel. In fact, Christine Thomas has argued that the *AAApos* are ultimately based upon some historical reality via oral tradition,[46] thus adding support to the presentation of a "real" life adventure.[47]

The most obvious misinterpretation of the *APTh* is how the relationship of Paul and Thecla has been understood after they left Iconium and were entering into Antioch (*AP* 3.26–4.1). Traditionally, this has been understood as Paul abandoning Thecla, leaving her to die on her own.[48] Within the commentary, I will demonstrate that this is not an abandonment of Thecla, but rather the trials of the young lovers are intensified in the same manner as that which one witnesses in the ancient novels. As their love intensifies, they end up having to delay their own gratifications, play word games with those who are imprisoning them, and finally separate temporarily and unwillingly as the trials intensify.[49] After a period of intense persecution, the lovers are finally rejoined, as Paul and Thecla rejoin after the trials of Antioch. The fact that Paul left Thecla in Antioch was not Paul *leaving* her, but his leaving out of necessity due to the situation. Consistent

---

Story of Pallene 5–6; Achilles Tatius, *Leuc. Clit.* 8.3; 8.6; and Heliodorus, *Aeth.* 10.7; 8.9.9–16; *contra* Anne Jensen, *Thekla – die Apostelin: Ein apokrypher Text neu entdeckt: Übersetzt und kommentiert* (Freiburg, Basel, and Wien: Herder, 1995), 69.

[44] Even the "abandonment" of Thecla can be explained on the grounds of similarities to the ancient novel, see note 6 under *4.1.1 Textual Notes*.

[45] The fight in the arena is very popular in the ancient novel. See *4.2.2 General Comment*.

[46] Thomas, Christine M., *The Acts of Peter, Gospel Literature, and the Ancient Novel: Rewriting the Past* (Oxford: Oxford UP, 2003).

[47] Holzberg, *Ancient Novel*, 10–11.

[48] See *3.25.1. Textual Notes*, note 12; *3.26.2 General Comment* and *4.1.1 Textual Notes*, notes 5 and 6. On the abandonment of Thecla, see Davies, *The Revolt*, 58–59 for an example of this common interpretation.

[49] For examples, I include some of the content of note 12 in *3.25.1 Textual Notes*. See Heliodorus, *Aeth.* 1.8.3; 1.19.7 (Thyamis threatens Theagenes and Charicleia) 1.25; 7 (especially Alsace's intervention into the relationship of Theagenes and Charicleia); 5.31.1–4 (While enjoying a feast devoted to Hermes, the priest Calasiris records another threat to Theagenes and Charicleia by Pelorus); Longus, *Daph.* 1.15–17; 3.20; Chariton, *Chaer.* 4.3.8–10; 8.1; 5.Achilles Tatius, *Leuc. Clit.* 5.16–17; 5.21; 5.22.8; 5.27; et. al.

with the ancient novel, all attempts of the hero and heroine to stay alive at
all cost are taken advantage of, in the hopes that the lovers, subject to Fate,
will be able to endure the trials and once again reunite. The idea that Paul
should have "stood up" for Thecla is inconsistent with the themes of the
ancient novel. Survival for the sake of love is the key virtue, not dying a
noble death. Also, the idea that Paul should have made such a stand is sus-
piciously consistent with individualistic, post-enlightenment philosophic
rationality that does not adequately take into account the importance that
Fate played within the Greco-Roman world.

In conclusion, some scholars have been hesitant to include the *AAApos*
into the same category as the other stock ancient romances for various reasons, primarily stemming from their lack of ability to mold neatly into the
anachronistically created designation of "ideal ancient novel." To narrow
the discussion, the crux of the disagreement in the ancient novel and the
ancient Christian novel focuses upon the role of marriage in the text. As
has been demonstrated, the *APTh* have all of the same motifs, a narrative
story following a chronological timeline, filled with adventures, erotic
tales, and finally a "happily ever after" ending with Thecla dying single
and in peace. But unfortunately, although meeting the technical require-
ments, it still does not meet the required form due to the variant approach
that the text takes. This variation is centered upon the issue of marriage
(albeit abstinence from marriage), thus allowing the *APTh* to be an anomaly solely based on issues of sexuality and what is defined as deviant and
normative in marriage. To close, I go back once again to Richard Pervo's
statement, that one must ask whether or not it is at all likely that individuals of the ancient world would show this degree of discrimination to the
point where they have such stringent definitions of the "novel?"[50] I find it
highly unlikely. As one uses this commentary, I think it is important to pay
careful attention to the notes and comments, so that one will be able to see
the numerous links and similarities between the major ancient novels and
the *APTh*.

1.3 Historical Reliability

Regarding the historical reliability of the *AP*, it seems safe to say that the
account was not written for the purpose of the preservation of historical
events, but rather to record a historical fiction relating the events of Paul
and Thecla (who may have never existed).[51] I am not suggesting that the

---

[50] "The Ancient Novel becomes Christian," 694.

[51] See Carolyn Osiek, Margaret Y. MacDonald with Janet H. Tulloch, *A Woman's Place: House Churches in Earliest Christianity* (Minneapolis: Fortress Press, 2006) 17; see also C. Schmidt, *Acta Pauli aus der Heidelberger koptischen Papyrushandschrift* with the *Tafelband.* Leipzig: J. C. Hinrichs, 1904., 206, who similarly voiced skepticism

author of the text was agendaless, but rather his motivation was not recording historical data. I will discuss the possible motivation of this writing later in the introduction, when I address the relationship of the *AP* to the Pastorals and other NT documents. Further, the *AP* has limited value in "recovering" the historical Paul and/or Thecla, although it may have more purpose in resurrecting the theology and ecclesiology of the Pauline churches of the first century.

I am not suggesting that there are no reliable historical elements to the story, but rather this is not the purpose that the document was written. It appears that there are a few historical elements. First, Queen Tryphaena of Pontus, who was a relative of the Caesar, did exist.[52] Second, there was a Falconilla that might be identified with the Falconilla of this text.[53] Third, the facts about Iconium and the "royal road" seem to represent first century Iconium accurately.[54] Fourth, there was a historical Paul, Nero, etc.

However, at a different level, in regard to the *sitz im leben* of the churches that produced the *AP*, I would suggest that the *APTh* provides important insights into: (1) house churches, (2) the role of women in the second century (possibly the first century also), (3) various theological nuances concerning asceticism and marriage, and (4) the role of apostolic authority in the church, among other things. This does not suggest that every historical element of the text is unreliable, nor does it discredit the text as a social and historical indicator of churches, cities, etc. that allows us to see a window of the ancient world. For instance, the legal practices, presentations of Thecla in the ampitheater, geographical descriptions, etc. all seem to suggest a somewhat high level of accuracy and familiarity with Asia Minor.[55] The primary discrepancies have been the differences in relation to

---

over 100 years ago, but was never well received. For a review of this skepticism, see Léon Vouaux, *Les Actes de Paul et ses lettres Apocryphes: Introduction, textes, traduction et commentaire* (Les Apocryphes du Nouveau Testament: Paris: Librairie Letouzey et Ané, 1913), 125–27. I think Willy Rordorf's assessment that there may have been someone who Thecla represents who was an historical figure, but the actual details of her life (name, betrothed virgin?, from Iconium, etc.) are beyond our grasp. I come to this conclusion by acknowledging that (1) Thecla's personality, character, and religious thinking are very underdeveloped and (2) the fact that the *APTh* is the earliest known document to ever even mention her name is considerably late. By the turn of the second/third century CE, the legendary material of the apostles is expanding rapidly, yet here Thecla is mentioned for the *first* time ever! Unlikely that she would be totally overlooked for over 100 years.

[52] See *2.2 Date of Composition*.

[53] Ibid.

[54] See *3.3.1 Textual Notes*, note 1 for more information.

[55] See William M. Ramsay, *The Church in the Roman Empire before 70 A.D.* (London and New York: G. P. Putnam's Sons, 1892), 30–46, who draws out several valuable points, but is probably overstating the argument for historicity. Also, compare the scenes of Thecla in the theater in Antioch to the situations presented by K. M. Coleman, "Fatal

the *AP vis-à-vis* the Acts of the Apostles and the Pastorals, when one is attempting to reconcile the two accounts with the *AP*.[56]

1.4 Intended/Actual Readers of the Ancient Novel

Regarding the readership of this literary genre, who would have read early Christian novels and the *AP*? [57] In order to answer this question, a more generic examination of the readers of the Ancient Novel and literacy rates in antiquity ought to be considered more closely. To begin, there is very little within the novels themselves that explicitly expresses who actually read books.[58] Having such little evidence internally, it becomes helpful to consider several other external factors.

In determining the readers of the ancient novel, the question of literacy within the ancient world becomes pertinent. It has already been established (though not conclusively and with critics opposed) that literacy could have been as high as 20–30 percent mainly within the males of an elite and wealthy status of antiquity, and somewhat less for women.[59] Obviously, determining a statistical analysis of ancient literacy is incredibly difficult, therefore the wide range of statistics that can be made, and therefore some caution must be exercised. What we do know is that the issue was compli-

---

Charades: Roman Executions Staged as Mythological Enactments," *JRS* 80 (1990): 44–73.

[56] See Dunn, "The *Acts of Paul*," 35 and the discussion below on the "4. *Acts of Paul and the New Testament*."

[57] Ewen Bowie, "The Ancient Readers," 89. In addition to these comments see the overview presented by Bremmer pertaining to early Christian novels in, "The Apocryphal Acts," 160. Other noteworthy contributions to the discussion have been provided by Ewen Bowie in "The Readership of Greek Novels in the Ancient World," 435–59; Tomas Hägg, "Orality, Literacy, and the 'Readership' and 'The Ancient Novel'," in Roy T. Eriksen, ed., *Contexts of Pre–Novel Narrative* (Berlin and New York: Mouton de Gruyter, 1994) 47–81; Stephens, "Who Read Ancient Novels?" *The Search*, 405–18; and J. Morgan, "The Greek Novel. Toward a Sociology of Production and Reception," *The Greek World* (ed. Anton Powell; London: Routledge, 1995), 134–39.

[58] Ewen Bowie, "The Ancient Readers," 88. One example from Achilles Tatius 1.6.6 (referred to by Bowie, "The Ancient Readers," 87) tells how when the young Clitophon, "drunk with love" (μεθύων ἔρωτι) was hoping to catch a glimpse of his new love, Leucippe, he "took a book, and bent over it, and pretended to read" (βιβλίον ἅμα κρατῶν καὶ ἐγκεκυφὼς ἀνεγίνωσκον), while using the book as a way to secretly glance below it to see his love.

[59] See Rosalind Thomas, "Literacy," *Oxford Classical Dictionary* (ed. Simon Hornblower and Antony Spawforth; 3rd rev. ed.; Oxford: Oxford UP, 2003), 868–69; William V. Harris, *Ancient Literacy* (Cambridge: Harvard UP, 1989); and Bremmer, "The Apocryphal Acts," 160. For a possible exception to Harris' statistics see James L. Franklin, Jr., "Literacy and the parietal inscriptions of Pompeii," *Literacy in the Roman World* (ed. Mary Beard, *et al.*; Journal of Roman Archaeology Supplementary Series Number 3; Ann Arbor, MI: Journal of Roman Archaeology, 1991), 77–98.

cated due to factors such as diverse languages throughout the empire,[60] expensive writing materials, the prevalence of rural patterns of illiteracy,[61] poor educational system, and other such limitations.[62] To add to this, a good example of an exception to these statistics is seen in Pompeii. Although Pompeii demonstrates a "widespread literacy," one must consider that this limited exception could very well be due to the location, status, and wealth accumulated within Pompeii.[63] Nonetheless, the point is well taken by Franklin that generic figures for literacy are not sufficient in regard to issues of readership when specific localities and communities are under consideration. So, what generalization can be made in regard to readership and literacy? First, literacy was widespread throughout the entire empire. Second, reading was treasured and implemented on a high level within the wealthy and socially elite.[64] Third, reading and writing was not restricted to males, but that literacy and the readership of novels is extended and applicable to females also.[65] Fourth, reading and writing are

---

[60] Harris, *Ancient Literacy*, 177–90.

[61] On page 190–91 in *Ancient Literacy*, Harris provides an example of/from *Daphnis and Chloe*, where the two having been raised in the country, who are then "educated in letters" so that they could be "brought up in a more delicate manner." Harris makes the conclusion that this is revealing that a typical rural education would not have involved an education in reading and writing, but rather that the foster–fathers Lamon and Dryas thought it necessary for these two exceptions to receive an education, which fits well with Longus' idealization of Greek education.

[62] See Harris, *Ancient Literacy*, 190–196 and a synopsis of Harris in Franklin, "Literacy," 97–98.

[63] Frankin, "Literacy," 97–98.

[64] Holzberg, *Ancient*, 34; This is merely a point recognizing the "benefits" and "advantages" to wealth and status. It is not suggesting that slaves and the poor could not read, but rather it was more difficult for them to acquire the necessary education, training, materials, and finances necessary to accomplish the tasks of reading and writing.

[65] Bowie, "The Readership," 436–40. See also Susan Guettel Cole, "Could Greek Women Read and Write?" *Reflections of Women in Antiquity* (ed. Helene P. Foley; New York: Gordon and Breach Science Publishers, 1981), 219–45. I find the picture of a woman holding a pen that is now housed in the museum located within the Colosseum in Rome to be a significant piece of material culture. Also see David L. Balch, *Roman Domestic Art and Early House Churches* (Tübingen: Mohr, forthcoming 2008), 33, footnote 251 in reference to a woman who is "represented selecting a scoll from an open basket." This can be seen in *PPM* IX:233. See also footnote 178, in reference to a "well–dressed woman, who holds an unrolled scroll with both hands" as can be seen in *PPM* VIII:340. See also the images in vol. II, page 13 and vol. VII, page 7 of women sitting, reading in one, writing in the other image; see Figures 1 and 2 below for such representations as recorded from the Accademia ercolanese di archeologia (Naples, Italy), Ottavio Antonio Baiardi, and Pasquale Carcani. *Le Pitture Antiche di Ercolano e Contorni Incise con Qualche Spiegazione.* (Le Antichità di Ercolano Esposte. In Napoli: nella Regia stamperia, 1760 and 79 respectively); Other images that are found in and around Pompeii include the common images of the muses, especially Clio, muse of history and Calliope, muse of lyrical poetry (also the believed muse of Homer for the inspiration of writing the

not exclusive to the wealthy and elite, but were probably widespread throughout those whou were poor and with non-elite status through those who were literate.[66] Fifth, location and region within the empire can have a profound impact upon one's ability to read or write.[67]

In regard to literacy and reading within early Christianity, consider now a few more details. According to Bowie, the papyrology suggests that the popularity and development of the ancient novel seem to have been greatest in the late second century.[68] He goes on to say, "The production of the genre could therefore cover as short a span as the years A.D. 60–A.D. 230, with a concentration in the second half of the second century and first half of the third..."[69] In addition to this one might add Bowie's comments on readership: "That the educated classes of *provincial Asia* were indeed foremost among the intended readership of novels in general would certainly suit what little can be inferred about the readership of *Daphnis and Chloe.*"[70] Consider also the comments by Bremmer, that the five major *AAA*, the *Acts of John*, *Acts of Paul*, *Acts of Peter*, *Acts of Andrew*, and the *Acts of Thomas*, were all most likely being composed over a span from

---

Odyssey), who are represented in the buildings in Moregine, near Mt. Vesuvius in southern Italy, among other places; see the images reproduced in Pier Giovanni Guzzo, *Pompeii: Tales from an Eruption*, (Milan: Mondadori Electa, 2007), 169–72. However, it can be acknowledged that these women are reading and writing, but it is difficult to assess the correlation between these images of the divine and the women of Pompeii.; for more images of Clio and Calliope (?) see also *PPM* X:558; 1: 325 (Casa del Sacello I:783 (shown standing in the Casa annessa alla Casa dell'Efebo o di P. Cornelius Tages, 1.7.19, cubicolo f); IV:382, (#18 in Casa d'Ercole, 6.7.6, ambiente 7); VI:562 (Casa di M. Gavias Rufus, 7.2.16–17, visually representing either Clio or Calliope seated, wrapped in a green mantle, which nevertheless leaves her right side bare, writing on a large surface (ditico) which rests on her legs; the writing surface she holds stretches from her legs as high as her head. Below her is a visual representation of a still life). Thanks are extended to Dr. Balch for these further references and examples found within Pompeii and represented in *PPM*.

[66] Stephens, "Who Read Ancient Novels," 414–15; Also one cannot forget that lower status and/or slavery is not the equivalent of uneducated, illiterate, or poor. Such studies as Thomas E. J. Wiedemann, *Greek and Roman Slavery* (Baltimore: John Hopkins Press, 1981); Keith R. Bradley, *Slavery and Society at Rome* (New York: Cambridge UP, 1994); Dale Martin, *Slavery as Salvation: The Metaphor of Slavery in Pauline Christianity* (New Haven: Yale UP, 1990), et al. demonstrate literacy and wealth within slavery. See also Bowie, "The Readership," 438. The text mentions (with Bowie wishing to express a different point than the one I am suggesting) that it was "the regular practice of reading aloud by slaves to their owners in some cases."

[67] Once again, consider the article by Franklin, "Literacy," 77–98.

[68] Bowie, "The Readership," 442–43; and Holzberg, *The Ancient*, 43. For an earlier dating, see Hägg, *The Novel*, 5–6. This is reinforced by Judith B. Perkins, "This World or Another? The Intertextuality of the Greek Romances, The Apocryphal Acts and Apuleius' Metamorphoses," *Semeia 80*, 248.

[69] Ibid., 443.

[70] Ibid., 451.

150–230 CE, corresponding to the time of greatest activity of the ancient novel in general.[71] To add to this evidence, it seems that the readers of the *AAA* were most likely some of the "upper-class of Asia Minor" and in particular, women in this category.[72]

1.5 Intended/Actual Readers of the Acts of Paul

In regard to the *APTh*, it makes sense to consider the subject from both external evidence from the manuscript and textual history of reception as well as the external literary testimony of the sources that discuss, refer to, or quote from the *APTh*. After these considerations, I will provide an analysis of some of the internal evidence from the text. In this way, I think that we will be able to consider the readership of this text from the perspective of the actual readers (as best can be determined) and the ideal readers as can be seen from the internal evidence. Of course, there is no definite connection between external evidence to actual readers and internal evidence to ideal readers. But the fact that ancient novels, including Christian novels, were received with popularity shows that the authors could and did hit their target audiences on certain occasions. This is due in part to the success of a genre in general. Part of the success of the replication of themes, motifs, and narrative techniques is due to the familiarity of the "story line" to the reader. This demonstrates that sometimes the ideal audience actually merges with the actual audience, a phenomenon not necessarily available to empirical examination and proof.

The first person to make any mention of the *APTh* is Tertullian, who comments on the writings in *De Baptismo* 17, between the years 196 and 206.[73] From Tertullian we can infer that both women (the ones baptizing in Asia Minor and the Cainite woman in Carthage that Tertullian is rebuffing) and men (Tertullian) were real readers. This also confirms readers in both North Africa and Asia Minor. The second most important source comes from Hippolytus, who refers to Paul and the lion without hesitation as an orthodox tradition in his *Commentarium in Danielem* 3.29, written sometime around 180.[74] If the Ephesian episode and the *APTh* have been brought together by this time, then it can be assumed that Hippolytus knows the *AP*. If this be the case, then readership has made it to Rome at approximately the same time it has so offended Tertullian in Africa around the year 200.

---

[71] Bremmer, "Apocryphal Acts," 154.

[72] Ibid., 167.

[73] See footnote 13 in the introductory section entitled "1.2 Date of Composition."

[74] In 3.29.4, the text states Εἰ γὰρ πιστεύομεν, ὅτι Παύλου εἰς θηρία κατακριθέντος ἀφεθεὶς ἐπ᾽ αὐτὸν ὁ λέων εἰς τοὺς πόδας ἀναπεσὼν περιέλειχεν αὐτόν, πῶς οὐχὶ καὶ ἐπὶ τοῦ Δανιὴλ γενόμενα πιστεύσομεν, εἴπερ καὶ αὐτὸς Δαρεῖος πᾶσιν ταῦτα διὰ γραμμάτων ἀποστείλας διηγήσατο καὶ ἐν ταῖς Περσῶν... For the date, see Vouaux, *Actes de Paul*, 27.

X

Another witness to the *APTh* is Origen, who in his *De Principiis* 1.2.3 quotes from the *AP*, namely a section that has now been lost.[75] In addition to the quote in *De Principiis*, there are also references found in his commentary on John 20.12,[76] *Hom. Jer.* 20.1, and in *On the Passover* 36.6.[77] Eusebius also makes one other note in *Hist. eccl.* 3.1.1–3 that suggests that Origen's commentary on Genesis also recorded the death of Paul in Rome under Nero after Paul traveled from Jerusalem to Illyria.[78] If nothing more is gathered from these references, it means that Origen has a text of the *AP*, and he wrote from Alexandria (*De Principiis*, 220–230 CE), visited Rome (211–212 CE) having some contact with Hippolytus, relocated to Caesarea Maritima and there wrote his *Comm. Jo.* 20 (231–254 CE), while also writing his *Hom. Jer.* and the *Comm. Gen.* somewhere in the midst of his journeys.[79] This allows us to be aware that readers in either Alexandria and (in all probability) Caesarea Maritima, were reading the *AP* by the early to middle third century. It is uncertain how Origen gained access to the *AP*, but it seems apparent that he had knowledge of the text before having met Hippolytus in Rome, especially considering that the *AP* would have spoken to the appropriate behavior and response of Christians before

---

[75] The *De Principiis* text reads, "And therefore that language which is found in the Acts of Paul, where it is said that "here is the Word a living being," appears to me to be rightly used." This is thought by some to possibly be a "corruption" of Heb 4.12, ζῶν γὰρ ὁ λόγος τοῦ θεοῦ (see *ANF* 4:246, footnote 8) or that the author of the *AP* borrowed this quote and the *Quo Vadis?* scene from the *APt* and from Peter's prayer on the cross; see discussion in Schneemelcher, *NTApoc* 2:215 and Schmidt Schubert, eds., *ΠΠ*, 128; but for the most thorough discussion of the matter, see Rordorf, "The Relation between the *Acts of Peter* and the *Acts of Paul*: State of the Question," *The Apocryphal Acts of Peter: Magic, Miracles, and Gnosticism* (Ed. Jan N. Bremmer; Leuven: Peeters, 1998), 178–91; who claims that both sayings that are also used by Origen are oral tradition, and no claim can be made as to the dating of either work. See also Christine M. Thomas, "Word and Deed. The *Acts of Peter* and Orality," *Apocrypha* 3 (1993) 125–64, who also agrees on the orality tradition.

[76] The text in Greek reads, Εἴ τῳ δὲ φίλον παραδέξασθαι τὸ ἐν ταῖς Παύλου πράξεσιν ἀναγεγραμμένον ὡς ὑπὸ τοῦ Σωτῆρος εἰρημένον· "Ἄνωθεν μέλλω σταυροῦσθαι, οὗτος ὡς μετὰ τὴν ἐπιδημίαν παρα... See footnotes 93 and 94 and the discussion that follows concerning the *Quo Vadis?* scene. See also the discussion of Vouaux, *Actes de Paul*, 27–29. See also François Bovon, "A New Citation of the *Acts of Paul* in Origen," *Studies in Early Christianity* (Wissenschaftliche Untersuchungen zum Neuen Testament; Tübingen: J.C.B. Mohr [Paul Siebeck], 2003), especially 265–66, footnote 4. This article was translated by David H. Warren having originally appeared as "Une nouvelle citation des Actes de Paul chez Origène," *Apocrypha* 5 (1994): 113–17.

[77] See Bovon, "A New Citation," 265–68.

[78] Ilyria or Illyricum is Dalmatia, mentioned in *AP* 14.1 as the place from where Titus has just traveled, but it is syntactically possible that Origen reading the *AP*, could have thought that the text was saying that Paul had just traveled from Dalmatia. The text states, Ἦσαν δὲ περιμένοντες τὸν Παῦλον ἐν τῇ Ῥώμῃ Λουκᾶς ἀπὸ Γαλλιῶν καὶ Τίτος ἀπὸ Δαλματίας. Incidentally, this also seems to come from 2 Tim. 4.10.

[79] See Quasten, *Patrology*, 2:43–58.

magistrates, since they were being persecuted under Septimus Severus at the turn of the third century, further reinforcing a possible reason for the growing popularity of the *AP*. It is also known and agreed that Origen was well-trained rhetorically in Alexandria (via Clement), and yet demonstrated an appreciation for the *AP,* thus reinforcing the plausibility and acceptability of this text within a wealthy, elite, highly intellectual environment.

As has been briefly mentioned above through Origen's comments in *Comm. Jo.* 20.12 above, there is the matter of the *Quo vadis?* scene that appears in both *AP* and *APt*.[80] While it has not been conclusively shown which text influences the other or if the relationship is based on an oral tradition, it is certain that there is some connection between the texts, and a common interest of readers between the two texts, thus providing reason to believe that the readers of one text would have been the readers of the other, especially if they are circulating the same oral traditions.[81]

In general, the external evidence seems to demonstrate that there were male and female readers, including within wealthy, elite, and educated circles, in Asia Minor, Africa, Egypt, and possibly Syria within the first 50–75 years of the compilation, corresponding to the same time period of the ancient novel in general. This just reinforces the conviction that the readers of the ancient novel very well might have been the readers of the ancient Christian novel, and vice versa.[82]

The next and last aspect to consider in this section deals with the internal evidence from the *APTh* that might suggest a possible audience for the ancient Christian novel. There are several particular perspectives that ought to be considered in determining such a question. How does the text present women, men, sexuality, wealthy, poor, and status? While this is obviously

---

[80] See, Dennis R. MacDonald, "Which Came First? Intertextual Relationships Among the Apocryphal Acts of the Apostles," *Semeia 80: The Apocryphal Acts of the Apostles in Intertextual Perspectives* (Atlanta: Scholars Press, 1997), 11–18.

[81] See Carl Schmidt, *ΠΠ*, 127–130. After mentioning Tertullian and Hippolytus (and the dates of the compositions of their work), Schmidt states: "Die neuen Stücke bringen kein weiteres Material für die chronologische Fixierung. Aber nach einer andern Richtung hat das neue Quellenmaterial Aufklärung gebracht, nämlich inbezug auf das chronologische Verhältnis der AP zu den alten APe...Bisher hatte man fast allgemein die AP für älter als die letzteren angesetzt und angenommen, daß der Verfasser der APe zur Abfassung seiner Πράξεις durch die AP angeregt worden sei." (127). Schmidt goes on to argue for placing the *APt* earlier, while Bremmer, Rordorf, and MacDonald later suggest *AP* as the earlier document (also see footnote 90 above). See Bremmer, "The Apocryphal," 154; and Rordorf, "The Relation between the *Acts of Peter* and the *Acts of Paul*," 178–91. With regard to location of these readers of the *APt*, it seems that *APt* is following the lead of the *AP*, and nothing specific is known beyond conjecture. See Jan N. Bremmer, "Aspects of the *Acts of Peter*: Women, Magic, Place, and Date," *The Apocryphal Acts of Peter*, 18–20.

[82] Bremmer, "Apocryphal," 165.

not a complete index of possible avenues for determining readership, looking for these various attributes might suggest some of the ideal readers.

First, the author of the *APTh* appears to authenticate the text through
the description of Paul. It has been generally accepted that this is not an
authentic description of Paul; it nonetheless gives the appearance of some
knowledge of Paul.[83] The description of Paul adds a level of authority required of someone who hopes to communicate a worthy story of Paul's activities as a missionary.[84] I do not think this means that the author is attempting to be considered part of a *corpus scriptorum* in the same manner
as the author of the prologue of *Ben Sirach*,[85] but rather is attempting to
authenticate a story of Paul for the purpose of preserving the memory of
this apostle, especially, in contrast the accounts presented in the Pastorals.

Second, one cannot help but notice the emphasis upon the role of the
sexual relationship between various individuals within the text. First, there
is the attraction of numerous individuals to Paul throughout the text. To
name a few, the text begins with Demas and Hermogenes, who are traveling with Paul, and they "were entreating Paul earnestly as if they loved
him."[86] This is followed by the disciple, Onesiphorus, who meets Paul for
the first time. Upon seeing Paul, he smiles, Paul and Onesiphorus exchange greetings, and this immediately precipitates a jealous and hypo-
critical response from Demas and Hermogenes.[87] This is followed by the
implied sexual interest of Thecla in Paul. Thecla is introduced as one of
many "virgins" who are betrothed to marry men, such as Thamyris, who
are "going in" to Paul.[88] One can hardly miss the overtones in 3.8,[89] where
Thecla is being criticizd by her mother, who has gone to tell Thecla's fiancé, Thamyris about Thecla's attraction to Paul.

This type of sexual metaphor continues throughout the dialogue by
eroticizing Thecla when fighting beasts in the arena. Thecla is forced to do
the fighting practically naked, only to be clothed again after her salvation

---

[83] Bollók, "The Description of Paul in the Acta Pauli," 14–15. See also Grant, "The
Description of Paul in the Acts of Paul and Thecla," 1–4; and Malherbe, "A Physical Description of Paul," 170–75.

[84] Bremmer, "Magic, martyrdom," 38.

[85] Notice how the grandson compares the writing of his grandfather to the Law, the
Prophets, and the Others.

[86] *AP* 3.1, "καὶ ἐξελιπάρουν τὸν Παῦλον ὡς ἀγαπῶντες αὐτόν." I am not implying homoerotic love, but rather the ancient novel tends to exaggerate relationships between friends
and/or lovers. This is also the case here, where the relationships between Paul and his
companions is intensified, quasi–homoerotic, seemingly for the purpose of elevating the
sensual element of the story, hence the designation of *ancient romance*. Cf. the relationship of Clitophon – who is heterosexual – to his homoerotic friend, Clinias in *Achilles
Tatius* 1.7. This is typical of the *ancient novel*.

[87] Ibid., 3.2–5.

[88] Ibid., 3.7.

[89] See section "1.2 The Ancient Novel and the *Acts of Paul and Thecla*" above.

by God from these events.[90] It is not merely the eroticization of Thecla that I am interested in, but rather how Thecla is construed within her relationship to Paul. It is a continual theme that attempts are made to exploit Thecla's virginity at every turn by numerous officials and individuals, but these attempts are continually rebuffed in numerous ways.[91] I mention these trials in combination with the sexual metaphor to suggest that the theme of the "lovers beset by misfortunes" is clearly present in the text.[92] The emphasis upon sexual abstinence does not destroy the parallel between the ancient novel and the ancient *Christian* novel, but interestingly the theme of sexual abstinence is played out through a sexual metaphor, thus expressing a new representation of the same theme, the sexual metaphor. What does this suggest in regard to readership? There is a strong possibility that the readers of the ancient novel are the same readers of the Christian novel.

In addition to this limited conclusion, one cannot overlook the emphasis upon the prominence of Thecla and other women, such as Tryphaena in the text. This reinforces the statements of Tertullian, that women were directly being targeted by this text as readers. The text presents Thecla, (1) essentially affirmed by God, rather than from "God's apostle" Paul[93], and (2) being affirmed through patronage by Tryphaena, over and against her Thamyris through marriage.[94] However, the evidence does not suggest a readership of exclusively women, but wealthy, upper class men also. Tertullian's awareness of the *APTh* is the first clear indication of male readership. The author of the *APTh* must have taken into account both women and men reading the text with the hopes of influencing the readers (or hearers) to realize the theological implications of Thecla's receiving baptism and receiving the "seal."[95] The acceptance of this text would have

---

[90] Ibid., 4.8–13.

[91] Magda Misset-Van de Weg argues that Tryphaena's attempts to protect Thecla from rape, are, in the perspective of patronage, a way of protecting Thecla's honor. See the article, "A wealthy woman named Tryphaena: patroness of Thecla of Iconium," *The Apocryphal Acts of Paul and Thecla*, 29.

[92] Holzberg, *Ancient*, 23.

[93] The story is being told on two levels. First, the narrative account is being told. Second, the theological message is being presented *via* the narrative. From the narrative perspective, the two "lovers" are cautioned to delay their sexual gratification until a more opportune time. From a theological perspective, this is the vehicle to explain Thecla's affirmation (and fulfillment) by God. Affirmation by God rather than Paul has less to do with being "anti-Pauline," and more to do with coherence with Thecla's emergence as a "called out" emissary of God, not by humans, but by God. See *3.26.2 General Comment* below.

[94] Bremmer, "Magic, Martyrdom, and Women's Liberation," *The Apocryphal Acts of Paul and Thecla*, 56–58; and Magda Misset-Van de Weg, "A wealthy woman named Tryphaena,", 16–35.

[95] *AP* 4.10–15.

been an endorsement within the second century of a Pauline tradition that
is consistent with female apostolic leadership.

One might also ask whether there is an ideal geographical location for
the readership. The shift in the text from location to location is not necessarily a clear indicator of the location of the readership of the text, but
rather reflects the genre of the ancient novel, where the setting of the texts
includes extensive travelogues and voyages throughout the Mediterranean
region.[96] Also, the location question is obviously difficult to answer with
accuracy due to a deficiency in the textual transmission of the *AP*. Nevertheless, a limited answer might be suggested. If one takes into consideration the *Martyrium* account, then it is plausible to consider Asia Minor
(namely the citites of Iconium, Seleucia, and Myra), Syria (Antioch, Tyre,
and Sidon), Achaia (Corinth), and Italy (Rome) as several options. Excluding the *Martyrium* and *3 Corinthians* as possibly coming down to readers
as initially separate documents, this leaves Asia Minor and Syria as found
within the *APTh*. Even narrowing the text to these two locations, there still
seems to be a refocusing tendency to look not to Syria, but to Asia Minor.[97]

In summary, I have only been able to address these issues in a brief account of the subject and the evidence. So much more has been said, can be
said, and will be said as to the readership of the *AP*. It is enough at this
time to draw several conclusions. First, in dealing with the real readers, I
am convinced from the evidence that the development of the ancient Christian novel coincides with the development of the ancient novel, and that
the Christian novel is *not* the antecedent of the other. Second, the ancient
Christian novel first found a home in the same location as the ancient
novel, namely Asia. The real readers can also be found in Eastern and
Western North Africa, Italy, and Palestine/Syria, with the composition of
the text falling between the beginning of the second century to possibly
180 CE (with 206 CE being the *terminus ad quem*). This includes both the
writing of the documents and the arrangement and compilation of the
broader text over the century. If the *AP* were originally intended to be an
ancient novel, then theology and doctrine would have been a secondary
issue for the author, as evidenced by his inconsistent usage of other Christian texts, such as the canonical Pastoral Epistles. However, it is also clear
that as women and men would have been readers of the text, both were
reading the *AP* with theological doctrine at stake and recognizing that this

---

[96] Supposedly the *AP* begins with Paul in Damascus, proceeding to Jerusalem, then
Antioch, and then the text moves to Iconium, which is the beginning of the narrative of
APTh. See Holzberg, *Ancient*, 1–6, 9–10; Hägg, *The Novel*, 118.

[97] Notice Thecla's identification of herself as "I am one of the chief persons of the
Iconians," in 4.1, and then after her baptism, she decides to return to Iconium with Paul's
blessing (4.15–17).

text carried the status of early Christian authority. Regarding the status of the readers, the sources indicate nothing more than that those who mentioned or acknowledged it were of a wealthy, educated, upper class position, but were likely writing to lay people (e.g. Tertullian's audience). The ideal readers of the *AP* appear to be readers located first and foremost in Asia Minor. Beyond this location, Syria, Achaia, and Rome are possible, but less likely. Women are given special attention in the text, but the alignment of this text with other ancient novels suggests a mixed audience, primarily coming from a wealthy and elite status, but also possibly including listeners and readers from the poor and with a lower status.

Chapter 2: The Historical Context

2.1 Authorship and Place

Some time near the turn of the second century, Tertullian wrote a tractate entitled *de Baptismo*, in which he attempted to address the error that had been set forth by a certain female Gnostic or Marcionite of the Cainite sect who had argued that baptism was not a necessary sacrament of the Christian faith. Of interest to the reader of the *Acts of Paul* (*AP*) is his statement in chapter 17:

> But if certain Acts of Paul, which are falsely so named, claim the example of Thecla for allowing women to teach and to baptize, let men know that in Asia the presbyter who compiled that document, thinking to add of his own to Paul's reputation, was found out, and though he professed he had done it for love of Paul, was deposed[98] from his position. How could we believe that Paul should give a female power to teach and to baptize, when he did not allow a woman even to learn by her own right? *Let them keep silence* he says, *and ask their husbands at home.*[99]

From this quote, we learn that a certain presbyter in Asia compiled the *AP*. The question pertains to how much of the *AP* was actually *written* by the presbyter or merely *edited* by the presbyter. This is difficult to assess for

---

[98] I would translate "was deposed" as "resigned from his place." The context suggests that "deposed" is an accurate interpretation, although it does not literally assert that he was made to resign.

[99] "quod si quae Acta Pauli, quae perperam scripta sunt, exemplum Theclae ad licentiam mulierum docendi tinguendique defendant, sciant in Asia presbyterum qui eam scripturam construxit, quasi titulo Pauli de suo cumulans, convictum atque confessum id se amore Pauli fecisse loco decessisse. Quam enim fidei proximum videtur ut is docendi et tinguendi daret feminae potestatem qui ne discere quidem constanter mulieri permisit? Taceant, inquit, et domi viros suos consulant." Quoted from Ernest Evans, ed. and trans., *Tertullian's Homily on Baptism* (London: SPCK, 1964) 36–37. The italics at the end of the quote are quotations from 1 Cor 14:35.

various reasons. Part of the problem deals with the history of reception of the *AP*, and the evidence that suggests that *3 Corinthians* (*3 Cor*), the *Acts of Paul and Thecla* (*APTh*), and the *Martyrdom of Paul* all circulated independently and some of this likely circulated independently previous to the completion of the *AP*.[100] Nonetheless, there has been a growing consensus that the *AP*, at least the *APTh* were originally penned or conceived orally by a woman or within communities of women.[101] This claim has initially been made on the assumption that Tertullian was not truly speaking of the *AP*, based on textual discrepancies, where Davies argues unconvincingly that the original text of *de Baptismo* was only *Pauli*, rather than the more likely *Acta Pauli quae*, which is the reading that Evans reproduces following Codex Trecensis 523 over the text edited by Mesnartius in 1545.[102] While the arguments that attempt to discredit Tertullian's knowledge of the *AP* or to discredit the critical text of *de Baptismo* may not be sufficiently argued, this does not ultimately discount female authorship of the *APTh*. I believe that it is still possible that parts of the *APTh* could have come from a female or female communities, written earlier in the second century, and then moved into the Asian presbyter's edited work entitled, the *Acts of Paul*.[103]

---

[100] See *3. History of Reception* for more details on this point.

[101] See first Stevan L. Davies dissertation entitled "The Social World of the Apocryphal Acts," (Ph.D. diss., Temple University, 1978); then republished as *The Revolt of the Widows: The Social World of the Apocryphal Acts* (Carbondale: Southern Illinois University Press, 1980) 104–09; and revisited in "Women, Tertullian, and the *Acts of Paul*," in *Semeia 38: The Apocryphal Acts of the Apostles* (Atlanta: Scholars Press, 1986) 139–43; Dennis Ronald MacDonald, *The Legend and the Apostle: The Battle for Paul in Story and Canon* (Philadelphia: Westminster Press, 1983) 34–53; Virginia Burrus, *Chastity as Autonomy: Women in the Stories of Apocryphal Acts* (Studies in Women and Religion Volume 23; Lewiston/Queenston: Edwin Mellon Press, 1987) 67–8. Some criticisms have been offered by P. Dunn, "Women's Liberation, the *Acts of Paul*, and Other Apocryphal Acts of the Apostles: A Review of Some Recent Interpreters," *Apocrypha* 4 (1993): 245–61 and Jean–Daniel Kaestli, "Les principales orientations de la recherche sur les Actes apocryphes des Apôtres," *Les Actes apocryphes des Apôtres*, 49–61 and "Fiction littéraire et réalité sociale: que peut–on savoir de la place des femmes dans le milieu de production des Actes apocryphes des Apôtres?" *Apocrypha* 1 (1990) 279–302.

[102] See text in footnore 109 above. Response of Thomas W. Mackay to Stevan L. Davies article, "Women, Tertullian and the *Acts of Paul*," *Semeia 38*, 139–49; and Willy Rordorf, "Tertullien et les Actes de Paul (à propos de *bapt*. 17,5) *Autour de Tertullien* (Hommage à René Braun; Nice: Association Publications de la Faculté des Lettres et Sciences Humaines de Nice, 1990) 2:153–60. Reprinted in *Lex Orandi – Lex Credendi: Gesammelte Aufsätze zum 60. Geburtstag*. (Paradosis 36: Freiburg: Universitätsverlag Freiburg Schweiz, 1993), 475–84. See also A. Hilhorst, "X. Tertullian on the Acts of Paul," *The Apocryphal Acts of Paul and Thecla* (Ed. Jan N. Bremmer; Kamen: Kok Pharos, 1996) 150–63.

[103] See Jeremy W. Barrier, "Tertullian and the Acts of Paul or Thecla? Readership of the Ancient Novel and the Invocation of Thecline and Pauline Authority" (paper presented at the annual meeting of the Society of Biblical Literature, Washington, D. C., 20

2.2 Date of Composition

De Baptismo was written sometime between the years 196 and 206.[104] It is the dating of *de Baptismo* that provides the *terminus ante quem* for the *AP*. On the other hand the *terminus post quem* is uncertain. Alfred von Gutschmid noted that a Queen Tryphaena, widow of King Cotys of Thrace, mother of King Polemon II, King of Pontus, and a relative to Caesar, has been proven to have existed (possibly having lived in Iconium) around 38–63 CE, which increases (but, by no way confirms) the likelihood of Thecla's historicity and provides a *terminus a quo* back to the time when the events were reported to have occured.[105] Jan Bremmer suggests a much narrower date of 160 CE, because of the evidence on a Roman inscription of a Pompeia Sosia Falconilla, the wife of a Roman consul in Sicily around the year 169 CE.[106] Bremmer is convinced that this Falconilla is the source that provides the name for the Falconilla mentioned in the *APTh*, who is the daughter of Queen Tryphaena.[107] If this were true, then the date for writing the *APTh* falls within a space of 30–40 years, with the *AP* being compiled within the peak of the popularity of the ancient novel.[108] On the

---

November 2006), where I argue Tertullian's use of *construxit*, in contrast to *scribo* as an important distinction to consider regarding authorship of the *AP*. See also Schneemelcher who translates this as "produced," in *NTApoc*, 2:214.

[104] See Evans, *Tertullian's Homily*, 35–37, 97–101; or *Tertulliani Opera: Pars I* (ed. J. G. Ph. Borleffs; CCSL; Turnholti: Typographi Brepols Editores Pontificii, 1954), 291–92. See also several translations together in one article with thorough discussion by A. Hilhorst, "Tertullian on the Acts of Paul," 150–53; and Hilhorst acknowledges that a more thorough discussion is provided by Willy Rordorf in "Tertullien et les Actes de Paul," 475–84.

[105] See Rordorf, "Tradition and Composition in the *Acts of Thecla*: The State of the Question," *Semeia 38*, 46 or "Tradition et composition dans les *Actes de Thècle*: Etat de la question." *Theologische Zeitschrift* 41 (1985): 276–78; Rordorf is stemming his comments from the earlier discussion of Gutschmid. "Die Königsnamen in den apokryphen Apostelgeschichten. Ein Beitrag zur Kenntnis des geschichtlichen Romans." *Rheinisches Museum für Philologie* 19 (1864): 161–83., 177–79; Theodor Zahn, *Göttingische Gelehrte Anzeigen*, (1877): 1307; Ramsay, *The Church in the Roman Empire*, 391; F. C. Conybeare, ed., *The Apology and Acts of Apollonius and other Monuments of Early Christianity* (London and New York: Swan Sonnenschein & Co. and Macmillan, 1894) 50–55.

[106] Jan N. Bremmer, "The Apocryphal Acts: Authors, Place, Time and Readership," *The Apocryphal Acts of Thomas* (Leuven: Peeters, 2001) 153; W. Eck, "Senatorische Familien der Kaiserzeit in der Provinz Sizilien," *ZPE* 113 (1996): 109–28; Bremmer, "Magic, Martyrdom, and Women's Liberation," 53; "Aspects of the *Acts of* Peter: Women, Magic, Place and Date," *The Apocryphal Acts of Peter*, 17.

[107] *APTh* 28–36 (4.3-11); Bremmer, "Apocryphal," 153. I do not find this evidence convincing due to the fact that the name Falconilla is common and the provenance of this inscription is Sicily, while the provenance of the *AP* is Asia.

[108] See the section entitled *1. The Ancient Novel* in this introduction below. See also Ewen Bowie's "The Readership of Greek Novels in the Ancient World," in *The Search for the Ancient Novel* (ed. James Tatum; Baltimore and London: John Hopkins UP, 1994)

other hand, Hilhorst suggests that the passage of Jerome, where he is commenting upon Tertullian's criticism of the *Acta Pauli* is significant regarding the composition of *AP*.[109] In addition to essentially repeating what Tertullian had to say, Jerome adds "conuictum apud Iohannem." If Jerome is not mistaken in his addition to Tertullian's comment, this addition leads Hilhorst to conclude that the *AP* must have been written after Paul's death and before the death of the apostle John. This would make the *terminus post quem* between 68 CE and 98 CE.[110] Peter Dunn makes several calculations regarding the age of Thecla (building on the work of J. Gwynn[111]) who would have met Paul in the late 40's, and in turn settles on the date of 120 CE as the *terminus post quem*..[112] The problem of this assessment is that the historicity of Thecla cannot be determined. Of significance to the dating question is the more recent conclusion, based largely on the find of Bodmer X, that suggests that *3 Corinthians* circulated independently previous to its incorporation into the *AP*, which allows for the possibility that the various parts of the *AP* were written at different times.[113] Therefore, it is possible that the writing and compiling of the *AP* spans a period of over 100 years. It seems likely that the final compilation would have come toward the last 30–40 years of the second century, due to the content and issues that are addressed,[114] while allowing for parts of the document to have originated at an earlier time.

442–43; and Niklas Holzberg, *The Ancient Novel: An Introduction* (trans. Christine Jackson-Holzberg; London and New York: Routledge, 1995), 43; For earlier dating see Tomas Hägg, *The Novel in Antiquity* (Berkeley and Los Angeles: U of Cal P, 1983) 5–6. This is reinforced by J. Perkins, "This World or Another?," 248; Bremmer, "Apocryphal Acts," 154.

[109] "Tertullian," 158–59; referring to Jerome, *Vir. ill.* 7.

[110] Ibid., 158–61.

[111] Gwynn, "Thecla," *Dictionary of Christian Biography, Literature, Sects and Doctrines: being a continuation of "The dictionary of the Bible".* (ed. William George Smith and Henry Wace; London: J. Murray, 1877–87) 4:892. Gwynn gives a date of 117.

[112] *Recension G* and *APTh* 45 have Thecla dying at age 90, therefore this is around 140, with a reduction to 12 C.E. "allowing for a more moderate date of ca. AD 120." See Dunn, "*The* Acts of Paul," 8–9.

[113] See M. Testuz for the *editio princeps*, *Papyrus X–XI, X,* 9 for a discussion, and third century dating. For a complete discussion, see Willy Rordorf, "Héresie et orthodoxie selon la Correspondance apocryphe entre les Corinthiens et l'apôtre Paul." *Lex Orandi – Lex Credendi: Gesammelte Aufsätze zum 60. Geburtstag.* (Paradosis 36; Freiburg: Universitätsverlag Freiburg in der Schweiz, 1993) 389–431.

[114] I am referring to the concern and mention made to the document by Tertullian (*Bapt.* 17) and also Hippolytus of Rome (*Comm. Dan.* 3.29).

Chapter 3: History of Reception

3.1 Canonicity

The question of canonicity is anachronistic at a certain level, demanding more of early Christianity than is fair.[115] On the other hand, the *AP* was used widely by the early church (see "2.4 Intended/Actual Readers of the *Acts of Paul*" above). The only early source that directly opposes the *AP* is Tertullian (*Bapt.* 17) at the turn of the second century, while Origen (quoting possibly five times),[116] Hippolytus (*Comm. Dan.* 3.29), then later Jerome (*Epist.* 22.3) all seem to have no problem with the text. It is only by the fourth century that hesitation is witnessed again. For instance, Jerome independently speaks of Thecla on one occasion (*Epist.* 22.3), and when he has a negative comment, he essentially has nothing more to say than to repeat Tertullian's comment (*Vir. ill.* 7). Also, Eusebius over 100 years after Tertullian mentions the *AP* as "not genuine" (Eusebius, *Hist. Ecc.*, 3.25). On the other hand, the sixth century Codex Claromontanus includes the *AP* within its canonical list.[117] This Codex, while representing the "Western" text type, indicates the length of time that the *AP* remained within canonical/authoritative lists of the church. In addition to this, it is clear that Ephrem's Syriac corpus of Pauline letters included *3 Corinthians* which locates this text in a canonical/authoritative position in the fourth century in Syria (representing the East as well).[118] Finally, one might also add that the Hamburg Papyrus ($\mathfrak{P}^1$), found in Egypt and dating to the third or fourth century, was bound as a Codex that included the Greek *AP*, Song of Songs in the Old Fâyyum Coptic dialect, Lamentations of Jeremiah in the same dialect, an unknown text, Ecclesiastes in Greek, and Ecclesiastes in the old Fâyyum Coptic. This, once again, places the text of the *AP* alongside other authoritative texts that were bound into a book that was obviously intended for a bilingual church in need of texts in both languages.[119]

---

[115] In particular, I am dealing with the fact that the issue of canonicity does not really develop for another 100–150 years after the second century. Therefore, it may be fair to say that these are really questions of proto-canonicity.

[116] *De Principiis* 1.2.3; *Comm. Jo.* 20.12, *Hom. Jer.* 20.1, *Pasch.* 36.6. Eusebius makes a note in *Hist. eccl.* 3.1.1–3 that suggests that the third volume of Origen's commentary on Genesis (now lost) knew of the *AP* and this apparently included the *MP* as well.

[117] Schneemelcher interprets the Claromontanus list much differently (*NTApoc* 2: 216) while altogether ignoring Ephrem's commentaries.

[118] See Willy Rordorf, "Hérésie et orthodoxie," 389–431; Walter Bauer, *Orthodoxy and Heresy in Earliest Christianity* (London/Philadelphia: SCM/Fortress Press, 1971) 39–42.

[119] Schmidt, *ΠΠ*, 6–8.

It is not coincidence that the point in time (fifth/sixth century) in which
the *AP* bore the most authority is also the time in which the artistic representations of Thecla are the greatest, and the Cult of Thecla is the strongest
also.[120] Seleucia of Isauria was probably the most important cult center,
where a basilica the size of a football field was devoted to Thecla. By the
end of the sixth century there were also several other shrines in Seleucia.
In addition to this, Justinian was known to have built two basilicas devoted
to Thecla in the city of Constantinople.[121] The manuscript history demonstrates that the *AP* were considered authoritative in certain circles of the
church from a very early time, eventually developing into canonical status
by the fifth/sixth century, and then finally purged from the Christian canon
of scriptures at some later date. The purging of the *AP* was a process beginning as far back as Tertullian, reinforced by others (Eusebius, Gelasian
Decree) and then slowly tipping the scales over time. Another example is
that of Ps.-Athanasius' *Synopsis Scripturae Sacrae* 76 (PG 28.432), where
the *AP* falls alongside other such περίοδοι as the *Didache*, the *Epistle of
Barnabas*, and the *Apocalypse of Paul*.[122] I do not think that there was any
one point in which it was definitively rejected. It is something that took
time, and most likely gained the greatest degree of momentum in the post-
enlightenment era, especially after the Council of Trent and other such
church decisions that further illuminated issues of canonicity and authority.

3.2 Manuscript History[123]

Following upon those early witnesses noted above, there were other attes-
tations, such as the Stichometry of Nicephorus,[124] which listed the *AP* as
having 3600 lines.[125] The apocryphicity of *AP* and the *APTh* continued to
develop over the years beginning with Tertullian, then Jerome's designation of the "περιόδους *Pauli et Theclae*" determined to be *apocryphas scrip-*

---

[120] MacDonald, Dennis R. and Andrew D. Scrimgeour, "Pseudo-Chrysostom's Panegyric to Thecla: The Heroine of the *Acts of Paul* in Homily and Art," *Semeia 38*, 51–52.

[121] Ibid., 153.

[122] See Kurt Niederwimmer, *The Didache: A Commentary*, (ed. Harold W. Attridge;
trans. Linda M. Maloney; Hermeneia; Minneapolis: Fortress Press, 1998), 4–6; and also
Johannes Quasten, *Patrology* (Utrecht, Holland: Spectrum, 1953; repr., Allen, Texas:
Christian Classics, 2003), 3.39, for more information on Ps.Athanasius, *Synopsis Scripturae Sacrae*.

[123] Consider other standard introductions to the manuscript history, such as Schneemelcher, *NTApoc* 2:213–218.

[124] Ninth century list compiled by the Patriarch Nicephorus of Constantinople (circa
758–828 CE).

[125] As a reference Acts of the Apostles has 2600 lines and Codex Claromantanus
claims that the *AP* has 3560 lines.

turas (Vir. ill. 7),[126] and then finally reinforced as rejected by the Gelasian Decree (fifth century CE) and the Stichometry of Nicephorus. However, it might be added that by the time of the Gelasian Decree, the *APTh* were circulating separately from the *AP* corpus and the *APTh* alone is the specific text rejected by the Decree.[127] The *AP* are sporadically witnessed through the middle ages with such writers as the fourteenth century Nicephorus Callistus Xanthopulus (*Historia Ecclesiastica* 2.25–26), as he recalls the Ephesian Episode and other aspects of the *AP*.[128]

During the fourth through the sixth century, the peak of Thecla's popularity, there were three writings that have preserved the memory and remnants of the *APTh*.[129] First, the *Travels of Egeria* (ca. 4th century) record the travelogue of a Spanish nun who traveled to Seleucia and witnessed the disciples of Thecla serving at the monastery there.[130] Second, the *Life and Miracles of St. Thecla*, a fifth century document, falsely attributed to Basil, summarizes the *APTh* and then goes on to tell 46 miracles performed by Thecla.[131] Third, the Pseudo-Chrysostom *Panegyric to Thecla*, which is a liturgical homily devoted to Thecla to be preached during the "Feast of St. Thecla, the Virgin Martyr" on September 23 in the West and September 24 in the East.[132]

The modern textual history essentially begins with the work of Joannes Ernest Grabe[133] who produced the first critical text in 1698, based on the

---

[126] *Igitur περιόδους Pauli et Theclae et totam baptizati Leonis fabulam, inter apocryphas scripturas computamus.* This is translated "Therefore the *Acts of Paul and Thecla* and all the fable about the Lion baptized by him, we reckon amoung the apocryphal writings."

[127] Pick, *The Apocryphal Acts,* 10.

[128] *Historia Ecclesiastica* begins:Ὡς ὁ Παῦλος ἐν Ἐφέσῳ θηριομαχήσας ἐπὶ ἄρχοντος Ἱερωνύμου, θείᾳ δυνάμει ὑπέρτερος ὤφθη. Οἱ δὲ τὰς Παύλου περιόδους ἀναταξάμενοι, ἄλλα τε πλεῖστα παθεῖν τε ἅμα καὶ δρᾶσαι τοῦτον ἱστόρησαν, καὶ δὴ καὶ τόδε, ἡνίκα δὴ τῇ Ἐφέσῳ παρῆν. Ἱερωνύμου γὰρ ἄρχοντος ...

[129] MacDonald, "Pseudo-Chrysostom's Panegyric to Thecla," 152.

[130] See Stephen J. Davis, *The Cult of Saint Thecla: A Tradition of Women's Piety in Late Anitquity* (Oxford: Oxford, 2001), 64–69.

[131] See Scott Fitzgerald Johnson, *The Life and Miracles of Thekla: A Literary Study,* (Cambridge: Harvard UP, 2006). The Greek text with a French translation can be found in Gilbert Dagron in collaboration with Marie Dupré La Tour. *Vie et miracles de sainte Thècle: texte grec, traduction et commentaire.* Subsidia Hagiographica 62. Brussels: Societe des Bollandistes, 1978.

[132] MacDonald, "Pseudo-Chrysostom's Panegyric to Thecla," 157. The *editio princeps* was published by Fronton du Duc in 1601; Then Michel Aubineau publishes "Le panéyrique de Thècle, attribué à Jean Chrysostome *(BHG* 1720): la fin retrouvée d'un texte motile." AnBoll 93 (1975): 349–62, based on the finding of a new manuscript.

[133] *Spicilegium SS. Patrum ut et Hæreticorum: Seculi post Christum natum I. II. & III. quorum vel integra monumenta, vel fragmenta, partim ex aliorum patrum libris jam impressis collegit, & cum codicibus manuscriptis contulit, partim ex MSS. nunc pr mum edidit, ac singula tam præfatione, quàm notis subjunctis illustravit : tomus I. sive seculum I* (Oxford: E Theatro Sheldoniano, 1698), 94.

Greek Codex Barocciano 180[134] (12th century)[135] and Latin Codex Digbaeno 39 (12th century) [136], which had been given to the Bodleian library in Oxford, England by a "Reverand" Dominus D. Millius. In addition, Grabe published a fragment of the *AP*, as recorded through Rufinus' transposition of Origen's *De Principiis*, and also the longer "martyrdom of the holy and glorious proto-martyr Thecla who died as an apostle."[137] At this point the *AP*, the *Martyrdom of Paul*, *3 Corinthians* (not yet recovered), and *APTh* are all thought to be separate documents. Grabe's work is then quickly followed by further publications of Johann Albert Fabricius (1703, 1719)[138] and then Jeremiah Jones (1798).[139] English translations working off of Jones were followed by Montague Rhodes James (1893 and 1924), and finally up to the present by the work of J. Keith Elliott.[140] Translations have similarly been done also in Italian, French, and German.[141] The manuscript becomes most interesting over the last 125+ years following a series of finds in Egypt and other places abroad.[142] It had not been known that the *AP* included *3 Corinthians*, the *Martyrdom of Paul*, and the *Acts of Paul*

---

[134] Also called *Codex G, Recension G, or G.*

[135] Dating found in the "Prolegomena," *AAA*, XCIX–C.

[136] See von Gebhardt, *Passio*, XXXIII, for the dating of this manuscript.

[137] Translation of the Latin heading in Grabe, *Spicilegium SS. Patrum ut et Hæreticorum*, 95, 128.

[138] Fabricius, Johann Albert. *Codex Apocryphus Novi Tesamenti* (Hamburg: B. Schiller, 1703); and *Codex Apocryphus Novi Tesamenti: Collectus, castigatus, testimoniisque, censuris & animadversionibus illustratus à Johanne Alberto Fabricio* (3 vols.; 2d ed.; Hamburg: B. Schiller & Joh. Christoph. Kisneri, 1719–43).

[139] Jeremiah Jones, *A New and Full Method of Settling the Canonical Authority of the New Testament to which is subjoined a Vindication of the Former part of St. Matthew's Gospel, from Mr. Whiston's Charge of Dislocations* (3 vols; Oxford: Clarendon Press, 1798).

[140] The Greek critical texts were continued in James' *Apocrypha Anecdota: A Collection of Thirteen Apocryphal Books and Fragments* (Texts and Studies 2.3; Cambridge: University Press, 1893); and in English translation in *The Apocryphal New Testament* (Oxford: Clarendon, 1924); J. Keith Elliot, *The Apocryphal New Testament: A Collection of Apocryphal Christian Literature in an English Translation* (Oxford: Clarendon Press, 1993).

[141] Most notably (1) German: Edgar Hennecke, ed., *Handbuch zu den Neutestamentlichen Apokryphen in Verbindung mit Fachgelehrten.* (Tübingen: J. C. B. Mohr [Paul Siebeck], 1904) 358–95; and *Neutestamentliche Apokryphen in Verbindung mit Fachgelehrten in deutscher Übersetzung und mit Einleitungen* (Tübingen and Leipzig: J. C. B. Mohr [Paul Siebeck], 1904), 357–82; and the subsequent 4 editions up until 1992 through the work of Wilhelm Schneemelcher and translated by R. McL. Wilson; (2) French: Vouaux, *Les Actes de Paul* and Rordorf, "Actes de Paul," in *ÉAC*, 1115–77; (3) Italian: Luigi Moraldi, *Apocrifi del Nuovo Testamento* (Turin: Unione Typigrafico–editrice torinese, 1971) 2:1061–1130.

[142] For a more complete description of the difficult manuscript history, I refer the reader first to Willy Rordorf's retracing of the history of the reception of *3 Corinthians*, which largely covers much of the textual history in "Hérésie et orthodoxie," 389–431.

and Thecla. First, it must be noted that a series of manuscripts began to be uncovered beginning in 1890 leading up to the discovery of a Coptic Papyus in Egypt in 1897 (Cop[1])[143] that included a sixth century manuscript that had sections of *APTh, 3 Corinthians*, an Ephesian episode (known to Hippolytus), and the *MP* all within the same manuscript, which suggested all of these writings were integrally incorporated into the text. This created quite a discussion over the relationship of the documents,[144] finally answered more thoroughly only with the finds of two Greek papyrii from Egypt; namely the Hamburg Papyrus ($\mathfrak{P}^1$) (ca. fourth century) and the Bodmer Papyrus ($\mathfrak{P}^7$) (ca. third century).[145] These two Greek manuscripts along with Ephrem's Syriac commentaries were able to (1) reinforce an original Greek document of a complete *AP* at a very early stage, (2) reaffirm the original independent circulation of *3 Corinthians* in the earlier part of the second century, and (3) demonstrate definitively a united *AP* including all subsequent writings mentioned above. As will be noted in the commentary below, Cop[1], $\mathfrak{P}^1$, $\mathfrak{P}^7$ have high priority in textual decisions due to their early dating.

Therefore, yet another critical edition will be necessary, i.e. that which is being produced by Willy Rordorf, Pierre Cherix and Rudophe Kasser

---

[143] This is not a complete listing, but see Bernard P. Grenfell, and Arthur S. Hunt, eds. and trans. *The Oxyrhynchus Papyri* (London: Egypt Exploration Fund, 1898) 1:9–10, papyrus number 6 and 13:23–25, papyrus number 1602; P. Vetter, "Der apokryphe dritte Korintherbrief neu übersetzt und nach seiner Entstehung untersucht," *TQ* 72 (1890): 610–39; A. Carrière, and S. Berger. "La Correspondance apocryphe de saint Paul et des Corinthiens." *Revue de Théologie et de Philosophie* 24 (1891): 333–51; Eduard Bratke, "Ein zweiter lateinischer Text des apokryphen Briefwechsels zwischen dem Apostel Paulus und den Korinthern," *Theologische Literaturzeitung* 17 (1892): 585–88; and then Carl Schmidt, *Acta Pauli aus der Heidelberger koptischen Papyrushandschrift* with the *Nr. 1: Tafelband* (Leipzig: J. C. Hinrichs, 1904) and supplemented by "Ein neues Fragment der Heidelberger Acta Pauli," *SPAW* (4 Feb. 1909): 216–20.

[144] Theodor Zahn, *Geschichte des neutestamentlichen Kanons* (Erlangen and Leipzig: A. Deichert, 1890; Reprint, Hildesheim and New York: Georg Olms, 1975), 2:595–611; Adolf von Harnack, "Untersuchungen über den apokryphen Briefwechsel der Korinther mit dem Apostel Paulus." *SPAW* 1 (1905): 3–35; D. de Bruyne, "Nouveau fragments des Actes de Pierre, de Paul, de Jean, d'André, et de l'Apocalypse d'Élie," *Revue Bénédictine* 25 (1908): 149–60; "Un nouveau manuscrit de la Troisième Lettre de Saint Paul aux Corinthiens." *Revue Bénédictine* 25 (1908): 431–34; "Un quatrième manuscrit latin de la Correspondance apocryphe de S. Paul avec les Corinthiens," *Revue Benedictine* 45 (1933): 189–95; Boese, H. "Über eine bisher unbekannte Handschrift des Briefwechsels zwischen Paulus und den Korinthern." *Zeitschrift für die neutestamentliche Wissenschaft* 44 (1952–53): 66–76.

[145] Testuz, M. *Papyrus Bodmer X–Xl. X*; and Schmidt and Schubart, *ΠΠ*, along with "Ein Berliner Fragment der alten Πράξεις Παύλου," *SPAW* (19 Feb. 1931): 37–40; and announced in 1929 in "Neue Funde zu den alten Πράξεις Παύλου," *SPAW* (28 Feb. 1929): 176–83.

through *Corpus Christianorum Series Apocryphorum*. In addition to the material mentioned above, there is a Coptic text entitled Bodmer CLI (Cop[B]) announced by Rudolphe Kasser in 1959 with the *editio princeps* finally published in 2004,[146] as well as an unpublished John Rylands Coptic manuscript (Cop[M]).[147]

Chapter 4: The *Acts of Paul* and the New Testament

4.1 APTh, Early Christian texts, ancient novels, and this commentary

There have been several studies conducted over the last few years that attempt to determine what knowledge the author of the *AP* had of the documents now found in the New Testament.[148] In general, it appears the author of the *AP* may have utilized several NT writings, while exhibiting some oral familiarity with the content or possibly the actual written documents of several additional NT writings. In particular, it appears that the author of the *AP* may have known several Gospels and Pauline letters, namely Matthew,[149] Mark, Luke, Acts, Romans, 1 Corinthians, 2 Corinthians,[150] Galatians, Ephesians, 1–2 Thessalonians, 1–2 Timothy, Titus, Philemon, 2 Peter, and Revelation. In addition, in *AP* 3.6, there is a strong possibility of a connection to 2 Clem 6.4, 7–9 (see note 6 in *3.6 Textual Notes*). However, there is a significant breach in interpretation of this relationship, primarily regarding the relationship of the *AP* to the canonical Acts of the Apostles and the Pastoral Epistles. The most significant discussions have developed surrounding the relationships of these documents. In particular, (1) what is the relationship of the *AP* to the Pastorals[151], and (2) what is the

---

[146] See Kasser and Luisier. "Le Bodmer XLI," 281–384.

[147] Kasser, Rodolphe, "Acta Pauli 1959." *Revue d'histoire et de philosophie religieuses* 40 (1960): 45–57; and Crum, "New Coptic Manuscripts," 501.

[148] The most thorough investigations have been completed by Julian Hills, "The Acts of the Apostles in the *Acts of Paul*," *SBL Seminar Papers, 1994* (ed. E. H. Lovering, Jr.; SBLSP 33; Atlanta: Scholars Press, 1994) 24–54; see also the articles by Willy Rordorf, Julian V. Hills, Richard Bauckham, and Daniel Marguerat in *Semeia 80,* 137–83; and P. Herczeg, "New Testament Parallels to the Acta Pauli Document," *The Apocryphal Acts of Paul and Thecla,* 142–49. Several of these summaries systematically identify the specific references under question.

[149] See *3.5.1 Textual Notes*, note 8 for an example.

[150] 1 Cor 15:32 was probably one of the sources that provided the basis for the Ephesian Episode in *AP*, but more telling is the use of 1 Cor 7.29 in *AP* 3.5

[151] See Dunn, *"Acts of Paul,"* 45–68; and MacDonald, *The Legend and the Apostle,* 54–77; and Jouette M. Bassler, "The Widows' Tale: A Fresh Look at 1 Tim 5:3–16." *JBL* 103 (1984): 23–41.

relationship of the *AP* to the Acts of the Apostles?[152] The relationship is incredibly difficult to determine, and the complexity of it matches the complexity of the synoptic Gospel problem. In general, with this is mind, I decided that I would overview some of the discussion dealing with the relationship of the *AP* to the canonical Gospels and Acts, and then provide an even more thorough discussion of the relationship of the *AP* to the Pastorals to demonstrate the complexity, and also to make some determinations as to how one might understand this relationship.

As one approaches this commentary, the questions of literary dependence upon various texts is one of my concerns. With this in mind, I made textual notes to address various concerns ranging from theological to text-critical, and beyond, but in particular I wanted to highlight the various possible connection points between the *APTh/AP* and other texts. In particular, I gave special attention to noticing the connections between (1) the *AP* and Acts, the (2) *AP* and the Pastorals, (3) the *AP* and the New Testament, (4) the *AP* and the ancient Christian novels, (5) the *AP* and other early Christian texts, and last (6) the *AP* and other ancient Greek texts in general. The first four received the most attention, while there was less concern for connections to other ancient Christian texts, and even less concern than that was my concern for the connections to other ancient Greek writers. With this in mind, it is common throughout the commentary for me to simply identify specific word connections or contextual similarities, theological similarities, or where thematic material overlaps. Showing these overlaps serves the purpose of accommodating future scholars who share an interest in the nature of the *APTh*, and a desire to understand the complex relationship that it has to other ancient texts.

4.2 Acts of Paul, *the Gospels and the Acts of the Apostles*

In regard to the relationship of the *AP* to the Acts of the Apostles, I will summarize the dominant theories. The major interpretations have stated that the *AP* is (1) a continuation of Acts, (2) dependent upon Acts, (3) a replacement of Acts or (4) independent of Acts. There are at least five possible connections that have been given an "A" rating by Julian Hills, and possibly one other connection (not mentioned by Hills) worthy of consideration.[153] Rordorf makes the strongest argument for suggesting that the author of the *AP* does not have a copy of Acts in his article, "Paul's Con-

---

[152] See Dunn's summary in "*Acts of Paul*," that overviews the major views and arguments on pages 36–44.

[153] Hills, "The Acts of the Apostles," 45–49. See also my discussion under *3.24.1 Textual Notes*, note 15. The references are *AP* 3.24=Acts 1:24 and 15:8; *AP* 6= Acts 4:29; *AP* 9=Acts 4:12; *AP* 13= Acts 2:30; and *AP* 14.6=Acts 1:5. I would add *AP* 3.2=Acts 6:8–15.

verson in the Canonical Acts and in the *Acts of Paul*," 137–43. Rordorf argues that the clearest event in Paul's life that both *Acta* record is the conversion of Paul, yet both accounts have almost nothing in common other
than the mention of the location of conversion being Damascus.[154] From
this perspective, it becomes difficult to understand how the accounts can
vary so significantly if the *AP* author had a copy of Acts sitting in front of
him/her. Second, if there is direct dependence, then why are there no clear
examples of dependence other than sharing one, two, or three words together? Also, if the *AP* is dependent on Acts, then what are they attempting
to do? A major problem for a dependency theory is that it is believed that
the *AP* is attempting to supplement the Acts of the Apostles with additional
material. If this is the case, then a dependency theory is lacking in detail
regarding where to place the material of the *AP* into the canonical Acts.[155]
There is no consistent way to harmonize the two accounts. Replacement
theories share many of the same problems. At this point, I hope it is sufficient to say that I have not been convinced of a literary relationship between the canonical Acts and the *AP*. However, I would add, I have simply
summarized this discussion, and I would direct you to consider some of the
more thorough discussions that I have footnoted.

If the *AP* is indeed a Christian version of the novel, then the recording
of historicity is not even a real consideration within the writing of such a
text. This would allow for the author of the *AP* to have some awareness or
knowledge of the Acts of the Apostles (while not actually having a copy),
while at the same time having no intention of critically attempting to supplement, continue, or replace the canonical Acts account. Historical docu-
mentation is not a relevant concern for the second century author(s) of the
AP. It is anachronistic for us to assume that the author of the *AP* would
have an interest in this. If the author has some knowledge of Acts
(oral/legend material), then this can account for some of possible influences or connections, overlap of specific locations (historical Paul details),
yet also explains why there are inconsistencies between the *AP* and Acts.
After considering the content as a novel, then it becomes clearer that the
main concern of the *AP* is the telling and elaboration upon the Pauline legend for church reading, exhortation to endure persecutions, entertainment,
Christian instruction, and likely for edification of the church through stories of early church leaders.

Just a brief word will be said concerning the *AP* and the Gospels.
Rather than seeing the *AP* as mimicry of the Acts of the Apostles, it might
be more useful to compare this early Christian novel to the Gospel ac-

---

[154] See also Richard I. Pervo, "A Hard Act to Follow: The *Acts of Paul* and the Canonical Acts." *Journal of Higher Criticism* (1995) 2/2:3–32.
[155] Dunn, "*Acts of Paul*," 36.

counts.[156] Indeed, the *AP* and the Gospels share a novelistic narrative about one set aside by God to bring salvation and deliverance to God's people. Even Paul has his passion narrative, rising from the dead and creating belief in those who witness his resurrection. Taking it one step further, it seems clear to me that the *APTh* also serve as a novelistic narrative of Thecla as a savior, where she is called and baptized by water and the spirit of God at the stake in Iconium, and then experiences her own death, burial, and resurrection in Antioch. Following this, she is not the resurrected dead in a literal sense, but she is one who is resurrected/transformed by God who can now be a witness and teacher for God. In many ways this "calling" of Thecla demonstrates how the Iconium and Antioch scenes are not simply repeated "cycles," but actually serve to develop one theme, leading from Iconium with the narrative climaxing in Antioch.[157] Other notable details in the stories shared by the Gospels of Jesus and the *AP*, are the passion of Jesus and the Sermon on the Mount, both of which find their way into the story of Thecla and the story of Paul, where the sermon on the mount is found in 3.5-6; Thecla's passion is in *AP* 4, and Paul's passion is in *AP* 14.[158] These details make it more evident that the author was most likely writing some kind of narrative, novel, or shall we say a "gospel."

4.3 Acts of Paul *and the Pastorals*

Introduction

The question of the dependence of the *APTh* upon the Pastorals has been an intriguing issue, albeit strong varying opinions have existed concerning the relationship between these texts.[159] In particular, the discussion has focused upon the nature of this relationship. Following Dennis R. MacDonald's three summation models as presented in *The Legend and the Apostle* the nature of the relationship has been described this way:

---

[156] Dennis Ronald MacDonald, "Apocryphal and Canonical Narratives about Paul," *Paul and the Legacies of Paul* (Ed. William S. Babcock; Dallas: Southern Methodist UP, 1990), 55–70.

[157] Against MacDonald, *Legend*, 30–31.

[158] See the notes and general comments in the commentary in 3.22 for more details.

[159] For further discussion and summation, see Dennis R. MacDonald, *The Legend and the Apostle: The Battle for Paul in Story and Canon* (Philadelphia: Westminster, 1983); see Peter W. Dunn, "Part Two: The Relationship between the *Acts of Paul* and the Pastoral Epistles," in "The *Acts of Paul* and the Pauline Legacy in the Second Century." Ph.D. diss., University of Cambridge, 1996.

Model One: The Author of the *Acts of Paul* knew and used the Pastorals[160]
Model Two: The Author of the Pastorals used a written source behind the *Acts of Paul*[161]
Model Three: The Authors knew the same oral legends[162]

MacDonald and Willy Rordorf prefer the third model, essentially suggesting that oral stories existed in Asia sometime around the end of the first or early second century, most likely originating from an historical Thecla (or at least a prominent female heroine in the region).[163] Rordorf essentially stops with this conclusion, while MacDonald takes it further. As MacDonald suggests, these "women's stories" are known in Asia, and sometime between 100 and 140 CE,[164] the Pastoral Epistles are written pseudonymously in response to these oral legends, with one of them being, in particular, the Thecla legend. In the Pastorals, we find an attack upon the public role of women in the churches of Asia, and other theological concerns. The democratic organizational structure of the *APTh* is further attacked by the insistence of the writings to Titus and Timothy to organize their churches by installing leaders in the roles of bishops, deacons, and organizing the widows.[165] As he continues to explain, following the writing of the Pastorals, sometime between 150–190 CE, the *Acts of Paul and Thecla* is written based upon the oral traditions of Thecla that were circulating.

The problem with this ingenious and intricate theory is that it is based upon multiple unlikely assumptions. First, a second century date of the Pastorals is highly unlikely. Consider the comments by James D. G. Dunn:

> If...the letters are pseudonymous, then a date sometime between the deaths of Paul (early 60s) and of Ignatius (c. 110s) seems appropriate. This is principally because the more devel-

---

[160] See MacDonald, *Legend*, 115, note 27; Adolf von Harnack, *Geschichte der altchristlichen Literatur bis Eusebius,* Part 2 ed ed. 1.498; Carl Schlau, *Die Acten des Paulus und die ältere Thekla-Legende: Ein Beitrag zur christlichen Literaturgeschichte.* (Leipzig: J. C. Hinrichs, 1877), 82–84; Schmidt and Schubart, *ΠΠ,* 108–12; Vouaux, *Les Actes de Paul,* 123–24; Schneemelcher, "The Acts of Paul," *NTApoc,* 2:348; William M. Ramsay, *The Church in the Roman Empire Before A.D. 170.* (New York and London: G. P. Putnam's Sons, 1893), 416–7.

[161] Richard Adelbert Lipsius, *Die Apokryphen Apostelgeschichten und Apostellegenden: Ein Beitrag zur Altchristlichen Literaturgeschichte* (Braunschweig: C. A. Schwetschke und Sohn, 1890); and Peter Corssen, "Die Urgestalt der Paulusakten," *ZNW* 4 (1903), 42.

[162] MacDonald, *Legend,* 65; Willy Rordorf, "In welchem Verhältnis stehen die apokryphen Paulusakten zur kanonischen Apostelgeschichte und zu den Pastoralbriefen?" *Lex Orandi – Lex Credendi: Gesammelte Aufsätze zum 60. Geburtstag.* (Paradosis 36. Freiburg: Universitätsverlag Freiburg in der Schweiz, 1993), 449–65; "Nochmals: Paulusakten und Pastoralbriefe." *Lex Orandi,* 466–74; "Tradition and Composition in the *Acts of Thecla.*" *Semeia 38: The Apocryphal Acts of the Apostles* (Atlanta: Scholars Press, 1986), 43–52.

[163] MacDonald, 20–21; Rordorf prefers the latter.

[164] Ibid., 54.

[165] Ibid., 65–73.

oped ecclesiology of the Pastorals seems to be in the process of formation... and still some way from the monoepiscopacy that Ignatius promotes but also was able to assume. Nor has the false teaching attacked in the Pastorals such clear shape as that attacked in the 110s by Ignatius.... Some have argued for a still later date, but the later the exercise the less likely that a pseudonymous writing would have been accepted as still genuinely Pauline.[166]

The Pastorals have been couched as a defense against Pauline opponents, Marcion, and finally the communities behind the oral legends of the *APTh* with various dates being attached to fit the argument.[167] Second, the basis that the *APTh* is based upon oral tradition is underdeveloped, and untenable for several reasons. MacDonald's theory of oral tradition, which is built upon the work of Olrik and Lord in folklore studies, has been seriously questioned by Peter Dunn in his 1996 Cambridge dissertation that I point you to, but do not repeat most of it here. [168] In the words of P. Dunn, "MacDonald's failure to apply what Olrik calls a 'strict' law gives the impression that he freely manipulates the methodology to fit the stories."[169] Dunn identifies several specific problems in relation to the application of the oral forms, but allow me to mention just one or two other additional problems. First, orality is much broader a field of discipline than MacDonald is giving it credit for. There are many other considerations that should be considered.[170] In particular, the structure and genre of the *APTh* is that of an ancient romance or novel, a literary production.[171] This does not suggest that there is not an oral tradition of

---

[166] "The First and Second Letters to Timothy and the Letter to Titus," *The New Interpreter's Bible Volume XI* (Nashville: Abingdon, 2000), 781.

[167] See Hans von Campenhausen, "Polykarp von Smyrna und die Pastoralbriefe," *Aus der Frühzeit des Christentums: Studien zur Kirchengeschichte des ersten und zweiten Jahrhunderts* (Tübingen: J. C. B. Mohr [Paul Siebeck], 1963); and again W. Bauer, *Orthodoxy and Heresy in Earliest Christianity* (London/Philadelphia: SCM/Fortress Press, 1971).

[168] Olrik, Alex, "Epic Laws of Folk Narrative," *The Study of Folklore* (Ed. Alan Dundes; Prentice–Hall, 1965), 131–41; and Albert B. Lord, *The Singer of Tales*, (Harvard: Harvard UP, 1978).

[169] Dunn, "The *Acts of Paul* and the Pauline Legacy," 50.

[170] See Casey Wayne Davis, "Chapter 1: The Principles of Orality," and "Chapter 3: Identification of Analysis of Units," *Oral Biblical Criticism: The Influence of the Principles of Orality on the Literary Structure of Paul's Epistle to the Philippians* (Sheffield: Sheffield, 1999), 11–63, 98–140; Pieter J. J. Botha, "Cognition, Orality–Literacy, and Approaches to First–Century Writings," *Orality, Literacy, and Colonialism in Antiquity* (Ed. Jonathan A. Draper; Semeia 47; Atlanta: SBL, 2004), 37–63; Compare some of the work that has been developed on issues of orality in Gospel studies in *Jesus and the Oral Gospel Tradition* (Ed. Henry Wansbrough; London: T & T Clark, 1991) and Birger Gerhardsson, *Memory and Manuscript: Oral Tradition and Written Transmission in Rabbinic Judaism and Early Chistianity* (Copenhagen: Villadsen og Christensen, 1961).

[171] See Pervo, Richard I. "Early Christian Fiction." Pages 239–54 in *Greek Fiction. The Greek Novel in Context.* (Edited by J. R. Morgan and R Stoneman. London and New York: Routledge, 1994) and see Pervo, "The Ancient Novel Becomes Christian," *Novel in*

some kind or stories that precede the document, but determining the orality or
the features of the text that are oral is very difficult. In particular, the text
lacks numerous features that would be apparent in an oral presentation, such
as some kind of rhythm, repetition, and redundancy to the text.[172] The
Iconium and Antioch scenes can hardly be said to represent repetition as
MacDonald determines;[173] names of individuals show no signs of oral struc-
turing or descriptions for memory recall (such as adjectives attached to names
like: The "noble" Paul, the "strong" Thecla, the "deceivers" Demas and Hermogenes); Also, there is very little evidence of redundancy, outside of a mar-
tyrology theme that repeats from town to town (which is better explained
from a literary perspective in connection to the *sitz im leben* of an audience
facing martyrdoms); Evidence of chiastic-structured thought is not present,
etc. Last, but not least, oral traditions often reaffirm "conservative, traditional" thought. Thecla's overthrow of the Roman household is hardly traditional for society nor can it be said to be traditional for early Christianity, thus
suggesting that these "old traditions" are, at best case scenario, less than 100
years of age and don't really reaffirm Greco-Roman or generally accepted
early Christian values.

If one is looking for signs of orality, the best evidence in the *APTh* is the
list of Beatitudes in 3.5–6 that Paul presents in Iconium, when Thecla first
hears Paul teach. While several of the beatitudes appear to come straight out
of the Gospel of Matthew,[174] such a phenomenon does not necessarily imply a
literary connection, but rather most likely this is the evidence of an oral connection. Compare some of the work being done on the *Gospel of Mary* or the
Gospel of Thomas, where some verbatim expressions overlap, but the evidence seems to indicate literary independence between the canonical Gospels
and the Gospels of Mary and Thomas.[175]

If MacDonald's thesis is not convincing, then where does that leave us? It
must be noted that MacDonald has clearly made the point, and well done, that
literary dependence between the *APTh* and the Pastorals does not adequately
explain the relationship, and scholarship must move beyond such a sugges-

---

the *Ancient World*, 694; Erwin Rohde, *Der griechische roman und seine vorläufer* (2d
ed.; Leipzig: Breitkopf and Hartel, 1900) and Rosa Söder, *Die apokryphen Apostelgeschichten und die romanhafte Literatur der Antike* (Würzburger Studien zur Altertumswissenschaft 3; Stuttgart: W. Kohlhammer, 1932); Melissa Aubin, "Reversing Romance? The *Acts of Thecla* and the Ancient Novel," 257–72.

[172] Davis, *Oral*, 18–20, 80–97.

[173] MacDonald, *Legend*, 30–31.

[174] Compare the *APTh* 3.5–6 to Matthew 5:3, 5, 6, and 10.

[175] Karen L. King, *The Gospel of Mary of Magdala: Jesus and the First Woman Apostle* (Santa Rosa, Ca.: Polebridge, 2003)115–18; Uwe-Karsten Plisch, *The Gospel of Thomas: Original Text and Commentary* (Trans. Gesine Schenke Robinson; Stuttgart:
Deutsche Bibelgesellschaft, 2008) 105–07, especially the footnotes that discuss the issue
of the possible "independence" of Logion 36.

tion. The following section serves the purpose of reconsidering the question of the relationship between the *APTh* and the Pastorals to determine how we can best understand this relationship in the context of the first and second centuries of Christianity. To do this, I will (1) provide a list of all of the possible connections between the *APTh* and the Pastorals providing a brief summation of the strongest links between the two texts. (2) I will then try to explain this relationship in a different way. To be more specific, I would like to suggest a new understanding that we can call "Model Four: The Pastorals and the *APTh* have no direct relationship," outside of a shared common Christian heritage, some shared oral traditions from Asia and/or Phrygia and possibly some shared texts from earliest Christianity and the Pauline corpus. In so saying, I am suggesting that there is no polemic of the Pastorals against the *APTh*, which was written much later, and no sufficient evidence to directly link the *APTh* to earlier folklore or oral accounts that were the target of the Pastorals. Nor do I think that the *APTh* were writing with the Pastorals specifically in mind. There just isn't enough evidence to suggest a literary connection or an intertextual connection, or even a polemic against the Pastorals. Neither the genre of the *APTh* which is the ancient romance, nor the content of the text suggests such a relationship. At most, the *APTh* presents an alternative vision of early Christianity outside of the vision of the Pastorals. The *APTh* understands the organization of the early church much less hierarchical[176], specific roles are absent (bishops, deacons, apostles), the role of purity and chastity are connected to a present resurrection, and there is a restructuring of the household. To prove that there is no specific relationship, I will begin by looking at the various possible connections between the *APTh* and the Pastorals.

The best evidence for a literary connection is found between *AP* 3.1 and 2 Tim 2:8 where both texts read ἐκ σπέρματος δαυίδ (trans. "from the seed of David"). While this is verbatim, notice that there are only three words to consider, and it is highly unlikely that this constitutes grounds to suggest a literary connection. Especially in regard to an expression that would have been common in early Jewish and Christian circles stemming from the Hebrew Scriptures in 3 Kgdms 11:39 and Jer 33:22 (אֶת־זֶרַע דָּוִד)[177] and represented verbatim in John 7:42 and Rom 1:3. This does not suggest literary dependence between the various texts, but represents common Christian thought of the early church.

The second possible connection is found in *AP* 3.14, in the discussion between Thamyris and Demas and Hermogenes, where the two, speaking in unison state: καὶ ἡμεῖς σε διδάξομεν, ἣν λέγει οὗτος ἀνάστασιν γενέσθαι, ὅτι ἤδη

---

[176] Initially, Thecla feels subordinate to Paul, however the text overwhelmingly affirms her legitimacy outside of Paul's recognition, after her baptism by God, and her commissioning from God to teach.

[177] Noticeably absent in the Septuagint, but showing up in Origen and Lucian's translation of the Hexapla.

γέγονεν ἐφ᾽ οἷς ἔχομεν τέκνοις, translated "And we will teach you, what this one says happens in (respect to) resurrection. Since it has already happened upon these children we have."[178] 2 Tim 2:18 reads Οἵτινες περὶ τὴν ἀλήθειαν ἠστόχησαν, λέγοντες [τὴν] ἀνάστασιν ἤδη γεγονέναι translated "who have wandered away from the truth. They say that the resurrection has already taken place..." One might notice that this is also reminiscent of Mark 12:18 (Matt 22:23; Luke 20:27) also that states καὶ ἔρχονται Σαδδουκαῖοι πρὸς αὐτόν, οἵτινες λέγουσιν ἀνάστασιν μὴ εἶναι, καὶ ἐπηρώτων αὐτὸν λέγοντες· translated "Then the Sadducees, who say there is no resurrection, came to him with a question" (Mark 12:18/Matt 22:23/Luke 20:27). It is possible that there is a connection, here, but to be frank, there are not two words that are identically represented in order that suggest a literary connection. In other words, this is still not a quotation, and more probably represents early Christian (and Jewish) thought along with the discussions concerning resurrection. However, it might be added that the author of the APTh argues the point that is in agreement with 2 Tim 2:18, in suggesting that Demas and Hermogenes are suggesting to Thamyris that Paul is teaching that the resurrection has already happened, and it is witnessed in their children, while 2 Timothy warns against those who would make such an argument.[179]

The third strongest connection is found in AP 4.9, where Paul speaks of the ὑστέρᾳ ἡμέρᾳ (latter day) while 1 Tim 4:1 speaks of the ὑστέροις καιροῖς (latter times). There is a single word shared by both, but both suggest a similar context. This is the Christian age of the "last times." This is a very generic overlap and suggests awareness of the concept of the "latter times," but does not constitute overlap in texts.

The fourth strongest connection is found in the expression Θεὸς ζῶν (genitive) while 1 Tim 4:10 speaks of the Θεῷ ζῶντι (dative). However it might be added that this expression and a contrast between the "true God" and idols is not unusual to early Christian literature (cf. 1 Thess 1:9; Acts 14:15; 1 John 5:20–21; Romans 9:26; Matt 16:16; 26:63; John 6:69)[180]

One Word Connections

Beyond these four tenous examples, the APTh share some 55–58 (depending on how you count) single word connections. These are shared names, verbs,

---

[178] Pál Herzog provides a recent article looking for New Testament parallels in "IX. New Testament Parallels to the Apocryphal Acta Pauli documents," *Apocryphal Acts of Paul and Thecla*, 142–9; and see AP 3.14 as presenting the opposite view of 2 Tim 2:18, and assumes that there is no knowledge of the canonical text.

[179] Dunn argues that Demas and Hermogenes misrepresent Paul. I find this difficult to accept, especially considering AP 3.14 and 4.14 seem to demonstrate a present form of resurrection in one way or another.

[180] See Julian V. Hills, "The Acts of the Apostles in the *Acts of Paul*," *SBL Seminar Papers, 1994* (Edited by E. H. Lovering, Jr. Atlanta: Scholars Press, 1994), 29.

nouns, that might be argued to be a connection between the texts. For instance, "ἀστοχῶν" is used in reference to Thecla, who, has been "led astray" or "lost" to Thamyris as a wife and daughter to Theocleia. This is the same verb that shows up in 2 Tim 2:16–18 mentioned above in relation to the resurrection. 2 Tim 2:18 specifically says that those who are "leading people astray" will argue that the resurrection has already occurred. Also in 1 Tim 6:20–21, Timothy is told to "guard what has been entrusted to you, avoiding worldly *and* empty chatter *and* the opposing arguments of what is falsely called "knowledge", which some have professed and thus *gone astray* from the faith (NAS). This warning against those who have "gone astray" is somewhat generic, and although, it could apply to what has been said of Thecla, it in no way can be ascertained with certainty whether or not this one word link, is actually a literary or oral connection that brings these two texts together. What makes this link strongest is the fact that the specific teaching mentioned by the Pastorals that leads astray is the teaching on the resurrection, and Thecla is described as having been led astray by Paul's teaching. However, once again, this is simply just not specific enough. Being "led astray" is very generic language, and can be found in all kinds of texts, religious or not, to describe numerous different attitudes of going away or being led astray. On the other hand, teachings on the resurrection, which is quite specific, is not a unique subject in early Christianity, since much of early Christianity is centered around the death, burial, and resurrection of Jesus Christ, and the resurrection of believers that ensues.

Most of the word connections are similar to this, such as the connection of the word ἐπιθυμία.(trans. *passion* or *desire*). One aspiring to the office of a Bishop "desires" a good work (1 Tim 3), while Thecla is drawn to a "new desire." ἐπιθυμία represents a word that shows up in both texts, yet the value of the word has been reversed or reassigned. In this case, Thecla could not possibly be a Bishop according to the criteria of the Pastorals, but yet, she exhibits a good and strong *desire* for Paul's teaching in the *APTh*. 1 Tim 6:9 warns that such who desire riches get trapped (as Thecla is stuck like a spider to the window in *AP* 3.9) by many senseless and harmful "desires." 2 Tim 2:22 warns to "flee youthful lusts," while 2 Tim 3:6 warns against those who will captivate "silly women" by sins and various "desires." Paul, the "teacher" (3.1, 5, 17) can be contrasted with 2 Tim 4:3, which warns against such teachers who will lead people away by their own desires. Tit 2:12 also warns against following after "worldly desires." Although, there seems to be a possible similarity, where one might could suggest that the *APTh* is presenting an alternative vision of Paul *against* that of the Pastorals, it makes more sense that the *APTh* presents an alternative vision of Paul, with some shared vocabulary, and general disagreement on the organization of church hierarchy and/or the role of women and what they can and cannot do. Additionally, the use of the word *desire* is not assigned a positive or negative value per se, but is defined contextually. There are some good desires and bad desires.

Contextual Similarities

Beyond one word overlap, and possible similarities in texts, it has also been argued that there is some level of intertextuality, or enough contextual similarities to suggest some kind of relationship or dependencies. Some examples have already been considered, and some exist that may be stronger. These sections have demonstrated a stronger possibility for a connection than the one word connections, but even these should be reconsidered more closely.

First there is the concern over the shared names between the Pastorals and the *APTh*, which has been covered quite extensively, so I will summarize and then focus upon one issue in particular. There is the shared relationship between the Pastorals (mostly 2 Timothy) describing events that took place in Paul's ministry in Antioch, Iconium, and Lystra (2 Tim 3:10–11) and the trials that Paul endured in Asia (2 Timothy 1:15), and the names of Alexander the Coppersmith who "did me great harm" (2 Tim 4:14; also in 1 Tim 1:20); and then "Phygelus and Hermogenes who, Paul states to Timothy "You are aware that all who are in Asia have turned away from me...;" and then Demas, "having loved this present world, has deserted me and gone to Thessalonica." Last, but not least, there are the companions of Paul, Onesiphorus and Titus, who are mentioned in the Pastorals (Onesiphorus is only found in the New Testament in the Pastorals). What I find interesting is how most of these names show up in the *APTh*. Demas is with Hermogenes, while Alexander is completely separate in Antioch. Most telling is the fact that in the *APTh*, Hermogenes is the χαλκεύς (blacksmith or coppersmith), and Alexander is not. MacDonald explains that if both the *APTh* and the Pastorals used the same oral legends, then this "can account for the different depictions of Paul in the *Acts of Paul* and the Pastorals without conjecturing earlier written sources, but it also can better account for the similarities than either of the other models."[181] If the composer of the tale actually had a copy of the Pastorals, then why does Hermogenes become the blacksmith, and Alexander not? This makes no sense. It is a simple mistake, one not to be overlooked, if the text were before the Presbyter. This can only suggest to us that the author of the text did not have the Pastorals. Beyond this, oral memory would probably have been quite strong, and such a mistake, such as reassigning the role of the blacksmith to Hermogenes, would have been highly improbable. I don't think it is possible to suggest that author would have been able to continuously hear or read the Pastorals, but rather had heard them maybe a few times, or even more, was aware of the Pastorals or oral remembrances of the Pauline legacy

---

[181] MacDonald, *Legend*, 65.

or even the legacy attached to the Pastorals. It needs to be remembered that the telling of an oral story is one that would have been told and retold within certain forms. I am doubtful that this is what we have here. Let me demonstrate this with a few other examples.

No Relationship? The Use of Names, Titles, and Locations

In both texts, we find Paul, Onesiphorus, Titus, Demas, Hermogenes, and Alexander, and the latter two are both Coppersmiths, depending on which text we are looking at. Also, there is the overlap of Antioch and Iconium. Is it possible, that the author of the *APTh* is aware of Paul's activities in this area of Phrygia or more broadly Western Turkey (including Asia, Phrygia, and Galatia), and that the traditions have been passed down, and they have simply been incorporated into the *romance*? After all, this is not an extensive amount of material for one to remember or know about. Essentially, in order to account for the similarities of texts, the shared knowledge of the Pastorals and the *APTh* includes 2 companions of Paul, 3 enemies of Paul, trials in Antioch and Iconium, and possibly Asia, and one of the opponents is a blacksmith. What is fascinating is that it makes more sense to suggest that this is independent verification of the historical Paul material. Independently, the Pastorals, *APTh*, and Acts of the Apostles testify to a metal worker who caused Paul problems in Asia Minor. Both texts testify to trials in Antioch and Iconium, and conflict between Paul and metal workers in service of local gods of Asia. In the canonical Acts, the metal worker is in Asia, in particular Ephesus, his name is Demetrius, and he is an ἀργυροκόπος and not a χαλκεύς (Acts 19:21–24). The Heidelberg Coptic text of the *APTh* calls Hermogenes a ⲡ2ⲁⲙⲕⲁ̄ⲗ̄ which is the combination of two words to give us a "craftsman of iron/metal."[182] This word shows up also in 2 Tim 4.14 as ⲫⲁⲙⲕⲁⲗ̄ⲗⲉ, indicating simply one who works with metal, but the Coptic reflects a different word for Acts 19:21–24. The mention of a blacksmith in all three texts can be understood as possibly providing remembrances of Paul and his legacy, while demonstrating the literary independence of these texts.

The most telling absence from the text cannot be missed. Where is Thecla? Wouldn't Thecla have been a prominent name to have been shared between texts that would have given us absolute certainty that the Pastorals were aware of the Thecla legends and folklore, however the all important link is not in the Pastorals. The connection between "silly women" in 2 Tim 3:6 and the name Thecla is just not strong enough to suggest that it is the same person. However, Alexander in the *APTh* is very prominent a character in Antioch, and certainly would not have been mistaken for a blacksmith. Considering it from

---

[182] Crum, *Coptic Dictionary*. (Oxford: Clarendon Press, 1939) 762, under definition of "2ⲁⲙ," on page 673 and "ⲕⲏⲗ," on page 102.

another perspective, the strongest argument to suggest a shared common tradition is the mention of 5 names, one occupational title, and two cities. This is hardly sufficient evidence to suggest a direct relationship from either a literary dependence or through oral tradition. This seems more like general remembrances of Pauline legends and miscellaneous facts and non-relational oral traditions.

Theological Similarities

But it is not simply these names that lead scholars to believe that the texts must share some kind of context or have a relationship whether direct or indirect. This overlap is best seen in the "butting of heads" between the texts theologically in terms of encratism, purity, marriage, and resurrection. However, this can be explained without too much trouble. The *APTh* present the case that followers of the "teachings" of Paul will need to devote themselves to a life of purity and self-control that leads the followers to reject marriage if they have not already become married. Dunn argues that the only section of the *AP* that can be said to support a strong teaching on continence is the *APTh* (namely the events in Iconium and Antioch). He cites the example of the marriage of Onesiphorus and Lectra (among others in the *AP*) arguing that the text "implicitly" endorses marriage and procreation.[183] However, I don't think this explanation is sufficient. Consider some of Paul's "beatitudes:"

> *Blessed are those who have kept the flesh chaste*, for they will be a temple of God. Blessed are the *self-controlled*, for God will speak to them...*Blessed are they who though having a wife, are as those not having a wife, for they will inherit God...Blessed are the bodies of the virgins*, for they shall be well pleasing to God and *they will not lose the rewards of their purity*, for *the word of the father shall be to them a work of salvation in the day of his son...*

I think Dunn's observant point is answered in the macarism, *Blessed are they who though having a wife, are as those not having a wife, for they will inherit God.* It is not Paul encouraging people to renounce their marriage, however, they are to refrain from sexual activity from this point forward. Obviously those who are not married should not get married, providing a greater opportunity to not remain chaste and pure. As follows, if one remains pure and chaste, then they will be resurrected. To reinforce this, in *AP* 3.12, Demas and Hermogenes claim that Paul is saying: "There is no other resurrection for you, if you do not remain pure and do not stain the flesh but keep it pure." Dunn suggests that "sexual asceticism is encouraged," yet marriage is not forbidden.[184] As Dunn argues, this places the *APTh* alongside other Christian writers, such as Ignatius, Justin or 1 Clement who also encourage "sexual asceticism" yet do not "require" a rigid asceticism "manifested by a total abstinence

---

[183] Dunn, "The *Acts of Paul*," 77–8.
[184] Dunn, "The *Acts of Paul*," 81.

from sexual intercourse."[185] Although Dunn argues that the *AP* is not encratite in a strict sense, his suggestion that sexual intercourse is not completely rejected in the *APTh* is not sustainable. Consider that the result of Thecla's activities in Iconium and Antioch result in the overthrow of marriage, which is accomplished by a total rejection of Thamyris, and then a rejection of Alexander's sexual advances in Antioch. These two facts combined with Paul's direct teachings in 3.5–6, and a redefining of *passion* for Paul's *teaching*, and not a *passion* for Paul, further serve to avert one's attention from marriage and sexual intercourse to continence and "fullfilment" through Christ.

This concept of purity and continence leading to resurrection is contrary to what the Pastorals present, but this theological view is generic enough that it does not necessitate or even suggest a dependence or polemic against the Pastorals, but rather reflects the independent views of a second century author. The condemnation of such teaching in the Pastorals is found, however it is not specific enough to any situation, nor are any of the other 101 "warnings" that are found in the numerous lists of the Pastorals. Once again, these views are not specific, but are rather generic in nature and could have been presented solely based on Christian tradition as found in Asia or Phrygia.

Having argued that the *APTh* does indeed have encratite teaching, I would suggest this particular teaching is part of the puzzle that leads one *from* (1) purity/chastity *to* (2) rejection of marriage = avoidance of sexual intercourse *to* (3) resurrection, that begins now and continues through the ages. What I am trying to say is that it is unlikely that the author of the *APTh* had three "separate" theological concerns in mind, but rather it was an interconnected concern, and the author is formulating this perspective on, say... "resurrection" and how one attains it. It is very likely that this understanding of resurrection and how to attain it is not interconnected with an opposing view, but is rather being presented by the author in a non-apologetic way. At least, we cannot detect a specific audience through the internal evidence.

In sum, I think it is safe to say that the overlap of names, titles, and locations, and the theological disagreements that exist between the text are simply not enough to suggest anything further than an independent understanding of the Christian heritage, albeit a disagreement on church hierarchy and organization, independent oral traditions from Asia and/or Phrygia and possibly some shared texts and remembrances from early Christians and the Pauline corpus.

Broader Implications

If one accepts Model Four, that suggests that there is no direct literary link and the oral background to each text is not a shared tradition, then this an-

---

[185] See Ignatius, *Polcarp* 5.2; Justin, *1 apology* 29.1; and 1 Clem 38.2; and Dunn, "The *Acts of Paul*," 69–88.

swers several questions. First, scholars have noticed the uniqueness of the
APTh versus the *AP*. Notably, Dunn points out that continence is advocated in
the *APTh*, however absent in the rest of the *APl*.[186] This uniqueness has been
addressed by noting that the *APTh* circulated independently.[187] Thus the relationship between the two has been a concern.[188] In particular, it has been the
recent consensus that the *APTh* must represent legendary material,[189] not an
earlier literary text (as Theodor Zahn, Adolf Harnack, and William Ramsay
and others assumed[190]). While acknowledging that there must be some kind of
historical kernel behind the text, possibly a Christian virgin who endured or
averted martyrdom, it is too much to say the Thecla legend is a full oral tradition. The best explanation to date has been that the Iconium/Antioch scene is
an oral tradition. If this is not the case, then I still have to account for why
Thecla emerges as such a prominent heroine, completely dominating the text,
and pushing Paul completely from the story in the Antioch scene. This problem can be answered if one looks to the ancient novel as the genre of the text.
It is not uncommon for ancient novels to give prime place to both the hero and
heroine of the text. From this perspective, the *APTh* (possibly written by the
Presbyter that Tertullian mentions or an earlier author), is incorporated into
the *AP* by the Presbyter, who is able to highlight an important part of the
Pauline tradition from Antioch and Iconium that he or she is aware of, via the
genre of the ancient novel. What this leaves is a fictionalized and sensational-
ized account of Paul and Thecla in the garb of historicity (this is the nature of
the *romances*), with faint traces of oral traditions (such as: a heroine from
Iconium; or the Macarisms of 3.5–6); historical awarenesses (such as the
"royal road" of the first century mentioned in *AP* 3.1–2; Queen Tryphaena;
Roman rule; etc.); and broader strokes of a Pauline legacy (oral legends of
Paul, remembrances and expressions from the Pauline corpus; names of com-

---

[186] Dunn, "The *Acts of Paul*," 77.

[187] This principle was further reinforced in the finding of an early, Greek, manuscript
of the 3 Corinthians: see M. Testuz, *Papyrus Bodmer X–Xl. X: Correspondance apocryphe des Corinthiens et de l'apôtre Paul. Xl: Onzième Odes Salomon. XlI: Fragment d'un
Hymne liturgique.* (Cologny and Genève: Bibliotheca Bodmeriana, 1959); and for a comprehensive discussion of the textual history of 3 Corinthians, see Rordorf, "Hérésie et
orthodoxie selon la Correspondance apocryphe entre les Corinthiens et l'apôtre Paul."
Pages 389–431 in *Lex Orandi – Lex Credendi*, 389–431.

[188] See Rordorf, "Tradition and Composition in the *Acts of Thecla.*" *Semeia 38: The
Apocryphal Acts of the Apostles* (Atlanta: Scholars Press, 1986), 43–52; see Carl
Schmidt, "Die Akten des Paulus und der Thekla." in *Acta Pauli aus der Heidelberger
koptischen Papyrushandschrift: Zusätze zur ersten Ausgabe* (Leipzig: J. C. Hinrichs,
1905), 145–61; Schmidt and Schubart. *ΠΠΙ*, 120–22.

[189] Schneemelcher, "The Acts of Paul," 221; see footnote 4 above.

[190] Zahn, Theodor. "Die Paulusakten," *Geschichte des neutestamentlichen Kanons.*
(Erlangen and Leipzig: A. Deichert, 1890. Repr., Hildesheim and New York: Georg
Olms, 1975) 2: 965–91; Harnack, *Geschichte der altchristlichen Literatur bis Eusebius*;
Ramsay, *The Church in the Roman Period*, 31–6.

panions and enemies, places, people), which are then synthesized in a second century novel filled with the theological language and bias of a second century author who is attempting to present a grand picture of the events, teach ings, and thought of Paul in his life, where entertainment and remembrance of a hero who has nearly been forgotten took precedence over doctrine, hierarchy, and church politics.

Conclusion and Purpose of Writing

In short, it makes more sense to argue that the Pastorals and the *APTh* share no direct link, but are related only through independent strains of early Christian oral traditions of Paul's activities in Iconium, Antioch, and/or Asia, and possibly some New Testament texts (namely Matthew). These contextual similarities are best seen in the way that purity and chastity are presented in the *APTh* as key concepts to attain to the resurrection into a new life. This in turns leads to a restructuring of the home, where those married act as unmarried (denying sexual relations), and those unmarried remain unmarried. The church is less hierarchical, more democratic, where titles are absent,[191] and women can teach, preach, and can be Christian missionaries as well, outside of official designation or a "handing down" of leadership in apostolic ascension. This, no doubt, was resisted, as Tertullian demonstrates, however, because of the distinctive character of these issues, and their acceptance in the early church, all the way back to Paul's letters, for instance, to the Corinthians, this text was not rejected within numerous circles spanning from Asia, to Syria, and even to Egypt. It appears that we have a novelistic story, in the garb of an ancient romance that attempts to address some second century concerns through the telling of the story of Paul and Thecla that most certainly would have provided encouragement to these early churches, not in combat ing other Christian writings, but in understanding that God delivers his followers, even as they face persecution and martyrdom before their opponents, even the Roman Empire.

Chapter 5: Feminist Criticism and the *Acts of Paul and Thecla*

Research interests of the *AP* have shifted somewhat over the last 30 years, not surprisingly, as postmodernity has continued to shift the foundations of academic studies. In particular, the impact of feminist studies has continued to demonstrate a remarkable amount of influence upon the reading and interpretation of various early Christian documents including the *AP*. In the words of Bernadette Brooten:

---

[191] There are no bishops, deacons, nor even ἀπόστολοι.

If the focus were on women, then one might be less inclined to compare Paul with his male Jewish contemporaries and their views on women and more interested in placing such Roman Jewish women as Prisca and Junia within their Jewish and Roman context.[192]

I would quickly add Thecla to this list, and especially the study of the *APTh*.[193] The phenomenon of feminist-critical studies of the *AP* has not taken place within a vacuum. I am not going to attempt to provide a thorough summary of all work on the Apocryphal Acts of the Apostles, but one might note that feminist studies on the *AP* began before the emergence of Elisabeth Schüssler Fiorenza's *In Memory of Her: A Feminist Theological Reconstruction of Christian Origins* (New York: Crossroads, 1983) and other such works.[194] From the perspective of Jean-Daniel Kaestli, three American scholars, Stevan L. Davies in 1980,[195] Dennis Ronald MacDonald in 1983,[196] and Virginia Burrus in 1987[197] moved the discussion of the *AP* into a new realm specifically revolving around the feminist social world.[198] This has shifted the discussion (1) from a question of literary sources to oral sources, (2) from philological, theological, and historical concerns to socio-cultural concerns and (3) from the perspective of a male author and audience to a female author and audience. This has continued up to the present with feminist critical interpretations, the most recent being Amy-Jill Levine's *A Feminist Companion to the New Testament Apocrypha*,[199] that includes five out of thirteen articles specifically dealing with

---

[192] Bernadette J. Brooten, "Early Christian Women in their Cultural Context: Issues of Method in Historical Reconstruction," *Feminist Perspectives on Biblical Scholarship* (ed. Adela Yarbro Collins; Chico, Ca.: Scholars Press, 1985), 65. Jean-Daniel Kaestli quotes a French translation of this in "Les Actes Apocryphes et la reconstitution de l'histoire des femmes dans le christianisme ancient," *FoiVie* 28 (1989): 71–79.

[193] See Shelly Matthews, "Thinking of Thecla: Issues in Feminist Historiography," *JFSR* 17 (2001): 39-55.

[194] See the commentary of Sheila E. McGinn, "The Acts of Thecla," *Searching the Scriptures: Volume 2, A Feminist Commentary* (ed. Elisabeth Schüssler Fiorenza with the assistance of Shelley Matthews and Ann Graham Brock; New York: Crossroads, 1994) 800–28.

[195] *Revolt of the Widows.*

[196] *The Legend and the Apostle.*

[197] *Chastity as Autonomy.*

[198] Jean–Daniel Kaestli, "Fiction littéraire et réalité sociale: que peut–on savoir de la place des femmes dans le milieu de production des Actes apocryphes des Apôtres?," *Apocrypha* 1 (1990): 290. Some methodological concerns have been raised both by Kaestli in his articles and by Peter W. Dunn, "Women's Liberation, the *Acts of Paul,* and Other Apocryphal Acts of the Apostles: A Review of Some Recent Interpreters," *Apocrypha* 4 (1993): 245–61.

[199] *A Feminist Companion to the New Testament Apocrypha* (ed. Amy–Jill Levine with Maria Mayo Robbins; Feminist Companion to the New Testament and Early Christian Writings, 11; Cleveland: The Pilgrim Press, 2006).

Thecla,[200] another article highlights the *APTh* in a subsection,[201] and remarkably every article in the entire book is devoted to the *AAA*, leaving the title to be somewhat of a misnomer.

The essential questions that are connected to feminist-critical inquiry have largely been addressed already in the introduction. Specifically, these questions are the concerns of female/male authorship, female audience, orality, and leadership issues revolving around Thecla. The impact of feminist criticism will also be evident with a focusing upon the life of Thecla within the commentary.

Chapter 6: Artistic Representations of the *Acts of Paul* and the *Acts of Paul and Thecla*

With regard to the artistic representations of the *AP* and the *APTh* as a more specific parameter, there have been no artistic representations from the first and second century (this is not unique to the *AP*, but is true of all early Christian artistic representations),[202] and very few examples of pre-Constantinian art dealing with the *AP* (if any at all).[203]

One can compare some of the images of the ampitheaters and wild beasts that have been discovered in such places as Pompeii that adequately demonstrate the topos presented in the *APTh* of Thecla defending herself within the amphitheater, but this speaks generically to the popularity of such writings, forms of entertainment, and the status quo of the Roman

---

[200] Namely the articles of *A Feminist Companion to the New Testament Apocrypha* are: Johannes N. Vorster, "Construction of Culture Through the Construction of Person: The Construction of Thecla in the *Acts of Thecla;*" Cornelia B. Horn, "Suffering Children, Parental Authority and the Quest for Liberation?: A Tale of Three Girls in the *Acts of Paul (and Thecla)*, the *Act(s) of Peter*, the *Acts of Nerseus and Achilleus* and the *Epistle of Pseudo-Titus*," Magda Misset–Van de Weg, "Answers to the Plights of an Ascetic Woman Named Thecla;" Susan A. Calef, "Thecla 'Tried and True' and the Inversion of Romance;" and Gail P. C. Streete, "Buying the Stairway to Heaven: Perpetua and Thecla as Early Christian Heroines."

[201] Richard Valantasis, "The Question of Early Christian Identity: Three Strategies Exploring a Third *Genos*," 67–68.

[202] Robin Margaret Jensen, *Understanding Early Christian Art* (London: Routledge, 2000); Paul Corby Finney, *The Invisible God: The Earliest Christians on Art* (New York and Oxford: Oxford, 1994); and Graydon F. Snyder, *Ante Pacem: Archaeological Evidence of Church Life before Constantine* (Macon: Mercer, 2003).

[203] For the most complete discussion of images of Thecla and Paul, and the *AP*, see David R. Cartlidge and J. Keith Elliott, "Paul, Thecla, and Peter," in *Art and the Christian Apocrypha* (London and New York: Routledge, 2001), 134–71; and David R. Cartlidge, "Thecla: The Apostle Who Defied Women's Destiny," *Bible Review* 20.6 (2004): 24–33; Stephen J. Davis, *The Cult of St. Thecla: A Tradition of Women's Piety in Late Antiquity* (Oxford: Oxford UP, 2001).

house.[204] Eleanor Winsor Leach demonstrates how numerous houses in Pompeii show evidence of supporters from the games, by way of posters (*venationes*) throughout the *domus* advertising the gladiatorial games.[205] For instance, in the house of Ceius Secundus (1.5.15), one will find frescos (*venationes*) on the walls of the hunting and killing of bulls and other animals by leopards and lions. In addition to this house, these *paradeisoi*[206] can be found in numerous locations in Pompeii.[207] I find this interesting, because the very sight that people wished to see as entertainment in the theaters and amphitheaters was transposed onto the walls of homes and gardens, essentially testifying to the popularity and familiarity that the *APTh* would have had to the average Roman citizen, essentially glorifying the violence of the amphitheater.[208] But the direction of influence is not just the ampitheater violence into the *domus*, but rather it is the influence of Greek mythology upon mass culture that is eventually reproduced in the amphitheater and on the walls of homes in Pompeii.[209] Some evidence of

---

[204] Look at the two images that are represented in the house of Ceius Secundus (or the House of the Ceii; 1.6.15) in Pompeii. See Figures 3–6 below. See also the image from Ida Baldassarre, ed., *Pompei: Pitture e Mosaici* (10 vols.; Roma: Instituto della Enciclopedia Italiana, 1994) 1:475; or the "House of the Hunt" (VII.4.48), with a nineteenth century reproduction found in Paul Zanker, *Pompeii: Public and Private Life* (trans. Deborah Lucas Schneider; Cambridge: Harvard UP, 1998) 188 which represents a "hunting scene" with animals killing animals, people killing animals, and animals hunting people.

[205] See Eleanor Winsor Leach, *The Social Life of Painting in Ancient Rome and on the Bay of Naples* (Cambridge: Cambridge UP, 2004) 131–32.

[206] This comes from the Avestan concept of פַּרְדֵּס (*Pardes*) or paradise (*HALOT*, 2:963) symbolizing an exotic garden from the East mixed with mythological elements presenting a garden like atmosphere for the *domus* or the courtyard peristyle. See also the discussion in Ernesto De Carolis, *God and heroes in Pompeii* (trans. Lori–Ann Touchette; Rome: "L'erma" di Bretscheider, 2001) 11; Annamaria Ciarallo, *Gardens of Pompeii* (trans. Lori–Ann Touchette; Rome: "L'erma" di Bretscheider, 2001); and Wilhelmina Mary Feemster Jashemski, *The Gardens of Pompeii: Herculaneum and the Villas destroyed by Vesuvius* (New Rochelle, N.Y.: Caratzas Bros., 1979–93) 68–73. Leach denies that these are *paradeisoi*, but are posters alone for the amphitheater.

[207] See the discussion by Balch, *Roman Domestic*, 22–25; in addition to the ones already mentioned see the house of M. Lucretius Fronto (5.4a; *PPM* 3:966–1032), the House of Centenario (9.8.3.7; *PPM* 9:903–1104), and the House of Orpheus (6.14.20; *PPM* 5.264–307). For color plates see *Domus: Wall Painting in the Roman House*, 274–96; and for the House of Orpheus see Figures 7–10 below, which I took upon personal observation and study of these images while in Pompeii in July of 2006.

[208] Another example provided by Leach is the poster of Aulus Rustius Verus, owner of the Case del Centenario, who had the remains of four posters extant on the walls of his house. See Leach, *The Social Life of Painting in Ancient* Rome, 132.

[209] Consider the fresco in the House of Sallust (VI.2.4) where Actaeon is being torn apart by dogs for having looked upon Artemis bathing. This mythological scene is one likely to have been recreated in the theater/ampitheater and also represented in a garden

this is found in the prevalence of the mythology being pressed upon the cultures through several mediums. One variation is found in Varro, who reports that Q. Hortentsius, in a place near Laurentum, was entertaining guests who were overlooking a large forest that was enclosed within a wall called a *therotrophium* (game-preserve), and he called for someone dressed as Orpheus. Orpheus then proceeded to come out of the woods dressed in robes and playing a harp and singing to the animals, which then came out of the woods to him.[210] This simply follows the mythological story of the great Orpheus musician who could charm the wild beasts. This is the Orphic image represented within the *domus* of Pompeii (witnessed in the House of Orpheus [see footnote 180] and the House of Epidius Sabinus in Pompeii[211]). A modification of this same theme exposes this mythological scene as one also appropriate for the amphitheater. *Liber Spectaculorum*, a collection of epigrams commemorating Titus' games in celebration of the dedication of the Flavian amphitheater (which is contemporary with the frescos of Pompeii), epigram 21 records a similar occasion, where at the conclusion, "Every kind of wild beast was there, mixed with the flock, and above the minstrel [Orpheus] hovered many birds; but the minstrel fell, torn apart by an ungrateful bear."[212] This variation on the theme of Orpheus symbolizes the prominence of mythology within daily life, and especially the emergence of such themes into the violent amphitheater.[213] In general, we see that the mythological themes show up (1) in the entertainment of the wealthy, (2) within the amphitheater, and (3) also in the *domus*. It must be noted that the role of Orpheus shows up in the *domus* and within the game-preserve true to the mythological accounts, and the variation of the theme is found in the amphitheater. I find that this evi-

---

space of one of the homes in Pompeii. See Zanker, *Pompeii,* 166–67. See also the discussion in K. M. Coleman, "Fatal Charades: Roman Executions Staged as Mythological Enactments," *JRS* 80 (1990): 44–73, where he argues convincingly that the activities within the ampitheater were often intended to be reenactments of mythological stories.

[210] Varro, *Res rusticate* (On Agriculture) 3.13.2–3; Zanker, *Pompeii,* 187.

[211] *PPM* 8:1029–33. See Figures 7–10.

[212] "adfuit inmixtum pecori genus omne ferarum et supra vatem multa pependit avis, ipse sed ingrate iacuit laceratus ab urso." See quote and commentary found within Coleman, "Fatal Charades," 62.

[213] I disagree with Leach's assessment (*The Social Life of Painting in Ancient* Rome, 132) of the fresco in the House of Orpheus. Leach denies that the image is a *paradeisoi* located on the wall of the peristyle. She suggests that there is little connection between the animals and Orpheus. In response, a lion and a leopard, sitting next to Orpheus, not attacking him of the deer and wild boar immediately before suggests strongly that this is portraying the mythological elements of the power of Orpheus. The literature from antiquity supports both a violent and nonviolent response to Orpheus depending on what source one reads. I think that the implications for what would have been witnessed of Orpheus in the amphitheater would have been familiar to those who viewed this fresco, but this does not suggest that this image is a *venationes*.

dence reinforces the influence of mythology within the culture to be one of the pervasive elements that then moves out into other forms within society, which in turn continue to provide reinterpretation to the myths and how they are manifested within the Roman world.

Regarding how this has bearing upon the *AP*, severals facts must be noted. (1) the *AP*, and specifically the *APTh*, report heavily the events of the Roman amphitheater and the *spectaculi* that took place there. (2) It is worth noting that the subject matter of the *APTh* (namely spectacles and erotic situations) is also one of the predominant themes found in *domus* frescos *and* literature.[214] (3) The fact that the *APTh* is an ancient romance further compounds the problem, due to the fact that the ancient novels are very erotic and salacious literature. This connection moves the *APTh* and the *AP* into a dangerous area regarding appropriate subject matter for Christians. All one has to do is to look at the writings of Tertullian. In *de spectaculis* 17, Tertullian, while giving proofs on why Christians are not to attend the games in the amphitheater, provides further evidence in comparing the pagan themes of the games to pagan literature. He states:

If, again, we despise the teaching of secular literature as being foolishness in God's eyes, our duty is plain enough in regard to those spectacles, which from this source derive the tragic or comic play. If tragedies and comedies are the bloody and wanton, the impious and licentious inventors of crimes and lusts, it is not good even that there should be any calling to remembrance the atrocious or the vile. What you reject in deed, you are not to bid welcome to in word.[215]

This quotation provides a further window into the *APTh* in that it becomes even clearer that the subject matter of the *APTh* is more than the reporting of a martyrdom (which it is not), but that it is the same erotic and secular subject matter as found within other novels and also found within the amphitheater. This possibly reinforces why the *APTh* were initially resisted by some.[216] The representation of beasts, amphitheaters, and the role of

---

[214] See Jürgen Hodske, *Mythologische Bildthemen in den Häusern Pompejis: Die Bedeutung der zentralen Mythenbilder für die Bewohner Pompejis* (Stendaler Winckelmann–Forschungen 6; Ruhpolding: Verlag Franz Philipp Rutzen, 2007), 135–39 for a printing and discussion of all of the Fourth (and final) Pompeiian Style mythological images, Hodske states on page 136, "the figures are now more scantily dressed, their clothes billow out behind them or are draped so that their beautiful, naked bodies are presented in a particularly flattering light." Then Hodske again on page 138 states, "The range of paintings was narrower in the Fourth Style, and combinations are often repeated. Combinations of large–scale mythological landscapes now vanish, and the most common themes involve naked figures in erotic situations...."

[215] The English text is taken from *ANF*; "Si et doctrinam saecularis litteraturae ut stultitiae apud Deum deputatam aspernamur, satis praescribitur nobis et de illis speciebus spectaculorum, quae saecuari litteratura lusoriam uel agonisticam secaenam dispungunt."

[216] Tertullian's explicit remarks of the *Acts of Paul* in *de Baptismo* 17, are concerning

mythology within the Roman world, allow us somewhat of a social background, and a visual representation of the themes that one reads in the *APTh*.

Moving on chronologically, the first two direct representations of the *AP* illustrate a scene recorded in *AP* 3.7–10, and the other illustrates the execution of Paul as recorded in *AP* 14, also known as the *Martyrdom of Paul*. The first image, represented upon a grave stone or sarcophagus fragment, dating from the fourth century, depicts Paul standing and holding the rudder of a ship entitled THECLA.[217] The meaning is uncertain although two different interpretations have been suggested.[218] In addition to this image there is also the fourth century stone sarcophagus of Junius Bassus (circa 359) now in the Museo Pio Cristiano, Vatican which depicted the arrest of Paul, with the guard withdrawing a sword in order to execute Paul.[219] This image is consistent with the story as told in the Martyrdom account. Once again, Paul's facial features, baldness, beard, and brow seem to be consistent with the description provided in the *AP* 3.2–3.[220]

Another noteworthy image is the fifth/sixth century ivory tablet (4.2 x 9.8 cm) from the British Museum (Catalog no. MME 1856.06–23) that depicts Thecla standing within a castle/home listening to Paul, who is seated and reading from a scroll outside the castle/home.[221] The tablet is divided in the center, and the right side portrays the stoning of Paul (Acts 14:19–

---

the issue of baptism and the appropriate administration of this sacrament. It must be added that Tertullian mentions that one of the explicit teachings within the baptismal liturgy addresses the Christians being willing to shun the public arena and the games!

[217] Found at the Musei Capitolini, Sala II, inv. Nr. 67. See Cartlidge and Elliot, *Art and the Christian Apocrypha*, 148–50. See Figure 11 below.

[218] Is Paul guiding and controlling the ship, or is Paul being carried by the ship? Possibly the interpretation of the image is meant to be deciphered based on the shared relationship and interdependence of the two. See Cartlidge and Elliott, *Art and the Christian Apocrypha*, 148–50; Cartlidge, "Thecla," *BR* 20.6 (2004): 32–33; also see Annewies van den Hoek and John J. Herrmann, Jr., "Thecla the Beast Fighter: A Female Emblem of Deliverance in Early Christian Popular Art," *The Studia Philonica Annual: Studies in Hellenistic Judaism*, 13 (2001): 212–49; and also Hermann and van den Hoek, *Light from the Age of Augustine* (Cambridge: Harvard Divinity School, 2002), plate 49.

[219] See Figure 12 below.

[220] It is also worth noting that the vast majority of inscriptions, artistic representations, and paintings come from the fourth through the sixth century at the height of Thecla's popularity. Therefore, those images mentioned above come from this era as well as several others, but I have not included all of the images because I believe that they are not necessarily a testimony or adequate source for understanding the *AP* in the second century. They are more helpful in understanding the tradition of Thecla, and later interpretations of the *AP* that sometimes might have bearing upon the text (See "2. The Use of Traditon in the AAA," within "Introduction: The Forgotten Novels of the Early Church," by Dennis R. MacDonald in *Semeia 38*, 3–4.

[221] See Figure 13 below.

20). Here the accounts of the *AP* and the Acts of the Apostles have been mixed, as the stoning of Paul that took place in Iconium is set against the conversion of Thecla. It might be noted that the details of Thecla's conversion are not following closely to the *APTh*, where Paul should be inside a house.[222] Although, it might be added that Paul being located outside of the *domus* might symbolically represent the socially public external space, while Thecla represents the domesticated internal space of women.

Last, I would like to mention the fresco that has been found within the "Paulusgrotte" about 80 meters above sea level[223] on the Bülbül dağ, a small hill located immediately to the southwest of Ephesus.[224] In 1906, the first mention was made of this cave.[225] In 1998, while the graffiti of the whitewashed walls were being studied, it was determined that there were indeed frescoes lying underneath the whitewash. At this point, a "comprehensive restoration and conservation" of the frescoes was begun.[226] It became known that there was a fresco representing a triptych of Thecla, Paul and Theocleia (the mother of Thecla). Thecla is sitting within a house, while Paul and Theocleia are both standing equally in height in teaching form with their right hand erect, lifting the index and middle fingers,

---

[222] In addition to these images mentioned, I will also note briefly a 6th–8th century fresco that was found in the necropolis at El Bagawat, Egypt (Figure 14 below; it can be seen at http://alain.guilleux.free.fr/khargha_bagawat/khargha_necropole_bagawat.html), on the dome of the "Peace Chapel" (Chapel 80). It is an image of Paul and Thecla sitting beside each other, with Paul apparently teaching Thecla. Also, there is an interesting Limestone roundel (5th century) in the Nelson–Atkins Museum of Art, Kansas City, Missouri that depicts the martyrdom of Thecla at Antioch (Figure 15). Thecla is shown wearing only a girdle (Cartlidge and Elliott call it a flowering skirt) with her hands tied behind her back. Also, there is an aura (halo) around her head with two angels flanking her to her left and right. Below the angels are a lion(ess) and a bear). Cartlidge and Elliott suggest an Eastern and perhaps an Egyptian provenance for the roundel. A number of images, such as the roundel, are reproduced in Cartlidge and Elliott, *Art and the Christian Apocrypha*, 148–55. For further information on other frescoes, flasks, etc. that have been found with Thecla's image see Davis, *The Cult of St. Thecla*, including the images found on pages 216–38.

[223] Ruth Ohm, "The Ambiguity of Interpretation: Paul and Thekla in Ephesos" (paper presented at the annual meeting of the SBL, Washington, D. C., 20 November 2006, 1.

[224] See Figure 16 below.

[225] O. Benndorf, *Forschungen in Ephesos* (1906): 105. For a more complete recounting of the history behind the cave see Renate Pillinger, "Neue Entdeckungen in der sogenannten Paulusgrotte von Ephesos," *Mitteilungen zur Christlichen Archäologie* 6 (2000) 16–29; and Ruth Ohm, "The Ambiguity of Interpretation, 1–11.

[226] Pillinger, "Neue Entdeckungen," 29. It became known in the research done in 2003–04 that there were indeed 5 levels of wall paintings, and the picture of Thecla, Paul, and Theocleia, may represent a 5th century painting, but the dating of the paintings has not been verified yet. See Renate Pillinger, "Vielschichtige Neuigkeiten in der sogenannten Paulusgrotte von Ephesus," *Mitteilungen zur Christlichen Archäologie* 11 (2005): 60–61.

clearly teaching Thecla.[227] Immediately publications began to emerge mentioning this painting ranging in dates from the fourth through the sixth century. Most noteable was the mention made by John Dominic Crossan and Jonathan L. Reed, who used the picture for the cover of their book *In Search of Paul: How Jesus's Apostle Opposed Rome's Empire with God's Kingdom* (San Francisco: HarperSan Francisco, 2004), and went on to say that the image of Paul was standing next to Thecla, whose eyes and hand had been burned and scratched out, representing a change in the ideology of women in the church. Crossan soon recanted his argument based on erroneous information that he had gained concerning the images, when he found out that the Thecla that he had mentioned was actually Theocleia.[228] Crossan went on to amend his case and argue that the picture is recording a variant interpretation of Theocleia than that which is recorded in the *AP*. In this new light, Crossan claims that rather than resisting the ministry of Paul, Theocleia is being presented as an advocate and preacher/teacher as well, which varies significantly from the Theocleia of the *APTh*, who wanted to burn her daughter at the stake. Interestingly enough, if one looks closely, the figures of Paul and Thecla are very similar to the fifth/sixth century ivory tablet of Paul and Thecla and the stoning of St. Paul.[229] In the Paul grotto of Ephesus, Thecla is depicted in a home, in a window listening to Paul. It should be noted that the iconography in the grotto has slightly adjusted the literal details as recorded in the literary text. In the *AP*, Theocleia is not teaching alongside Paul in the text, but symbolically this is exactly what Theocleia is doing. From this symbolic perspective, they are quite consistent with the *AP* depending on the interpretation. It is plausible to argue that Theocleia and Paul are teaching competitively to Thecla, presenting Thecla with two different messages. On the one hand, Paul is exhorting Thecla, who will decide whether she will leave the symbolic "home" and renounce her fiancé, or whether she will heed the message of Theocleia, and fulfill her social duty in Iconium. If this be the case, the abuse that has been witnessed on Theocleia's hand and eyes is a testimony to the renouncement of her message.[230]

---

[227] See Pillinger, "Vielschichtige," 56–62. See also Mary Heuser, "Gestures and their Meaning in Early Christian Art," (Ph.D. diss., Radcliffe College, 1954), 152.

[228] This is reported in John D. Crossan, "A Woman Equal to Paul: Who Is She?" *BR* 21.3 (2005): 29–31, 46, 48.

[229] See Cartlidge and Elliott, *Art and the Christian Apocrypha*, 148; See the discussion above and Figure 16 below. Pillinger notes this connection also; see "Neue Entdeckungen," 26–27.

[230] Ruth Ohm, in "The Ambiguity of Interpretation," 3, defends the position that Theocleia could be presented as equal "opposition" to Paul. Ohm goes on to say that the context of the cave, the determining of the various layers of the cave, and the dating of the various paintings in the cave are still too recent to be able to determine any further conclusions on the interpretation of the image.

Acts of Paul 3.5-6:

1. Μακάριοι οἱ καθαροὶ τῇ καρδίᾳ, ὅτι αὐτοὶ τὸν θεὸν ὄψονται.
2. μακάριοι οἱ ἀγνὴν τὴν σάρκα τηρήσαντες, ὅτι αὐτοὶ ναὸς θεοῦ γενήσονται.
3. μακάριοι οἱ ἐγκρατεῖς, ὅτι αὐτοῖς λαλήσει ὁ θεός.
4. μακάριοι οἱ ἀποταξάμενοι τῷ κόσμῳ τούτῳ, ὅτι αὐτοὶ εὐαρεστήσουσιν τῷ θεῷ.
5. μακάριοι οἱ ἔχοντες γυναῖκας ὡς μὴ ἔχοντες, ὅτι αὐτοὶ κληρονομήσουσιν τὸν θεόν.
6. μακάριοι οἱ φόβον ἔχοντες θεοῦ, ὅτι αὐτοὶ ἄγγελοι θεοῦ γενήσονται.
7. μακάριοι οἱ τρέμοντες τὰ λόγια κυρίου, ὅτι αὐτοὶ παρακληθήσονται.
8. μακάριοι οἱ σοφίαν λαβόντες Ἰησοῦ Χριστοῦ, ὅτι αὐτοὶ υἱοὶ ὑψίστου κληθήσονται.
9. μακάριοι οἱ τὸ βάπτισμα τηρήσαντες, ὅτι αὐτοὶ ἀναπαύσονται πρὸς τὸν πατέρα καὶ τὸν υἱόν.
10. μακάριοι οἱ σύνεσιν Ἰησοῦ Χριστοῦ χωρήσαντες, ὅτι αὐτοὶ ἐν φωτὶ γενήσονται.
11. μακάριοι οἱ δι' ἀγάπην θεοῦ ἐξελθόντες τοῦ σχήματος τοῦ κοσμικοῦ, ὅτι αὐτοὶ ἀγγέλους κρινοῦσιν καὶ ἐν δεξιᾷ τοῦ πατρὸς εὐλογηθήσονται
12. [μακάριοι οἱ ἐλεήμονες, ὅτι αὐτοὶ ἐλεηθήσονται] καὶ οὐκ ὄψονται ἡμέραν κρίσεως πικράν.
13. μακάρια τὰ σώματα τῶν παρθένων, ὅτι αὐτὰ εὐαρεστήσουσιν τῷ θεῷ καὶ οὐκ ἀπολέσουσιν τὸν μισθὸν τῆς ἁγνείας αὐτῶν ὅτι ὁ λόγος τοῦ πατρὸς ἔργον αὐτοῖς γενήσεται εἰς ἡμέραν τοῦ υἱοῦ αὐτοῦ, καὶ ἀνάπαυσιν ἕξουσιν εἰς αἰῶνα αἰῶνος.

Matthew 5:3-12:

1. μακάριοι οἱ πτωχοὶ τῷ πνεύματι, ὅτι αὐτῶν ἐστιν ἡ βασιλεία τῶν οὐρανῶν.
2. μακάριοι οἱ πενθοῦντες, ὅτι αὐτοὶ παρακληθήσονται.
3. μακάριοι οἱ πραεῖς, ὅτι αὐτοὶ κληρονομήσουσιν τὴν γῆν.
4. μακάριοι οἱ πεινῶντες καὶ διψῶντες τὴν δικαιοσύνην, ὅτι αὐτοὶ χορτασθήσονται.
5. μακάριοι οἱ ἐλεήμονες, ὅτι αὐτοὶ ἐλεηθήσονται.
6. μακάριοι οἱ καθαροὶ τῇ καρδίᾳ, ὅτι αὐτοὶ τὸν θεὸν ὄψονται.
7. μακάριοι οἱ εἰρηνοποιοί, ὅτι [αὐτοὶ] υἱοὶ θεοῦ κληθήσονται.
8. μακάριοι οἱ δεδιωγμένοι ἕνεκεν δικαιοσύνης, ὅτι αὐτῶν ἐστιν ἡ βασιλεία τῶν οὐρανῶν.
9. μακάριοί ἐστε ὅταν ὀνειδίσωσιν ὑμᾶς καὶ διώξωσιν καὶ εἴπωσιν πᾶν πονηρὸν καθ' ὑμῶν [ψευδόμενοι] ἕνεκεν ἐμοῦ·
10. χαίρετε καὶ ἀγαλλιᾶσθε, ὅτι ὁ μισθὸς ὑμῶν πολὺς ἐν τοῖς οὐρανοῖς· οὕτως γὰρ ἐδίωξαν τοὺς προφήτας τοὺς πρὸ ὑμῶν.

Chart 1: A Comparison of Matthew 5:3-12 and AP 3.5-6

Figures

Figure 1. Image of woman reading from a scroll. Sketch of a fresco in Herculaneum as found in Accademia ercolanese di archeologia (Naples, Italy), Ottavio Antonio Baiardi, and Pasquale Carcani, *Le Pitture Antiche di Ercolano E Contorni Incise con Qualche Spiegazione* (Le Antichità di Ercolano Esposte. In Napoli: Nella Regia stamperia, 1760), 2:13.

Figure 2. Image of a woman painting. Scretch of a fresco in Herculaneum as found in Accademia ercolanese di archeologia (Naples, Italy), Ottavio Antonio Baiardi, and Pasquale Carcani, *Le Pitture Antiche d'Ercolano E Contorni Incise con Qualche Spiegazione* (Le Antichità di Ercolano Esposte. In Napoli: Nella Regia stamperia, 1760), 7:5.

Figure 3. A scene common to the amphitheater. Lions chasing after a bull and wild boars. The image is found in the House of Ceii. Photo Credit: Jeremy W. Barrier.

Figure 4. A close-up image of the lion chasing the bull in the House of Ceii. Photo Credit: Jeremy W. Barrier.

Figure 5. Another close-up image of the lion chasing the bull in the House of Ceii. Photo Credit: Jeremy W. Barrier.

Figure 6. Two lioness' attacking a wild boar. Another wild boar is to the left, and a leopard is above the two lioness on the right in the House of Ceii. Photo Credit: Jeremy W. Barrier.

Figure 7. Picture taken from the *fauces* of the House of Orpheus, looking over the *impluvium*, through the *tablinum*, and into the *peristyle*, where an image of Orpheus surrounded by animals in a *paradesios*. Photo Credit: Jeremy W. Barrier.

Figure 8. Orpheus, with a leopard to his left and a lion to his right. Below Orpheus, on the left is a wild boar, and a deer on the right. All the animals remain calm due to the influence of Orpheus' powerfully soothing music. Photo Credit: Jeremy W. Barrier.

Figure 9. Close-up picture of the deer in the House of Orpheus. Photo Credit: Jeremy W. Barrier.

Figure 10. Close-up picture of Orpheus and the leopard in the House of Orpheus. Photo Credit: Jeremy W. Barrier.

Figure 11. The so-called "Thecla Ship." The lid from a fourth century marble sarcophagus with a ship symbolizing Thecla and Paul, via Flaminia; wall from the Basilica de San
Velentino, Rome; Capitoline Museum. Photo Credit: David L. Balch.

Figure 12. The arrest of Paul. Sculpture from the sarcophagus of Junius Bassus (circa
359); found at the Vatican, Museo Pio Cristiano. Photo credit: Erich Lessing/Art Resource, NY.

Figure 13. A fifth/sixth century ivory tablet (4.2 x 9.8 cm) from the British Museum (Catalog no. MME 1856.06–23) that depicts Thecla standing within a castle/home listening to Paul, who is seated and reading from a scroll outside the castle/home. The panel is divided in the center, and the right side portrays the stoning of Paul (Acts 14:19–20). Photo Credit: Erich Lessing/Art Resource, NY.

Figure 14. A 6th–8th century fresco that was found on the dome of Chapel 80 (Peace Chapel) of the necropolis at El Bagawat in the Kharga Oasis. It is an image of Thecla (far left) being taught by Paul (center) while sitting beside each other. Photo Credit: Alain Guilleux.

Figure 15. *Saint Thecla with Wild Beasts and* Angels depicting the martyrdom of Thecla in Antioch, 5th century C.E. Limestone, 3 3/4 x 25 ½ inches (9.5 x 64.8 cm). Photo Credit: The Nelson-Atkins Museum of Art, Kansas City, Missouri. Purchase: William Rockhill Nelson Trust, 48–10. Photograph by Jamison Miller.

Figure 16. Paul and Theocleia teaching Thecla. Image taken from Renate Pillinger, "Vielschichtige Neuigkeiten in der so genannten Paulusgrotte von Ephesus," *Mitteillungen zur Christlichen Archäologie* 11 (2005): 60–61. Photo Credit: N. Gail/ÖAI, Vienna.

Part II

Commentary on the *Acts of Paul* 3–4

Acts of Paul 3.1–26

Πράξεις Παύλου καὶ Θέκλης

3.1

Ἀναβαίνοντος[1] Παύλου εἰς Ἰκόνιον μετὰ τὴν φυγὴν τὴν ἀπὸ Ἀντιοχείας[2] ἐγενήθησαν σύνοδοι αὐτῷ Δημᾶς καὶ Ἑρμογένης ὁ χαλκεύς,[3] ὑποκρίσεως[4] γέμοντες, καὶ ἐξελιπάρουν τὸν Παῦλον ὡς[5] ἀγαπῶντες αὐτόν. ὁ δὲ Παῦλος ἀποβλέπων εἰς μόνην τὴν ἀγαθοσύνην τοῦ Χριστοῦ οὐδὲν φαῦλον[6] ἐποίει αὐτοῖς, ἀλλ' ἔστεργεν αὐτοὺς σφόδρα, ὥστε πάντα τὰ λόγια κυρίου καὶ τῆς δι- δασκαλίας[7] καὶ τῆς ἑρμηνείας [τοῦ εὐαγγελίου][8] καὶ τῆς γεννήσεως καὶ τῆς ἀναστάσεως τοῦ ἠγαπημένου[9] ἐγλύκαινεν[10] αὐτούς, καὶ τὰ μεγαλεῖα[11] τοῦ Χριστοῦ, πῶς ἀπεκαλύφθη[12] αὐτῷ,[13] κατὰ ῥῆμα διηγεῖτο αὐτοῖς,

Codex M

καὶ ἐκ μαρίας τῆς παρθένου καὶ ἐκ σπέρματος δαυὶδ ὁ χριστός ἐστιν.[14]

Cop[1]

ⲛⲉϥϫⲟⲩ ⲙ̄ⲙ[ⲁⲩ ⲛⲉⲩ ϫⲉ ⲡⲉⲭⲣ̄ⲥ̄ ⲛ̄ⲧⲁⲩ ϫⲡⲁϥ] ⲁⲃⲁⲗ' ϩⲙ̄ ⲙ[ⲁ]ⲣⲓⲁ ⲧⲡ[ⲁⲣⲑⲉⲛⲟⲥ ⲙ̄ⲛ ϩⲙ̄ ⲡⲉⲥⲡ]ⲉⲣⲙⲁ ⲛ̄ⲇⲁⲩⲉⲓⲇ':

Reconstruction

ὅτι[15] ἐκ μαρίας τῆς παρθένου καὶ ἐκ σπέρματος δαυίδ[16] ὁ χριστός ἐστιν.[17]

Translation

As Paul was going up into Iconium after the flight from Antioch, traveling with him were Demas and Hermogenes, the blacksmith. Being full of hy- pocrisy, they were entreating Paul earnestly as if they loved him. But Paul, who was steadfastly looking into the goodness of Christ alone, was doing nothing bad to them, but he was loving them greatly, so that all the words

of the Lord and the teachings and the interpretation [of the Gospel] and of
the birth and of the resurrection of the beloved one, he was sweetening
them even with the great things of Christ, as they were revealed to him,
according to the word passed over to them. He was telling them that the
Christ was born of Mary the virgin and of the seed (sperm) of David.

3.1.1 Textual Notes

[1] From ἀναβαίνω – "to go up, ascend" BDAG, 58. This is a genitive absolute. This is the only time ἀναβαίνω appears in the *AP*. Cop[1] uses the
Second Future Verb (*imperfectum futuri*), ϥⲛⲁⲃⲱⲕ, with a translation, "As
Paul was about to." This is a very common word in the New Testament;
used with εἰς to refer to entering into a place (Acts 2:34). Also used in reference to *ascending* to a place such as a temple. See Acts 10:4, 11:2,
18:22, and 21:6. An ascent of elevation is clear. But an ascent from which
Antioch is under question. The most likely conclusion is the ascent in elevation from Antioch of Syria versus Antioch of Pisidia (*ÉAC*, 1128, footnote II,3 "*Ils lui jetèrent des pierres et l'expulsèrent de leur ville*: on cher-
cherait en vain ici des parallèles avec les événements racontés en Ac 13–
14, qui se situent à Antioche de Pisidie."). The canonical Acts of the Apostles does not help to clarify, since Paul travels from both locations to
Iconium (Acts 14:1 and 16:2). None of the texts clarify for us. See discussions in Dunn, "*Acts of Paul*," 19–20; Rordorf, *Lex Orandi – Lex Credendi*, 452–54; Schneemelcher, *NTApoc* 2:218–20; Schmidt, *ΠΠ*, 115–16;
Ernst Rollfs, "Paulusakten," *Neutestamentliche Apokryphen in Verbindung
mit Fachgelehrten in deutscher Übersetzung und mit Einleitungen* (ed. Edgar Hennecke; Tübingen and Leipzig: J. C. B. Mohr [Paul Siebeck], 1904),
192; and Peter Corssen, "Die Urgestalt der Paulusakten," *ZNW* 4 (1903):
46, for further discussion. Nicetas has Paul imprisoned in Syrian Antioch
on the Orontes (*Panegyric* 82). Cherix identifies the Antioch in the *AP*
with Antioch of Syria, also basing his translation on Cop[1], although Cop[1]
does not clarify at all. *ATit* follows *AP*. In my opinion, the deciding factor
lies in the usage of this genitive absolute, which distinctly forces the reader
to understand this going as an ascent (LSJ, 98). Unfortunately Cop[1] does
not help us here. The text only states, "after he fled away (ⲁⲃⲁⲗ' [Ach-
mîmic Dialect for ⲉⲃⲟⲗ, Crum, *Coptic Dictionary* (Oxford: Clarendon
Press, 1939), 2.]) from Antioch and he will go up/down (ⲁⲅⲣⲏⲉⲓ) to
Iconium." Although, I would add that this title itself is partially reconstructed from the first two lines of Cop[1] in which it is easy to reconstruct
the content of the words. It seems likely if one is traveling from the coastal
region of Syrian Antioch into the mountainous regions of Asia Minor, and
in particular, entering upon the Central Anatolian plateau, a region where
both Antioch of Pisidia and Iconium are located. I find it more difficult for

this description to be inserted if traveling from Pisidian Antioch, and I also find it difficult to believe that the Asian author would have been ignorant of such a geographical distinction. The only other alternative for insisting upon a Pisidian location is to follow the later *ATit* that suggests Paul travels "again" (πάλιν) to Antioch of Pisidia (Schneemelcher supports this reading, *NTApoc* 2:219) or that the author cannot be trusted for such particular details (Schneemelcher again, *NTApoc* 2:219–220).

² See 2 Tim 3:11. In 2 Tim 3:11, Paul mentions sufferings and trials he endured in Antioch, Iconium, and Lystra. In future notes, I will often cite specific references to the Pastorals, ancient novels, other early Christian texts, where, typically, I will be noting verbatim word connections or intertextual similarities. However, I make an effort to note the relevant verbatim connections, sometimes without further comment, but solely for the purpose of facilitating the readers pursuit of these connections.

³ Or "coppersmith" (LSJ, 1973). See 2 Tim 4:9, 10, 1:15, 4:14 for the connections of Demas and Hermogenes in the Pastorals, both of whom wronged the Pastoral's Paul.

⁴ Not found in Acts, but in 1 Tim 4:2, Luke 12:1; 20:20 (participial verb form; ὑποκρινομένους), and Gal 2:13. Most of the language here in *AP* finds no similarities with Acts, although the possible connection to the Pastorals seems more probable. This is similar to ὁ ὑποκριτής, οῦ, as found in Luke 6:42, 11:39, and in Achilles Tatius, *Leuc. Clit.* 8.8.14; 8.17.3 (BDAG, 1038).

⁵ "ὡς may be rendered *as if. . .*" when translated with the participle. (Smyth, *Greek Grammar* [rev. Gordon M. Messing; Cambridge: Harvard UP, 1920], §2086). Cop¹ translates ⲉⲅⲕⲱⲣ︤ⲱ︥ as the circumstancial "flattering."

⁶ On the use of φαῦλον in "household of God" instructions, see Titus 2:8 and 3:2. The author of *AP* appears to be presenting Paul as obedient to his own instructions to Titus. See also Romans 9:11 that contrasts the ἀγαθός with the φαῦλον (cf. BDAG, 1050). This word is unknown to any New Testament writings other than John 3:20 and James 3:16. 2 Tim 2:24-26 deals with instructions on how to deal with those who are hostile to God, similar to Paul's treatment of Demas and Hermogenes.

⁷ See *AP* 3.9 and 13; 2 Tim 3:16.

⁸ Bracketed text is not original here. Schneemelcher claims that the line "of the doctrine and of the interpretation of the Gospel" is missing from the text, based on the work of A. F. J. Klijn, "The Apocryphal Correspondence between Paul and the Corinthians." *VC* 17 (1963): 19–20. To the contrary, Cop¹ includes the line with the exception of "of the Gospel." Klijn's discussion is on page 13–14, (not 19–20 as Schneemelcher suggests; *NTApoc* 2:266, footnote 4). In addition, it seems evident that Schneemelcher only looked at Klijn's quoting of the *AAA* (which has

bracketed the Greek text "and of the teaching and the explanation of the Gospel"). If one continues to read Klijn's comments, he goes on to say, "Probably it is not necessary to put the words 'and of the teaching ...Gospel' between brackets, but the words 'of the Gospel' must be considered secondary, since they are omitted in some Greek manuscripts and the Coptic text," (Klijn, *VC* 16, 1963, 14).

[9] See Hills, "The Acts of the Apostles in the *Acts of Paul*," 29. Using similar textual ratings than that of the Nestle-Aland Greek New Testament with the grades of A, B, C, and D, Hills gives the phrase τοῦ ἠγαπημένου here in *AP* 3.1 a "D" reading regarding being connected to ἐν τῷ ἠγαπημένη in Ephesians 3:1.

[10] Most of the verbs throughout this paragraph are in the imperfect active indicative, leaving the text with the telling of a past situation, but anticipating something further in the story. This is preliminary narration for what is to come.

[11] Acts 2:11, where Peter tells everyone in Jerusalem at Pentecost about the "τὰ μεγαλεῖα τοῦ θεοῦ." τὰ μεγαλεῖα is in the neuter gender and plural in number, but taking a first aorist passive indicative, third person singular verb.

[12] Reconstructed tenuously by Schmidt as ⲉⲛ[ⲧⲁⲅϭⲱⲗ]ⲡ̄.

[13] Translated from Cop[1] as: (17) as so that he told them many words of the Lord (18) and teachings and interpretation: with the birth (19) and resurrection of the beloved one; and of the (20) great things (greatness) of Christ in the manner of which they were offered (21) to him: he was telling to them that the Christ (22) was born of Mary the virgin and of (23) of the seed (sperm) of David.

[14] See *AAA*, 236, for the textual transmission of this text. The text of manuscripts *A*, *B*, *C*, *E*, *F*, *H*, *I*, *K*, *L*, and *M* are essentially the same with minor additions and subtractions; therefore I produced only *M* as one representative. The reconstructed text takes into consideration the Greek manuscripts, and I have also added the textual influence of Cop[1]. The text of *AAA* lacks this section of the text, but it appears to be much earlier than thought by Lipsius and Bonnet, and the theological content is very early and not a latter addition as previously thought.

[15] ὅτι is supported by Greek manuscripts *A*, *B*, *C*, *E*, *F*, *H*, *I*, *K*, *L*, and the Latin *m*.

[16] ἐκ σπέρματος δαυίδ – see 2 Tim 2:8.

[17] *AAA* follows Tischendorf, the Greek manuscript *G*, the latin manuscript *d*, and the Syriac versions listed as *s*, against the other manuscripts, but after having found Cop[1], it appears that the manuscript *M* is the superior rendering, but with minor alterations needed. I have provided a reconstruction that I believe is more consistent with both the Greek manuscripts and the Coptic.

3.1.2 General Comment

Within this first passage, we are introduced to several individuals, but most notably, we are introduced to Paul. This introduction, consistent with other ancient novels, allows us to begin the tale by introducing the major figures, themes, plot, love triangles, etc. This "introduction" will span the first several chapters, as Paul, Thecla, Onesiphorus and his family, and the opponents of the hero and heroine are also introduced.

As we are introduced to Paul, the question might arise, "is this Paul the apostle?" Only in the latter addition (*APTh* 45) to the *APTh* and within $\mathfrak{P}^7$ does the designation of ἀπόστολος appear in the Greek text, and the $\mathfrak{P}^7$ reference is found in 3 Corinthians in reference to the other apostles, who came before Paul (Note the contrast between Gal and 3 Cor, where the canonical texts never have Paul quoting from anything that he had received from "the apostles who were before me"). However, Paul is given the designations of ξένος (3.13), μάγος (3.15), and Χριστιανός (3.14, 17), but never ἀπόστολος. Even when Paul is asked directly, Τίς εἶ, καὶ τί διδάσκεις (3.16), Paul diverts the discussion away from himself, and defends his message. However, while I think it important to note the absence of the designation, I also think it important to realize that a fair assumption in the late second century is that the *AP* is dealing with the apostle Paul in the same way that the other *AAApos* deal with the other apostles.

In regard to geographical location of these events, I would argue that Paul is presented as coming up to Iconium from Syrian Antioch (for further discussion see footnote 1 above), so that he might begin teaching the word of God there also. At this point, we are not told whether Paul has been to Iconium before, but that he is simply going into Iconium (See *3.2.2 General Comment* for further discussion on this point). The text is recounted in the imperfect (incomplete past) tense, providing a backdrop for the events that are soon to come. Some of the strongest connections to the Pastoral Epistles begins in this chapter, in particular the names of people and places, and also the reference to ἐκ σπέρματος δαυίδ (2 Tim 2:8). Also some awareness of the Pauline corpus is possible here (specifically Romans 9:11; see note 6 above). Outside of this, there is one reference to the "Great things of Christ," (Acts 2:11) but no literary relationship to the canonical Acts is evident. Interestingly, Demas and Hermogenes are mentioned as false companions of Paul. These are some of the same individuals mentioned in 2 Timothy, while also mixing the Pastoral individuals of "Alexander, the coppersmith," with "Hermogenes, the blacksmith." Nonetheless, some kind of connection to the material of 2 Timothy is probable (see *Chapter 4: Acts of Paul and the New Testament* for a detailed discussion). The Latin manuscript *d* sees a connection to the Pastorals and actually added the name "Alexander," before the title, ὁ χαλκεύς, in order to be consistent with 2 Timothy. More names shared with the Pastorals surface in 3.2, where we realize that Paul is also headed to the house of Onesiphorus (See 3.2 and 2 Timothy 1:16; see *3.2 1 Textual Notes*, note 1, and *3.2.2 General Comment*).

3.2

Καί τις ἀνὴρ ὀνόματι Ὀνησιφόρος[1] ἀκούσας τὸν Παῦλον παραγενόμενον[2] εἰς Ἰκόνιον,[3] ἐξῆλθεν σὺν τοῖς τέκνοις αὐτοῦ Σιμμίᾳ καὶ Ζήνωνι καὶ τῇ γυναικὶ αὐτοῦ Λέκτρᾳ εἰς συνάντησιν Παύλου, ἵνα αὐτὸν ὑποδέξηται· διηγήσατο[4] γὰρ αὐτῷ Τίτος ποταπός ἐστιν τῇ εἰδέᾳ[5] ὁ Παῦλος· οὐ γὰρ εἶδεν αὐτὸν σαρκί[6] ἀλλὰ μόνον πνεύματι.[7]

Translation

And a certain man named Onesiphorus, having heard that Paul was arriving into Iconium, went out to meet Paul with his children, Simmias and Zenon, and his wife, Lectra, so that he could receive him. For Titus had described to him what sort of image Paul had, for he knew him not by flesh, but only in spirit.

3.2.1 Textual Notes

[1] 2 Timothy 1:16–18; 4:19. See also *AP* 3.2; 3.4; 3.5; 3.7; 3.15; 3.23; 3.25; 3.26. Onesiphorus is known to Paul as the one who has greeted him on several occasions, namely in Ephesus and Rome, but now in Iconium according to the *APTh*. See also the later traditions from the *Acts Pet. And.* 13–21, where the name of Onesiphorus is picked up in the story as a comforting figure who provides housing for the apostles Peter and Andrew. Possible connections begin with 2 Timothy and the τὸν Ὀνησιφόρου οἶκον, which is a source of comfort for the Paul of the Pastorals, whose role is further expanded upon in *APTh*. This role is developed into a full scene which follows in the *APTh*, where Onesiphorus' home is the center of teaching and the home where the events of Iconium take place. An expansion of the tradition of Onesiphorus, as stated above, is found in *Acta Petri et Andreae*, which develops the tradition of the conversion of Onesiphorus as a rich man who finally converts to the apostles and is baptized in addition to 1,000 others in one night. The story concludes in *Acts Pet. And.* 21 with Πέτρε εἴσελθε εἰς τὸν οἶκον μου καὶ ἀναπαύου. One difference is the inability to conclude that the city of the barbarians (πόλει τῶν βαρβάρων) is indeed Iconium. It is unlikely to be the same location.

[2] On παραγενόμενον (second aorist middle deponent participle, accusative masculine singular), see Luke 7:4, 20; 8:19; 11:6; 12:51; 14:21; 19:16; 22:52; Acts 5:21, 22, 25; 9:26, 39; 10:33; 11:23; 13:14; 14:27; 15:4; 17:10; 18:27; 20:18; 21:18; 23:16, 35; 24:17, 24; 25:7; 28:21. This word is preferred by Luke-Acts, being found outside of Luke-Acts in the New Testament only nine times. There is a possible borrowing of the *AP* from the language of Luke-Acts.

[3] For a discussion on the disagreement with the canonical Acts account of Paul's coming to Iconium, see W. Rordorf, "In welchem Verhältnis stehen die apokryphen Paulusakten zur kanonischen Apostelgeschichte und zu den Pastoralbriefen?," *Lex Orandi – Lex Credendi,* 453–54.

[4] διηγήσατο – second aorist middle deponent indicative, third person, singular, from διηγέομαι – meaning to "set out in detail, describe" (LSJ, 427). Onesiphorus has clearly never seen or met Paul. Contrast 2 Tim 1.16, where it appears that Onesiphorus has seen Paul before.

[5] On εἰδέᾳ, see Matt 28:3 for the sole NT usage in reference to Jesus figure in the tomb after the resurrection. See also LXX Genesis 5:3 which uses both ἰδέαν and εἰκόνα in reference to how Adam's son Seth was in the same form and image of Adam. The form of the word, ἰδέα, is the older form with the present form characteristic of later Greek. This term is probably not suggesting the actual appearance of Paul (εἰκών), but rather the "appearance" of Paul or the type of form, the elemental shape of Paul (e.g. Platonic Philosophic language of forms, see Plato's *Phaedrus* 265d) from a Physiognomistic perspective. In particular, the connections that can be drawn from Paul's outer features that enlighten us upon his "inner qualities." For more discussion of Physiognomics, see Mikeal C. Parsons, *Body and Character in Luke and Acts: The Subversion of Physiognomy in Early Christianity,* Grand Rapids: Baker, 2006), 17–37, and 51–56; see also the discussion under "description of Paul" in the *3.3 Textual Notes,* notes 5 and 8; *3.3 General Comment*; and LSJ 485, 817; BDAG, 466. See *TDNT* 2:373–75, and the cognates represented in the NT, such as εἶδος in 2 Cor 5:7 or 1 Thess 5:22.

[6] See Gal 5:16–26. See also Fred O. Francis and J. Paul Sampley, *Pauline Parallels,* (Philapelphia: Fortress, 1984), 243, for further possible Pauline connections in the contrast of the fleshly and the spiritual.

[7] On the expression, οὐ γὰρ εἶδεν αὐτὸν σαρκὶ ἀλλὰ μόνον πνεύματι, compare Gal 1:22–23, which states "ἤμην δὲ ἀγνοούμενος τῷ προσώπῳ ταῖς ἐκκλησίαις τῆς Ἰουδαίας ταῖς ἐν Χριστῷ. μόνον δὲ ἀκούοντες ἦσαν ὅτι ὁ διώκων ἡμᾶς ποτε νῦν . . ." Hills gives the literary dependency of these two texts a "B" rating (Hills, "The Acts of the Apostles," 33). The textual allusion appears to be there, and consistent with Galatians, but the only literary connection is μόνον, which makes the connection possible, but unlikely. In addition, the use of εἰδέᾳ instead of προσώπῳ makes the connection even

less likely. On the contrary, if the author of *3 Corinthians* happened to be
the same author of the *APTh*, then an awareness of Gal could be proven,
but at this point, there is not enough evidence to support the argument that
the two documents are written by the same hand (See the Introduction sections *Chapter 2. Historical Context* and *Chapter 3. History of Reception*).

3.2.2 General Comment

Here, Onesiphorus comes with his family to greet Paul as he enters into
Iconium (as was his custom according to 2 Tim 1:16–18). Interestingly
enough, Rordorf argues that the church already exists in Iconium, but the
members there do not recognize him, suggesting that Paul did not plant the
church in this place. This would clearly be in conflict with the canonical
Acts account (Acts 13:51–14:6; see *3.2.1 Textual Notes*, note 3). Rordorf is
not convincing. Onesiphorus is not one who is *from* Iconium, but rather is
residing there itinerantly for the planting of a church in Iconium. It is evident from the account in 2 Tim 1:16, that Onesiphorus is presented as a
coworker of Paul, who has often *refreshed* him (Compare 2 Tim 1:16 and 2
Tim 4.19) in various cities under various circumstances. Paul, in 2 Tim
1:16–18 mentions the house of Onesiphorus, a prison in Rome, and finally
services rendered in Ephesus. It seems appropriate that Onesiphorus, the
traveling coworker could meet Paul in Iconium, expecting him, so as to
begin his work with Paul.

   As the text continues, Simmias, Zenon, the children and Lectra, the
spouse of Onesiphorus, join him to meet Paul, but they are no where spoken of again in the *AP*, so their significance is minimized from a literary
perspective. In fact, their introduction into the text allows for them to hold
minor roles (although their names are no longer mentioned) in the *AP*
3.23–26. It is due to the complaining of the hungry children from their fast
for Thecla that Paul allows them to go seek food, and they cross paths with
Thecla. Nonetheless, the family does not know Paul, but Titus has described the image of Paul to Onesiphorus. There seems to be a subtle ma-
nipulation of the wording by the author of the *AP* to suggest that this is not
a literal description of Paul's features. The author claims that this is the
"form" or "image" of Paul, and when one considers the description presented in 3.3, it appears that this is not a description of Paul's actual appearance, but a description of a persona that Paul possessed (See *3.3.2
General Comment* for further explanation). However, Onesiphorus knows
Paul from a connection in the Spirit, but has yet to see him in the flesh.

3.3

Καὶ ἐπορεύετο κατὰ τὴν βασιλικὴν ὁδὸν¹ τὴν ἐπὶ Λύστραν, καὶ εἱστήκει²
ἀπεκδεχόμενος³ αὐτόν, καὶ τοὺς ἐρχομένους ἐθεώρει κατὰ τὴν μήνυσιν Τίτου.⁴
εἶδεν δὲ τὸν Παῦλον ἐρχόμενον, ἄνδρα μικρὸν τῷ μεγέθει, ψιλὸν τῇ κεφαλῇ,
ἀγκύλον ταῖς κνήμαις, εὐεκτικόν, σύνοφρυν,⁵ μικρῶς ἐπίρρινον, χάριτος πλήρη⁶·
ποτὲ μὲν γὰρ ἐφαίνετο ὡς ἄνθρωπος, ποτὲ δὲ ἀγγέλου πρόσωπον εἶχεν⁷.⁸

Translation

And he was going down the king's way, the one from Lystra, and he stood
eagerly awaiting him, and he was looking over the ones coming by according to the description passed on by Titus. And he saw Paul coming, a man
small of stature, bald headed, a crook in the legs, healthy, a brow meeting
in the middle, a small nose, a gracious presence; for some times he appeared as a man, but at other times he had the face of an angel.

3.3.1 Textual Notes

¹ Cop¹ breaks at this point, and 16 lines are missing. The "Royal Road,"
most likely the one built by Augustus from Antioch to Lystra. Ramsay argues convincingly that the Royal Road from Lystra to Iconium would have
fallen out of use after 74 CE after the dissolution of the Pisidian colonial
system (*The Church in the Roman Empire*, 30–35.). Afterward, the road
from Antioch directly to Iconium would have been the road familiar to
people who traveled through this region. This indicates that the author of
the *AP* must have had some documents or particular knowledge of the first
century road system allowing for such an insight.

² εἱστήκει – This is the second pluperfect form (third singular) of ἵστημι,
"to stand," lit. "stood." William M. Ramsay (*The Church in the Roman
Empire*, 31, note †) adds "'he proceeded along the Royal Road,' but the
following εἱστήκει implies that the first clause indicates the point to which
Onesiphorus went and where he stood."

³ ἀπεκδεχόμενος – In "our lit(erature). Always of Christian hope w(ith).
Its var(ious). Objects...," BDAG, 100. See Rom 8:19, 23, 25; 1 Cor 1:7;
Gal 5:5; Phil 3:20; Heb 9:28; and 1 Pet 3:20.

⁴ The canonical books of the New Testament provide no biographical
description of Paul. The best information that provides us with a possible
description is found in 1 Cor 2:3–5; 2 Cor 10:8–11; 12:1–10 and Gal 4:12–
16, which seem to suggest that Paul was weak in appearance, suffered
from poor vision, and suffered from some form of health problems (thorn
in the flesh?). If this is accurate, then there is still a discrepancy in the way
that Malherbe and Grant interpret the author of the *AP* description and the

information provided by Paul himself. See also Cartlidge and Elliott, "5 Paul, Thecla, and Peter," *Art and the Christian Apocrypha*, 138–40 for a discussion of a comparison of the description of Paul to that of Socrates.

[5] σύνοφρυν – See Malherbe's discussion in "A Physical Description of Paul," 174; Bruce J. Malina and Jerome H. Neyrey, *Portraits of Paul: An Archaeology of Ancient Personality* (Louisville: Westminster/John Knox Press, 1996), 100–52. *Portraits of Paul* provides a thorough comparison of the characteristics of Paul through the lens of Physiognomics. See also footnote 8 below.

[6] Elliott translates this more literally as "full of grace," (*ANT*, 364), while Schneemelcher (*NTApoc* 2:239) translates the expression as "full of friendliness." This expression χάριτος πλήρη is also found in John 1:14 and Acts 6:8. This expression is further complicated by the fact that Luke-Acts uses πλήρης in discussing how different ones are "full of the Holy Spirit" (Luke 4:1; Acts 7:55), "full of the "faith" and the "Spirit" (Acts 6:5, 11:24) "full of the spirit and power" (Acts 6:8), and "full of spirit and wisdom" (Acts 6:3). John 1:14 is a theologically loaded expression, so "full of Grace and Truth" seems justified, but does this represent the language of the author of the *AP* (see Raymond E. Brown, *The Gospel according to John I–XII: A New Translation with Introduction and Commentary* [Anchor Bible 29; New York: Doubleday, 1966] 14). Acts appears to suggest a theologically motivated usage also. There are possibly two touchstones within this brief description of Paul in comparison to Stephen. The comparison below will hopefully help elucidate this connection.

Acts 6:8:
Στέφανος δὲ <u>πλήρης χάριτος</u>
καὶ δυνάμεως ἐποίει τέρατα
καὶ σημεῖα μεγάλα ἐν τῷ λαῷ.

AP 3:2:
εἶδεν δὲ τὸν Παῦλον ἐρχόμενον,
ἄνδρα μιχρον...<u>χάριτος πλήρη</u>·

Acts 6:15:
Καὶ ἀτενίσαντες εἰς αὐτὸν πάντες οἱ καθεζόμενοι ἐν τῷ
συνεδρίῳ εἶδον τὸ <u>πρόσωπον αὐτοῦ ὡσεὶ πρόσωπον ἀγγέλου</u>

ποτὲ μὲν γὰρ ἐφαίνετο ὡς ἄνθρωπος, ποτὲ δὲ <u>ἀγγέλου πρόσωπον</u>
εἶχεν

Hills overlooks the parallel expression of πλήρης χάριτος. Hills gives the latter connection of *AP* 3.2 and Acts 6:15 a "B" rating. I think that the connection is strengthened significantly by the connection of these two in at least three points. The connection can be seen in that the text compares Paul to Stephen as (1) full of grace, (2) a comparison of their faces that look like the face of an angel, and (3) both texts seem to suggest the dichotomous nature of Paul and Stephen, who looks as (ὡς) a man, and all those who saw his face (the *man* Stephen) saw it as if (ὡσεὶ) the face of an

angel. See Grant, "The Description of Paul in the Acts of Paul and Thecla," 1. Hans Conzelmann says "the idea of an angel-like face here is
found frequently in Judaism" referring to the comments of Str-B 2.665–66
(see *Acts of the Apostles*, 48). The primary problem is that the evidence
seems to be most suggestive of an awareness of the content of the canonical Acts at an *oral* level, while at the same time arguing against *literary*
dependence. In order to be clear, I think that an awareness of Acts is apparent, but the author of the *AP* does not have a copy before him or her. In
regard to πλήρης χάριτος, BDAG suggests *favor, grace, goodwill* (*terminus
technicus*) in the sense of "reciprocity known as Roman patronage, in
which superiority of the donor over the client is clearly maintained," 1079,
definition 2. Although, the act of reciprocity is not directly being referred
to in this passage in *AP*, the reference to Paul's χάρις is imbedded in the
term (see also Malina, Bruce J., *The New Testament World: Insights from
Cultural Anthropology* [3ʳᵈ ed., Philadelphia: Westminster John Knox,
2001], 93–7; Ekkehard W. Stegemann and Wolfgang Stegemann, *The Jesus Movement: A Social History of the First Century*, [trans. O. C. Dean
Jr.; Minneapolis: Fortress Press, 1999], 34–5).

[7] ποτὲ μὲν γὰρ ἐφαίνετο ὡς ἄνθρωπος, ποτὲ δὲ ἀγγέλου πρόσωπον εἶχεν –
Hills gives this a "B" rating as a possible connection to Acts 6:15, which
reads, εἶδον τὸ πρόσωπον αὐτοῦ ὡσεὶ πρόσωπον ἀγγέλου. ("The Acts of the
Apostles," 42). Hills cites *BiPa* which draws a connection between Tertullian's *Res.* 55.9 and Acts 6:15.

[8] Neither Malherbe nor Grant understand this description as historical or
biographical. Building off the work of Grant, Malherbe sees the description as painting Paul in heroic language ("A Physical Description," 170–
75.), while Grant lays the groundwork for seeing the description connected
to descriptions of military generals, and that this one comes from Greek
poetry by way of Greek rhetoric ("The Description," 2). Compare Elizabeth C. Evans, "Physiogmonics in the Ancient World," *TAPA* (1969): 51–
58; and the origin of Malherbe and Grant's argument, a fragment of Ar-
chilochus (frg. 58 Bergk⁴) with a translation in J. M. Edmonds, *Elegy and
Iambus,* 2.127. This is consistent with the *Martyrdom of Paul* and other
portions of the *AP* that describe Paul and the Christian Church as an an-
tithesis to the Roman Empire. See Grant, "The Description," 3. This is also
consistent with 2 Tim 2.3–4. In this rhetoric, Paul is the general of Christ
entering Iconium and later Rome (see *AP* 10–11). From this perspective,
Paul the general comes recruiting soldiers (especially *AP* 10–11 in Rome).
The military image is much subdued here in comparison to that which is
stated in the martyrdom account in Rome. However, the confrontation between Rome and Christianity surfaces consistently throughout this section
as Paul comes, and then Demas and Hermogenes twice attempt to make the
teaching of Christianity an issue before the governor (3.14–16). For a more

recent evaluation of the description in light of the physiognomists, see Bollók, "I. The Description of Paul in the Acta Pauli," 1–15.

3.3.2 General Comment

The text begins with a description of Paul. Here we find Paul traveling down the Roman highway connecting Lystra to Iconium, as he moves toward Iconium from the South. Finally, the "hero" and "general" Paul (see *3.3.1 Textual Notes*, note 8) moves into Iconium, and is identified by Onesiphorus from the description provided to him by Titus. The description (discussed in *3.3.1 Textual Notes*, notes 4–7) then presents Paul as one who is worn, but is gracious in appearance, and sometimes has the appearance of an angel. In the *AP* 3.3, we see the strongest possible connection between the *AP* and Acts, primarily in seeing the language to describe Stephen applied to Paul here (See *3.3.1 Textual Notes*, note 6). The text has spent two paragraphs introducing the male hero of this tale, and having done so, it is now time to move back into the introduction of the text, in order that the reader will be given a context that incorporates Paul, Onesiphorus and his house as a setting sufficient to introduce the true hero in this tale, namely Thecla. It is important, at this point to realize that most of the facts leading up to 3.7, are also the features in the narrative that have specific bearing upon the latter in events in the *APTh*, regarding the development of Thecla's persecutions, and eventually the development of Thecla as a leader.

3.4

Καὶ ἰδὼν ὁ Παῦλος τὸν ᾿Ονησιφόρον ἐμειδίασεν, καὶ εἶπεν ὁ ᾿Ονησιφόρος Χαῖρε, ὑπηρέτα τοῦ εὐλογημένου θεοῦ· κἀκεῖνοςεῖπεν ῾Η χάρις μετὰ σοῦ καὶ τοῦ οἴκου σου. Δημᾶς δὲ καὶ ῾Ερμογένης[1] ἐζήλωσαν καὶ πλείονα τὴν ὑπόκρισιν ἐκίνησαν, ὥστε[2] εἰπεῖν τὸν Δημᾶν, ῾Ημεῖς οὐκ ἐσμὲν τοῦ εὐλογημένου, ὅτι ἡμᾶς οὐκ ἠσπάσω[3] οὕτως; καὶ εἶπεν ὁ ᾿Ονησιφόρος Οὐχ ὁρῶ ἐν ὑμῖν καρπὸν δικαιοσύνης·[4] εἰ δὲ ἔστε τινές,[5] δεῦτε καὶ ὑμεῖς εἰς τὸν οἶκόν μου καὶ ἀναπαύσασθε.

Translation

And Paul, seing Onesiphorus, smiled and Onesiphorus said, "Greetings, servants of the blessed God, and he replied, "Grace be with you and to your house." But Demas and Hermogenes being jealous and full of hypocrisy were disturbed, so that Demas said, "Are we not of the blessed one, that you did not greet us in the same way?" And Onesiphorus said, "I do not see fruit of righteousness in you, but if you are such ones (bearing fruit of righteousness), then come into my house and you will be refreshed."

3.4.1 Textual Notes

[1] Here in this text, Demas speaks independently of Hermogenes, although he appears together with Hermogenes. In the language of epic folk narrative laws, the two are represented as "twins" in 3.1, 4, 12, 14, and 16. In 3.1, they have no voice; 3.4, Demas speaks alone, and both speak in unison in the remaining sections. See Alex Olrik, "Epic Laws of Folk Narrative," *The Study of Folklore* (ed. Alan Dundes; Prentice-Hall, 1965), 131–41; and the application of the laws of folktales as applied to the *APTh* in MacDonald's *The Legend and the Apostle*, 26–33. Demas speaking alone argues against the thesis of MacDonald, while the occurrence of Hermogenes and Demas as twins, only appearing in the *APTh*, supports MacDonald and Viriginia Burrus' argument for a folklore analysis of the *APTh*. See Burrus, *Chastity as Autonomy*, 33–38. If this be the case, then this possibly demonstrates the oral predecessor to the writing of the text in it's present state.

[2] ὡς εἰπεῖν τὸν Δημᾶν – Elliott, *ANT*, 365 and Schneemelcher *NTApoc* 2:239 (probably following Edgar Hennecke's *Neutestamentliche Apokryphen*, 369), translates this "so that Demas said." See Smyth, *Greek Grammar*, 508. Smyth states in §2260a that "ὥστε with the infinitive means *as to, so as to;* but with a subject necessary in English it must often be translated by *so that*." This is said in the framework of a discussion on "Result Clauses." It is important to notice that although the Greek texts preserve ὡς, it is the Coptic text that possibly preserves the earlier Greek (within the Coptic document) form as ϩⲱ[ⲥⲧⲉ]. It appears that there is a space within the manuscript that suggests that the word could not have only been ϩⲱ[ⲥ, but must have been the suggested ϩⲱⲥⲧⲉ. ὥστε is also supported by *G*, a 12th century codex.

[3] ἠσπάσω – aorist middle, second singular verb. The implication being that Paul has not given the same type of treatment to Demas and Hermogenes at any point in the past, as he is showing to Onesiphorus at this point. This is the turning point, where the role of Demas' and Hermogenes' jealousy overflows into a series of actions that lead to the eventual trials and persecutions of both Paul and Thecla in Iconium.

[4] Compare Phil 1:11 (identical phrase); Heb 12:11; Jas 3:18; LXX Prov 3:9; 11:30; 13:2; Amos 6:2; Hos 10:12. Hills gives this a "D" rating ("The Acts of the Apostles in the *Acts of Paul*," 29) in connection to Phil 1:11.

[5] τινές – Referring back to the fruit of righteousness. Awkward phrasing, but attested also in Cop[1].

3.4.2 General Comment

Upon arrival in Iconium, Paul and Onesiphorus see one another, smile and greetings soon follow. This warm greeting and blessing that includes an exchange of blessings called upon by God, is followed by a response by Hermogenes and Demas. The simple, seemingly insignificant exchange between Paul and Onesiphorus is precisely the impetus for the chain of events that follow. If this is a folklore tale, these evil "twins" of Paul, who are posing as his comrades, are now pushed to frustration and the jealously overflows with an exchange with Onesiphorus, where the latter calls them out as charlatans and lacking true "fruit of righteousness." The twins, while being present at the events in the remainder of the *APTh*, lose all of their characteristics except for their driving voice of jealousy and hypocrisy. Their behavior becomes pivotal for the attempted demise of Paul and Thecla. It is their voice that suggests to the jealous Thamyris in 3.12 that Paul is responsible for Thecla's leaving him. Then they reappear with Thamyris and suggest "Bring him (Paul) before the Governor Castellius because he persuades the multitudes to embrace the new teaching of the Christians, and he will destroy him and you shall have Thecla as your wife..." Finally, the twins also suggest to Thamyris the appropriate accusation against Paul to the governor that will result in the death penalty.

3.5

Καὶ εἰσελθόντος Παύλου εἰς τὸν τοῦ Ὀνησιφόρου οἶκον[1] ἐγένετο χαρὰ μεγάλη, καὶ κλίσις γονάτων[2] καὶ κλάσις ἄρτου[3] καὶ λόγος θεοῦ περὶ ἐγκρατείας[4] καὶ ἀναστάσεως,[5] λέγοντος τοῦ Παύλου Μακάριοι[6] οἱ καθαροὶ τῇ καρδίᾳ, ὅτι αὐτοὶ τὸν θεὸν ὄψονται.[7] μακάριοι οἱ ἁγνὴν τὴν σάρκα τηρήσαντες, ὅτι αὐτοὶ ναὸς θεοῦ γενήσονται.[8] μακάριοι οἱ ἐγκρατεῖς, ὅτι αὐτοῖς λαλήσει ὁ θεός. μακάριοι οἱ ἀποταξάμενοι τῷ κόσμῳ τούτῳ, ὅτι αὐτοὶ εὐαρεστήσουσιν τῷ θεῷ. μακάριοι οἱ ἔχοντες γυναῖκας ὡς μὴ ἔχοντες, ὅτι αὐτοὶ κληρονομήσουσιν τὸν θεόν.[9] μακάριοι οἱ φόβον ἔχοντες θεοῦ, ὅτι αὐτοὶ ἄγγελοι θεοῦ γενήσονται.

Translation

And Paul having entered into the house of Onesiphorus, there was great joy, and bending of knees, breaking of bread, and the word of God concerning self-control and resurrection with Paul saying,
"Blessed are the pure in heart, for they shall see God.
Blessed are those who have kept the flesh chaste, for they will be a temple of God.
Blessed are the self-controlled, for God will speak to them.

Blessed are they who are set apart from this world, for they will be well pleasing to God.

Blessed are they who though having a wife, are as those not having a wife, for they will inherit God.

Blessed are they who have a fear of God, for they will be angels of God."

3.5.1 Textual Notes

[1] εἰς τὸν τοῦ Ὀνησιφόρου οἶκον – See *3.2.1 Textual Notes*, note 1. On οἶκος in the *AP*, see *4.16.1 Textual Notes*, note 2. For more information on οἶκος as a center for early Christianity, see Carolyn Osiek and David L. Balch, *Familes in the New Testament World: Households and House Churches* (Philadelphia: Westminster John Knox Press, 1997) 193–214; Balch and Osiek, eds., *Early Christian Families in Context: An Interdisciplinary Dialogue* (Grand Rapids: Eerdmans, 2003). See also Robert Jewett's discussion and overview of the four potential locations of meeting, *Romans* (ed. Eldon Jay Epp; Hermeneia; Philadelphia: Fortress, 2007), 64–69; Hans-Josef Klauck, *Hausgemeinde und Hauskirche im frühen Christentum* (SBS 103; Stuttgart: Katholisches Bibelwerk, 1981), 15–20.

[2] κλίσις γονάτων – Generally, this term can simply be referring to sitting and resting, *bending the knees* in order to sit down, but this reference is more theological in nature (see *AP* 9.14 also). 3.24 clarifies the meaning suggesting a posture for prayer filled with joy. While *AP* 9.14 suggests submission, in opposition to prayer and rejoicing (the two features associated with bending the knees in 3.5).

[3] This is most likely an agape feast of the Christians. See Matt 14:19; 15:36; 26:26; Mark 8:6, 19; 14:22; Luke 22:19; 24:30; Acts 2:46; 20:7, 11; 27:35; 1 Cor 10:16; 11.24. Also, see Didache 9.1–10.7; Niederwimmer, *The Didache*, 139–143. See also Peter Lampe, "The Eucharist: Identifying with Christ on the Cross," *Int* 48.1 (1994): 36–49; and Dennis E. Smith, *From Symposium to Eucharist: The Banquet in the Early Christian World* (Minneapolis: Fortress, 2003), 176–85. See also the discussion in Jewett, *Romans*, 64–69; and Matthias Klinghardt, who sees no distinction between the love feast and the eucharist in the first two centuries, see *Gemeinschaftsmahl und Mahlgemeinschaft: Soziologie und Liturgie frühchristlicher Mahlfeiern* (Texte und Arbeiten zum neutestamentlichen Zeitalter 13; Tübingen and Basel: A. Francke Verlag, 1996) 8, 518–21. In *AP* 9.5, the Coptic text refers explicitly to Paul leaving ⲧⲁⲅⲁⲡⲏ with Lemma after his conversion in Damascus (See the *editio princeps*, Rudolphe Kasser and Philippe Luisier, "Le Bodmer XLI en Édition Princeps l'Épisode d'Èphèse des *Acta Pauli* en Copte et en Traduction," *Le Muséon* 117 (2004): 281–384).

⁴ See other remarks in *APTh* concerning this issue in the beatitudes of the *AP* 3.5–6 and also 3.12, where the testimony of Demas and Hermogenes appears to forbid marriage. The Lukan Paul addresses the subject of *self-control* in a positive light in Acts 24:25. Also found as a virtue in Gal 5:23; 2 Pet 1:6; 1 Cor 7:9; 9:25; Titus 1:8. See also Henry Chadwick, "Enkrateia," *Reallexicon für Antike und Christentum* (vol. 5; Stuttgart: Hiersemann, 1962), 343–65; H. Strathmann, "Askese II (christlich)," *Reallexicon für Antike und Christentum* (vol. 1; Stuttgart: Hiersemann, 1950), 758–63; J. Gribomont, "Askese IV," *TRE* (vol. 4; Berlin and New York: Walter de Gruyter, 1970), 204–225; see also chapter four in Dunn, "The *Acts of Paul*," 69–88.

⁵ λόγος θεοῦ περὶ ἐγκρατείας καὶ ἀναστάσεως – This appears to be the core of the teaching of Paul that leads to Paul's dilemma in *AP* 12. See also 4.1 and 14 (*MP*). For further discussion concerning the Pastoral Epistles, encratism and marriage, see *3.6.1 Textual Notes* and *3.6.2 General Comment*.

⁶ Μακάριοι – See Joseph Fitzmyer, *Dead Sea Scrolls and Christian Origins* (Grand Rapids: Eerdmans, 2000), 117–18, for connections between macarisms from 4Q525, Luke 7, Matthew 5, 2 Enoch 13.64–70, and Qoh 10:16–17, etc. *AP* is most likely dependent primarily upon a Matthean formula/oral tradition or even possibly the Matthean text here (see Chart 1). This macarism is in the literary form of ascription (see T. Y. Mullins, "Ascription as a Literary Form," *NTS* 19 (1972–73): 194–95.). See also Hauck, F. "Μακάριος," *TDNT*, 4:362–64; G. Bertram, "Μακάριος," *TDNT*, 4:364–67; H. Cazelles, *TDOT*, 1:445–48. See also *ATh* 94 for a similar list of beatitudes. The *ATh* seems to capitalize on the beatitudes of Matthew that the *AP* ignores, especially those pertaining to οἱ πραεῖς, τῆς βασιλείας τῆς ἐπουρανίου, and οἱ πεινῶντες in Matthew 5:3, 5, 6, and 10.

⁷ This is verbatim to Matthew 5:4.

⁸ See 2 Clem 8:6; 1 Cor 3:16 (2x), 17; 6:16–19; 2 Cor 6:16.

⁹ See 1 Cor 7:29 and Rom 8:17. Origen quotes this passage from the *AP* in *On the Passover* 36.6. See note III,5 by Willy Rordorf in "Actes de Paul," in the *ÉAC*, 1130. See also François Bovon, "A New Citation of the *Acts of Paul* in Origen," in *Studies in Early Christianity* (ed. Jörg Frey; WUNT 161; Tübingen: J. C. B. Mohr [Paul Siebeck], 2003); originally published as, "Une nouvelle citation des *Actes de Paul* chez Origène." *Apocrypha* 5 (1994): 113–17. Bovon proves that Origen is dependent upon *AP* and not 1 Cor 7:29, while the *AP* are dependent upon Paul. Note the textual variant in *AAA*, 238, and the referencing of the 13ᵗʰ century codex K, *Parisinus graecus* 769, which omits any reference to the γυναῖκας when stating μακάριοι οἱ μὴ ἔχοντες ὡς οἱ ἔχοντες.

3.5.2 General Comment

Within this text, we see Paul finally reaching the point of destination in Iconium, which becomes the central point of focus within chapter three of the *AP*, where this is the place of Christian focus, recalling the memory of the earlieast Christians from the first and early second century. The house of Onesiphorus, a place recalled warmly by Paul (2 Tim 1:16; 4:19), is the location chosen for the celebration of joy by believers, prayer, and the breaking of break (whether an *agape* or eucharistic meal is uncertain as no distinction is made, possibly reinforcing the thesis of Klinghardt, see note 4 above), recalling the celebration and centrality of the Christian message, although the *APTh* centers this Christian message on two features: resurrection and self-control. It is evident that the *APTh* upholds a form of "love-patriarchalism," unlike Jewett's evaluation of the community in Rome's egalitarian communalism, as the text centers on the house of Onesiphorus here and later the house of Queen Tryphaena as a form of "love-matriarchalism;" see Jewett, *Romans*, 64–65; Gerd Theissen, *The Social Setting of Pauline Christianity: Essays on Corinth* (trans. J. H. Schütz; Philadelphia: Fortress, 1982).

As Paul begins to teach this message, locating Paul physically and socially within the house can be somewhat difficult. The image of Thecla (3.7) sitting near an opening (window) in the house (καθεσθεῖσα ἐπὶ τῆς σύνεγγυς θυρίδος τοῦ οἴκου) is challenging to imagine in a Greco-Roman dwelling. The question is what window would have been open to the *atrium* or the *peristyle* in the back of a house. Paul must have been stationed in an adjoining workshop owned by Onesiphorus that would have been outward facing to the street (See *4.17.2 General Comment*) or perhaps an upper storey room as Thecla looks on from an adjoining house or from a location with a different elevation. One of these two options must be the case, because if this were strictly the *domus* of Onesiphorus then locating external windows to the house would have been difficult, since they are not a customary feature of the *domus*, with exception being given to small vertical slits made to the exterior to allow light (and air) into the dwelling. One must remember that a window to the outside would be a safety concern, and also would allow the elements to enter the home in an uncontrolled way. More comment will be made on this issue in 3.7 *Textual Notes* and *General Comment*; see also *2.11.1 Textual Notes*, note 1.

If Paul were indeed inside the *domus*, then Paul begins teaching the people who are coming and going into the house of Onesiphorus, probably beginning his lesson located in the medium-sized *atrium* with people filling the area around the *impluvium*, and sitting within the small *cubicula* located around the *atrium*, and also sitting and standing in the *fauces* and the *tablinum*, with the people coming and going in and out of the house

through the *fauces*. Otherwise, if a workshop, the coming and going would
have been much simpler.

At this point, Paul begins to teach by means of the literary form of *ascription* (see *3.5.1 Textual Notes*, note 7). Interestingly, beatitudes 1, 2, 3,
4, 5, 8, 9, 10, and 13 are directly connected to the teaching on *self-control*,
but any teaching explicitly related to the resurrection is absent in 3.5–6
(See Schneemelcher's assessment, *NTApoc* 2:234), although the implicit
discussion is intricately connected to resurrection. Further comments on
the marcarisms will be made in *3.6 General Comment*.

3.6

Μακάριοι[1] οἱ τρέμοντες τὰ λόγια κυρίου,[2] ὅτι αὐτοὶ παρακληθήσονται.[3]
μακάριοι οἱ σοφίαν[4] λαβόντες Ἰησοῦ Χριστοῦ, ὅτι αὐτοὶ υἱοὶ ὑψίστου
κληθήσονται.[5] μακάριοι οἱ τὸ βάπτισμα τηρήσαντες, ὅτι αὐτοὶ ἀναπαύσονται
πρὸς τὸν πατέρα καὶ τὸν υἱόν.[6] μακάριοι οἱ σύνεσιν Ἰησοῦ Χριστοῦ χωρήσαντες,
ὅτι αὐτοὶ ἐν φωτὶ γενήσονται. μακάριοι οἱ δι᾽ ἀγάπην θεοῦ ἐξελθόντες τοῦ
σχήματος τοῦ κοσμικοῦ, ὅτι αὐτοὶ ἀγγέλους κρινοῦσιν[7] καὶ ἐνδεξιᾷ τοῦ πατρὸς
εὐλογηθήσονται[8] καὶ οὐκ ὄψονται ἡμέραν κρίσεως πικράν. μακάρια τὰ σώματα
τῶν παρθένων, ὅτι αὐτὰ εὐαρεστήσουσιν τῷ θεῷ[9] καὶ οὐκ ἀπολέσουσιν τὸν
μισθὸν[10] τῆς ἁγνείας αὐτῶν.[11] ὅτι ὁ λόγος τοῦ πατρὸς ἔργον αὐτοῖς γενήσεται
σωτηρίας εἰς ἡμέραν τοῦ υἱοῦ αὐτοῦ, καὶ ἀνάπαυσιν[12] ἕξουσιν εἰς αἰῶνα[13]
αἰῶνος.[14]

Translation

Blessed are those who tremble over the words of the Lord, for they shall be
comforted.

Blessed are those who receive the wisdom of Jesus Christ, for they shall be
called sons of the most high.

Blessed are those who have kept their baptism, for they shall be refreshed
by the Father and the Son.

Blessed are those who have taken hold of the knowledge of Jesus Christ,
for they shall be in the light.

Blessed are they who have come out of the image of this world through the
love of God, for they will judge angels, and they will be blessed on the
right hand of God and will not see a bitter day of judgment.

Blessed are the bodies of the virgins, for they shall be well pleasing to God
and they will not lose the rewards of their purity, because the word of the
father shall be to them a work of salvation in the day of his son, and they
shall have rest forever.

3.6.1 Textual Notes

[1] Cop[1] begins here after a break of 16 lines.

[2] *AAA* reads as τὰ λόγια τοῦ θεοῦ (the words of God). Cop[1] has ⲛ̄ⲛ̄ϣⲉⲭⲉ ⲙ̄ ⲡⲭⲗⲉⲓⲥ (words of the Lord) instead of τὰ λόγια τοῦ θεοῦ (the words of God). This reading is also attested by the 10th century codex *B, Parisinus graecus* and the Latin codex *Casinensi* 142 (*c*). Compare *Did.* 3.8 (Niederwimmer, *Didache*, 101).

[3] See Matthew 5:4.

[4] σοφίαν – This is reminiscent of some of the Gnostic literature. See *Soph. Jes. Chr.* NHC III, 108.10–14 and III, 117.8–118.2. In *Soph. Jes. Chr.*, a connection is drawn to sex as a means for enslavement to the subordinate powers, and that the "pure knowledge" of the father, shared through Jesus Christ breaks the bond of the subordinate powers (See Douglas M. Parrott, *The Nag Hammadi Library* [ed. James M. Robinson; rev. ed.; New York: Harper Collins, 1978, 1990], 220–221); the two articles, "D. Gnosticism," and under "E. The New Testament," see "2. The Logia," by Ulrich Wilckens under the heading, "σοφία, σοφός, σοφίζω," *TDNT*, 7.509–517.

[5] See Matthew 5:9; On αὐτοὶ υἱοὶ ὑψίστου see *AP* 3.6; *AP* 4.4 (!); Mark 5:7; Luke 1:32; 6:35 (!); 8:28.

[6] See *2 Clem* 6.4, 7–9. There is a possibility of a literary connection between the *APTh* here and *2 Clem* 6, where the author of *2 Clem* commends the readers to τηρήσωμεν τὸ βάπτισμα ἁγνὸν καὶ ἀμίαντον. If one does this then ποιοῦντες γὰρ τὸ θέλημα τοῦ Χριστοῦ εὑρήσομεν ἀνάπαυσιν. According to *2 Clem* 6.4, one keeps their baptism pure by avoiding "adultery, depravity, avarice, and deceit." (Bart D. Ehrman, trans., *The Apostolic Fathers: Volume 1* (LCL 24; Cambridge: Harvard, 2003), 172–3.

[7] See 1 Cor 6:3 and 2 Pet 2:4.

[8] The *AAA* includes Matthew 5:7, (via the support of a number of textual witnesses) μακάριοι οἱ ἐλεήμονες, ὅτι αὐτοὶ ἐλεηθήσονται although this is missing from Cop[1]. Cop[1] (and the Greek Codices *G* and *I*) continues without breaking the text as stated above in the Greek text, ...τοῦ πατρὸς εὐλογηθήσονται καὶ οὐκ ὄψονται... This reading is further supported by the substance of the two connected statements, the indications being that the completion of the thoughts on judgment make more sense roled into one macarism, rather than spanning the two. The reason for the addition of Matthew 5:7 with the statement added to it can be explained in two ways; first, it makes sense by suggesting that those who are receiving mercy at judgment will consequently experience a satisfying rather than a bitter judgment. But this does not provide a motive for adding Matthew 5:7. The motivation for a scribe could be that he is possibly making an attempt to complete the Matthean list of beatitudes. Notice that Matt 5:4, 5, 7, 8, 9,

and 10 are represented. This leaves only 5:3 and 5:5 off the list. Matthew
5:4–9 would be represented in this text, if it were not for the lack of 5:6.
The question remains, why would the original author leave 5:6 off of the
list? In my judgement Matthew 5:6 uses language that suggests something
other than *self-control* and encratic behavior, therefore leaving it inappropriate for the list. This leaves only 5:3 and 5:9–10 remaining. Is it possible
that the author of the *APTh* resists the eschatological view of Matthew and
the βασιλεία τῶν οὐρανῶν mentioned only in 5:3, 9, and 10? For a comparison of Matt 5:3–12 and *AP* 3:5–6, see Chart 1 above. For an expansion of
this chart, see Peter Dunn's addition of the comparison to 1 Cor 6:2-3;
6:18-19; and 7.29-34 at http://actapauli.files.wordpress.com/2009/04/com-
parison-of-acts-of-paul-iii-with-1-cor-and-matt.pdf.

[9] ὅτι αὐτὰ εὐαρεστήσουσιν τῷ θεῷ – See macarism 4 (*AP* 3.5).

[10] See Matthew 10:42.

[11] τῆς ἁγνείας αὐτῶν – See macarism 2 (*AP* 3.5).

[12] Compare the last line of *AP* 3.4.

[13] On καὶ ἀνάπαυσιν ἕξουσιν εἰς αἰῶνα αἰῶνος, see Matthew 11:29.

[14] For a fuller discussion of encratism, especially regarding *APTh*, see
Schneemelcher, *NTApoc* 2:2335–35; Dunn, "The *Acts of Paul*," 70–88; for
the discussion over whether or not the *APTh* is encratite, see Erik Peterson,
"Einige Bemerkungen zum Hamburger Papyrusfragment der *Acta Pauli*."
VC 3 (1949): 142–62; P. Devos, "Actes de Thomas et Actes de Paul."
AnBoll 69 (1951): 119–30; H. J. W. Drijvers, "Der getaufte Löwe und die
Theologie der Acta Pauli," *Carl-Schmidt-Kolloquium an der Martin-
Luther-Universität 1988* (ed. Peter Nagel; Kongress und Tagungsberichte
der Martin-Luther-Universität, Halle-Wittenberg; Halle: Abt. Wissen-
schaftspublizistik der Martin-Luther-Universität, 1990), 181–89; A. Ham-
man, "'Sitz im Leben' des actes apocryphes du Nouveau Testament,"
StPatr (TUGAL 93; Berlin: Academie-Verlag., 1962), 8:61–69; Jean-
Daniel Kaestli, "Les principales orientations de la recherche sur les Actes
apocryphes des Apôtres," *Les Actes apocryphes des Apôtres,* 49–61; Yves
Tissot, "Encratisme et Actes Apocryphes." *Les Actes apocryphes des Apôtres,* 109–19. Those who have assumed encratism are P. Vielhauer,
*Geschichte der urchristlichen Literatur. Einleitung in das Neue Testament,
die Apokryphen und die Apostolischen Väter* (Berlin: De Gruyter, 1975),
703; Ernst Dassmann, *Der Stachel im Fleisch: Paulus in der frühchristlichen Literatur bis Irenäus* (Münster: Aschendorff, 1979); Walter Rebell,
Neutestamentliche Apokryphen und Apostolische Väter (München: Chr.
Kaiser Verlag, 1992), 192; Andreas Lindemann, *Paulus im ältesten Christentum. Das Bild des Apostels und die Rezeption der paulinischen Theologie in der frühchristlichen Literatur bis Marcion* (BHT 58; Tübingen: J. C.
B. Mohr [Paul Siebeck], 1979), 6 and Philip Sellew, "Paul, Acts Of," *ABD*
(New York and London: Doubleday, 1992), 5:202.

3.6.2 General Comment:

As one reads through the list of macarisms the connections to Matthew 5 are strong. Yet, this is not Jesus speaking, but rather is a profound introduction of the Gospel according to Paul. I think it important to note arguments made by MacDonald, which suggest linking the genre of the *AP* with a Gospel passion (see "Apocryphal and Canonical Narratives about Paul," *Paul and the Legacies of Paul* [ed. William S. Babcock; Dallas: Southern Methodist UP, 1990], 62). As Paul first begins his teachings on encratism and resurrection, he provides twelve macarisms (it is possible that there might only be eleven [the same number as Matthew], if one takes into consideration that the first six are lost from Cop[1], and there is not unanimous agreement from the Greek and Latin manuscripts that all of these six are present) that are almost wholly devoted to a life of sexual purity and self control. This seems to be most important in the presentation by Paul, especially after considering the final macarism that states plainly, "Blessed are the bodies of the virgins, for they shall be well pleasing to God and they will not lose the wages of their purity, because the word of the father shall be to them a work of salvation in the day of his son." The most likely conclusion from this is that those who keep themselves sexually pure (i.e. *self control*) will receive the "wages of their purity" which is salvation with God (i.e. implying resurrection from the dead consistent with the remainder of the *APTh*, in particular *AP* 4.14). Dunn argues that the PE and the *AP* do not conflict with regard to sexual purity, and likewise suggests that the hermeutical key cannot be taken from the statement that Paul was preaching *self-control* and *resurrection*. Dunn cites Onesiphorus and Lectra as the prime example in the *APTh*, while mentioning other examples from the *AP* (See Dunn, "The *Acts of Paul*," 78–79). I have a hard time accepting the silence of the *APTh* in regard to the future relations of these two, especially when the conversion of Thecla centers on her rejection of marriage with Thamyris as constituting her grounds for acceptability to receive the seal of baptism in *APTh* 3.25. In fact, it is on the grounds of sexual compromise that Paul withholds baptism from her, suggesting that she might not be in a position to receive the seal, hence not properly prepared for an eventual resurrection and/or salvation with God.

3.7

Καὶ ταῦτα τοῦ Παύλου λέγοντος ἐν μέσῳ τῆς ἐκκλησίας ἐν τῷ Ὀνησιφόρου οἴκῳ,[1] Θέκλα τις παρθένος Θεοκλείας μητρὸς μεμνηστευμένη ἀνδρὶ Θαμύριδι, καθεσθεῖσα ἐπὶ τῆς σύνεγγυς θυρίδος τοῦ οἴκου[2] ἤκουεν νυκτὸς καὶ ἡμέρας[3] τὸν περὶ ἁγνείας λόγον λεγόμενον ὑπὸ τοῦ Παύλου·[4] καὶ οὐκ ἀπένευεν ἀπὸ τῆς θυρίδος, ἀλλὰ τῇ πίστει ἐπήγετο ὑπερευφραινομένη. ἔτι δὲ καὶ βλέπουσα πολλὰς γυναῖκας⁵ καὶ παρθένους εἰσπορευομένας⁶ πρὸς τὸν Παῦλον, ἐπεπόθει⁷ καὶ αὐτὴ καταξιωθῆναι κατὰ πρόσῶπον στῆναι Παύλου καὶ ἀκούειν τὸν τοῦ Χριστοῦ λόγον· οὐδέπω γὰρ τὸν χαρακτῆρα⁸ Παύλου ἑωράκει, ἀλλὰ τοῦ λόγου ἤκουεν μόνον.

Translation

And as Paul was saying these things in the midst of the assembly in the house of Onesiphorus, a certain virgin Thecla (whose mother was Theocleia) who had been betrothed to a man, Thamyris, was sitting at a nearby window of the house listening night and day to the things concerning purity which were being said by Paul. And she was not turning away from the window, but was being lead on in faith with an overabundant joy. But yet seeing many women and virgins going in to Paul, she herself desired to be made worthy to stand in the presence of Paul and to hear the word of Christ, for she had not yet seen the characteristics of Paul, but was only hearing his speech.

3.7.1 Textual Notes

¹ See *3.2.1 Textual Notes*, note 1 and *3.5.2 General Comment*.

² Vorster ("Construction of Culture through the Construction of Person," 110), in evaluating the "spatial restriction of women" in this text suggests that Thecla was "sitting and staring from the window of her mother's home." Thecla is possibly looking down from above or across from Paul teaching on the second floor; see *3.5.2 General Comment*.

³ See 1 Thess. 2:9. Also, see Peterson, "Einige Bemerkungen," 142; and Peterson cites Ernst von Dobschütz, *Die Thessalonicher-Briefe* (Meyer's Kommentar; Göttinger: Vandenhoek and Ruprecht, 1909), 97.

⁴ See *AP* 9, the Ephesian Episode; and *ATh* 92–95. See also Schmidt, *ПП*, 27–30. See discussion of Peterson, "Einige Bemerkungen," 144–45. Peterson believes that the *AP* and the *ATh* are "entweder sind die Thomas- und Paulus-Akten aus demselben Milieu hervorgegangen und von ein- und demselben Verfasser geschrieben worden oder aber der Verfasser einer dieser Akten hat den andern kopiert" ("Einige Bemerkungen," 154–55). This is also the *Ausgangspunkt* for the response of Devos, "Actes de Thomas," 119, who demonstrates that the *AP* predates the *ATh*.

⁵ A couple of lines are missing from Cop¹.

⁶ A sexual play on words.

⁷ See note 6 above.

⁸ τὸν χαρακτῆρα – This suggests more than just Thecla not having seen Paul. Χαρακτήρ is used in reference to the impression or stamp on the face of a coin (s.v. "Χαρακτήρ," LSJ, 1977; Euripides, *Electra*, 559; Plato, *Poli-*

tics, 289b). It can also refer to features of the face, but the theology of the text suggests more (see s.v. "Χαρακτήρ," LSJ, 1977; Heroditus 1.116), especially in light of arguments made by Malherbe and Grant (See *3.3.1 Textual Notes*, Note 4 and Note 8).

3.7.2 General Comment

Here, we are told more about the circumstances of Paul' preaching of the Gospel in the house of Onesiphorus. It appears that as Paul is preaching, numerous women (possibly translated as *wives*) and virgins are scandalously "going in" (εἰσπορευομένας) to Paul to see him, yet Thecla, the story's heroine, will not go in. Here, Thecla anxiously desires (ἐπεπόθει) to see Paul, as the other women are doing, but as the text suggests, the problem is that she is already betrothed to be married to a man by the name of Thamyris.

This is best understood as the introduction of characters and the development of the plot of this ancient Christian novel (Christine M. Thomas, *The* Acts of Peter, *Gospel Literature, and the Ancient Novel: Rewriting the Past* [Oxford: Oxford UP, 2003]; Niklas Holzberg, *The Ancient Novel*, 1–27; Perkins, "This World or Another?," 247–60; Ewen Bowie, "The Ancient Readers of the Greek Novel,", 88). Regarding the *AAA* being novels proper, Holzberg states,

the anonymous authors of the various apocryphal *Acts*, which first appeared in the second century. . .increased considerably the thematic similarities to 'secular' novels. . . they undeniably created a new type of fictional prose narrative which can in an certain sense quite legitimately be labeled the 'early Christian novel'. However they cannot be included in the genre 'ancient novel', because they represent more properly the beginnings of its reception and influence." (*The Ancient Novel*, 23).

This is reinforced via Holzberg in "The Genre: Novels Proper and the Fringe," *The Novel*, 25. A more moderate stance is presented by Tomas Hägg (*The Novel in Antiquity*, 160), who says of the ancient Christian novel, "the designation 'novels of the apostles' would be more appropriate," but then goes on to dumb this down by adding "However, these similarities in narrative structure and motifs do not imply that the Acts of the Apostles should be regarded as 'novels' *tout court*. They have other important elements. . ." See also the discussions in Christine Thomas, *The Acts of Peter*, 1–7; Jan N. Bremmer offers an assessment of the inclusion of the Apocryphal Acts of the Apostles into the category of the Ancient Romance as current as 2001 in "The Apocryphal Acts: Authors, Place, Time and Readership," *The Apocryphal Acts of Thomas*, 149–50 (See introduction, "1. The Ancient Novel").

Within the framework of this novel, Thecla is in the process of falling for Paul as she sits night and day listening to his teaching, anticipating seeing him fully. The absence of Thecla seeing Paul further emphasizes the fact that Thecla's infatuation for Paul is connected to her conversion to Paul's encratic message, but couched in a romantic language to heighten the excitement of text. Thecla desires to go in to Paul to experience a more intimate (i.e. sexual) relationship to Paul. Compare Chariton *Callirhoe* 1.3–4, where Callirhoe confined to home as a newlywed, who has yet to bore her husband a child, is wrongly perceived by her husband on two accounts to be unfaithful to him. This is due to the fact that it appears that various lovers are coming in to her home at night. Here, in the *APTh*, Thecla desires to also go in to Paul.

3.8

'Ὡς δὲ οὐκ ἀφίστατο¹ ἀπὸ τῆς θυρίδος, πέμπει² ἡ μήτηρ αὐτῆς πρὸς τὸν Θάμυριν· ὁ δὲ ἔρχεται περιχαρής,³ ὡς ἤδη λαμβάνων αὐτὴν πρὸς γάμον. εἶπεν οὖν ὁ Θάμυρις πρὸς Θεοκλείαν Ποῦ μού ἐστιν ἡ Θέκλα, ἵνα ἴδω αὐτήν ;⁴ Καὶ εἶπεν ἡ Θεοκλεία Καινόν σοι ἔχω εἰπεῖν θεώρημα,⁵ Θάμυρι. καὶ γὰρ ἡμέρας τρεῖς καὶ νύκτας τρεῖς⁶ Θέκλα ἀπὸ τῆς θυρίδος οὐκ ἐγήγερται,⁷ οὔτε ἐπὶ τὸ φαγεῖν οὔτε ἐπὶ τὸ πιεῖν,⁸ ἀλλὰ ἀτενίζουσα⁹ ὡς πρὸς εὐφρασίαν, οὕτως πρόσκειται¹⁰ ἀνδρὶ ξένῳ ἀπατηλοὺς καὶ ποικίλους¹¹ λόγους διδάσκοντι,¹² ὥστε με θαυμάζειν πῶς ἡ τοιαύτη αἰδὼς¹³ τῆς παρθένου χαλεπῶς¹⁴ ἐνοχλεῖται.

Translation

But since she was not departing from the window, her mother sent for Thamyris; and he came gladly, as one already receiving her for marriage. Therefore Thamyris said to Theocleia, "Where is my Thecla that I might see her?" And Theocleia said, "I have a new spectacle to tell you about, Thamyris. For three days and three nights, Thecla has not risen from the window, neither to eat nor to drink, but she is gazing intently as though enraptured, thus she is closely attached to a foreign man who is teaching deceptive and divisive words, so that I marvel how the one of such virginal modesty is being burdened (so) painfully."

3.8.1 Textual Notes

¹ ἀφίστατο – imperfect middle indicative of ἀφίστημι meaning "to distance oneself from some person or thing," (BDAG, 157–58, definition 2). Specifically in regard to *withdraw* or *fall away* with a figurative sense referring to moral qualities, teachings, or conditions from which one needs to be withdrawn. See 1 Tim 4:1; Wis 3:10; Luke 8:13, et. al. (BDAG, 158).

² Historical Present (Smyth, *Greek Grammar*, 422, §1883).

[3] περιχαρής – *overjoyed,* (BDAG, 808). Ptolemy is overjoyed in the success of military exploits (Diodorus Siculus 20.76.6), etc. (see *ATh* 24.1). For similarities with the ancient romance, *overjoyed* is used in relation to the rejoining of lovers or spouses. See Chariton, *Callirhoe* 6.5; Achilles Tatius, *Leuc. Clit.* 7.14; Longus, *Daphn.* 3.28; Heliodorus *Aeth.* 10.11.1; and Josephus, *Ant.* 1.284.

[4] Cop[1] reads, ⲭⲉ ⲉⲉⲓⲛⲁⲛⲉⲩ ⲁⲣⲁⲥ. Gebhardt offers a possible reconstruction of the text, based on the textual witnesses of several Latin manuscripts that read *Vbi est mea Thecla, ut illam uideam?* (*Passio,* XC; See also Carl Schmidt, *Acta Pauli,* 31; Vouaux, *Actes de Paul,* 162, note 3).

[5] *AAA* reads διήγημα. Correction: P. Oxyrhynchus 6 states, KAINON ΣΟΙ ΕΧΩ ΕΙΠΕΙΝ *ΘΕΩΡΗΜΑ*. See Schmidt, *Acta Pauli,* 31.

[6] See Jonah 2:1; and Matt 12:40.

[7] ἐγήγερται replaces ἐγείρεται (Schmidt, *Acta Pauli,* 31; "Attic reduplication" [Smyth, *Greek Grammar,* 149, §446). This is most likely an allusion to the Christian story of Christ in the tomb for three days and three nights. Is this Thecla's "death" and resurrection (οὐκ ἐγήγερται)? The new information is told in the form of a *sight* (καινόν θεώρημα) that has been witnessed. It seems more clear in the Antioch scene.

[8] See 1 Kgdms 30:11–15. Thecla's response probably represents a fast and commitment to the beatitudes that Paul has been teaching. See *Joseph and Aseneth* 15.4–5.

[9] See *AP* 3.9, 10, 20, 21; see also Luke 4:20; 22:56; Acts 1:10; 3:4, 12; 6:15; 7:55; 10:4; 11:6; 13:9; 14:9; and 23:1. In the early Jewish romance, see *Joseph and Aseneth* 8.8 (BDAG, 415). This is quite possibly the "evil eye." See Heliodorus, *Aeth.* 3. This chapter is largely about the evil eye and lovesickness.

[10] See *Joseph and Aseneth* 15.6 and 16.7.

[11] P. Oxyrhynchus 6 adds καὶ κενούς. Cop[1] omits any further adjectives (See Schmidt, *Acta Pauli,* 32).

[12] See Tit 1:10 (Vouaux, *Actes de Paul,* 162).

[13] See 1 Tim 2:9. αἰδώς is absent in P. Oxyrhynchus 6. Cop[1] has preserved in the form of ⲧⲉⲉⲓⲡⲁⲣⲑⲉⲛⲟⲥ ⲛ̄ⲭⲡⲓⲟ ⲛ̄ⲧⲉⲉⲓ̈ⲅⲉ meaning *this virgin with shame (abuse) of this kind.* The textual critics have preserved it in the Greek text (see Schmidt, *Acta Pauli,* 32; bracketed by Schneemelcher, *NTApoc,* 2:240; Rordorf, *Actes de Paul,* 1131; Vouaux, *Acts de Paul,* 163).

[14] See 2 Tim 3:1–16, especially 3:1, 6–7, 11, and 16.

3.8.2 General Comment

The connections between the *AP* and the ancient romance are beginning to become clearer. This chapter is the most sexually explicit chapter up to this point, as the connection that Thecla is making to Paul becomes more and more pronounced. The chapter could possibly be a dialogue with the Pastorals (although I think it not convincing) as it begins with a possible theological gloss (1 Tim 4:1) that suggests that Thecla is *falling away* from the truth, and then the chapter ends with the realization that the burdensome/troublesome (χαλεπῶς/ χαλεποί) times have arrived (see note 14 above). Thecla has fallen prey to the warning of 2 Tim 3:6–7, "For among them are those who make their way into households and captivate silly women, overwhelmed by their sins and swayed by all kinds of desires (ἐπιθυμίαις – see *3.9.1 Textual Notes*, note 5), who are always being instructed and can never arrive at a knowledge of the truth." This is further reinforced by 2 Tim 3:10–11, that appeals for the reader of the Pastorals to look to the example, teaching, and persecution of Paul in "Antioch, Iconium, and Lystra." This then leads to Paul commending Timothy to avoid deceivers through the use of the τὰ ἱερα γράμματα which will (among other things) lead Timothy to the correct teaching (διδασκαλίαν; 2 Tim 3:15–16 and *AP* 3.1, 9 and 13). Thecla is described by her mother as falling into the trap that the Paul of the Pastoral Epistles has said to avoid. This is Thecla's falling away/conversion story, in particular a conversion to Paul. Thecla can not take her eyes away from Paul (ἀτενίζουσα). This expression is used four times in describing Thecla's unwavering commitment to Paul (see note 9 above). This is a favorite verb/participle of Luke-Acts, and also finds a comparison between lovers in the ancient Jewish novel, *Joseph and Aseneth*, as Aseneth, who is in love with Joseph, cannot pull her eyes from him. The delicate situation is intensified when Thamyris overjoyed (περιχαρής – see further connection to the ancient novel in note 3 above) comes to see his Thecla, only finding his loved one falling in love with another. Metaphorically speaking, Thecla has first heard of her savior, she then hears his sermon of the beatitudes, and longing to see him, she stays for three days and three nights and her resurrection is yet to come. The theological gloss of this passage is strong. It is highly unlikely that Paul taught continuously for three days and three nights, nor did Thecla sit for three days and three nights. It is symbolic of a complete amount of time, and also mirrors the conversion of disciples to Jesus, but in this case a conversion to Paul and his message. It is more than a conversion; it is love that is developing at an intimate level. The fact that the story that Theocleia refers to suggests Thecla has gone without eating and drinking furthers this connection, as the conversion of Aseneth to God is filled with denial of physical food and drink and the embrace of spiritual feasting with God (See 15.4–5). Theocleia's sexual description becomes most acute within the next sentence, where the imagery suggests Thecla being sexually united to Paul (see note 10 above). This imagery is a paradox. Sexual imagery is implied, but the union with God is the connotation that is also intended. Thecla is commited to God, albeit sexually with Paul, ironically embracing fasting, sexual abstinence, and self control. The image is advanced further with Theocleia completing the infinitive result clause in amazement that Thecla can be a virgin of shame/modesty, yet is so *closely attached* to Paul even to the point that she has been fooled by his deceptive words and is allowing Paul to attach himself to her in a painful, burdensome way. Theocleia is suggesting a theological, spiritual raping of Thecla, via the sexual metaphor.

The Jewish novel and the Christian novel, as noted above, fall in harmony with the intentions, motifs, and genre of the ancient novel. The irony of the *Christian* (and Jewish) novel is that the love relationship that is being promoted and advocated is rather salacious, and paradoxically advocates such a sensual relationship with God alone (albeit through Paul). Thecla's desire to be with Paul is not really a physical desire, but a spiritual desire as Paul is posing as the Jesus figure of this "Gospel" that concludes with a passion of its own in the martyrdom account in Rome (AP 14). This account is much more explicit and graphic though than the canonical Gospel accounts of Jesus.

3.9

Θάμυρι, ὁ ἄνθρωπος οὗτος τὴν Ἰκονιέων πόλιν ἀνασείει,[1] ἔτι δὲ καὶ τὴν σὴν Θέκλαν· πᾶσαι γὰρ αἱ γυναῖκες καὶ οἱ νέοι εἰσέρχονται πρὸς αὐτόν, διδασκόμενοι[2] παρ' αὐτοῦ ὅτι Δεῖ, φησίν, ἕνα καὶ μόνον θεὸν φοβεῖσθαι καὶ ζῆν ἁγνῶς.[3] ἔτι δὲ καὶ ἡ θυγάτηρ μου ὡς ἀράχνη ἐπὶ τῆς θυρίδος δεδεμένη[4] τοῖς ὑπ' αὐτοῦ λόγοις κρατεῖται ἐπιθυμίᾳ[5] καινῇ καὶ πάθει[6] δεινῷ. ἀτενίζει γὰρ τοῖς λεγομένοις ὑπ' αὐτοῦ[7] καὶ ἑάλωται[8] ἡ παρθένος. ἀλλὰ πρόσελθε αὐτῇ σὺ καὶ λάλησον· σοὶ γάρ ἐστιν ἡρμοσμένη.[9]

Translation

"Thamyris, this man will shake up the city of the Iconians, and yet even your Thecla; for all the women and the young men are going in to him, being taught by him that 'it is necessary,' says he, 'to fear the one and only God and to live purely.' But yet, even my daughter, being bound to his words as a spider in the window, is being held to a new desire and a fearful passion. For she is holding intently to the things being said by him and the virgin has fallen. Go and speak to her, for she is…was betrothed to you."

3.9.1 Textual Notes

[1] Similarly, Jesus is accused of political disturbance, when stirring up the people (Luke 23.5), and the high priest stirs up the crowd against Jesus in order to release Barabbas (Mark 15.11).

[2] See *3.1.1 Textual Notes*, note 7. See also *3.8.2 General Comment*.

[3] See *3.6.1 Textual Notes*, note 6 and 8; *3.6.2 General Comment*. This word is important to the theology of the *APTh* that is being advocated. See *AP* 3.5, 6, 7, 9, 12 (twice); 4.2, 6. See also 1 Tim 4:12, 5:2, 22, Titus 2:5 for comparison.

[4] See 2 Tim 2:9.

[5] ἐπιθυμία – found here and *AP* 13.6. See Joachim Jeremias, "ἐπιθυμία, ἐπιθυμέω," *TDNT* 3:168–72. Used here in a negative context, unlike 1 Tim 3:1. See especially 1 Tim 6:9; 2 Tim 2:22, 3:6, 4:3; Titus 2:12, and 3:3. See Gal 5:16, 24 where ἐπιθυμία and πάθει are combined. See also Col 3:5 and 1 Thess 4:5 for ἐπιθυμία and πάθει together. It should be added that in Herm. *Mand.* 12.1, ἐπιθυμία carries both positive and negative meanings (see Carolyn Osiek, *The Shepherd of Hermas* (ed. Helmut Koester; Hermeneia; Minneapolis: Fortress, 1999), 148–9.

[6] See note 5 above. See also BDAG, 748; Athenagoras 21.1.

[7] ἀτενίζει γὰρ τοῖς λεγομένοις ὑπ’ αὐτοῦ – "car elle fait attention à ses paroles et à sa doctrine." (Vouaux, *Actes de Paul*, 164).

[8] Schmidt translates this as "es ist gefallen (gefangen) die Jungfrau…" (*Acta Pauli*, 32) based on ϩⲁⲉⲓⲉ, which is the Achmîmic form of the verb ϩⲉ (meaning *to fall*) from Cop[1]. It should be noted that the state of Thecla's "falleness" as a virgin is also combined with a tension in the use of the second perfect verb form with the present indicative of εἰμί, that suggests that Thecla is no longer betrothed to Thamyris, but is now "was" betrothed to Thamyris (see also note 9 below).

[9] Cop[1] reads ⲛ̄ⲧⲁⲩϣ̄ⲡⲧⲟⲟⲧⲥ̄ ⲛ̄ⲅⲁⲣ ⲛⲉⲕ, *for, to you, they betrothed her.* This is the second perfect verb form, allowing for the emphasis to be placed upon *to you*.

3.9.2 General Comment

As the story develops, Theocleia is continuing to make Thamyris aware of the seriousness of the situation, and how Thecla *has fallen* for Paul (see notes 8 and 9 above). This coincides with a tension in referring to the state of Thecla's betrothal to Thamyris. It appears that Thecla's falling/loss of virginity (at least symbolically) coincides with Thamyris' loss of betrothal. Theocleia is compelling Thamyris to respond to this situation, for he is about to lose (has lost) his espoused wife. Interestingly enough, Thecla continues to fall into the category that the Pastorals warn people to avoid (see *3.9.1 Textual Notes* notes 3–5). As an example that might serve as a hermeneutical key to explaining the relationship between the two texts, 2 Timothy 2:22 states, "Shun youthful passions (ἐπιθυμίας) and pursue righteousness, faith, love, and peace, along with those who call on the Lord from a pure heart." In 2 Tim 2:17, the text says that Hymenaeus and Philetus have "swerved from the truth" in teaching that the resurrection has already taken place. Then, it goes on to say that some vessels have been kept pure, especially those that have done as stated in 2:22. The author of the *APTh* has a much different understanding of passions and fauthfulness to God than the Pastorals. First, in the *APTh*, Thecla is described as falling into new passions, but the Pastorals warned against this. Second, Hermogenes and Demas suggest that Paul is teaching that the resurrection has already taken place (3.12, 14). The evidence suggests that the *APTh* has a different understanding than the Pastorals concerning the teaching on *self control* and *resurrection*. Dunn and Kaestli deny this, but the text suggests otherwise, as has been noted (See *3.6.1 Textual Notes*, note 14 and *3.6.2 General Comment*). 1 Tim 4:3 (i.e. forbidding of marriage) and 2 Tim 2:17, respectively conflict with (1) the last macarism that specifically connects the ability of the virgin to remain pure as having an effect upon resurrection and then (2) *AP* 3.12 and 14 suggest that Paul teaches that the resurrection has already taken place. The question is: do both Theocleia and Demas and Hermogenes accurately represent what Paul is teaching and representing in the text and what Thecla will teach and represent in the text? The text leaves no indication that they are misrepresenting them, but rather seems to affirm that these beliefs are worth dying for. It is a much more difficult question to determine why the author of the *APTh* would want to (1) describe Thecla's behavior with the same wording that the Pastorals condemned, if the text is not contrary to the Pastorals. (2) Why would the author allow Theocleia and then Demas and Hermogenes to misrepresent Paul and Thecla without ever presenting clearly the truth of Paul and Thecla as in agreement with the Pastorals? (3) If the Pastorals are in agreement, then how does one explain their close association? The most likely explanation is that the author of the *APTh* is attempting to write a document that represents a text in harmony with the undisputed Pauline letters. In this case, *harmony* with the undisputed epistles simply means that both a present resurrection that takes place now is evident in the *APTh*, while an expectation of a continuation or future resurrection is also present (see *APTh* 3.12, 14 and 4.13 [i.e. day of Judgment]), while on the other hand, the Pastorals deny a present form of resurrection. Apparently, the author of the *APTh* is presenting his own understanding of Paul, and is attempted to present a text that (s)he (they?) perceived to be in harmony with the Pauline texts, especially in regard to encratism (1 Cor 7:26–28), a resurrection for the present and future, *contra* Pastorals, and the role of women in the church.

3.10

Καὶ προσελθὼν Θάμυρις, ἅμα μὲν φιλῶν αὐτήν, ἅμα δὲ καὶ φοβούμενος τὴν ἔκπληξιν[1] αὐτῆς, εἶπεν Θέκλα ἐμοὶ μνηστευθεῖσα, τί τοιαύτη κάθησαι;[2] καὶ ποῖόν σε πάθος κατέχει ἔκπληκτον;[3] ἐπιστράφηθι πρὸς τὸν σὸν Θάμυριν καὶ αἰσχύνθητι.[4] Ἔτι δὲ καὶ ἡ μήτηρ αὐτῆς τὰ αὐτὰ ἔλεγεν Τέκνον, τί τοιαύτη κάτω βλέπουσα κάθησαι, καὶ μηδὲν ἀποκρινομένη ἀλλὰ παραπλήξ;[5] Καὶ οἱ[6] μὲν ἔκλαιον δεινῶς ἐν τῷ οἴκῳ,[7] Θάμυρις μὲν γυναικὸς ἀστοχῶν,[8] Θεοκλεία δὲ τέκνου, αἱ δὲ παιδίσκαι[9] κυρίας· πολλὴ οὖν σύγχυσις ἦν ἐν τῷ οἴκῳ[10] πένθους. καὶ τούτων οὕτως γινομένων Θέκλα οὐκ ἀπεστράφη, ἀλλ᾽ ἦν ἀτενίζουσα τῷ λόγῳ Παύλου.[11]

Translation

And Thamyris, entering, now on the one hand loving her, but on the other hand fearing her mental disturbance, said, "My espoused Thecla, why are you sitting in such a way? And what sort of suffering takes hold of you terror-stricken? Turn to your Thamyris and be ashamed." Yet, even her mother said the same, "Child, Why are you sitting in such a way looking downward, and not answering but stricken?" And those in the house were weeping bitterly, Thamyris, for the loss of a wife; Theocleia, (for the loss) of a child, but the female slaves (for the loss) of a mistress. Therefore a great confusion of mourning was in the house. And these things having thus come to pass, Thecla did not turn, but was gazing intently to the word of Paul.

3.10.1 Textual Notes

[1] Etymologically connected to ἐκπλήσσω. Commonly used in reference to one's reaction to a teaching of Christ or an apostle (BAGD, 308); see Matt 13:54; 19:25; Mark 6:2; 10:26, etc. See also *Mart. Pol.* 7.3.

[2] τοιαύτη κάθησαι – See *AP* 3.7–8 with regard to her posturing and sitting to listen to Paul for such lengthy periods of time.

[3] See note 1 above.

[4] This appeal to "turn back and be ashamed," is probably best understood from a cultural-anthropological perspective. See Malina, "Honor and Shame: Pivotal Values of the First-Century Mediterranean World," *The New Testament World*, 27–57; see especially pages 46–49. Thecla is defending her newly understood honor, while at the same time, Thamyris is

trying to convince her to maintain her shame, through allowing him to maintain his honor.

⁵ See note 1 and 3.

⁶ This text serves the purpose of demonstrating a challenge to the shame of Thecla (see note 4). The collective group (Thamrys, Theocleia, and the female slaves) represent the group who stand to be dishonored in the exchange. Thamyris offers a challenge first (ascribed honor), Theocleia follows (blood honor), and finally the slaves (it is unclear if their honor comes from the honor of Thamyris or Theocleia). Vorster would argue: "To be a woman is to be a person only associated with a man" (106); and "[o]ne of the probable motivations for Theocleia's extremely aggressive attitude towards her own daughter (20.6) also lies in the loss of a prospective son-in-law. Societal marginalization and a diminishing of her status as a person stared her in the face" ("Construction of culture through the contruction of person,"*A Feminist Companion to the New Testament Apocrypha*, 108). Nonetheless the slaves are directly connected to the shame of Thecla. Thecla does not respond, indicating her dishonoring of the three groups. They respond indignantly. Their being dishonored by Thecla is only worsened later in 3.14, when Thecla is proven honorable by God. Thecla wins the challenge.

⁷ ἐν τῷ οἴκῳ – This has only been preserved through Cop¹, *E*, *s*, and *C*. See also Schmidt, *Acta Pauli*, 33, note on 12.4.

⁸ See 1 Tim 1:6; 6:21; 2 Tim 2:18. See also *AP* 10 (*3 Cor* 4.21) in connection with 2 Tim 2:18.

⁹ For further information on παιδίσκη see BDAG, 749. Compare *AP* 4.14–15. The implications are that Thecla is seemingly not alone in various settings of the text, 3.6–10 being the first experience where Thecla has a host of "maidservants" with her. Noticably different are the conversion of the maidservants in 4.14, and their assistance in supporting Thecla's ministry and commission in 4.15. For more on female slaves, see Richard Saller, "Women, Slaves, and the Economy of the Roman Household"; Carolyn Osiek, "Female Slaves, *Porneia*, and the Limits of Obedience," in *Early Christian Families in Context*, 185–204, 255–74; Jean-Daniel Kaestli, "Les Actes Apocryphes et la reconstitution," 76, and "Fiction littéraire et réalité sociale, 291–94; Justin, *2 Apol.* 2.

¹⁰ Thecla is located in the house of Thamyris, Theocleia, and the female slaves (see note 6 and 9), and the mourning takes place here.

¹¹ See *3.8.1 Textual Notes*, note 1; and *3.8.2 General Comment*. Thamyris says, ἐπιστράφηθι πρὸς τὸν σὸν Θάμυριν καὶ αἰσχύνθητι, but then Thecla οὐκ ἀπεστράφη. Thecla is clearly fixed on Paul. In particular, she is transfixed upon the "word," and does the exact opposite of what is requested of her, thus she is disobeying and dishonoring Thamyris. It is not completely certain, but I would assume that the "word" here is Chris-

tological. This is reinforced by her encounter with Christ in *AP* 3.20-21, where she and Christ exchange gazes. However, the synthesis of Christ/Paul can hardly be overlooked also. The two are intended to essentially be one and the same in the text. So, as she gazes intently to the "word," it is also clear that she is intently gazing at Paul (3.20).

3.10.2 General Comment

The die is cast. Thecla is transfixed upon Paul. The negotiations in the text are easily understood from the perspective of cultural anthropological insights of *honor* and *shame*. Thamyris is concerned over the behavior of Thecla and challenges her. She does not respond, thus dishonoring Thamyris. Apparently, Thecla has fallen for the word of Paul (i.e. Jesus), thus the dishonor of Thamyris is due partly to the fact that Paul has successfully penetrated Thecla (double entendre intended) with his embodied words (See Vorster, "Construction of culture through the contruction of person," *A Feminist Companion to the New Testament Apocrypha*, 106–09). This is obvious by the way that Paul has transfixed her (τί τοιαύτη κάθησαι) and bewitched Thecla (ποῖόν σε πάθος κατέχει ἔκπληκτον). From the perspective of Thamyris and Theocleia, Thecla has been given the evil eye, but from the perspective of Thecla, she is being called to God! Great mourning within the house ensues, as it is evident that a moral and social breach of their betrothal has occured.

3.11

Ὁ δὲ Θάμυρις ἀναπηδήσας ἐξῆλθεν εἰς τὸ ἄμφοδον,[1] καὶ παρετήρει τοὺς εἰσερχομένους πρὸς τὸν Παῦλον καὶ ἐξερχομένους. καὶ εἶδεν δύο ἄνδρας εἰς ἑαυτοὺς μαχομένους πικρῶς.[2] καὶ εἶπεν πρὸς αὐτούς "Ἄνδρες, τίνες ἐστὲ εἴπατέ μοι, καὶ τίς οὗτος ὁ ἔσω μεθ᾽ ὑμῶν, πλανῶν[3] πλάνος ἄνθρωπος[4] ψυχὰς νέων καὶ παρθένων[5] ἀπατῶν,[6] ἵνα γάμοι μὴ γίνωνται ἀλλὰ οὕτως μένωσιν[7]· ὑπισχνοῦμαι οὖν ὑμῖν δοῦναι πολλὰ χρήματα, ἐὰν εἴπητέ μοι περὶ αὐτοῦ· εἰμὶ γὰρ πρῶτος τῆς πόλεως.[8]

Translation

But Thamyris, having started up, went out into the street, and he was watching closely those who were entering in and going out from Paul. And he saw two men quarreling sharply amongst themselves, and he said to them, "Men, tell me, who are you, and who is this man of deception who is inside with you, deceiving the souls of young ones and defrauding virgins, in order that they might not become married but that they should remain as they are? Therefore I promise to give you much money, if you might tell me concerning him, for I am the first man of the city.

3.11.1 Textual Notes

[1] ἄμφοδον – a street. Possibly in reference to a "block of houses surrounded by streets," (LSJ, 95) which might suggest typical Roman housing, akin to Pompeii, where it is a block of interconnected houses. See also *AP* 3.26–4.1.

[2] πικρῶς – a favorite adverb of the author of the *AP*. See also *AP* 3.6, 26, 4.3, 6, 7, 8; 9.15.

[3] Paul is accused of false teaching here. In 3.17, Paul proclaims to the proconsul that the world is in error (πλανωμένῳ κόσμῳ). This is also mentioned in *AP* 9.13, where Paul makes his defense in the theater in Ephesus before the governor, and then again before Nero in *AP* 14.4. The *AP* presents a case where Paul is arguing for an alternative worldview that perceives the world to be ignorant and mislead ("Ανδρες οἱ ὄντες ἐν τῇ ἀγνωσίᾳ καὶ τῇ πλάνῃ ταύτῃ), while Thamyris understands him as one who is upsetting the social norms of society.

[4] πλάνος ἄνθρωπος – see Cop[1] (see note 5), and *C, E, G,* ℰ̅ *(d), s*, and Tischendorf. *AAA* and Vouaux leave this out following other manuscripts.

[5] παρθένων – *virgins*; playing a key role in the *APTh*. The word is found in 3.6, 7 (2x), 8, 9, 11, 12, 16, 22; *APTh* 3.44, 45 (5x).

[6] νέων – probably mistranslated by Schmidt (*Mensch*, see *Acta Pauli*, 34), Elliott (*young men, ANT*, 366), and Schneemelcher (*young men, NTApoc* 2:241). Vouaux and *ÉAC* are more accurate (*jeunes gens* in *ÉAC*, 169). Cop[1] translates the passage as ογεγ πε πεειρωμε [Ϻ]πλανος ετΝ ϩογΝ ΝϺΜΗΤΝ: εϥ̄ρλπ[λ]τλ ΝϺφγχΗ ΝΝⲱϩρεⲱⲏⲙ' ϻΝ ϻπλρθενος χεκλλςε ενογχι ϩεει (who is this man of deception who is inside with you? He is deceiving the souls of young ones and virgins so that they are rejecting a husband). It is equally likely that the *young children, young ones* are young girls, and not young men. There is nothing in νέων (genitive plural of νέος, α, ον) or the remaining context to indicate that these individuals are male (such is also the case with ⲱⲏⲣⲉⲱⲏⲙ see Crum, *Coptic Dictionary*, 584 for further definitions and examples; Exod 2:8; Mark 9:36, etc.). The term refers to a young individual 30 or younger (see Behm, "νέος, ἀνανεόω," *TDNT*, 4:897; Xenophon, *Mem.* 1.2.35). It is possible that in the context, it is synonymous with παρθένος, thus possibly indicating young women and virgins. This would be consistent to 3.7 which states πολλὰς γυναῖκας καὶ παρθένους εἰσπορευομένας πρὸς τὸν Παῦλον. See also 3.9, αἱ γυναῖκες καὶ οἱ νέοι, translated "women and young people" (*NTApoc* 2:240); see also 3.12 that clearly specifies "young ones" in a masculine tense (νέους

γυναικῶν καὶ παρθένους ἀνδρῶν). 3.12 suggests that 3.11 is dealing with both sexes that are suffering from the sexual and marital prohibition, thus the *young ones* and *virgins*.

[7] οὗτως μένωσιν – See 1 Cor 7:8, 11, 20, 40; 1 Tim 2:15; 2 Tim 3:14.

[8] The leading people in a city (BDAG, 894).See *AP* 4.1. See also Chariton, *Callirhoe* 2.4.4, 2.11.2; Mark 6:21; Luke 19:47; and Acts 17:4, 25:2, 28:17.

3.11.2 General Comment

After having grieved over Thecla, Thamyris goes outside only to find Demas and Hermogenes quarrelling with one another. Somehow Thamyris connects these two individuals to Paul, and asks the two about Paul. Most likely, Thamyris sees the crowd around the house of Onesiphorus and simply asks these two men standing outside to fill him in on the details of what is happening. Thamyris accuses Paul of being a false teacher. Contrast this accusation with Paul's accusation of some in the world who are leading people astray (See 1 Tim 4:1; 2 Tim 3:13 (2x); Tit 3:3). The specific problem, according to Thamyris, is Paul's teaching on marriage (see also *AP* 3.16). Demas and Hermogenes include Paul's claim to be a follower of Christ (3.16), and his view on the resurrection (3.14) to be potential problems to get Paul in trouble, but Thamyris does not seem to care about these theological concerns. It also appears that the governor is only concerned with the social order and law, and the theological matters are of no concern (*AP* 3.20–21). The question that is difficult to answer is whether or not Thamyris is talking about the *young men and virgins* or the *young girls and virgins* (See note 7 above). It is possible that the author of the text implies that Paul was teaching in such a way to encourage young girls and virgins to remain chaste (obviously this applies to the men also). This means that 3.7, 9, and 11 are referring solely to women. Then in 3.12, Demas and Hermogenes intensify the obvious problem in which Paul is not just teach chastity, but is denying "*young men* of wives and *virgins* of husbands" highlighting the aspect that Thamyris can use in a court of law. The limits of the text have been reached.

3.12

Καὶ ὁ Δημᾶς καὶ Ἑρμογένης[1] εἶπον αὐτῷ Οὗτος μὲν τίς ἐστιν, οὐκ οἴδαμεν·[2] στερεῖ δὲ νέους γυναικῶν καὶ παρθένους ἀνδρῶν,[3] λέγων "Ἄλλως ἀνάστασις ὑμῖν οὐκ ἔστιν, ἐὰν μὴ ἁγνοὶ μείνητε καὶ τὴν σάρκα[4] μὴ μολύνητε ἀλλὰ τηρήσητε ἁγνήν.[5]

Translation

And Demas and Hermogenes said to him, "On the one hand, this one, who is he? We do not know, but on the other hand, he takes away wives from young men and virgins from husbands, saying, "There is no other resurrection for you, if you do not remain pure and do not stain the flesh but keep it pure."

3.12.1 Textual Notes

[1] See *3.1.1 Textual Notes*, note 3 and *3.4.1 Textual Notes*, note 1.

[2] This is a justification of what the text stated in 3.1, ὑποκρίσεως γέμοντες, καὶ ἐξελιπάρουν τὸν Παῦλον ὡς ἀγαπῶντες αὐτόν.

[3] See *3.11.1 Textual Notes*, note 7 and *2.11.2 General Comment*.

[4] See Rev 14:4.

[5] See *AP* 3.5. This is the negative statement of beatitude 13, "μακάρια τὰ σώματα τῶν παρθένων, ὅτι αὐτὰ εὐαρεστήσουσιν τῷ θεῷ καὶ οὐκ ἀπολέσουσιν τὸν μισθὸν τῆς ἁγνείας αὐτῶν." See *3.6.1 Textual Notes*, notes 9–11. There is no good reason, based on the other texts mentioned above to conclude that Demas and Hermogenes are misrepresenting Pauline teaching in the *APTh*. If they are misrepresenting Paul, then the *APTh* are not encratite. See *NTApoc* 2:234; Dunn argues that Demas and Hermogenes misrepresent Paul of the *APTh* in, "The *Acts of Paul*," 78–79. Further support that rejects this text as encratic are Tissott, "Encratisme et Actes Apocryphes," 116; and Kaestli, "Fiction littéraire," 283–84 for an opposing view. See Irenaeus, *Haer.* 1.28.1; Epiphanius, *Pan.* 47.1 on encratism. Tissot takes Irenaeus and Epiphanius to task on their accuracy. Also, in regard to μολύνω/μολυσμός (BDAG 657), this verb (and noun form) are found only in the interpolation to 2 Cor 7:1 (μολυσμός) and then μολύνω in 1 Cor 8:7; Acts 5:38 (variant reading of Manuscript E [which Metzger considers of Montanist origin!]). See Metzger, *A Textual Commentary on the Greek New Testament* (2d ed.; Stuttgart: United Bible Societies, 1971), 292–93; Rev 3:4, and 14:4.

3.12.2 General Comment

Demas and Hermogenes (with voice in unison) address the question of Thamyris, beginning first with a lie, "This one, who is he? We do not know." This is the response that bypasses the first question, "who are you" while quickly addressing the second, "who is he" with a claim of ignorance. Reasons for this lie are unexplained, other than to separate themselves from Paul as they could easily see the mood of Thamyris, and possibly to gain access to the promised money. They follow this by quickly explaining the teaching of Paul that has allowed Thecla to withdraw herself from him, highlighting the theological motivation of abstinence, namely the promise of the resurrection hinges upon one's ability to remain sexually pure. This statement is consistent with Paul's earlier teaching on the "resurrection and encratism" in *AP* 3.5–6 and with 3.1 which explains that Paul was active in teaching Demas and Hermogenes about "all the words of the Lord and the teachings and the interpretation [of the Gospel] and of the birth and of the resurrection of the beloved one...." In regard to this Vouaux states:

La réponse de Démas et d'Hermogènes montre qu'en somme ils ne connaissent pas saint Paul; pourquoi donc se sont-ils unis à lui? C'est un point assez obscur; l'auteur les suppose peut-être attires par les miracles accomplis par les mains de l'apôtre. En tout cas, ils l'ont entendu exposer sa doctrine, et il n'y a pas de raison de soupçonner qu'ils experiment ici à ce sujet leur proper pensée plutôt que celle de Paul; leur indication concorde bien avec celle du début du c[hapitre] v, où Paul parle «sur la continence et la resurrection.» (*Actes de Paul,* 171, note 1*).

3.13

'Ο δὲ Θάμυρις εἶπεν αὐτοῖς Δεῦτε, ἄνδρες, εἰς τὸν οἶκόν μου καὶ ἀναπαύσασθε[1] μετ' ἐμοῦ. καὶ ἀπῆλθον εἰς πολύτιμον δεῖπνον[2] καὶ πολὺν οἶνον καὶ πλοῦτον μέγαν καὶ τράπεζαν[3] λαμπράν· καὶ ἐπότισεν[4] αὐτοὺς ὁ Θάμυρις, φιλῶν τὴν Θέκλαν καὶ θέλων τυχεῖν γυναικός.[5] καὶ εἶπεν ἐν τῷ δείπνῳ ὁ Θάμυρις "Ανδρες, εἴπατέ μοι, τίς ἐστιν ἡ διδασκαλία αὐτοῦ, ἵνα κἀγὼ γνῶ·[6] οὐ γὰρ μικρῶς ἀγωνιῶ περὶ τῆς Θέκλης,[7] ὅτι οὕτως φιλεῖ τὸν ξένον[8] καὶ ἀποστεροῦμαι γάμου.[9]

Translation

But Thamyris said to them, "Come, men, into my house and refresh yourselves with me. And they came to a highly priced meal with much wine, great wealth, and a splendid table. And Thamyris gave them to drink, while loving Thecla and wishing to have a wife. And Thamyris said in the meal, "Men, tell me, what is his teaching, in order that even I might know? For I am agonizing greatly concerning Thecla, because she loves the stranger thus and I am being robbed of marriage.

3.13.1 Textual Notes

[1] ἀναπαύω – See 3.4, 6 (2x), 13, *APTh* 45, and 9.23. This term connotes both a metaphysical eternal "rest" (1 Cor 16.18; Phlm 7, 20; BDAG, 69, note 1 and 3b) and a physical rest from travel.

[2] δεῖπνον – The first part of the meal proper. See Dennis E. Smith, *From Symposium to Eucharist,* 27–31.

[3] the *splendid* table is in reference to a fine meal. See Leonhard Goppelt, "τράπεζα," *TDNT*, 209–215. For δεῖπνον being used in conjunction with τράπεζα see Plutarch, *Alex.* 20.13.6, where Alexander, after routing Darius, finds his tent with a large banquet with much wealth fit for a king. See also Plutarch, *Quast. Conv.* 632F, 635B, 643A, 643D, etc.

[4] ποτίζω – "to give to drink" (LSJ, 1455); to give οἶνος (Aeneas Tacticus 27.14); to give *nectar* (νέκταρ) Plato, *Phaedr.* 247E. Jesus was offered to drink from the sponge, while on the cross (Mark 15:36; Matt. 27:48). In the Ephesian episode in *AP* 9.21, Paul offers Artemilla to drink (ἐπότισεν) from the word.

[5] This may be more sexually explicit than the Greek suggests. Manuscript *E* (*AAA*, 244) suggests only to "have her as a wife," but Cop[1] seems to be a more difficult text that reads ⲉϥⲟ]ⲩⲱ[ϣ]ⲉ ⲁⲅⲙⲉⲥ[ⲧ ⲛ̅ⲙ̅ⲙⲉⲥ, translated *he was wishing to be with her*. ⲁⲅⲙⲉⲥⲧ̅ (Achmîmic Dialect for ⲅⲙⲟⲟⲥ, Crum, *Coptic Dictionary,* 679) The text (Greek and Coptic) suggests that he would like to be with her, notably as his wife (see discussion by Schmidt, *Acta Pauli*, 35).

[6] γνῶ – present active subjunctive verb, first person singular of γιγνώσκω (Smyth, *Greek Grammar*, 197, §682).

[7] οὐ γὰρ μικρῶς ἀγωνιῶ – literarlly *for no little agony* [I am having] *concerning Thecla*.

[8] οὐ γὰρ μικρῶς ἀγωνιῶ περὶ τῆς Θέκλης, ὅτι οὕτως φιλεῖ τὸν ξένον. See *3.11.2 General Comment*; Chariton, *Callirhoe* 5.10.7, and the *General Comment* below.

[9] In Coptic the repetition of Thamyris' concern for not *being with her* to espouse her is a concern (ⲧⲛⲁⲣ̅ⲅⲁ[ⲉⲓⲉ ⲅⲙⲉⲥⲧ̅). This is also connected to the reason for the textual variants in the Greek and Latin, possibly a homoioteleuton.

3.13.2 General Comment

After Thamyris leads Demas and Hermogenes to his house, he provides for them an extravagant banquet and meal. At the point in the meal when conclusion to the δεῖπνον is at hand and the wine is being poured, the *convivium* ("drinking party," Smith, *From Symposium to Eucharist*, 27) has begun. Thamyris brings up the first philosophical question of the evening, "Tell me, what is his teaching?" (See Smith, *From Symposium to* Eucharist, 13–65; Plutarch, *Quaest. conv.* 613–14.). Thamyris' concern is quickly identified; he is attempting to understand what sort of teaching might lead Thecla to deny him in marriage. Also, one must consider that as Thamyris and his guests increase the amount of the aphrodisiac that they are drinking, Thamyris is probably sexually aroused, consistent with the tone of the *AP*, and quite simply might be wishing to have Thecla there with him at the time for sexual favors, and more generally, her accompaniment (Osiek, "Female Slaves," 264; Smith, *From Symposium to Eucharist*, 35–6). It is interesting to note that the question is so pointed as to understand why Thecla is breaking the social norms, while at the same time appearing to be less interested in the theological teaching of the *stranger* (see *3.11.2 General Comment*).

In regard to Thecla as ξένος (*stranger*), this designation is not unfamiliar to the genre of the ancient novel. For a very similar text in genre, motif, and same wording, see Chariton, *Callirhoe* 5.10.7, where Chaereas is mourning the potential loss of Callirhoe to a foreigner (ξένος) in marriage, and is feeling no little anxiety (οἶδα ὅτι μικρὸς ἀνταγωνιστής εἰμι Διονυσίου, ξένος ἄνθρωπος) as a match for Dionysus, the man he thinks has taken Callirhoe. ξένος is consistently used to identify Paul (see *AP* 3.8, 13, and 19). After leaving Iconium, Thecla is henceforth referred to as ξένος in 4.1 and 3. It could simply be the word/definition to identify the outsiders from a particular city (see Acts 17:18–21) or this could also have some theological gloss behind it, identifying Paul and Thecla as separate from their surroundings. Ξένος was firmly entrenched in the Greek language, often suggesting that the ξένος "implies the status of a suppliant who ought to be treated as a guest" (see "ξένος," BDAG, 684). Nonetheless the connection to the ancient novel should not be overlooked.

3.14

Εἶπον δὲ Δημᾶς καὶ Ἑρμογένης[1] Προσάγαγε[2] αὐτὸν τῷ ἡγεμόνι Καστελίῳ[3] ὡς ἀναπείθοντα τοὺς ὄχλους ἐπὶ καινῇ διδαχῇ Χριστιανῶν,[4] καὶ οὕτως ἀπολεῖ αὐτὸν καὶ σὺ ἕξεις τὴν γυναῖκά σου Θέκλαν. καὶ ἡμεῖς σε διδάξομεν, ἣν λέγει οὗτος ἀνάστασιν γενέσθαι, ὅτι ἤδη γέγονεν[5] ἐφ᾽ οἷς ἔχομεν τέκνοις [, καὶ ἀνέστημεν[6] θεὸν[7] ἐπεγνόντες[8] ἀληθῆ].[9]

Translation

And Demas and Hermogenes said, "Lead him before the governor Castellius as one who is persuading the crowds over to a new Christian teaching, and thus destroy him, and *you*[10] will have your wife Thecla. And *we*[11] will teach you, what this *one* says happens in (respect to) resurrection. For (since) already it has happened upon these children we have,[12] and we have been risen knowing the true God.

3.14.1 Textual Notes

[1] See *3.4.1 Textual Notes*, note 1, on Demas and Hermogenes as "twins."

[2] See Acts 16:20. Notice, they are accused of being Ἰουδαῖοι, not Χριστιανόι, who are yet "disturbing" the city of Philippi and "advocating customs that are not lawful" for Romans to accept.

[3] There is no archaelogical evidence or outside literary evidence for a governor Castellius. The textual manuscripts spell Castellius in various ways: Καστελίῳ (*A* and *C*), Καστηλίῳ (*B*), Κατελλίῳ (*G*), Καστελλίῳ (*F*), κεϲϲιλοϲ (Cop¹), etc. See *AAA*, 245; Vouaux, *Actes de Paul*, 172.

[4] This is presented by Demas and Hermogenes as a reason to bring an individual before a court of law, but the response of Thamyris and Castellius is neutral toward their religious belief. This is similar to responses in Acts 18:12–15; 25:24–25. The *APTh* does not seem to be impacted in the same way as what is mentioned in Pliny the Younger, *Ep. Tra.* 10.96; 1 Pet 4.16. Nor does the *APTh* seem to reflect the same attitude of Nero as presented in Tacitus, *Ann.* 15.44.2–8. Nor is the *APTh* consistent with the latter part of the *AP*, namely the *MP*, which presents an intensely divided relationship between Christianity and Rome. See *AP* 14.2; Rordorf, Willy, "Die neronische Christenverfolgung im Spiegel der apokryphen Paulusakten," *Lex Orandi – Lex Credendi*, 370. This probably suggests a different author in the *APTh* than the *MP*.

[5] Compare 2 Tim 2:18, Mark 12:18 (Matt 22:23/Luke 20:27), καὶ ἔρχονται Σαδδουκαῖοι πρὸς αὐτόν, οἵτινες λέγουσιν ἀνάστασιν μὴ εἶναι, καὶ ἐπηρώτων αὐτὸν λέγοντες for similar texts. In this sentence, ἥν is a relative pronoun, agreeing in gender (feminine) and number (singular), that refers back to καινῇ διδαχῇ and it's case (accusative) is determined by the function it has in its own clause: "This one says *what*" similar to "whom you have crucified."

[6] Changed to manuscript *G* (confirmed by Cop¹ [see note 7 and 8]) reading, ἀνέστημεν θεὸν ἐπεγνόντες from *AAA* reading of ἀνιστάμεθα. Ἀνέστημεν which is second aorist active indicative, third person plural of ἀνίστημι; see Schmidt, *Acta Pauli*, 35.

[7] θεὸν...ἀληθῆ – See Hills, "The Acts of the Apostles," 29. She gives the connection to Rom 3:4; 1 Thess 1:9; John 3:33, 17:3 a "D" rating.

[8] ἐπεγνωκότες (*AAA*) is changed to ἐπεγνόντες following manuscript *G* and Cop¹. ἐπεγνόντες is second aorist active participle, nominative masculine plural from ἐπιγιγνώσκω.

[9] The textual transmission is difficult; *ÉAC* translates the text *et que nous ressuscitons en reconnaissant le vrai Dieu* (1133). Cop¹ has ⲁⲅⲱ ⲁⲛⲧⲱ[ⲱⲛⲉ ⲉ(?)] ⲁⲛⲥⲟⲩⲱⲛ ⲡⲛⲟⲏⲧⲉ, translated *and we were resurrected having known God*. The vowels of ⲁⲛⲥⲟⲩⲱⲛ are somewhat interesting as this is a Bohairic spelling of ⲥⲟⲟⲩⲛ̄, meaning "to know." Vouaux sees

Gnostic tendencies in this statement (*Actes de Paul*, 173). This assessment is unlikely. There are no other specific details to suggest Gnostic origins. Pieter J. Lalleman ("VIII. The Resurrection in the Acts of Paul," in *The Apocryphal Acts of Paul and* Thecla, 134–35), states that "P. W. Dunn informs me that Rordorf's forthcoming edition in *CCSA* retains the phrase." See also Bauckham, R. J. "The *Acts of Paul* as a sequel to Acts," *The Book of Acts in Its Ancient Literary Setting* I (eds. B. W. Winter and A. D. Clarke; Grand Rapids and Carlisle: Eerdmans and Paternoster, 1993), 128.

[10] Emphasis added in order to express the Greek σὺ ἕξεις.

[11] Emphasis added in order to express the Greek ἡμεῖς...διδάξομεν.

[12] Schneemelcher (*NTApoc* 2:241) and Elliott (*ANT* 366–67) translate this as "is to come." While *ÉAC* avoids the dispute with "Et nous t'enseignerons que cette resurrection" (1133).

3.14.2 General Comment

Demas and Hermogenes, continuing to speak in a *twin* voice, further give counsel to Thamyris on how to treat the situation with Paul. They finally present a plan for Thamyris to prosecute Paul. They encourage Thamyris to identify Paul with the new teaching, Christianity. This is partly in answer to Thamyris question, (3.13, εἴπατέ μοι, τίς ἐστιν ἡ διδασκαλία αὐτοῦ) and partly a continued assault by Demas and Hermogenes against Paul. Interestingly, the attack is not adopted by Thamyris (3.15–16; see also *3.11.2 General Comment*), but is continued unsuccessfully by Demas and Hermogenes (3.17). This is ironic considering the language of the *MP*, which is very confrontational between Christians and the Empire. This demonstrates a lack of continuity in the *AP*, and deepens the possible seams between the texts, possibly indicating various authors with a compiler as the unifying thread. It is also worth noting that this progressive resistance to the Roman Empire (in the *MP*) is not reciprocal at all here in the *APTh*, especially in the lack of response by the governor in respect to the public pronouncement of one being a Χριστιανός (see note 4 above; and *3.16.1 Textual Notes*, note 8).

Demas and Hermogenes emphasize that this plan of action will result in Thamyris regaining Thecla. They intend to instruct further Thamyris on the resurrection that Paul claims has taken place, but Thamyris seems to be compelled by the first statement of regaining Thecla, for he does not wait for any more of ἡ διδασκαλία αὐτοῦ (3.15). Demas and Hermogenes then give us further insight into the theology of Paul on the resurrection in explaining that he teaches concerning a present resurrection. This resurrection extends to Christ in a bodily fashion (see *AP* 3.1), and deals with the resurrection of believers also. Demas and Hermogenes claim that Paul teaches that their children have experienced this (2 Tim 2:18) and that they experience it also. This resurrection, that begins now in a bodily fashion and continues toward an eschatological completion, appears to be in conflict with the understanding of the Pastorals which demonstrate a resistence to a present, embodied resurrection (*AP* 3.5–6; see *3.9.2 General Comment* and *3.14.1 Textual Notes*, note 9).

3.15

Ὁ δὲ Θάμυρις ἀκούσας παρ᾽ αὐτῶν ταῦτα, καὶ πλησθεὶς¹ ζήλου² καὶ θυμοῦ³ ὄρθρου⁴ ἀναστὰς⁵ εἰς τὸν οἶκον Ὀνησιφόρου⁶ ἀπῆλθεν μετὰ ὄχλου καὶ [μετὰ]⁷ ξύλων καὶ ἀρχόντων καὶ δημοσίων⁸,⁹ λέγων τῷ Παύλῳ Διέφθειρας¹⁰ τὴν Ἰκονιέων πόλιν καὶ τὴν ἡρμοσμένην μοι, ἵνα μὴ γαμηθῆναι με ·¹¹ ἄγωμεν ἐπὶ τὸ βῆμα¹² τοῦ ἡγεμόνος¹³ Καστέλιον.¹⁴ Καὶ πᾶς ὁ ὄχλος ἔλεγεν Ἀπάγαγε τὸν μάγον·¹⁵ διέφθειρεν γὰρ ἡμῶν πάσας τὰς γυναῖκας.¹⁶

Translation

But Thamyris, having heard these things from them, being full of envy and an angered heart, rising up in the morning, he departed to the house of Onesiphorus with a crowd with clubs and the rulers and public officials, saying to Paul, "You have destroyed the city of the Iconians and the one who has been joined to me, so that she does not marry me; Let us go to the Bema of governor Castellius." And the whole crowd was saying, "Take away the magician; for he has destroyed all of our wives.

3.15.1 Textual Notes

¹ See especially 9.16; 3.3, 12.2; 14.3. See also 3.22, 4.9, 10, *Recension G*; 9.23 (not in any English versions, see *ÉAC*, 1159); 9.25; 12.1; 13.4; and 14.1.

² See 3.1 and 3.4. See also *G*; 3.17 (describing God); 9.16 (Diophantes becomes envious of Paul); 12.3 (some must suffer *envy* before going to the father [see *NTApoc* 2:258, note 10 noting connections to Rom 8:15, 23; 9:4; Gal 4:5; and Eph 1:5). *AP* 14.1 describes the devil as τοῦ δὲ πονηροῦ διαβόλου ζηλοῦντος τὴν ἀγάπην τῶν ἀδελφῶν.

³ See Eph 4:31.

⁴ See 3.15; 4.5; 9.21 (2x); 14.5, 7. This is possibly a theologically motivated choice of wording drawing a parallel to the passion narrative (*ATh* 3, 13, 29, 92; *AJ* 18, 48. See especially Luke 24:1 (24:22 also has ὄρθριος) and Acts 5:21.; See also John 8:2 and *Gos. Pet.* 12. Possible connections can be drawn between this text and Hesiod *Op.* 577; Diodorus Siculus

14.104.1; *Papiri Fiorentini* 305.11; *4 Baruch* 5.5; Josephus *Ant.* 11.37 (BDAG, 722).

[5] Interesting choice of words, since, "rising up" or "resurrection" is part of the problem for Thamyris.

[6] On Onesiphorus, see *3.2 Textual Notes*, note 1, and *3.2 General Comment*.

[7] Uncertain if this was in the original text. See Schmidt, *Acta Pauli*, 36, note on 14.2.

[8] ἀρχόντων καὶ δημοσίων – Only here in *AP*. Also not attested in this way in any New Testament writings. For δημόσιος see Acts 5:18, 16:37, 18:28 (Codex *E* contrasts δημοσίᾳ with καὶ κατ᾽οἶκον probably following 20:20), and 20:20. δημόσιος – meaning *belong to the people or the state* (LSJ, 387); generic term used to imply a mass public outcry siding with Thamyris against Paul making an issue εἰς τὸν οἶκον Ὀνησιφόρου into a public concern. εἰς being a spatial usage of the preposition, indicating a movement of the public *into* the space of the οἶκος. It is uncertain in meaning whether or not this implies a literal entering into the house of Onesiphorus (see *AP* 3.18; compare Acts 9:17 that adds εἰσῆλθεν to clearly indicate an *entering into* the house of Ananias).

[9] μετὰ ὄχλου καὶ [μετὰ] ξύλων καὶ ἀρχόντων καὶ δημοσίων replaces μετὰ ἀρχόντων καὶ δημοσίων καὶ ὄχλου ἱκανοῦ μετὰ ξύλων according to *AAA*, but following Cop[1] which is ⲙⲛ̄ ⲟⲩ[ⲙ]ⲏϣⲉ: [ⲙⲛ̄ ϩ]ⲛ̄ⲟ̄ⲉⲣⲟⲟⲃ ⲙⲛ̄ ϩⲛ̄ⲁⲣⲭⲱⲛ ⲙⲛ̄ ϩⲛ̄ϩⲩ̄[ⲡⲏⲣⲉ]ⲧⲏⲥ (ὑπηρέται).

[10] Said twice in 3.15, in reference to (1) destroying the city of the Iconiums, (2) the one who has been joined to Thamyris, and (3) the wives of the crowd.

[11] θελήσῃ με is changed to γαμηθῆναι με based on manuscripts Cop[1] (ϩⲙⲉⲥⲧ̄, See Schmidt 36, 9*), *E*, ⓖ, *m*, (*d*) (See *AAA*, 245).

[12] ἄγωμεν ἐπὶ τὸ βῆμα for other examples of the prominent role of the court room, governors, etc. in the resolution of love disputes, see other examples of the ancient novel (e.g. Achilles Tatius, *Leuc. Clit.* 7.7–16; Chariton *Chaer.* 5.4–8. See also *3.16.2 Textual Notes*, note 2; and *4.2.1 Textual Notes*, note 6).

[13] ἐπὶ τὸ βῆμα τοῦ ἡγεμόνος Καστέλιον instead of ἐπὶ τὸν ἡγεμόνα Καστέλιον based on Cop[1] ([ⲉⲛⲓϥ ϣ]ⲁ ⲡⲃⲏⲙⲁ ⲙ̄ⲫⲛⲅⲉⲙⲱⲛ ⲕⲉⲥⲧⲓⲁ[ⲟⲥ], Schmidt, *Acta Pauli*, 36, 9*).

[14] See *3.14.1 Textual Notes*, note 3 for further discussion of Castellius. In the accusative, the name of Castellius appears as Καστέλιον (*A, C*, preferred by *AAA* text and Tischendorf), Καστήλιον (*B*), Καστέλλιον (*F, G*), and Κεστιλλίον (*E*).

[15] On μάγος, "(m)ore generally 'the possessor and user of supernatural knowledge and ability' " (see Delling, "μάγος," *TDNT* 4:356–8; and A. D. Nock, *Essays on Religion in the Ancient World* [ed. Zeph Steward; Cam-

bridge: Harvard, 1972], 1:308–30). See *AP* 3.20; 9.21; Acts 13:6, 8; *APt* 31 (2x), 32. See also Léon Vouaux, *Les Actes de Pierre: Introduction, textes, traduction et commentaire* (Paris: Librairie Letouzey et Ané, 1913); Gerard Luttikhuizen, "Simon Magus as a narrative Figure in the Acts of Peter," and Tamás Adamik's "The Image of Simon Magus in the Christian Tradition," in *The Apocryphal Acts of Peter,* 39–64; See also footnote 7 on page 147 of Misset-van de Weg, "Answers to the Plights."

[16] *καὶ συνεπείσθησαν οἱ ὄχλοι* has been excerpted from the text, not being found within Cop[1] (See Schmidt, *Acta Pauli,* 36, 10*).

3.15.2 General Comment

This section signals a turning point in the text, where the domestic matter of Thamyris and the disruption of his home becomes a public and civic affair (See Misset-van de Weg, "Answers to the Plight," 151, n(n). 20 and 21). This is signaled in the text (see *3.15.2 Textual Notes*, note 7), where the scene moves from within the house of Onesiphorus to the Bema of the governor Castellius. This is very similar to the shift that is evident in Acts 18:28 and 20:20. This is also true of *ὄρθρου* (see *3.15.1 Textual Notes*, notes 3 and 4) which is also a key word signaling a change in the situation. Night has ended, and the dawning of the day is beginning. This proves to be a significant word in Luke 24:1, bringing on the dawn of a new era, possibly picked up by Christian writers, beginning with Acts 5:21. This is supported by the choice of wording of the author of this text (*δὲ Θάμυρις...ὄρθρου ἀναστὰς*). This is also evident in the usage found in the *Gosp. Pet.* 12, where this new era is indicated also. More broadly the *AP* and other acts (namely the *Acts of Thomas*) use this word not only to indicate a significant beginning, but to signal significant changes in the apostolic ministries, consistent with the earlier usage as found in Luke-Acts. In the *AP*, it always falls at very important transition points, such as the first case brought against Paul in a public sphere (3.15); the second persecution of Thecla in Antioch by Alexander (4.5); Paul's raising of Artemilla (9.21 (2x)); and Paul's martyrdom and resurrection from the dead (14.5, 7). Due to the connection of this word with the time of gathering for prayer by Christians at dawn, this may be an illusion to the coinciding of the resurrection of Christ, the tradition that continued to meeting at dawn, and consequently the significance placed upon the events of dawn as presented by the author of the *AP* (See the article on "*ὄρθρος, ὁ*," Lampe, *Patristic Greek Lexicon*, 973).

The criticism of Thamyris and the crowd with him is not directed toward Paul's religious faith or ideology. They are attacking Paul on the grounds of his exceptional ability to upset the social order of Iconium, especially regarding marriage. Demas and Hermogenes only partially succeed in their attack on Paul (see *3.14.2 General Comment*). In addition, Paul is called a μάγος, which, ironically is the title given to the opponents of the apostle Paul in Acts 13:6 and 8 (Bar-Jesus/Elymas). I also find it interesting that in many early Christian artistic representations of Jesus and Moses (Jesus feeding the five thousand and Moses striking the rock) from the catacombs of Rome that both are represented with the magician's wand. This is not necessarily a derogatory term, but rather helps elucidate early perceptions of Christianty and the miracululous elements of early Christianty. While Paul is in Ephesus, ὁ ὄχλ]ος ἐβόα· ἆραι τὸν μάγον, ἆραι τὸν φ[αρμακόν] (*AP* 9.21; the crowd also calls Paul a μάγος again in 3.20). This is also the title given to Simon *Magus*, opponent of Peter in the *Acts of Peter*. Thus as the transition is completed, Paul has now left the domestic sphere of Onesiphorus, entered the civic sphere before the Bema, is now a magician, and is disrupting the social order of Iconium, and a mass crowd has gathered to deal with the problem.

3.16

Καὶ στὰς[1] πρὸ τοῦ βήματος[2] ὁ Θάμυρις κραυγῇ μεγάλῃ εἶπεν ᾽Ανθύπατε,[3] ὁ ἄνθρωπος οὗτος οὐκ οἴδαμεν πόθεν ἐστίν,[4] ὃς οὐκ ἐᾷ γαμεῖσθαι τὰς παρθένους·[5] εἰπάτω ἐπὶ σοῦ τίνος ἕνεκεν[6] ταῦτα διδάσκει. Ὁ δὲ Δημᾶς καὶ Ἑρμογένης[7] εἶπον τῷ Θαμύριδι Λέγε αὐτὸν Χριστιανόν,[8] καὶ οὕτως ἀπολέσεις αὐτόν.[9] Ὁ δὲ ἡγεμὼν ἔστησεν τὴν διάνοιαν αὐτοῦ καὶ ἐκάλεσεν τὸν Παῦλον λέγων αὐτῷ Τίς εἶ, καὶ τί διδάσκεις;[10] οὐ γὰρ μικρῶς σου κατηγοροῦσιν.[11]

Translation

And having stood before the Bema, Thamyris said with a great shout, "Proconsul, this man, we do not know where he is from, who does not allow virgins to marry; Let him tell you for what (reason) he is teaching these things." But Demas and Hermogenes said to Thamyris, "Say that he is a Christian, and thus you will destroy him." And the Governor stood firm in his thought and called out to Paul saying to him, "Who are you and what are you teaching? For, they are accusing you of no small matter."

3.16.1 Textual Notes

[1] This is the second aorist active participle, nominative masculine singular of ἵστημι, translated *having stood*.

[2] Also, *judicial bench* (BDAG, 175) where legal cases would have been heard. See the usage in 3.15, 20 (2x), and 4.2 also. Similar to Jesus in the Gospels (Matt 27:19; John 19:13) and Paul in Acts (Acts 18:12, 16; 25:6,

10, and 17). See also *3.15.1 Texual Notes,* note 12; and *3.15.2 General Comment.*

³ See also *AP* 3.17 (2x), and 4.7.

⁴ Thamyris is repeating the information given to him from Demas and Hermogenes in 3.12 (See *3.12.2 General Comment*). Hills, "The Acts of the Apostles," 33, gives ὁ ἄνθρωπος οὗτος οὐκ οἴδαμεν πόθεν ἐστίν a "B" rating, regarding a connection with John 9:29; 7:27, 28; 8:14.

⁵ See *AP* 3.16, 20, 26. See also *3.14.2 General Comment* and *3.15.2 General Comment.* On παρθένους see also *3.11.1 Textual Notes,* note 6. παρθένος shows up specifically at 3.6, 7 (2x), 8, 9, 11, 12, 16, 22, 44, 45 (5x). Misset-van de Weg, "Answers to the Plight," 162, for a discussion of the social effects of a second-century woman becoming an ascetic Christian "in a society in which the institution of marriage (and procreation) was of fundamental importance."

⁶ ἕνεκα, ἕνεκεν is postpositive *on account of what, for what* (Smyth, *Greek Grammar,* 369).

⁷ See *3.1.1 Textual Notes,* note 3 and *3.4.1 Textual Notes,* note 1.

⁸ Χριστιανός is found in the *AP* here, 3.14, 14.2, 3 (2x) (Χριστιανοὺς is spelled as Χρηστιανοὺς in 𝔓¹; Acts 11:26; 26:28; 1 Peter 4:16) (BDAG, 1090). See also Lucian *Alex.* 25, 38; *Peregr.* 11, 12, 13, 16; Tacitus, *Ann.* 15.44; Suetonius, *Nero* 16; Pliny the Younger, *Ep.* 10.96.1, 2, 3; Ignatius, *Eph.* 11.2; *Magn.* 4; *Rom.* 3.2; *Pol.* 7.3; *Mart. Pol.* 3; 10.1; 12.1, 2; *Did.* 12.4; *Pre. Pet.* 2; etc. (see Walter Grundmann, "Χριστιανός" and "Χριστιανισμός," *TDNT,* 9:576–80). See also comments under *3.14.1 Textual Notes,* note 4.

⁹ See 3.14, "...οὕτως ἀπολεῖ αὐτὸν καὶ σὺ ἕξεις τὴν γυναῖκά σου Θέκλαν...". ⲅⲛ ⲟⲩ6ⲉⲡⲏ has been added to ⲁⲅⲱ ϥⲛⲁⲙ[ⲟ]ⲅ ⲅⲛ ⲟⲩ6ⲉⲡⲏ in Cop¹ (See Schmidt, *Acta Pauli,* 36, footnote 14.17, 10*).

¹⁰ On the διδαχή (and other verb forms [such as διδάσκω] with the same root as διδαχή), see *AP* 10 (*3 Cor* 3 and 5.24); 3.1, 8, 9, 13, 14, 16 (2x), 17 (3x), 20; 4.16, *Recension G*; 12.1; 13.4 (2x); 14.1. See *3.5.1 Textual Note,* note 6, *3.9.2 General Comment,* *3.14.2 General Comment* concerning more on the *teaching* of Paul.

¹¹ Cf. Mark 15:4

3.16.2 General Comment

Thamyris begins by addressing the proconsul. It is unclear why Thamyris is shouting. On the one hand, he might be addressing the crowd there also. However, if Thamyris' address is intended primarily for the Proconsul, then his shouting simply illuminates and itensifies the anger and frustration of Thamyris. Thamyris identifies Paul as an unknown quantity/foreigner, not knowing anything about Paul (see note 4). Otherwise, Thamyris does not take the advice of Demas and Hermogenes, who suggest twice (3.14 and 16) that the mention of Paul as a Christian will bring about his destruction. In neither case does Thamyris do so, but presses forward in arguing that Paul is disrupting marriages and prohibiting marriage.

Demas and Hermogenes insert their opinion again to Thamyris, but the governor is not easily swayed in mind, and he waits to hear Paul's defense of himself. Paul is finally asked, "Where are you from?" yet Paul does not respond. He only answers the question of the nature of his teaching. It is also worth noting that the offense of teaching women not to marry is no small issue to the governor, who accepts this as a grave concern.

3.17

δὲ[1] ἦρεν[2] τὴν φωνὴν αὐτοῦ ὁ Παῦλος λέγων Εἰ ἐγὼ[3] σήμερον ἀνακρίνομαι τί διδάσκω, ἄκουσον, ἀνθύπατε. Θεὸς ζῶν,[4] θεὸς ἐκδικήσεων,[5] [θεὸς ζηλωτής],[6] θεὸς ἀπροσδεής,[7] χρῄζων [μεγάλως][8] τῆς τῶν ἀνθρώπων σωτηρίας ἔπεμψέν με, ὅπως ἀπὸ τῆς φθορᾶς[9] καὶ τῆς ἀκαθαρσίας ἀποσπάσω αὐτοὺς καὶ πάσης ἡδονῆς[10] καὶ θανάτου, ὅπως μηκέτι ἁμαρτάνωσιν· διὸ ἔπεμψεν ὁ θεὸς τὸν ἑαυτοῦ παῖδα, ὃν ἐγὼ εὐαγγελίζομαι καὶ διδάσκω ἐν ἐκείνῳ ἔχειν τὴν ἐλπίδα τοὺς ἀνθρώπους,[11] ὃς μόνος συνεπάθησεν[12] πλανωμένῳ κόσμῳ, ἵνα μηκέτι ὑπὸ κρίσιν ὦσιν οἱ ἄνθρωποι, ἀλλὰ πίστιν ἔχωσιν καὶ φόβον[13] θεοῦ καὶ γνῶσιν σεμνότητος[14] καὶ ἀγάπην ἀληθείας. εἰ οὖν ἐγὼ τὰ ὑπὸ θεοῦ μοι ἀποκεκαλυμμένα διδάσκω, τί ἀδικῶ, ἀνθύπατε;[15] Ὁ δὲ ἡγεμὼν ἀκούσας ἐκέλευσεν δεθῆναι τὸν Παῦλον καὶ εἰς φυλακὴν βληθῆναι,[16] μέχρις ἂν εὐσχολήσας καλῶς[17] ἀκούσῃ αὐτοῦ.[18]

Translation

And Paul lifted up his voice saying, "If *I* am being judged today concerning what I teach, then listen, Proconsul. The living God, a God of vengeance, [a jealous God], a God who is needing no one, needing [greatly] the salvation of people, he sent me, in order that I should withdraw them from the corruption and uncleanness and from every pleasure and death, so that they might not sin any longer; Therefore God sent his own child, whom I proclaim as good news and I teach people to have hope in that one, who alone sympathized with a deceived world, in order that humans might not be under judgment any longer, but they might have faith, the fear of God, a knowledge of holiness and a love of truth. Therefore, if I teach things revealed to me by God, what injustice do I do, Proconsul? But the Governor having heard *these things* called to have Paul bound and to be placed into prison, until having a time of leisure, he might hear him thoroughly.

3.17.1 Textual Notes

[1] δὲ instead of καὶ (Schmidt, *Acta Pauli*, 37, footnote on line 20; παγλοc Δε...," 10*).

[2] From αἴρω, *to lift up, take up* (BDAG, 28). See *AP* 3.20; 4.7; 9.26 (Matt 24:39); 14.3. Primarily used in the sense of *to destroy, to perish* by the author of the *AP*.

[3] Emphasis added to the English translation by italization.

[4] Acts 14:15; *AP* 4.12; *Recension G* (2x); 9.17; 14.2, 4 (5x), 5 (2x), 6, 7. This is connected to the ongoing language and discussion of the resurrection. Hills, "The Acts of the Apostles," 29, gives this a "D" rating regarding the possible connection to the New Testament texts of Rom 9:26; Matt 16:16, 26:63; John 6:69. Note also the "traditional contrast (e.g., in 1 Thess 1:9; Acts 14:15; 1 John 5:20–21) between 'idols' and 'the true God'", as in *AP* 9.17. No reason is provided by Hills for this rating, but in support of the rating, it must be noted that there is not a single verbatim cross-reference between these texts, namely none of the NT passages refers to the Θεὸς ζῶν with the nominative noun for God with the nominative form of the participle as demonstrated above.

[5] See Ps 94:1 (93:1 LXX).

[6] See Exod 20:5; *AP* 3.15; *APTh* 45; 14.1. θεὸς ζηλωτής is probably added to the text. It is not found within Cop[1] (see Schmidt, *Acta Pauli*, 37, 10*).

[7] θεὸς ἀπροσδεής can be translated as *a God without want*. I followed a more literal translation of Cop[1] on this passage that states ΠΝΟΥΤΕ ΝϥΡ̄ΧΡΙΑ ΕΝ Ν̄ΛΑΑΥΕ. Schmidt translates *der Gott, der nichts bedarf* (*Acta Pauli*, 37). Rordorf has *le Dieu qui se suffit à lui-même* (*ÉAC*, 1134).

[8] μεγάλως might be a better addition than the text of *AAA*, following Cop[1], ΜΜΕΤΕ, which can be translated as *only, greatly*. Schmidt inserted μόνον here, translating it as *nur* (*Acta Pauli*, 37), although *greatly* seems to be more consistent with the contrast that Paul is setting up concerning the salvation of humanity.

[9] Used in *APTh* 44 and 45, regarding those who are attempting to *corrupt* or *molest* Thecla in her virginity. See also Rom 8:21; 1 Cor 15:42, 50; Gal 6:8; Col 2:22; 2 Pet 1:4; 2:12 (2x), 19. The Pauline usage indicates that the *corrupt* is contrasted with the *incorruptible*, paralleled by "flesh and blood" not entering the kingdom of God (being considered corrupt).

[10] Compare the cosmology of *AP* 10.4.11 (*3 Cor* 4.11).

[11] Compare 1 Tim 4:6–11 to this section. In particular, notice τῆς τῶν ἀνθρώπων σωτηρίας ἔπεμψέν με and ἐγὼ εὐαγγελίζομαι καὶ διδάσκω ἐν ἐκείνῳ ἔχειν τὴν ἐλπίδα τοὺς ἀνθρώπους.

[12] Cop[1] has ΕΝΤΑϥΡ̄ϹΥΜΠΑϹΧΕ (συμπάσχειν)

[13] See *AP* 3.5.

[14] See also *AP* 9.22, καὶ ἀπαχθεὶς [ε]ὐθέως ἐβλήθη εἰς τὸ στάδιον, ὡς πάντας ἄχθεσθαι ἐπὶ τῇ σεμνότητι Παύλου; Compare 1 Tim 2:2; 3:4; Tit 2:7 (only time in NT). Schmidt translates καὶ γνῶσιν σεμνότητος as "*und die Erkenntnis* (γνῶσιν) *der Heiligkeit*" based on Cop[1], which states ⲙⲛ̄ ⲧⲉⲅⲛⲱⲥⲓⲥ ⲛ̄ⲧⲙⲏⲛⲧⲥⲉⲙⲛⲟⲥ.

[15] τί ἀδικῶ, ἀνθύπατε; Contrast the example of Achilles Tatius, *Leuc. Clit.* 7.3–6, in which Clitophon plans his demise in court due to his love sickness for Leucippe.

[16] Cop[1] states ⲁⲧⲣⲟⲩⲙⲟⲩⲅⲣ ⲙ̄ⲡⲁⲩⲗⲟⲥ: ⲛ̄ⲥⲉⲛⲁⲝⲋ̄ ⲁⲡⲉϣⲧⲉⲕⲟ, translated *so that they bound Paul, and they seized him away to prison*. Codices *F* and *G* have the reading of βληθῆναι which is more consistent with the Coptic verb ⲝⲓ, rather than the preferred reading of *AAA*, ἀπαχθῆναι, following *C*.

[17] καλῶς (Cop[1] – ⲕⲁⲗⲱⲥ) replaces ἐπιμελέστερον (*AAA* following Greek manuscripts).

[18] See Acts 24:25; Hills, "The Acts of the Apostles," 43, gives the connection between this text and Acts as a "B" rating.

3.17.2 General Comment

As Paul comes before the Proconsul, in similar fashion to the Acts of the Apostles, Paul is able to make his appeal before the Proconsul. After the Proconsul hears the message of Paul, he sends Paul away to listen to him at a more convenient time, seemingly ending the hearing (e.g. Acts 24:25). At this juncture, Paul is able to explain in his own words, similar to being able to teach in 3.5–6, the content of his "teaching" (See *3.16.1 Textual Notes*, note 10). Paul begins by explaining the nature of his God as a *living God* (Acts 14:15). This term, theologically loaded within the context of the *AP* is intricately tied to the issue of the resurrection, which becomes most explicit in the martyrdom accounts of the *AP* (*AP* 14). The idea of the *living God* of resurrection, and salvation from death is seen clearly in the report of Thecla to the Governor of Antioch (4.12), in response to ""Who are you and what is it about you, that none of the beasts touched you?" that the God who saved her from death by the wild beasts is the *living God*, and Thecla is his *handmaid*.

This reference to the *living God* is followed by several other titles that have later significance, such as a God of vengeance (Ps 94:1 [93:1 LXX]), and a God who *wants nothing*, but needs only/greatly the salvation of humanity. Several key concepts that emerge here include: God can resurrect and sustain life, he avenges his people, he has no need of anything/anyone (ⲗⲁⲁⲩ), yet paradoxically needs the salvation of humanity. As the text unfolds, Thecla becomes the example of God's intervention as *living, vengeful*, and as an agent of human salvation *par excellence*, thus demonstrating these characteristics through her life. In Paul's speech, these are the reasons that he has been sent to them. Paul understands even his presentation to the Proconsul as divine intervention, thus one needs to understand that the following sequence of events with Thecla is interpreted as predetermined by God.

Paul's wish to *withdraw* humanity from the corruption/deterioration and uncleanness that is filled with pleasures and incidentally death, further strengthens the ties of resurrection being associated with the abstinence of sexual pleasure as hedonistic (key to the cosmology of *AP* 10.4.11 [*3 Cor* 4.11]), leading to death as product of sin. The message of Paul is consistently conflicted as Paul points people to himself, and then to Jesus. Paul mentions the sending of God's son (ἔπεμψεν ὁ θεὸς τὸν ἑαυτοῦ παῖδα), although leaving off any names or titles, while at the same time presenting the core Christian message that God sent his son, and Paul is the emissary who proclaims this Good News (εὐαγγελίζομαι) and continues to teach people.

There appears to be some overlap in thought between this section and 1 Tim 4:6–11, where the essential doctrinal elements are presented on how one produces faith leading to godliness in the household of God: (1) It must be taught (1 Tim 4:6), (2) it produces faith (1 Tim 4:6), (3) an interest in knowledge that produces godliness as contrasted with the corruptible present is mentioned (1 Tim 4:7–8). (4) a *living God* (1 Tim 4:10), (5) our hope is placed upon this savior/salvation (1 Tim 4:10), and (6) you must insist on and teach these things (1 Tim 4:11).

3.18

Ἡ δὲ Θέκλα νυκτὸς περιελομένη τὰ ψέλια ἔδωκεν τῷ Πυλωρῷ,[1] καὶ ἤνοιξεν[2] αὐτῇ τῆς θύρας ἀπῆλθεν[3] εἰς τὴν φυλακήν· καὶ δοῦσα τῷ δεσμοφύλακι[4] κάτοπτρον ἀργυροῦν[5] εἰσῆλθεν πρὸς τὸν Παῦλον,[6] καὶ καθίσασα παρὰ τοὺς πόδας αὐτοῦ[7] ἤκουσεν τὰ μεγαλεῖα τοῦ θεοῦ.[8] καὶ οὐδὲν ἐδεδοίκει[9] ὁ Παῦλος, ἀλλὰ τῇ τοῦ θεοῦ παρρησίᾳ[10] ἐνεπολιτεύετο· κἀκείνης ηὔξανεν ἡ πίστις, καταφιλούσης τὰ δεσμὰ αὐτοῦ.[11]

Translation

But Thecla, at night, having loosened her bracelets, gave them to the gatekeeper, who opened the gate for her, and she entered into the prison. And giving to the jailer a silver mirror, she entered to Paul, and she sat by his feet listening to the great things of God. And Paul feared nothing, but living as a free citizen with the confidence of God. And her faith grew, as she was kissing his bonds.

3.18.1 Textual Notes

[1] Found here and in 3.19 (2x) also.

[2] ἤνοιξεν (F, G [ἤνυξεν], Syriac, Cop[1] [ⲁϧⲟⲅⲏⲛ]) instead of ἀνοιγείσης.

[3] See the discussion pertaining to ἀπῆλθεν, in *3.15.1 Textual Notes*, footnote 8; and *3.19.1 Textual Notes*, note 5. Here simply connoting that she entered the prison; possibly adding clarity to 3.15.

[4] δεσμοφύλαξ – see Acts 16:23. See also Achilles Tatius, *Leuc. Clit.* 7.1. 4–5, for the role of the jailer (δεσμῶν ἄρχων) as the "gatekeeper" for lovers.

[5] Cf. *Acts of Xanthippe and Polyxena* 13, where Xanthippe bribes her "porter" with gold and underpants. For similarities between the two texts, see M. R. James, *Apocrypha Anecdota* (Texts and Studies 2.3; Cambridge: University Press, 1893), 48; see also Lucian, *Peregr.* 12.

[6] See Achilles Tatius, *Leuc. Clit.* 2.19, where Leucippe and Clitophon join one another in the night for love. Also notice that the "prison" metaphor, προσθῶμεν ἤδη τι καὶ ἐρωτικόν. Φέρε ἀνάγκην ἀλλήλοις ἐπιθῶμεν πίστεως, translated "Let us add to them something with real love in it. Let us fetter one another with an indissoluble bond." See also Heliodorus, *Aeth.* 8.9.20.

[7] On the sitting at someone's feet, see *4.8.1 Textual Notes*, note 6.

[8] On τὰ μεγαλεῖα τοῦ θεοῦ see *AP* 3.1, τὰ μεγαλεῖα τοῦ Χριστοῦ (see *3.1.1 Textual Notes*, note 11). In *APTh* 45, Artemis is called τῆς μεγάλης θεᾶς.

[9] ἐδεδοίκει – pluperfect, active indicative, 3rd person, singular from δείδω.

[10] Also translated as *boldness* or following Schmidt (*Acta Pauli*, 38), *freiheit*. See Phil 1:14, 20; Phlm 8 [Eduard Lohse, *Colossians and Philemon*. (ed. Helmut Koester; trans. William R. Poehlmann and Robert J. Karris; Hermeneia; Philadelphia: Fortress, 1971). 198.]. παρρησία carries overtones in this passage of the political and legal world (specifically for males; "παρρησία, παρρησιάζομαι," *TDNT* 5:871–86), but carries a double entendre with Paul's confidence in his faith as the alternate meaning. This is also true of Paul's speech in 3.17 (ἀδικῶ). Notice also the connection made between παρρησία and πολιτεύομαι, similar to Paul's imprisonment, and impending defense referred to in Phil 1.12–30 (especially 20 and 27); "πολιτεύομαι," *TDNT* 6:534–5. Also, it must be noted the rich NT heritage that contrasts the πολιτεία with the ξένοι (Eph 2.12; Acts 22.28; Herm. *Sim.* 50.1–6; *Diogn.* 5.5.

[11] The erotic motif is intentional. Cf. Achilles Tatius, *Leuc. Clit.* 2.9; Chariton *Chaer.* 1.14.9. Compare also Thecla (see also *AP* 3.21; 4.7–9) to the the image presented of Andromeda as described in Achilles Tatius, *Leuc. Clit.* 3.6–7. See especially Achilles Tatius, *Leuc. Clit.* 4.4–5.

3.18.2 General Comment

After Paul is taken out of Onesiphorus' house, he is immediately carried to the Bema for a public hearing. As the hearing is dismissed, Paul's "lover/admirer" finds her way to him by bribing her way into the prison, making it through two "gate-keepers," who accept her bracelets and silver mirror as payment. Playing on the popular motif as found within other ancient novels, the "courtroom scene" is followed by imprisonment, and then, in this case the reunification of "lovers" (Holzberg, *Ancient Novel*, 9–10, 45), lovers of one another metaphorically, being consistent with the motif, but lovers of Christ demonstrated through vows of chastity (23). Contrary to the character of some of the heros and heroines of other ancient novels, Paul sits confident and proud as a freeborn citizen innocent of charges, and ready to present his case again before a magistrate if necessary (cf. Phil 1:14, 20) but more importantly living boldy and confidently before God. The bond between Paul and Thecla can be illustrated by Thecla's willingness to join him in prison, yet Paul is not able to reciprocate (*AP* 3.21–23), but later counterbalanced, almost chiastically by Queen Tryphaena to Thecla (*AP* 4.4). The reason for the lack of reciprocation has been understood as Paul's abandonment of Thecla (Davies, *The Revolt*, 58–59). This interpretation seems to be too dismissive, too quickly. One might ask, "Where was Thecla during the climax of the trial before the Proconsul?" She comes to Paul afterwards, with little difference from when Paul fasts and prays for several days looking for Thecla. Paul's response is admittedly more passive, but the text continually stresses one's unwavering commitment to Christ. This is demonstrated in Thecla's attentiveness to Paul (3.7, 18) as a Christ figure, and Paul's attentiveness to God (Paul continues to preach the τὰ μεγαλεῖα τοῦ θεοῦ with παρρησίᾳ). The scene concludes with the erotic motif paradoxically continued as Thecla takes hold of Paul's bonds while kissing them (compare Heliodorus *Aeth.* 6.9.7; once again similar to the example of young lovers witnessed in the ancient romance).

3.19

Ὡς δὲ ἐζητεῖτο[1] Θέκλα ὑπὸ τῶν ἰδίων καὶ Θαμύριδος, ὡς ἀπολλυμένη[2] ἐδιώκετο κατὰ τὰς ὁδούς, καί τις τῶν συνδούλων τοῦ πυλωροῦ ἐμήνυσεν ὅτι νυκτὸς ἐξῆλθεν.[3] καὶ ἐξελθόντες ἀνήτασαν τὸν πυλωρόν, καὶ εἶπεν αὐτοῖς ὅτι εἶπεν· πορεύομαι πρὸς τὸν ξένον[4] εἰς τὸ δεσμοτήριον· καὶ ἀπῆλθον[5] καθὼς εἶπεν αὐτοῖς καὶ εὗρον αὐτὴν τρόπον τινὰ συνδεδεμένην τῇ στοργῇ.[6] καὶ ἐξελθόντες ἐκεῖθεν τοὺς ὄχλους ἐπεσπάσαντο καὶ τῷ ἡγεμόνι ἐνεφάνισαν.

Translation

But as Thecla was being sought out for by her own *people* and Thamyris, thus she was being pursued in the streets as one who was lost. And a certain one of the fellowslaves of the gatekeeper was making it known that she went out in the night. And going out they questioned the gatekeeper, and he told them that she said, "I am going to the stranger in the prison." And just as he had told them, they departed and found her in a certain place, having been united by means of love. And having gone out from there, they attracted the crowd and reported *these things* to the Governor.

3.19.1 Textual Notes

[1] *AP* 3.21, 26; 4.15; 10.4.8; 14.2. There appears to be a light theological gloss in the language of this section (Matt 2:13; 6:33; 7:7, etc.)

[2] This word can mean either *lost* or *perished*, and it is not clear whether the text is indicating that they thought that she was merely lost or dead, but nonetheless she was gone, and possibly (socially) lost or dead. See also *AP* 10.4.8, 15. See note 1 above ("ἀπόλλυμι or -ύω," LSJ, 207, which states, in *NT*, *perish*, in a theological sense; John 3:16; 1 Cor 1:18 for opposite [οἱ σῳζόμενοι]).

[3] τις τῶν συνδούλων τοῦ πυλωροῦ ἐμήνυσεν ὅτι νυκτὸς ἐξῆλθεν – The question is, where was Thecla before she went out? Either (1) she was at the house of Onesiphorus or her mother, (2) she followed the crowd to the public hearing, or (3) she had been taken home by Thamyris and her own. The text is ambiguous regarding this point, but the implications are that she is sneaking out from under the supervision of her own people and Thamyris to see Paul, as the text indicates in 3.18 (see note 5 under *3.18.1 Textual Notes*). However, the implications are that Thecla's actions are incredibly scandalous and justice must be served. See also Chariton, *Chaer.* 1.3–6.

[4] ξένον – The text consistently presents Paul in paradoxical language. He is clearly a known entity to the Christian reader of this text, and the text presents Paul as standing confidently in τὰ μεγαλεῖα τοῦ θεοῦ (See *3.1.1 Textual Notes*, note 11; *3.18.2 General Comment*; and *3.18.1 Textual Notes*, notes 6 and 8), but at the same time Paul is unknown, strange, and from nowhere (see 3.3; 3.11: Ἄνδρες, τίνες ἐστὲ εἴπατέ μοι, καὶ τίς οὗτος ὁ ἔσω μεθ᾽ ὑμῶν); 3.12 (*3.12.2 General Comment*); 3.16. For a contrast of πολιτεία with ξένον see *3.18.1 Textual Notes*, note 10.

[5] On ἀπῆλθον, Cf. *3.15.1 Textual Notes*, footnote 8; *3.18.1 Textual Notes*, note 3. This is a commonly used word by the author of the *AP*. See *AP* 3.13, 15, 18, 19; 4.15, 17, 18; *APTh* 44, 45; 9.16 (2x); 12.1; 14.1, 5, 6.

[6] συνδεδεμένην τῇ στοργῇ – This phrase, while not necessarily suggesting a sexual union (Cf. *Anth. Pal.* 5.165; 190; 7.476; "στοργή," LSJ, 1650), at-

tempts to demonstrate the interwoven union that Paul and Thecla share ("συνδέω," LSJ, 1700). I believe that the sexual overtones, consistent with the remainder of the *APTh* continue to create a document that is speaking of chastity in the language of the romance.

3.19.2 General Comment

This chapter attempts to draw Thecla into the center of the dispute as Thamyris and Thecla's people (τῶν ἰδίων καὶ Θαμύριδος) attempt to locate the problem, and provide solutions to that which has caused upheaval within the social fabric of Iconium. First, Thecla has relocated to the prison to be with Paul, and "kiss his bonds." Afterwards, with some space of time, Thecla is now *lost* and potentially socially dead, and those who represent the status quo and her family are attempting to locate her. It quickly becomes known through the gatekeeper that she has gone to be with the *stranger*. Here the text seems to illuminate the strangeness of Paul ("τὸν ξένον," Cf. *3.19.1 Textual Notes*, note 4), a man without home, no social, geographical, or political bearings within the entity of the Roman Empire, yet he is causing the undoing of the social fabric of this small city. This is consistent with the parallel account recorded in Chariton's novel, *Callirhoe*, when Chaereas (falsely) discovers that his lover Callirhoe has been involved in a scandalous affair in the night, he responds violently, kicking Callirhoe unconscious for several days, even to the point where she is buried alive, being thought dead (1.3–6). From this perspective, Thamyris is actually somewhat more civilized and gracious about the entire affair.

Once Thecla has been located, it becomes apparent that she is indeed lost and is intricately woven and united to Paul. Interestingly enough, the verb, συνδέω, is used in the sense of binding or wrapping materials together, such as binding a wound (Homer, *Il.* 13.599). It attempts to demonstrate the level of connection that exists between Paul and Thecla. I find it difficult to relegate a secondary status to Paul as one who has abandoned Thecla (Kaestli, "Fiction Littéraire," 291; Davies, *The Revolt*, 58–59), but at the same time realizing that the text will consistently shift toward a featured presentation and narrative of Thecla. I think it important to note that in 3.21, Paul is flogged and cast out of Iconium (καὶ τὸν μὲν Παῦλον μαστιγοῦν ἔξω τῆς πόλεως ἐξέβαλεν), not even given a choice as to whether he will stay with Thecla. Up to this point, Thecla and Paul are being presented as two who have been quickly drawn together with a seemingly inseparable bond. In all likelihood, the misunderstanding that Paul is abandoning Thecla is due to the ability of the author of the *AP* to fully develop the plot of this ancient Christian romance. This appears to be the portion of the text that is developing the plot and providing the basis and understanding of the relationship of Paul and Thecla as the "star crossed lovers" in similar manner as the very brief portion (in relation to the length of the text) of Chariton's *Chaeraeas and Callirhoe* 1.1 (Hägg, Tomas, *The Novel*, 5–6; Holzberg, *Ancient Novel*, 9, 26, 44–5). The reference to their being *united by means of love* (συνδεδεμένην τῇ στοργῇ; see *3.19.1 Textual Notes*, note 6) is not necessarily erotic (but not necessarily intending to preclude such an interpretation, either), but simply makes the point clear that Paul and Thecla are now clearly united in their devotion to one another. Through Thecla's domestic union with Paul, she has allowed herself also to be brought into the civic sphere, and thus essentially remain there for the duration of most of the narrative. Thecla has left the sphere of the private home in exchange for the civic center of Iconium and eventually Asia.

3.20

Καὶ ἐκέλευσεν ἄγεσθαι τὸν Παῦλον ἐπὶ τὸ βῆμα·[1] ἡ δὲ Θέκλα ἐκυλίετο[2] ἐπὶ τοῦ τόπου οὗ ἐδίδασκεν ὁ Παῦλος καθήμενος ἐν τῇ φυλακῇ.[3] ὁ δὲ ἡγεμὼν ἐκέλευσεν κἀκείνην[4] ἀχθῆναι ἐπὶ τὸ βῆμα·[1] ἡ δὲ μετὰ χαρᾶς ἀπίει ἀγαλλιωμένη[5] ἔμπροσθεν (ἐνώπιον) πάντων.[6] ὁ δὲ ὄχλος προσαχθέντος πάλιν τοῦ Παύλου περισσοτέρως ἐβόα Μάγος ἐστίν,[7] αἶρε αὐτόν. Ἡδέως γάρ, ὡς δὲ ἤκουεν αὐτοῦ ὁ ἀνθύπατος τοῦ Παύλου ἐπὶ τοῖς ὁσίοις αὐτοῦ ἔργοις τοῦ Χριστοῦ[8].[9] καὶ συμβούλιον ποιήσας ἐκάλεσεν τὴν Θέκλαν καὶ εἶπεν αὐτῇ ὁ ἡγεμών, Διὰ τί οὐ γαμεῖ κατὰ τὸν Ἰκονιέων νόμον τῷ Θαμύριδι[10]; ἡ δὲ εἱστήκει Παύλῳ ἀτενίζουσα·[11] τῆς δὲ μὴ ἀποκρινομένης, Θεοκλεία ἡ μήτηρ αὐτῆς ἀνέκραγεν[12] λέγουσα Κατάκαιε τὴν ἄνομον, κατάκαιε τὴν ἄνυμφον ἐν μέσῳ θεάτρου, ἵνα πᾶσαι αἱ ὑπὸ τούτου διδαχθεῖσαι γυναῖκες φοβηθῶσιν.[13]

Translation

And he[14] commanded to have Paul brought before the Bema: But Thecla was groveling in the place where Paul was teaching while having sat in prison. But the Governor commanded that she be brought before the bema also. But she departed with joy while rejoicing exceedingly before everyone. But the crowd, having brought Paul forward again, cried out even more, "He is a magician, take him away!" For willingly the Proconsul was listening to Paul concerning the holy work of Christ. And having taken counsel, the Governor called Thecla and said to her, "For what reason are you not marrying Thamyris according to the Iconian law?" But she stood there gazing intently at Paul: but when she did not answer, Theocleia, her mother, cried out saying, "Burn the lawless one! [Burn the one who is no bride in the midst of the theatre, in order that all the women who have been taught by this one might be afraid."]

3.20.1 Textual Notes

[1] Cf. *3.16.1 Textual Notes*, note 2.

[2] Interesting choice of verb (second person singular, aorist passive indicative from κυλίω) meaning *to roll up, to grovel, to wallow, to roll over* "of the embryo" ("κυλίω," [later form of κυλίνδρω] and "κυλίνδρω ," LSJ, 1008). Cf. Mark 9:20 for a NT *Hapax legomenon*.

[3] The implications are that Paul may have been teaching others also. Cf. *AP* (within the *Martyrdom* account) 14.4–7; Acts 16:25; Phil 1:12–13; *APt* 36–37, Peter preaches from the cross; *ATh* 159–68, Thomas preaches in prison and to the guards who take him away to be executed. Φυλακή is also found in 3.18.

[4] A word used frequently by the author of the *AP*. Κἀκείνην is also found in 3.4; 18; 20; 4.2; *APTh* 45; 10.2.5 (*3 Cor*); 14.6.

[5] Cf. also *AP* 3.25; 9.14; 19; Acts 16:34; Rev 19:7; Luke 10:21; 1 Pet 1:6, 8; 4:13.

[6] ἔμπροσθεν (ἐνώπιον) πάντων added based on Cop[1] (Schmidt, *Acta Pauli*, 39, 12*)

[7] On ὁ δὲ ὄχλος...περισσοτέρως ἐβόα Μάγος ἐστίν, see *3.15.1 Textual Notes*, note 15; and *3.15.2 General Comment*.

[8] Cf. 3.25 for another example of τοῖς ὁσίοις ἔργοις τοῦ Χριστοῦ, which implies that the recovery and salvation of Thecla is such a *holy work of Christ*. In contrast, it is unclear and unstated concerning about what Paul is speaking in this text, possibly his former travels and adventures, in which he had been saved.

[9] Ἡδέως δὲ ἤκουεν ὁ ἡγεμὼν τοῦ Παύλου ἐπὶ τοῖς ὁσίοις ἔργοις τοῦ Χριστοῦ – the Governor Castellius has consistently been presented as an even tempered fair judge of Paul, and if to be judged partial, then he has favored Paul. Here, the text even points out that Paul's discussion of the work is *holy* and even *pleasant* to the governor. The text is ambiguous on just who thinks the work to be *holy work*. Does this include Castellius? Possibly best explained in light of Mark 6:20 (Hills, "The Acts of the Apostles," 36 gives the connection an "A" rating, implying that the author of the *AP* knows this text of Mark with certainty). See also Mark 12:37; 2 Cor 11:19; 12:15; and Acts 13:8 (variant reading in Codex Bezae [*D*]. Hills remarks that "*TLG* database grants fewer than a dozen uses of this combination before the third century, and none with the exact Markan adverb + imperfect" (36). I am not sure if this can be offered as a support for the "A" rating, as this seems to suggest that the expression occurs almost a dozen times indicating common usage. First of all, there are at least a dozen examples of the combination in Plutarch alone, not even considering other authors (*Phil.* 15.11.2; *Nic.* 9.7.5; *Cic.* 25.3.4; *Sept. sap. Conv.* 147F.5; 158B.9; *Curios.* 519C.8; 519C.9; 519D.3; *Quaest. Conv.* 673C.2; 676C.12;

712D.12; *Amot.* 756A.1; *fac.* 937D.6). The expression was common. In addition, one ought to consider with equal weight the possibility of a connection between the Codex Bezae reading of Acts 13:8 and *AP* 3.20, which both have (1) an Apostle (Paul in both) (2) giving a defense before a proconsul (Sergius Paulus and Castellius), (3) who (the proconsul, that is) is listening gladly, and (4) who is attempting to determine whether a "magician is before him" (Paul in *AP* and Paul and Elymus in Acts). The striking similarities seem to be even stronger between these two texts than that of Mark. The verbatim connection between Mark and *AP* is strong testimony, but if anything, the connection between the *AP* and Mark or Acts is probable, although I would be hesitant to rank one above the other. The language seems to be common, and the author seems to have familiarity with one or both, but some kind of familiarity with the content of Acts seems the more probable (See István Czachesz, "The Acts of Paul and the western text of Luke's Acts: Paul between canon and apocrypha," *The Apocryphal Acts of Paul and Thecla* [ed. Jan Bremmer], 107–25). One might notice that ἡδέως ἤκουεν (with ἀκούω in the Imperfect) even shows up in Chariton (*Chaer.* 2.1.5 and 5.9.4); See also the *Acts of Xanthippe and Polyxena* 20.4.

[10] Once again, the Christian teaching is not the source of the problem, but rather the practical implications of the teaching of chastity. See *3.14.2 General Comment*.

[11] On ἀτενίζουσα see *3.8.1 Textual Notes*, note 9.

[12] See 4.1; 4.2, 5. (1) Theocleia cries out against her daughter Thecla to be burned (3.20); (2) Thecla cries out against Alexander to not harm her (4.1); (3) the women cry out against the Governor of Antioch not to condemn Thecla (4.2); and (4) Tryphaena cries out for the Governor to have mercy and not throw Thecla to the wild beasts (4.5).

[13] Theocleia demonstrates the value placed upon (1) the good of protecting one's honor and shame and (2) protecting the social group over the individual, even at the expense of her own daughter. Theocleia's reason has the "penal aim" of "deterrence" and quite possibly also prevention. See K. M. Coleman, "Fatal Charades," 44–73; esp. 48–49. See also Vorster, "Construction of culture through the contruction of person," 108; and *3.10.1 Textual Notes*, note 6. See also Cornelia B. Horn, "Suffering Children, Parental Authority and the Quest for Liberation?," 126.

[14] The Governor (ὁ ἡγεμών) Proconsul Castellius mentioned in the last line of 3.19.

3.20.2 General Comment

Once again Paul is called before the Proconsul, but this time it is due to the scandalous discovery of Thecla having been united with him within the prison after Thecla had bribed the gate keeper and jailer. Thecla's behavior is described in the same language of water rolling and tossing in the ocean, so Thecla also grovels, rolls up, and places herself upon the place where Paul sat teaching in the prison. As Thecla leaves the private sphere, the text overemphasizes her joy to remain with Paul even before the Bema as she faces her judgment. Once again, the proconsul saves Paul from the crowd who insistently call Paul a magician. At this point the text appears to demonstrate some connection to the Acts of the Apostles (Codex *Bezae* in particular) 13.8, most likely some strong oral familiarity based upon the text.

The proconsul withholds judgment until Thecla can be heard, but Thecla once again responds to her questioning by gazing intently (ἀτενίζουσα – note 11; reminiscent of Jesus' silence in Matt 26:63) at Paul. This leads Thecla's own mother to call down a judgment for execution by burning her. This appears to be the first real shift in the text, where Thecla will now move from passive, suppliant disciple of Paul to slowly developing apostle of God sealed by baptism and the Holy Spirit. This chapter also signals the beginning of the fading of Paul from the center of the text to the periphery as Thecla takes center stage. Note that the burning of Thecla is advocated not as decision of justice against Thecla, but in order to make an example of Thecla for the many other women who might be following Paul.

3.21

Καὶ ὁ ἡγεμὼν[1] ἔπαθεν μεγάλως,[2] καὶ τὸν μὲν Παῦλον μαστιγοῦν[3] ἔξω τῆς πόλεως[4] ἐξέβαλεν,[5] τὴν δὲ Θέκλαν ἔκρινεν κατακαῆναι.[6] καὶ εὐθέως ὁ ἡγεμὼν ἀναστὰς ἀπίει εἰς τὸ θέατρον· καὶ πᾶς ὁ ὄχλος ἐξῆλθεν ἐπὶ τὴν ἀνάγκην τῆς θεωρίας[7]. ἡ δὲ Θέκλα ὡς ἀμνὸς[8] ἐν ἐρήμῳ περισκοπεῖ τὸν ποιμένα, οὕτως ἐκείνη τὸν Παῦλον ἐζήτει.[9] καὶ ἐμβλέψασα εἰς τὸν ὄχλον εἶδεν τὸν κύριον[10] καθήμενον ὡς Παῦλον, καὶ εἶπεν Ὡς ἀνυπομονήτου μου οὔσης ἦλθεν Παῦλος θεάσασθαί με.[11] Καὶ προσεῖχεν αὐτῷ ἀτενίζουσα·[12] ὁ δὲ εἰς οὐρανοὺς ἀπίει.

Translation

And the Governor was affected greatly, and (on the one hand) he flogged Paul and cast him outside of the city, but (on the other hand), he condemned Thecla to be burned. And immediately the Governor rose up, departing into the theater, and all the crowd went out by necessity to the public spectacle. But Thecla was as a lamb in a desert looking around for the shepherd, so she sought for Paul. And having looked into the crowd, she saw the Lord sitting as Paul, and she said, "As if I am not enduring, Paul gazes upon me." And she held fast to him, gazing intently, but he went away into the heavens.

3.21.1 Textual Notes

[1] Codex *E* has ὁ δὲ ἀνθύπατος, but present reading is supported by Cop[1].

[2] On τὰ μεγαλεῖα τοῦ θεοῦ see *AP* 3.1, τὰ μεγαλεῖα τοῦ Χριστοῦ (See *3.1.1 Textual Notes*, note 11); see also *3.18.1 Textual Notes*, note 7. Words with the root μεγα – are especially popular with the author of the *AP*. See 3.1, 3, 5, 13, 16, 18, 21, 22; 4.8, 9, 13, 14, *APTh* 45; 9.14, 15, 17 (2x), 20, 23, 25, 27(2x); 12.1 (2x), 3, 5 (2x), 6; 13.2, 3, 4, 7, 8; 14.1, 2, 3, 6.

[3] Replace φραγελλώσας with μαστιγοῦν (following Cop[1], see Schmidt, *Acta Pauli*, 40, 12*).

[4] Cf. Acts 13:50; 14:19. Hills "Acts of the Apostles," 41, suggests a "C" rating.

[5] καὶ τὸν μὲν Παῦλον μαστιγοῦν ἔξω τῆς πόλεως ἐξέβαλεν – Considering the extraction of φραγελλώσας as indicated in note 3, then the judgment of Hills is incorrect ("The Acts of the Apostles," 36), who gives this reading an "A" rating, when comparing καὶ τὸν μὲν Παῦλον φραγελλώσας to Mark 15:15/Matt 27:26; "So Pilate wishing to satisfy the crowd, released Barabbas for them; and after flogging (φραγελλώσας) Jesus, he handed him over to be crucified." Hills also goes on to note that the author of the *AP* "was likely unaware that scourging was regularly a punishment inflicted *after a sentence of death* (see BAGD, *s. v.*[p. 865b])." It seems clear that the author did not make this mistake, therefore allowing that the connection to the passion narratives may still have been the underlying comparison being made by the author of the *AP*, with the amendation of the choice of beating (μαστιγοῦν) knowing that φραγελλώσας would not have made sense. This further strengthens the comparison to the *AP* in 9.14 where φραγελλώσας is used appropriately after Paul is sentenced to death. See also D. R. MacDonald, "Apocryphal and Canonical Narratives about Paul," 60–70.

[6] The proconsul finds Paul innocent and sympathizes with his message, but yet condemns Thecla for her crimes against the Iconians.

[7] See Aeschylus, *Prom.* 802; Aristophanes, *Vesp.* 1005 (LSJ, 797). The spectacle of beasts fighting beasts (and sometimes humans being killed by beasts; see *4.10.1 Textual Notes*, note 8) in the amphitheater is common in Greco-Roman wall paintings from Pompeii. See the image from house 1.3.23 now found in the National Archaeological Museum in Naples (see a good image in *Pompeii: guide to the site* [ed. Silvia Cassani; trans. Mark Weir; Napoli: Electra, 2002] 151.). See also "The House of the Hunt," in *Pompei: Pitture e Mosaici* (ed. Ida Baldasarre; 10 vols.; Roma: Instituto della Enciclopedia Italiana, 1994), 5:285; a picture of a hunt in the garden

of the house of Ceius Secundus (Region 1.6.15), found in *Pompei*, 1:475. See also Wilhelmina M. F. Jashemski, *The Gardens of Pompeii: Hercula-neum and the Villas Destroyed by Vesuvius* (New Rochelle, N.Y.: Caratzas Bros., 1979–93) 71–72; Paul Zanker *Pompeii: Public and Private Life* (trans. Deborah L. Schneider; Cambridge, MA: Harvard, 1998), 187–88, for further examples in the houses of Lucretius Fronto, Loreius Tiburtinus and the *House of the Hunt*. Regarding the involvement of the crowd in the fights in the ampitheatre, see Apuleius, *Metam.* 3.2–10; Fergus Millar, "The World of the Golden Ass," *JRS* 71 (1981) 70 and footnote 44 for fur-ther literature on "meetings in the theatre"; see also K. M. Coleman, "Fatal Charades," 44–73 especially 56 for connections of the form of execution that sound similar to Thecla's; and Donald G. Kyle, *Spectacles of Death in Ancient Rome* (New York: Routledge, 1998); and Kyle, *Sport and Specta-cle in the Ancient World* (Malden, MA: Blackwell, 2007), 312–29.

[8] In *AP* 9.23, the lion in Ephesus is also referred to as a lamb who re-clines next to the body of Paul ὡς ἀμνὸς εὐδίδακτ[ος καὶ ὡς δοῦ]λο[ς] αὐτοῦ. See also John 10:2, 11 (2x), 12, 14, and 16.

[9] See *AP* 3.19.

[10] εἶδεν τὸν κύριον – Thecla has an encounter with Jesus. Compare Acts 1:21; 9:4–6; 22:4–16; 26:9–18; 1 Cor 11:23; Gal 1:1, 11.

[11] See Aristotle, *Mir. Ausc.* 843A.15, as he describes *beholding* the waves that crash against the cliffs at the straight of the sea that separates the Sicilian coast from the Rhegium, on the Italian side; ...καὶ ποιεῖν συγκλυσμὸν ἄπιστον μὲν διηγεῖσθαι, ἀνυπομόνητον δὲ τῇ ὄψει θεάσασθαι· ποτὲ δὲ διισταμένους ἐκ τῆς πρὸς ἀλλήλους συρράξεως οὕτω βαθεῖαν καὶ φρικώδη τὴν ἄποψιν ποιεῖν τοῖς ἐξ ἀνάγκης θεωμένοις.... Θεάομαι; "gaze at, behold, mostly with a sense of wonder," (LSJ, 786).

[12] On ἀτενίζουσα see *3.8.1 Textual Notes*, note 9.

3.21.2 General Comment

The chapter might be best characterized by seeing that (1) *Thecla departed* (ἀπίει) *with joy while rejoicing exceedingly* (3.20), when led to the Bema; (2) the Proconsul *departed* (ἀπίει) to the theater, leading Thecla to be burned; and (3) Paul (actually the Lord καθήμενον ὡς Παῦλον) *departed* (ἀπίει) into the heavens leaving Thecla to be burned. The language of chapter 21 is very mixed with regard to the relationship of Paul and The-cla. While I think it is important to note that Paul is forced out of Iconium, and does not willingly leave Thecla, the text still seems to imply that there is some degree of abandonment, whether intentionally done by Paul or not is beside the point, and will be clarified in later notes and comments (see *3.25.1 Textual Notes*, note 12; *3.25.2 General Comment*; *4.1.1 Textual Notes*, note 6; and *4.1.2 General Comment*). Thecla has been left by all, so it seems. In fact, Thecla has been chosen by God to face these trials alone as will be explained more clearly in the text later as Thecla being separated for ministry. Thecla has followed Paul intently grasping and holding her attention upon him (ἀτενίζουσα – see note 11), yet to no avail up to this point. It has only brought upon her more intense difficulties. Thecla's facing the trial alone is actually something of the prophetic voice of Paul fulfilled from the very first time the beatitudes proceeded from his mouth. Thecla was attracted to just such a message (*AP* 3.5–6) that indicated that the lifestyle choices of those who followed the path of chastity, leading to resurrection, would be a path full of many tests. Although difficult, Paul stated "Blessed are the bodies of the virgins, for they shall be well pleasing to God and they will not lose the wages of their purity, because the word of the father shall be to them a work of salvation in the day of his Son, and they shall have rest forever." While anticipated, the response is seen in 3.22. This ἔργον of Christ is also connected to the "work" mentioned by Paul in 3.20.

3.22

Οἱ δὲ παῖδες[1] καὶ αἱ παρθένοι ἤνεγκαν ξύλα καὶ χόρτον ἵνα Θέκλα κατακαῇ.[2] ὡς δὲ εἰσήχθη γυμνή,[3] ἐδάκρυσεν ὁ ἡγεμὼν[4] καὶ ἐθαύμασεν τὴν ἐν αὐτῇ δύναμιν.[5] ἔστρωσαν δὲ τὰ ξύλα καὶ ἐκέλευσαν[6] αὐτὴν οἱ δήμιοι ἐπιβῆναι τῇ πυρᾷ.[7] ἡ δὲ τὸν τύπον τοῦ σταυροῦ[8] ποιησαμένη ἐπέβη τῶν ξύλων·[9] οἱ δὲ ὑφῆψαν.[10] καὶ μεγάλου πυρὸς λάμψαντος[11] οὐχ ἥψατο αὐτῆς τὸ πῦρ.[12] ὁ γὰρ θεὸς σπλαγχνισθεὶς ἦχον[13] ὑπόγαιον ἐποίησεν, καὶ νεφέλη ἄνωθεν ἐπεσκίασεν ὕδατος πλήρης[14] καὶ χαλάζης, καὶ ἐξεχύθη πᾶν τὸ κύτος,[15] ὡς πολλοὺς κινδυνεῦσαι καὶ ἀποθανεῖν,[16] καὶ τὸ πῦρ σβεσθῆναι τὴν δὲ Θέκλαν σωθῆναι.[17]

Translation

And the young ones and virgins brought wood and hay, in order that Thecla might be burned. But as she was brought in, naked, the Governor wept and marveled at the power in her. But the executioners spread the wood and commanded her to go up upon the pyre. But Thecla, making the sign of a cross, went upon the wood. But they set it on fire from underneath. Even though a great fire was shining, it did not touch her. For God who has compassion caused an underground roaring, and a cloud from above full of water and hail, and all of the contents were poured out, so that many were at risk and died, and the fire was extinguished and Thecla was saved.

3.22.1 Textual Notes

[1] Dunn, "The Acts of Paul," 58–59, supports his arguments against "Davies, MacDonald, et. al." that the *APTh* are not androcentric by also translating οἱ δὲ παῖδες καὶ αἱ παρθένοι as *the young men and virgins*. This appears to be inconclusive, but the most probable. See *3.10.1 Textual Notes*, note 9; *3.11.1 Textual Notes*, note 6; and *3.11.2 General Comment* for further discussion. See also the excellent observations of the children in the account of the *APTh* by Horn, "Suffering Children, Parental Authority, and the Quest for Liberation?," 121–30.

[2] See 3.20 (2x), 21 for events leading up to this point. See also *AP* 14.3.

[3] See Acts 16:22.

[4] In the same way that Proconsul Castellius ἔπαθεν μεγάλως (3.21) by Paul, now he is moved by Thecla. See *3.21.1 Textual Notes*, note 5; the passion narrative continues with Thecla as the Christ-figure.

[5] Alexander of Antioch attempts to overpower (δυνάμενος) Thecla in *AP* 4.1.

[6] ἐκέλευσαν... οἱ δήμιοι – It is no longer the Governor who is ordering people (via the executioner selected by the people), the people are doing the ordering (3.17, 20 (2x); but in the *APTh*, it is finally the governor (of Antioch) who orders to have Thecla restored (4.13). This is followed by the conversion of the maidservants, in essence the conversion of the οἱ δὲ παῖδες καὶ αἱ παρθένοι/ οἱ δήμιοι (see note 1).

[7] *damnati ad crematio*; see Coleman, "Fatal Charades," 55–56. Notice similarities to Blandina in Eusebius, *Hist. eccl.* 5.1.36–42. See also *4.1.1 Textual Notes*, note 1.

[8] τὸν τύπον τοῦ σταυροῦ – See *AP* 10.4.6.

[9] See Parthenius, *The Story of Pallene* 5–6; Achilles Tatius, *Leuc. Clit.* 8.3; 8.6; Heliodorus, *Aeth.* 10.7; 8.9.9–16 (!), for comparisons between the testing of Thecla and the testing of women and virgins in the ancient novel.

[10] ὑφῆψαν – aorist active indicative, third person plural from ὑφάπτω meaning *to set on fire from underneath*, (LSJ, 1907).

[11] See Acts 10:30.

[12] Cf. *Mart. Pol.* 15.1.

[13] See Luke 4:37; 21:25; Acts 2:2; and Heb 12:19.

[14] Cf. Matt 17:5, ἔτι αὐτοῦ λαλοῦντος ἰδοὺ νεφέλη φωτεινὴ ἐπεσκίασεν αὐτούς, καὶ ἰδοὺ φωνὴ ἐκ τῆς νεφέλης λέγουσα ; suggesting another example of a connection to Matthew. See the quotations in *AP* 3.5–6.

[15] Cf. Hos. 5:10 (BDAG, 312).

[16] Cf. Plato, *Apol.* 28B, τοιοῦτον ἐπιτήδευμα ἐπιτηδεύσας ἐξ οὗ κινδυνεύεις νυνὶ ἀποθανεῖν.... See also *Apol.* 28E (LSJ, 952).

[17] See *AP* 4.9. First, Thecla is saved through water, and then she is saved through fire. Cf. Clement of Alexandria, *Strom.* 5.1.9.

3.22.2 General Comment

The comparison of the *APTh* grows stronger to the passion narratives as the author strengthens allusions to the Gospel of Matthew and other texts and stories of early Christianity, but it is most explicit when Thecla makes the shape of a cross before getting onto the pyre of wood that will soon engulf her in flames. The very mobs of people (οἱ παῖδες/αἱ παρθένοι), who will eventually be Thecla's strongest following (*AP* 4.13–14) are yet still enemies and supporting the mob mentality to burn Thecla, having been instigated by Thecla's own mother to set an example for future followers of the new teaching (See *3.20.1 Textual Notes*, note 13).

As the fire is set beneath Thecla, God comes, out of compassion for Thecla (σπλάγχνον – Phlm 7, 12, and 20), with an apocalyptic presence and empties the heavens of hail and water. Thecla's salvation via fire and water only precedes her later submergence into water and salvation by fire (4.9). Considering that Thecla may have deserved a less degrading death, such as beheading (see note 7 above), then it seems plausible that Thecla's death by *crematio* is best explained literarily by the contrasting of water and fire as mentioned above. Interestingly, in both instances, the salvation of Thecla requires the death of others. The concept of the outpouring of "God's wrath" as found in Hos 5:10 is found here although no direct reliance upon Hosea is being suggested other than of the author's general awareness of this prophetic motif, implying some familiarity with Judaism. Most striking are the similarities of the trial of the *virgin* Thecla to other virgins in the ancient novels. It is a common theme that divine intervention brings about the salvation of pure maidens, who then are able to unite with their true love. In this case, the first trial only foreshadows the second trial, which leads directly to the unification of Thecla to Christ.

3.23

Ἦν δὲ ὁ Παῦλος νηστεύων[1] μετὰ Ὀνησιφόρου[2] καὶ τῆς γυναικὸς αὐτοῦ καὶ τῶν τέκνων ἐν μνημείῳ ἀνοικτῷ,[3] ἐν ὁδῷ ἐν ᾗ ἀπὸ Ἰκονίου εἰς Δάφνην πορεύονται. ἡνίκα δὲ ἡμέραι πολλαὶ διῆλθον, νηστευόντων αὐτῶν εἶπον οἱ παῖδες[4] τῷ Παύλῳ Πεινῶμεν. Καὶ οὐκ εἶχον πόθεν ἀγοράσωσιν ἄρτους·[5] κατέλιπεν γὰρ τὰ τοῦ κόσμου ὁ Ὀνησιφόρος καὶ ἠκολούθει Παύλῳ πανοικί.[6] Παῦλος δὲ ἀπεδύσατο τὸν ἐπενδύτην[7] καὶ εἶπεν Ὕπαγε, τέκνον, ἀγόρασον ἄρτους πλείονας καὶ φέρε.

Ὡς δὲ ἠγόραζεν ὁ παῖς, εἶδεν Θέκλαν τὴν γείτονα [ϱι πϱιρ],[8] καὶ ἐθαμβήθη καὶ εἶπεν Θέκλα, ποῦ πορεύῃ; ἡ δὲ εἶπεν Παῦλον διώκω,[9] ἐκ πυρὸς σωθεῖσα. Καὶ ὁ παῖς εἶπεν αὐτῇ,[10] Δεῦρο, ἀπαγάγω σε πρὸς αὐτόν· στενάζει γὰρ περὶ σοῦ καὶ προσεύχεται καὶ νηστεύει ἡμέρας ἤδη ἕξ.

Translation

But Paul was fasting with Onesiphorus, his wife, and the children in an opened tomb, on the road which leads from Iconium to Daphne. But after many days passed, the children, while they were fasting, said to Paul, "We are hungry!" And they did not have anywhere that they might buy bread; For Onesiphorus left the things of the world and was following Paul with his whole household. But Paul stripped off his outer garment and said, "Go, child. Buy more bread and bring it here." But as the child was buying bread, he saw Thecla, his neighbor, upon the street, and being afraid, said, "Thecla, where are you going?" But Thecla said, "I am pursuing Paul, having been saved from a fire. And the boy said to her, "Come, I will lead you to him; for he moans for you and he has been praying and fasting already for six days.

3.23.1 Textual Notes

[1] νηστεύω appears three times in 3.23.

[2] See *3.2.1 Textual Notes*, note 1; and *3.2.2 General Comment*.

[3] The passion narrative is being continued here. μνημεῖον is the same term as found in Luke 24:2. In this case, the *post-resurrection* discovery of Thecla is when the boy chances upon her in the market place.

[4] οἱ παῖδες – I have decided to translate this masculine plural noun as *children*, instead of *boys* (*NTApoc* 2:243) for several reasons. First, although the term is masculine, it is written from a generally patriarchal perspective, with gendered words being inclined to the masculine gender. If either Zenon or Simmia happened to be female, then the noun would still be written οἱ παῖδες and not αἱ παῖδες. Second, the text is consistently ambiguous about the gender of the young people referenced throughout the text (See *3.22.1 Textual Notes*, note 1; *3.10.1 Textual Notes*, note 9; *3.11.1 Textual Notes*, note 6; and *3.11.2 General Comment* for further discussion). Third, it appears that the children are not historical entities, but rather literary tools for setting up the situation to allow for Paul and Thecla to once again find each other (*3.2.2 General Comment*). For instance, it is the children (plural) who speak in unison (law of twins – see *3.4.1 Textual Notes*, note 1). Then, Paul responds, "Go, child" in the singular, addressing only one child. Only one child (masculine) goes to buy bread, speaks with Thecla, and leads her to Paul. *ÉAC* translates this *les enfants*, which inci-

dentally sustains the original better by not making a distinction between masculine and feminine in French.

⁵ Καὶ οὐκ εἶχον πόθεν ἀγοράσωσιν ἄρτους – Hills gives this a "B" reading when compared to John 6:5.

⁶ τὰ τοῦ κόσμου – Hills suggests giving this a "C" rating as a parallel to 1 Cor 7:33–34, only being attested in Clement of Alexandria (*Strom.* 4.7.51.3; 4.13.94.3; 6.8.68.1; *Quis. Div.* 37.5) and Tertullian amoung writers of the second century ("Acts of the Apostles," 31). Also found in Marcus Aurelius Antonius, *Imperator*, 9.28.1; Philo, *Somn.* 1.135.2, *Abr.* 46.3; *Aet.* 32.5; Plutarch, *Stoic. Rep.* 1054F; also found in the writings of Chrysippus (*Fragmenta logica et physica*, 550.11). For an interesting connection to "leaving the things of this world" and widows, see also *T. Job* 14.1–5; 9–13; 33.3, 4, 8; 34.4; 47.3; 53.3; see also the introduction by R. P. Spittler, "Testament of Job," *The Old Testament Pseudepigrapha* (ed. James H. Charlesworth; New York: Doubleday, 1983), 1:835–36; and the comments by Robert A. Kraft, ed. on *T. Job* 47.3 and 49.2 in *The Testament of Job*, (SBLTT 5; Pseudepigrapha Series 4; Atlanta: Scholars Press, 1974), 80–83.

⁷ ἀπεδύσατο τὸν ἐπενδύτην – Paul is providing the child with a garment, which will allow him or her to be able to buy bread in the place of Paul. See 1 Kgdms 18:4 (LXX), where Jonathan gives David his cloak representing his royal lineage and transfers it to David; The ἐπενδύτης represents much more than just a garment for warmth or protection, it symbolizes the fullness of Paul and his apostleship. Compare 4.15, where Thecla devises a way to ῥάψαι τὸν χιτῶνα εἰς ἐπενδύτην σχήματι ἀνδρικῷ, so that she will appear before Paul donning the appropriate attire of the apostle of God, and bearing the news of God himself that she has been selected. It is as much the garment as it is the news that convinces Paul. The contrast that should be seen is how flippantly Paul allows this young child to don the garment, while withholding it from Thecla through multiple trials (See McGinn, "The Acts of Thecla," *Searching the Scriptures*, 827; Vorster, "Construction of Culture," 110–11

⁸ There is no Greek translation or original for this expression. The Latin manuscript *c* has *in platea*. See Schmidt, *Acta Pauli*, 40–41; 13*; and *AAA*, 251.

⁹ Cf. 3.19; 14.7 (2x), Cestus and Longus *pursue* Titus and Luke, in the same way that they *pursued* Paul seeking life (εἰς ζωήν).

¹⁰ αὐτῇ added to the *AAA* text based on Cop¹, which has ⲡⲁⲭⲉ ⲡϣⲏⲣⲉ-ϣⲏⲙ ⲛⲉⲥ ⲭⲉ.

3.23.2 General Comment

The text here leaves numerous questions unanswered. To begin, how does Paul end up with Onesiphorus, Lectra, and their children. Secondly, how does Thecla end up in the market and why is she there? I find it surprising that Thecla has been involved with the possible destruction of numerous people in the center of the city, in the theatre, yet afterwards she is found in the forum. The theological point of 3.22 is clear, God delivered Thecla from the judgment, and in turn allowed her deliverance to be a moment of God's wrath coming down upon an unjust city and rulers. Obviously, unimportant to the author of the text, did the Proconsul acquit Thecla? Nonetheless, the point is clear that the narrative driven by a theological agenda is more important than historical inconsistencies and gaps. History writing is not the preeminent agenda.

The next chapter begins with a resurrection sequence that involves several twists to the traditional Gospel passions. First, the empty tomb is found, but the players are reversed with the disciples hiding and praying in the tomb. Paradoxically, Paul is presented as a friend and companion of Thecla, but not at the level that he remained at the trial of Thecla. He fled (?) also. The group, having fasted for six days suggests that the trial of Thecla elapsed a week ago, and yet no word of Thecla. It appears also that the text implies that this small band has been in hiding for six days, while Thecla had to go through any other legal harassments and difficulties alone. Nevertheless, the children call to end the fast, speaking in unison, "we are hungry ($\pi\epsilon\iota\nu\hat{\omega}\mu\epsilon\nu$), and we have no bread to eat." At this point, the major theological string is plucked in the next line Παῦλος δὲ ἀπεδύσατο τὸν ἐπενδύτην.... The implications of this action, while being ever so simple, carry a much greater significance, especially in light of Thecla's actions in *AP* 4.13–15. Paul casually gives the cloak that bears his authority and apostleship and hands it over to a child, yet withholds it from women to possess any responsibilities as an apostle. This could also be a foreshadowing of the emergence and blessing of Thecla as transitioning from childhood to womanhood without the rite of passage of sexual activity with a man (See Vorster, "Construction of Culture," 105–108; and Horn, "Suffering Children, Parental Authority and the Quest for Liberation?, 126). This will later be changed by the second direct personal intervention of God in Antioch (4.9–10). As the *children* initially speak to Paul, from this point forward there is only one child, suggesting that the children are merely serving the role of the "twins" (see *3.4.1 Textual Notes*, note 1; *3.23.1 Textual Notes*, note 4 above), and lack any real historical value, but serve as the instigators of reuniting Thecla to Paul. Upon coming to the market, Thecla sees the child, asks for Paul, and the child explains that Paul has been grieving, praying, and fasting for six days for her.

3.24

Ὡς δὲ ἐπέστη ἐπὶ τὸ μνημεῖον[1] Παύλῳ κεκλικότι[2] τὰ γόνατα[3] καὶ προσευ-χομένῳ καὶ λέγοντι Πάτερ[4] Ἰησοῦ[5] Χριστοῦ, μὴ ἁψάσθω[6] Θέκλης τὸ πῦρ, ἀλλὰ πάρεσο[7] αὐτῇ, ὅτι σή ἐστιν, ἡ δὲ ὄπισθεν ἑστῶσα ἐβόησεν[8] λέγουσα[9] Πάτερ,[10] ὁ ποιήσας τὸν οὐρανὸν καὶ τὴν γῆν,[11] ὁ τοῦ ἁγίου παιδὸς πατήρ,[12] εὐλογῶ σε ὅτι ἔσωσάς Με,[13] ἵνα Παῦλον ἴδω πάλιν.[14] Καὶ ἀναστὰς Παῦλος εἶδεν αὐτὴν καὶ εἶπεν Θεὲ καρδιογνῶστα,[15] ὁ πατὴρ Ἰησοῦ[16] Χριστοῦ, εὐλογῶ σε ὅτι ὃ ᾐτησάμην[17] ἐτάχυνάς δοῦναι[18] μοι καὶ εἰσήκουσάς μου.

Translation

But as she came upon the tomb to Paul, who had bent his knees and was praying and saying "Father of Jesus Christ, do not let Thecla be overtaken in the fire, but be with her, because she is yours." But Thecla, who was standing behind, cried aloud, "Father, the one who made the heavens and the earth, the father of the holy child, I thank you because you saved me, in order that I might see Paul again." And Paul, having risen, saw her and said, "God, knower of hearts, the father of our Lord Jesus Christ, I thank you because you hastened to give to me and responded to me that which I asked."

3.24.1 Textual Notes

[1] Text could possibly be τάφος instead of μνημεῖον based on Cop[1] (ⲁⲡⲧⲁⲫⲟⲥ).

[2] κεκλικότι – perfect active participle, dative masculine singular, from κλίνω meaning *to rest, lean, recline* (LSJ, 961).

[3] Bending the knees to pray, see *AP* 3.5 (*3.5.1 Textual Notes*, note 3); Mark 15:19; Luke 5:8; 22:41; Acts 7:60; 9:40; 20:36; 21:5; Phil 2:10.

[4] Πάτερ shows up three times in this verse alone, emphasizing the con-nection between Thecla and the father. This is consistent with a *post-resurrection* account of Thecla. Yet, Paul is unconvinced until after the Antiochene trial.

[5] Ἰησοῦ added based on textual evidence of Cop[1] (ⲛ̅ⲓ̅ⲥ̅). There are also numerous variations in the other manuscripts (*AAA*, 252; Schmidt, *Acta Pauli*, 41).

[6] See *AP* 3.22, καὶ μεγάλου πυρὸς λάμψαντος οὐχ ἥψατο αὐτῆς τὸ πῦρ.

[7] πάρεσο – present middle imperative, second person singular from πάρειμι (Smyth, *Greek Grammar*, 210–11, §768; 152, §462)

[8] βοάω (and other cognates such as βοήθησις) are common for the *AP*; see 3.20, 24; 4.5 (2x), 7, 8 (2x), 17 (4x); *APTh* 45; 9.15 (2x), 19, 21, 23, 25, 27, 28; 12.3 (2x), 4, 5.

[9] Added based on evidence of *G,C d*, and Cop¹ (ⲁⲥⲗⲩⲟⲏⲗ' ⲁⲃⲁⲗ' ⲉⲥⲭⲟⲅ
ⲏⲘⲁⲥ ⲭⲉ ⲡⲗⲉⲓⲱⲧ).

[10] Cop¹ reads ⲡⲗⲉⲓⲱⲧ, but Schmidt argues for the reading of *AAA* (based
on A,C F, and Latin B_b, C_abc, Syr., Arm.). See Schmidt, *Acta Pauli*, 41.

[11] Acts 4:24 and 14:15. Hills gives this reference a "C" rating ("Acts of
the Apostles," 41). See also 10.4.9 (*3 Cor*). "This expression, of course,
conveys a central biblical affirmation." (Ibid.). See Gen 1:1; 2:4; 14:19,
22; Exod 20:11 (Deut 5:14 LXX Vaticanus); 31:17; 4 Kgdms 19:15; 2 Chr
2:11 (12); LXX 1 Esd 6:13; Neh 9:6; Jdt 13:18; Esth 4:17; Add Esth 4:17
(=13:10); Ps 113:23 (115:15); 120 (121):2; 123 (124):8; 133 (134):3; 134
(135):6; 145 (146):6; Zech 12:1; Isa 37:16; 42:5; 51:13; Jer 39 (32):17;
LXX Dan 4:34; Bel 5.

[12] See Schmidt, *Acta Pauli*, 41, for text critical reasons for the amendation from ὁ τοῦ παιδὸς τοῦ ἀγαπητοῦ σου ᵉἸησοῦ Χριστοῦ πατήρ.

[13] ἐκ πυρός – following A, B, Syr., Arm., Lat. Versions, Cop¹.

[14] πάλιν – following Cop¹, ⲛ[ⲕⲉ]ⲥⲁⲡ (Schmidt, *Acta Pauli*, 42, 13*).

[15] Θεὲ καρδιογνῶστα – Cf. Acts 1:24; 15:8; Herm. *Mand.* 4.3.4; Clement
of Alexandria, *Strom.* 5.14.96 (=5.96.4); *Apos. Con.* 2.24.6; 3.7.8; 4.6.8;
6.12.4; 8.5.6. This is the strongest indication within the section of the
APTh, other than possibly 3.2, that the author of the *AP* could have had
some familiarity with the content of the canonical Acts. See Hills, "The
Acts of the Apostles," 45, who gives the connection an "A" rating, and
adequately critiques reservations to the connection made by Haenchen,
Cadbury, and Lake. For arguments against the two being compatible, see
Ernst Haenchen, *The Acts of the Apostles: A Commentary* (trans. Bernard
Noble, Gerald Shinn, and R. McL. Wilson; Philadelphia: Westminster
Press, 1971), 162; Cadbury, H. J., and Kirsopp Lake, *Part 1: The Acts of
the Apostles.* (F. J. Foakes Jackson and Kirsopp Lake, eds.; Vol. 1 of *The
beginnings of Christianity*; Grand Rapids: Baker, 1920–33, 1979), 4.15, n.
24.

[16] Alteration of *AAA* based on textual evidence of Cop¹ (ⲛⲓⲏⲥ). The decision made by Hills, "Acts of the Apostles," 30 which suggests a "D" rating in the connection between ὁ πατὴρ τοῦ κυρίου ἡμῶν ᵉἸησοῦ Χριστοῦ and
texts such as 2 Cor 1:3; Eph 1:3; 2 Cor 11:31; should be further disre-
garded, realizing that the text as quoted from *AAA* has an inferior reading
once amended with Cop¹ as indicated above.

[17] ᾐτησάμην being a form of αἰτεῖσθαι found in manuscripts A and B.
The change is based on textual evidence of Cop¹ (ⲡⲉⲛⲧⲁⲉⲓⲣ̄ⲁⲓⲧⲉⲓ). See
Schmidt, *Acta Pauli*, 42.

[18] δοῦναι added based on textual evidence of Cop¹ (ⲁⲧⲉⲉϥ).

3.24.2 General Comment

In this chapter, which provides one of the two best examples for a possible touchpoint for the *AP* author relying upon some form of the Acts of the Apostles (or possibly an oral knowledge, see note 15), the chapter takes the opportunity of combining two types of scenes as found in the ancient novel: (1) the scene, in which the hero or heroine goes to the temple to pray to the gods to be reunited to their lover (Chariton, *Chaer.* 2.2.5–8) and (2) the scene where the lovers are reunited (Ibid., 8.1.1–10). This Christian blend of the ancient novel creates the reunification of the *lovers* who paradoxically are truly lovers of God. Therefore upon reunification, instead of exchanging embraces and vows of love for one another, there is a series of prayers offered up to God, the father (Πάτερ...εὐλογῶ σε ὅτι...), giving thanks for this great occasion. Interestingly enough the scene does not take place at a μνημεῖον, but rather at a τάφος, comparible to the post-resurrection manifestations of Jesus to the disciples (Matt 27:61, 64, 65; 28:1; compare μνημεῖον in Mark 16:2; Luke 24:2), possibly demonstrating a preference for Matthew's Gospel. As the two *lovers* reunite, Thecla makes clear her desire in the words of her prayer, ἵνα Παῦλον ἴδω πάλιν. This line of celebration and reunification is continued in the first lines of *AP* 3.25 also, where we learn that there was much love (ἀγάπη πολλή) within the tomb, shared rejoicingly between Paul, Thecla, Onesiphorus, Lectra, Simmias, and Zenon.

3.25

Καὶ ἦν ἔσω ἐν τῷ μνημείῳ[1] ἀγάπη πολλή,[2] Παύλου ἀγαλλιωμένου[3] καὶ Ὀνησιφόρου καὶ πάντων. εἶχον δὲ ἄρτους πέντε[4] καὶ λάχανα καὶ ὕδωρ,[5] καὶ εὐφραίνοντο[6] ἐπὶ τοῖς ὁσίοις ἔργοις τοῦ Χριστοῦ.[7] καὶ εἶπεν Θέκλα τῷ Παύλῳ Περικαροῦμαι[8] καὶ ἀκολουθήσω σοι ὅπου δὰν πορεύῃ.[9] Ὁ δὲ εἶπεν Ὁ καιρὸς αἰσχρός,[10] καὶ σὺ εὔμορφος·[11] μὴ ἄλλος σε πειρασμὸς[12] λήψεταί χείρων τοῦ πρώτου,[13] καὶ οὐχ ὑπομείνῃς ἀλλὰ δειλανδρήσῃς.[14] καὶ εἶπεν Θέκλα Μόνον δός μοι τὴν σφραγῖδα[15] ἐν τῷ κυρίῳ,[16] καὶ οὐχ ἅψεταί μοι πειρασμός.[17] καὶ εἶπεν Παῦλος τῇ Θέκλῃ[18] μακροθύμησον,[19] καὶ λήψη τὸ ὕδωρ.[20]

Translation

And within the tomb there was much love, as Paul Onesiphorus and everyone were rejoicing. But they had five loaves of bread, vegetables, and water, and it caused them to be gladdened concerning the holy works of Christ. And Thecla said to Paul, "I will cut my hair and follow you wherever you should go." But he said, "O, shameless time, and you are beautiful." May another trial not leave you worse than the first, and you might not endure but you might be cowardly." And Thecla said, "Only give to me the seal in the Lord, and no temptation will touch me. And Paul said to Thecla, "Be patient, and you will receive the water."

3.25.1 Textual Notes

[1] τάφος could replace μνημεῖον again (see *3.24.1 Textual Notes*, note 1) based on Cop[1] (ϯ̄ΠΤΑΦΟϹ).

[2] Cop[1] has ΟΥΝΑϬ, therefore it is possible that it could have been μεγάλη instead of πολλή.

[3] Thecla's feelings of rejoicing in 3.20, ἡ δὲ μετὰ χαρᾶς ἀπίει ἀγαλλιωμένη[5] ἔμπροσθεν (ἐνώπιον) πάντων, are reciprocated by all (see *3.20.1 Textual Notes*, note 5).

[4] Possible Eucharistic or agape meal language; see *3.5.1 Textual Notes,* note 4. See also Matt 14:17, 19; 16:9; Mark 6:38, 41; 8:19; Luke 9:13, 16; John 6:9, 13. Compare also the bowing of prayer in 3.24 with 3.5 (see *3.5.1 Textual Notes*, note 3). See also Dunn, "The *Acts of Paul*," 86–7; Clement of Alexandria, *Paed.* 2.1.3–5. See Thomas M. Finn, "Agape (Love Feast)," *Encyclopedia of Early Christianity* (ed. Everett E. Ferguson; New York and London: Garland Publishing, 1990) 16–17, for the development of *love feasts* apart from the *eucharist*.

[5] The addition of ⟨καὶ ἅλας⟩ as found in *AAA* has been cut from the text, based on the absence of such a reading in Cop[1], and further explained by Schmidt as: *Lipsius* ⟨καὶ ἅλας⟩ *auf Grund des Syr. Hinter* ὕδωρ (Syr.c salt and water, *ebenso* Arm.), *aber dieser Zusatz sicher im Syr. entstanden, da er vom Schreiber nach dem Ritus der syrischen Kirche eingefügt ist...* (*Acta Pauli*, 42, note 20.2). He then suggests *Apos. Con.* 45.18 for comparison.

[6] Cf. Luke 15:23, 29, 32; Acts 7:41.

[7] Cf. *AP* 3.20, *3.20.1 Textual Notes*, notes 8 and 9.

[8] Cf. Heliodorus, *Aeth.* 6.9.7; 6.11.3.

[9] Cf. Matt 8:19; Lk 9:57. Hills, "Acts of the Apostles," 31, gives this a "C" rating.

[10] Cf. Tit 1:11; 1 Cor 11:6; 14:35; *1 Clem* 47.6. This term is enveloped with honor-shame overtones, "generally, in reference to that which fails to meet expected moral and cultural standards [opp. καλός] pertaining to being socially or morally unacceptable, *shameful, base...*" ("αἰσχρός, ά, όν," BDAG 29). See also Achilles Tatius, *Leuc.* 1.10.2; 5.11.3; 7.6.4; Chariton, *Chaer.* 4.2.2; 5.7.3. Also, may be translated as "ugly." Also see Tertullian, *Bapt.* 17. as a pivotal repudiation of Thecla's question, and how the *AP* deals with this discussion.

[11] Cf. Philo, *Virt.* 110; *T. Jud.* 13.3; Justin, *Dial.* 134.1; et. al. (BDAG, 409). Thecla is being accused of having made a shameless and "ugly" suggestion, when Paul is implying that this is such a shameless time.

[12] This is playing off the motif found in the ancient novel of the two lovers desiring to fulfill their sexual gratification, while abstaining until the appropriate time. This is intensified by numerous *temptations* that press in upon them from other individuals. For examples in the ancient novel see Heliodorus, *Aeth.* 1.8.3; 1.19.7 (Thyamis threatens Theagenes and Charicleia) 1.25; 7 (especially Alsace's intervention into the relationship of Theagenes and Charicleia); 5.31.1–4 (While enjoying a feast devoted to Hermes, the priest Calasiris records another threat to Theagenes and Charicleia by Pelorus); Longus, *Daph.* 1.15–17; 3.20; Chariton, *Chaer.* 4.3.8–10; 8.1; Achilles Tatius, *Leuc. Clit.* 5.16–17; 5.21; 5.22.8; 5.27; et. al.

[13] This is referring to the trials that she has just undergone in Iconium and the one to come in Antioch (chapter 4).

[14] Paul fears the renunciation of faith, when one is on the verge of martyrdom. See 2 Macc 8:13; 4 Macc 10.14.

[15] Cf. 9.20; 14.5, 7. The *seal* is baptism. See Robin M. Jensen, "Baptismal Rites and Architecture," *A People's History of Christianity: Volume 2, Late Ancient Christianity* (ed. Virginia Burrus; Minneapolis: Fortress, 2005), 120–22; Willy Rordorf, "Tertullien et les *Actes de Paul,*" 475–84. It appears that a connection developed quickly between the σφραγίς and βαπτίζω. The "seal" is connected to the seal of the Holy Spirit. In 2 Cor 1:21–22, Paul states, "But it is God who establishes us with you in Christ and has anointed us, by putting his seal on us and giving us his Spirit in our hearts as a first installment." In time this develops into the Christian rite, in which the application of holy oil, water immersion and *sealed* with ointment (this latter part is equated with the participation of the Holy Spirit). This development can be seen in the *Didache* 7, *Didascalia* 16, Hippolytus' *Trad. ap.* 22, and finally 7.22.2, where the text (and *Didascalia*) makes clear that the seal is baptism.

[16] τὴν ἐν Χριστῷ σφραγίδα has been changed to τὴν σφραγῖδα ἐν τῷ κυριῳ. See Schmidt, *Acta Pauli*, 43, note 20.11.[17] This is a continuation and response to the events from 3.22 (καὶ μεγάλου πυρὸς λάμψαντος οὐχ ἥψατο αὐτῆς τὸ πῦρ), 3.24 (μὴ ἀψάσθω Θέκλης τὸ πῦρ), 3.25 (μὴ ἄλλος σε πειρασμὸς λήψεται χείρων τοῦ πρώτου), and here.

[18] τῇ Θέκλῃ has been added, based on the evidence of Cop[1].

[19] μακροθύμησον – aorist active imperative (§390 and §543 in Smyth, *Greek Grammar*, 125 and 173 respectively) coming from μακροθυμέω, meaning *have patience*, *be patient* (BDAG, 612), *long-suffering* (LSJ, 1074); see also μακρόθυμος, ον (BDAG, 613) which means "pert(aining) to being self-controlled in the face of provocation, *patient, forbearing, toler-*

ant, even-tempered." See also Matt 18:26; 1 Tim 1:16; 2 Tim 3:10, 4:2; James 5:7 is suggestive of the eschatological *patience* for the coming of Christ (*AP* 4.9).

[20] "The water" means "baptism." Cop[1] reads ᄆᄑᄁΒΑΠΤΙϹΜΑ. Schmidt suggests *die Taufe* following Cop[1] (*Acta Pauli*, 43), but the change from τὸ ὕδωρ to τὸ βάπτισμα is unjustified. τὸ ὕδωρ is the more difficult reading with a higher degree of uncertainty as to the meaning of Paul's statement (*ÉAC*, 1136). No extant Greek manuscripts have the reading of τὸ βάπτισμα.

3.25.2 General Comment

Paul, Thecla, Onesiphorus, and his family all join with great love at the beginning of the chapter. While all are joined, there seems to be special emphasis upon the rejoining of Paul and Thecla (see 3.25; *3.25.2 General Comment*). As this blended passion narrative is combined with the characteristics of the ancient novel, one begins with the first *agape* meal following Paul's resurrection with a simple meal of bread, water, and vegetables (see Dunn, "The *Acts of Paul*," 86–7, for a discussion on the *AP* and aquarianism; compare also *ATh* 29, 49–59, and 158; *Did.*9; *Ign.* Phld. 4; *contra* 1 Tim 5:23; and *3.6.1 Textual Notes,* note 3; where the Eucharist includes the bread and a cup, but the text never specifies wine.). Eucharistic overtones can also be seen to the extent that Jesus' miracle of feeding the five thousand (Matt 14:17, et. al.) is possibly alluded to here, and equally represents the example of having a *meal with Jesus*, with the last supper being the meal *par excellence*.

As they eat this meal, and meditate on how the holy works of Christ have been represented in their lives, Thecla makes a pointed and anticipated statement; "...I will follow you wherever you should go." This statement seems innocent, but Thecla says this only after attempting to determine ways that she can be an apostle/disciple to Paul, even if it means going as a man. Thecla is making a request that is later repudiated on the basis of the Pauline witness in Tertullian, *de Baptismo* 17, who quotes Paul in 1 Cor 14:35. Her statement is clearly based on her desire to cut her hair and disguise her figure (see *AP* 4.14 where Thecla finally succeeds after the second πειρασμός).

There are at least two ways to interpret Paul's response to Thecla: (1) Paul is suggesting that the times are shameless and bad, and Thecla would be tempted beyond what she can bear or forced, and (2) Thecla's request is inappropriate, and Paul is suggesting that Thecla desires something that is *ugly* and *shameless*. I tend to believe that the second option is the more valid of the two, considering that the cutting of a woman's hair was culturally a shameful act (Cf. Paul's response in 1 Cor. 11:6). Paul boldly, but

wrongfully resists the desire of Thecla (and God) and will not ratify Thecla's request, although God himself has defended Thecla, on account of the
fact that ὁ θεὸς σπλαγχνισθεὶς ἦχον. At this point, the reader ought to antici-
pate that Paul has been represented in an inferior light to Thecla on at least
two counts; (1) He did not stay with Thecla for the trial, (2) he has denied
Thecla what God desires of her. Interestingly enough, Paul appears to be
presented as consistent with the canonical Paul of 1 Corinthians and the
Pastorals here (Tit 1:11; 1 Cor 11:6; 14:35; and *1 Clem* 47.6), yet is also
presented as lacking divine insight and ability to comprehend the intentions of the Spirit of God. It is almost as if the author of the text is presenting a Paul, who, formerly being ignorant concerning the role of women in
the church is now beginning to understand what Paul once thought shameless (αἰσχρός – 1 Cor 11:6). What he thought should be simply a custom of
the churches of God (συνήθειαν οὐκ ἔξομεν οὐδε αἱ ἐκκλησίαι – 1 Cor 11:16)
is incorrect information that God has to forcefully teach to Paul, by means
of Thecla (4.16 against 1 Cor 14:35). Thecla is naturally led to the conclusion that she should have the authority to teach and to baptize after receiving the seal of approval, *via* Paul baptizing her (see *4.16.2 General Comment*; and Barrier, "Tertullian and the Acts of Paul or Thecla?." Therefore
the issue at hand is not simply Paul withholding baptism from Thecla, but
rather, Paul is hesitant to issue the approval to be baptized, and therefore to
teach and baptize others with authority, i. e., apostolic authority. This is
the exact point that the *AP* will eventually make as one moves on through
AP 4 which concludes the story of Thecla (See *4.13.2 General Comment*).

3.26[1]

Καὶ ἀπέπεμψεν[2] Παῦλος τὸν Ὀνησιφόρου[3] πανοικὶ[4] εἰς Ἰκόνιον, καὶ οὕτως
λαβόμενος τὴν Θέκλαν εἰς Ἀντιόχειαν[5] εἰσῆλθεν.

Translation

And Paul sent away Onesiphorus with all of his household into Iconium,
and thus having received Thecla, he entered into Antioch.

3.26.1 Textual Notes

[1] Following the traditional numeration stemming from the first critical
edition prepared by R. A. Lipsius (1891), this short "chapter" is now somewhat displaced. According to the *AAA* text, 3.26 constituted what now en-
compasses 3.26 and 4.1 according to the numeration prescribed (for the
first time) by Rordorf in *ÉAC*. For the first time the *APTh* have been sub-

divided into chapters 3 (Iconium) and 4 (Antioch). This is based upon the evidence demonstrated provided by Cop[1] which constitutes this change. On the 20th leaf of the manuscript there is a clear break in the text with the words ...ⲉⲛⲧⲁϥⲃⲱⲕ ⲁⲧⲁⲛⲧⲓⲟⲭⲓⲁ (Greek, εἰς Ἀντιόχειαν εἰσῆλθεν) followed by a break and a new section with the chapter heading ⲁ[1]. The Coptic text then begins again with ⲍ̄ⲙ ⲡⲧⲣⲟⲩⲃⲱⲕ... (Greek, ἅμα δὲ τῷ εἰσέρχεσθαι αὐτούς). This break now divides chapter 26 in *AAA* into two halves. The first line of *AAA* critical edition of *APTh* 26 is now 3.26, and the remainder of *AAA*'s *APTh* 26 is now 4.1. In hindsight, it makes more sense to roll 3.26 into 3.25, and do away with 3.26 altogether, but for the present 3.26 will be retained to avoid confusion.

[2] See *AP* 14.1.

[3] See 2 Tim 1:15–16.

[4] See *AP* 3.23.

[5] The most recent arguments suggest Antioch of Pisidia (*ÉAC*, 1137); see also discussion in *3.1.1 Textual Notes*, note 1; Dunn, "The *Acts of Paul*, 21–22; Ramsay, *The Church in the Roman Empire*, 390–91, Gebhardt, *Passio*, xcviii–xcix; *NTApoc* 2:219; et. Al. This seems to be most reasonable based on the knowledge that Paul travels next to Myra (*AP* 4.15). This would allow Paul to have followed a highway in Pisidia connecting Iconium to Antioch, and then moving down the valley following the Catarrhactes and Cestrus rivers, possibly through Perga and Attalia in Pamphylia, and then along the coast or by ship to Myra in Lycia. The strongest argument against Pisidian Antioch is the Greek and Coptic evidence for Alexander being a Syrian and possibly a "president of the provincial capital of Syria" ("συριάρχης," LSJ, 1731). Cop[1] which supports a reading "immediately as they entered a Syrian (ⲥⲩⲣ[ⲟⲥ]) by the name of Alexander, one of the first of the Antiochenes...". This argues for Alexander being a Syrian, but does not necessarily locate him in Syrian Antioch for this series of events that follow. See also *4.1.1 Textual Notes*, note 1. In the same way that writing history is not the pre-eminent concern, it is also possible that neither is geography (see *3.23.2 General Comment*; Schneemelcher, *NTApoc* 2:219–220).

3.26.2 General Comment

At the close of 3.25, Thecla brings two requests before Paul. First, Thecla asks if she might be able to follow after Paul, in which Paul responds in the negative. Thecla then pushes forward in her request to receive the seal in Christ, being baptism, and Paul then cautions her again to wait with patience for baptism. The question is whether Paul has foresight into the future in which he has divine knowledge that anticipates Thecla's baptism, or if Paul is delaying to respond to Thecla's request? Although it is possible that Paul has divine foresight, it seems more likely that Paul is stalling. It appears that as Thecla is denied to follow Paul, then she seeks baptism for the sole purpose of going out on her own as a representative of Christ. Paul sensing that if he is to maintain any control over Thecla, then he must submit to the first request in order to (1) divert attention away from her request for baptism, which would eventuate in Paul's endorsement of Thecla as a teacher and apostle and (2) delay responding to the inevitable, that Thecla has been endorsed by God even in a miraculous way. When one learns in 3.26 that Paul is sending Onesiphorus and his family back to Iconium, and then takes Thecla along with him, it becomes apparent that Paul has submitted to the first request, in order to avoid the second request.

The motif that is being modeled here comes from the ancient novel (See *3.25.1 Textual Notes*, note 11). It is typical within the ancient novel for lovers to have to delay gratification of sexual desire until the appropriate time. As sexual gratification and union is prolonged, the temptations and attempts by others to fulfill sexual desires with one or both members become greater and greater. As the pressures externally are relieved, then the temptation by the lovers to maintain purity intensifies. As for the case of Thecla within the Christian novel context, Thecla maintains her purity by resisting Thamyris, only to then want to fulfill her desire for Paul/Christ. At this point, Paul cautions for patience. This delays the fitting union of lovers until the appropriate time, but (un)expectedly another greater temptation comes from the outside, namely through Alexander who emerges in the text only a few lines from here. After emerging from this situation, then Thecla's pure union with Jesus will eventually be complete as found in chapter 4.

Acts of Paul 4.1–18

4.1

ἅμα δὲ τῷ εἰσέρχεσθαι αὐτούς, συριάρχης[1] τις Ἀλέξανδρος ὀνόματι Ἀντιοχέων πρῶτος[2] πολλὰ ποιῶν ἐν τῇ πόλει ἐκείνῃ ἐν ὅλῃ τῇ ἀρχῇ αὐτοῦ[3] ἰδὼν τὴν Θέκλαν ἠράσθη αὐτῆς, καὶ πείθειν[4] τὸν Παῦλον χρήμασι καὶ δώροις.[5] ὁ δὲ Παῦλος εἶπεν Οὐκ οἶδα τὴν γυναῖκα ἣν λέγεις,[6] οὐδὲ ἔστιν ἐμή. ὁ δὲ πολὺ δυνάμενος, αὐτὸς αὐτῇ περιεπλάκη[7] εἰς τὸ ἄμφοδον[8] ἡ δὲ οὐκ ἠνέσχετο,[9] ἀλλὰ Παῦλον ἐζήτει. καὶ ἀνέκραγεν πικρῶς λέγουσα Μὴ βιάσῃ τὴν ξένην,[10] μὴ βιάσῃ τὴν τοῦ θεοῦ δούλην.[11] Ἰκονιέων εἰμὶ πρώτη,[12] καὶ διὰ τὸ μὴ θέλειν με γαμηθῆναι Θαμύριδι, ἐκβέβλημαι τῆς πόλεως.[13] καὶ λαβομένη τοῦ Ἀλεξάνδρου[14] περιέσχισεν αὐτοῦ τὴν χλαμύδα καὶ περιεῖλεν αὐτοῦ τὸν στέφανον,[15] καὶ ἔστησεν αὐτὸν θρίαμβον.[16]

Translation

But at the same time that they were entering, a certain Syrian named Alexander, a leading member of the Antiochenes, having accomplished many matters in that city by all of his leadership seeing Thecla, he felt passionately for her, and attempted to persuade Paul with money and gifts. But Paul said, "I don't know the woman of whom you speak, nor is she mine. But he, having much power, embraced her in the city quarter. But she did not put up with it, but sought out Paul. And she cried out bitterly, "Do not force the stranger! Do not force the servant of God. I am a leading woman of the Iconians, and on account of my not wishing to marry Thamyris, I was cast out of the city." And having been taken by Alexander, she took hold of him by the mantle and she took his wreath, and she stood by him triumphant.[17]

4.1.1 Textual Notes

[1] *AAA* (253, notes on sect. 26; following Tischendorf's preference for manuscript *C*) has συριάρχης, (see *3.26.1 Textual Notes*, note 5), meaning "president of the provincial council of Syria." Against manuscript *C* is Cop[1], *A, B, E, F, G,* and *m*.

[2] Ἀντιοχέων πρῶτος – See *3.11.1 Textual Notes*, note 8. See Heliodorus *Aeth.*, 1.22.2. This is not found in *AAA*, 253, but is found in some Greek manuscripts. Cop[1] supports such a reading.

[3] πολλὰ ποιῶν ἐν τῇ πόλει ἐκείνῃ ἐν ὅλῃ τῇ ἀρχῇ αὐτοῦ – following Cop[1] (ⲉϥⲉⲓⲣⲉ ⲛ̄ϩⲁϩ ⲛ̄ϩⲱⲃ ⲋⲛ̄ ⲧⲡⲟⲗⲓⲥ ⲛ̄ⲛⲁⲣⲭⲱⲛ ⲧⲏⲣⲟⲩ), *F*, *G*, *m*, and *s*.

[4] Changed from ἐξελιπάρει (*AAA*, 253), based upon Cop[1].

[5] This passage continues the motif of the lovers (Paul/Christ and Thecla), who are forcefully separated based upon the heroine drawing attention from others by her beauty. See *3.26.2 General Comment*. See also Vorster's social analysis regarding whether or not Thecla "belongs" to Alexander or Paul. Yet, Vorster admits through Paul's denial of Thecla, "in a strange, ironic manner his actions confirmed her autonomy." ("Construction of Culture," 115).

[6] This has been grossly misinterpreted. Often this has been interpreted as the abandonment of Thecla by Paul. On the contrary, this is continuing to follow the motif of the ancient novel, when upon facing external pressures the lovers will often create some story in order to protect themselves from possible death or even worse problems, with the untruth possibly extending their time in order to discover a more appropriate response to the dilemma (see Heliodorus *Aeth.* 6.9.7). For instance, Theagenes and Charicleia tell everyone consistently throughout the Ethiopian Romance that they are brother and sister, in order to avoid the execution of Theagenes, and avoid the direct jealousy of those who have fallen passionately in love with their betrothed, such as is the case with Arsace. In fact, this is clearly explained as such by Charicleia, when speaking to Theagenes (Heliodorus, *Aeth.* 1.22.2–1.25.6; see also 7.12.7–7.13.1). This is the most likely explanation of Paul's behavior toward Thecla, although the telling of the story has been greatly abbreviated in comparison to the typical ancient novel. Compare also Abraham and Sarah, Gen 20:1–18 and Isaac and Rebehah in Gen 26:6–11. An alternative interpretation is that found visually, where Paul's "abandonment" of Thecla is borrowing from such images as the fresco of Aeneas abandoning Dido in Africa (See PPM 4.843–44; 6.240, 245; and 4.187, 279) or Theseus' abandonment of Ariadne (PPM 3.992 referring to a fresco in the Casa di M. Lucretius Fronto). From this perspective, one must realize that a contrast in these two abandonment episodes from the Thecla episode is that in the case of Aeneas, the story follows the male who founds Rome, while in the case of the *APTh*, the story follows Thecla, the female heroine. However it is possible that similar to the reversal and reinterpretation of the ancient romance "love" story, this is also a reversal. In particular a reversal of which "hero" is to be followed after the abandonment takes place. In one case, the story of the male hero is continued, while in the other case the story of the female heroine is continued.

[7] See *Jos. Asen.* 16.14, Codex *A* (BDAG, 804).

[8] See *AP* 4.11 (center of outrageous activity on the part of both Thamyris and Alexander, Thecla's two admiring adversaries. There are possible theological/sociological overtones regarding social boundaries that may be intended); Acts 19:28.

[9] See 2 Cor 11:1, 4, 19, 20; 2 Tim 4:3.

[10] Paul's anxiety (Ὁ δὲ εἶπεν Ὁ καιρὸς αἰσχρός, καὶ σὺ εὔμορφος· μὴ ἄλλος σε πειρασμὸς λήψεται χείρων τοῦ πρώτου, *AP* 3.25) for Thecla is now being realized. Now Thecla is the alien (important designation for the author of the *AP* and used in the ancient novel [see Heliodorus 7.11.7]; *AP* 3.8, 13, 19; 4.1, 3; see especially *3.13.1 Textual Notes*, note 8 for connections to the ancient novel), not Paul, and the threat extends beyond possible physical abuse, but also forced rape, which would compromise the integrity of Thecla's purity.

[11] τὴν τοῦ θεοῦ δούλην – Luke 1:38 (ἡ δούλη κυρίου); 48 (τῆς δούλης αὐτοῦ [in reference to θεῷ from the preceding line]). See also *APTh* 45 (3x); 4.12 (Thecla says εἰμι τοῦ ζῶντος δούλη); and 4.13. This seems to be somewhat of a specific formal title given to Thecla preceding her commission from Paul in 4.16 selected by Thecla first and finally recognized by the governor in 4.13.

[12] This claim of "I am first of the Iconiums" should have suggested to the governor that the execution of Thecla should have been something less degrading than *damnati ad bestias* (Coleman, "Fatal Charades," 55, footnote 105: This footnote references P. Garnsey, "Why penalties become harsher: the Roman case, late Republic to fourth century Empire," *Natural Law Forum* 13 (1968): 141–62, especially 20, note 72; and F. Millar, "Condemnation to hard labour in the Roman Empire, from the Julio-Claudians to Constantine," *PBSR* 52 (1984): 124–47, especially 134.), such as execution by beheading. For a plausible explanation of this more "aggravated" form of punishment, see *3.22.2 General Comment*.

[13] ἐκβέβλημαι τῆς πόλεως – This is a small detail that is not mentioned in the conclusion to the accounting of the events that took place in Iconium in 3.22–26.

[14] See 2 Tim 4:14.

[15] Knocking the crown off Alexander's head embodies a greater symbolic value than actually bringing any physical harm to Alexander. The loss of the symbol can carry the meaning of a loss of divinity (possibly intended by the author of the *AP* to demonstrate the inferiority of the "leading man" to the Christ), or the loss of honor/dignity (also intended here). See "στέφανος, ου, ὁ," BDAG, 943–44; Grundmann, "στέφανος, στεφανόω," *TDNT* 7:620–22, 29–36. For an early refutation of the wearing of crowns see Tertullian, *de Corona*. In the gospels, only Christ wears a crown, but only in mockery, see Matt 27:29; Mark 15:17; John 19:2, 5; *Gos. Pet.* 3.8.

142 Part II: Commentary

¹⁶ Text changed to manuscript *C* reading (περιεῖλεν αὐτοῦ τὸν στέφανον¹³, καὶ ἔστησεν αὐτὸν θρίαμβον) from preferred reading of *AAA*, 254 (supported by manuscripts *A, B, E, F, G*, and Latin, Syriac, and Armenian versions), τὸν στέφανον ἀφείλετο ἀπὸ τῆς κεφαλῆς αὐτοῦ, καὶ ἔστησεν αὐτὸν θρίαμβον, based on evidence of Cop¹ (ⲁⲅⲱ ⲁⲥϥⲓ ⲙ̄ⲡⲉϥⲕⲗⲁⲙ' ⲁⲥⲕⲁⲁϥ ⲉϥⲁⲛ̄ⲱ̄).

¹⁷ Schmidt, *Acta Pauli*, 44 translates this as "*(und) stellte ihn erstaunt (sprachlos) hin*;" while Rordorf, *ÉAC*, 1137, carries the connotations of the triumphal parade farther with their free translation (including ἀπὸ τῆς κεφαλῆς αὐτοῦ, either for clarification of meaning in the translation or in support of the alternate reading) that reads that "Thècle arracha la couronne de sa tête et l'exposa au mépris public." It is possible that the image of the triumph leading up to the spectacle is possibly connected to the procession of the prisoners (Kyle, *Sport and Spectacle,* 313); see also θρίαμβος (LSJ, 805; BDAG, 459) regarding connections between this triumph of Thecla to *one in a triumphal procession*, where it appears that Thecla is truly this conqueror, who is claiming the στέφανος as her own in this triumph (compare 2 Cor 2:14; Col 2:15; similar to the athlete who wears a στέφανος in Aelian, *Var. hist.* 2.41, 9.31; contrast 2 Tim 4.8 [!]).

4.1.2 General Comment

Contrast Thecla's bankrupt declaration in the present tense, "I am a leading woman of the Iconians" to her present circumstance. This desperate plea to her newly lost social designation adequately demonstrates Thecla's hesitancy to accept her newly suggested title of ξένη and the baggage that comes with the title (same for Paul, see note 10 above). It should also be noted that such a claim by Thecla ought to have led the governor not to condemn Thecla *ad bestias*, but rather to have allowed Thecla a more noble and respectable death of beheading which would have been less degrading for Thecla (See note above). In fact, even Paul is offered this form of execution in *AP* 14.5 under the wrath of Nero. Interestingly Paul is able to embrace the title for his advantage as one who lives by a different standard as advocated in the beatitudes. It is possible that Thecla is bearing out the exact course of action that Paul would have anticipated in 3.25–26, and Thecla appears not to be ready. At this point, Paul is in no position to make any change in circumstance against the leading man of the Antiochenes, namely Alexander. However, Paul's removal from the situation combined with Thecla's near inadequacy to bear the mark, via the title of a 'stranger,' is finally reaffirmed when Thecla embraces the title of ξένη. When this is happens, she is once again socially accepted into the role of a daughter to Queen Tryphaena by means of a vision of the Queen's dead daughter telling the Queen to embrace Thecla as her daughter. The effect of Thecla equating the two terms "stranger" and slave/servant of God" through her appeal for salvation from a rape, "Μὴ βιάσῃ τὴν ξένην, μὴ βιάσῃ τὴν τοῦ θεοῦ δούλην, is powerfully redefined first through the reaffirmation of her being "strange," yet very socially and spiritually alive and secondly through the formal designation that Thecla is pronounced "servant/slave of God" by the governor of Antioch. This proclamation eventuates in the completion of Thecla's conversion story and her commissioning and affirmation as prophetess *par excellence* with rights of apostolic authority to carry out the great commission of Jesus to "go and teach the word of God" (Matt 28:19–20/*AP* 4.16; See *4.15.2 General Comment*).

Thecla begins to realize her ability in the closing lines of this passage, in which she successfully knocks the crown/wreath of Alexander from his head. This symbol of dignity (and for Thecla a threat to her God), is removed from his head (ⲁⲅⲱ ⲁⲥϥⲓ ⲙ̄ⲡⲉϥⲕⲗⲁⲙ') and Thecla realizes the potential for a triumph over such threats as Thamyris and now Alexander. This is also a declaration that Thecla is truly the one deserving of the triumphal procession into Antioch as a heroine of the faith (2 Tim 4.8), as Thecla is not given a crown, but rather has to take hers. As the text continues, her dignity and right to the crown will be borne out.

4.2

Ὁ δὲ ἅμα μὲν φιλῶν αὐτήν, ἅμα δὲ καὶ αἰσχυνόμενος[1] τὸ γεγονὸς αὐτῷ, προσήγαγεν αὐτὴν τῷ ἡγεμόνι, κἀκείνης[2] ὁμολογησάσης ταῦτα πεπραχέναι κατέκρινεν αὐτὴν εἰς θηρία,[3] Ἀλεξάνδρου συλλαμβάνοντος.[4] αἱ δὲ γυναῖκες τῆς πόλεως[5] ἀνέκραξαν παρὰ τὸ βῆμα[6] Κακὴ κρίσις, ἀνοσία κρίσις.[7] Ἡ[8] δὲ ᾐτήσατο τὸν ἡγεμόνα ἵνα ἁγνή[9] μείνῃ μέχρις οὗ θηριομαχήσῃ.[10] γυνὴ δέ τις ὀνόματι Τρύφαινα[11] πλουσία,[12] ἧς ἡ θυγάτηρ ἐτεθνήκει, ἔλαβεν αὐτὴν εἰς τήρησιν, καὶ εἶχεν εἰς παραμυθίαν.

Translation

But he, on the one hand loving her, but at the same time also dishonored by the things that had happened to him, brought her before the governor, and when she had confessed to have done these things, he condemned her to the wild beasts, which had been brought together by Alexander. But the women of the city cried out before the bema, "Evil judgment! Profane judgment!" But Thecla asked the governor, if she might remain pure until she should fight with wild beasts. But a certain wealthy woman, named Tryphaena, whose daughter had died, received her into her keeping, and she held her in consolation.

4.2.1 Textual Notes

[1] See also *AP* 3.10 (ἅμα μὲν φιλῶν αὐτήν, ἅμα δὲ καὶ φοβούμενος τὴν ἔκπληξιν αὐτῆς). Alexander is filled with mixed emotions, similar to other examples in the ancient novel. For instance, see Heliodorus, *Aeth.*, 7.10.6 (love and jealousy). On αἰσχυνόμενος see also 3.10 (ἐπιστράφηθι πρὸς τὸν σὸν Θάμυριν καὶ αἰσχύνθητι).

[2] See *3.20.1 Textual Notes*, note 4.

[3] See Coleman, "Fatal Charades," 44–73; esp. 48–49; and *3.21.1 Textual Notes*, note 7. What is the crime of Thecla? It is spreading social discord and upsetting the moral and social fabric against the leading man of the city. This case necessitates a punishment that effects the "permanent removal of the offender from society" (Coleman, "Fatal Charades," 48; Seneca, *Clem.* 1.22.1) and also deters others from committing the same "crime." The governor's decision is not wholly supported by the populous, as is demonstrated in the next sentence and further in *AP* 4.3. The size of the crime is initially assessed by the governor on the grounds of an offense to a very public official. This in turn would necessitate the public demonstration of Thecla going before the populous in the ampitheater fighting against wild beasts.

[4] The addition of ʾΑλεξάνδρου συλλαμβάνοντος (or more precisely, παγιδεύοντος αὐτά [see Schmidt, *Acta Pauli*, 44]) is made based upon Cop[1] and the Latin manuscripts (*c*, *d*, and *m*) and the Syriac *s*[ac]. This small addition demonstrates that Alexander had been a *munerarius* (patron of the animals for the arena) within Antioch, and on this occasion, when he had been dishonored, he had legitimate influence to insist that the magistrates rectify the shaming that had been brought upon him. See Coleman, "Fatal Charades," 50–54. On Alexander as a patron, see note 11 below.

[5] Cut ἐξεπλάγησαν καί and replace with τῆς πόλεως based on Cop[1], against *A*, *B*, *E*, *F*, and *H*.

[6] or translated as "judgment seat." Cf. 3.15, 16, 20. See *3.16.1 Textual Notes*, note 2; see also *3.15.1 Texual Notes,* note 12; and *3.15.2 General Comment*.

[7] See Luke 23.18. The crowd has an active role in the trial as to whether the actions ought to be carried out or dismissed. This is common to the ancient novel. See Heliodorus, *Aeth.* 10.17.1; Chariton, *Chaer.* 3.4.11–18; Apuleius, *Metam.* 3.2–10.

[8] *AAA* also includes the name Thecla here, but is absent from Cop[1], which is the more difficult reading.

[9] See *3.6.2 General Comment*; and *3.12.1 Textual Notes*, note 5.

[10] See 1 Cor 15:32; *1 Clem* 6.2; Ignatius, *Romans*, 5.2.

[11] Romans 16:12. See Misset-Van de Weg, Magda, "II. A Wealthy Woman Named Tryphaena," 16–35; Dunn, "The *Acts of Paul*," 22; On

Tryphaena as first cousin to the emperor Claudius, see Gutschmid, Alfred von, "Die Königsnamen in den apokryphen Apostelgeschichten. Ein Beitrag zur Kenntnis des geschichtlichen Romans," *Rheinisches Museum für Philologie* 19 (1864): 161–83., 177–79; Zahn, Theodor, *Göttingische Gelehrte Anzeigen*, (1877), 1307; Ramsay, *The Church in the Roman Empire*, 391. Conybeare, F. C., ed., *The Apology and Acts of Apollonius,* 50–55; Rordorf, Willy, "Tradition and Composition in the *Acts of Thecla*," 46–47 or "Tradition et composition dans les *Actes de Thècle*: Etat de la question." *Theologische Zeitschrift* 41 (1985): 276–78. Moving beyond questions of historicity, on Tryphaena and Alexander as patron and patroness respectively, see Misset-Van de Weg, "Answers," 156–62.

[12] γυνὴ καί τις ⟨βασίλισσα⟩ πλουσία, ὀνόματι Τρύφαινα changed to γυνὴ δέ τις ὀνόματι Τρύφαινα πλουσία based upon Cop[1] and *B, E, F,* and *H.* See *AAA*, 255 and Schmidt, *Acta Pauli*, 45.

4.2.2 General Comment

As Thecla brings dishonor upon Alexander, she quickly realizes that there are consequences for bringing offence against the "leading man of the city," who is also a patron for the production and funding of the public games for the city. This consequently places him in a position to be able to hold an unusual amount of weight with the governor, who against the cries of the women of the city condemns Thecla to the beasts. This chapter brings us the second trial of Thecla at the judgment seat, but this time Thecla takes center stage from beginning to end. Paul's role is removed from this account (not uncommon in the ancient novels to highlight a narrative concerning only one of the actors in the story) as she presents a possible answer to Alexander.

One might notice that throughout the *AP* the crowd seems to play an important role in each of the trials that take place, especially with Thecla in Antioch and Iconium. The collaboration of the crowd in a trial is common within the ancient novel. But at a level beyond the ancient novel, one only has to witness the large events in theaters and stadiums (musical concerts, sporting events, etc.) today to realize that the activity and commotion of a crowd within a theater would have been an incredibly exciting event to participate in, and the author of the *AP* and the ancient novels are trying to pass on this common event and genre of antiquity that would have been a favorite activity for entertainment for the people of the ancient world. At an elementary level, the activity of the crowd and how they support and reject Thecla at different points can be easily understood in light of the shifts and changes expected of the mob mentality of the masses within the theater.

This chapter continues to follow closely after the pattern of the ancient novel in presenting Alexander as torn between jealousy and love, the subsequent trial, the intervention of the crying crowd, the continuation of the theme of virginity and purity, and the introduction of a counterbalance of patron Alexander in the form of Patroness Tryphaena. Here the struggle for survival, which appears always to be consistent in the ancient novel finds an unexpected salvation through a quite curious woman, Tryphaena.

There has been a considerable amount of discussion over the historicity of Tryphaena (see note 11 for further reading). While the possibility for a historical Tryphaena exists, it is unlikely that much may be said about her beyond the remains of a coin, and a reference to her here, which offers little about her other than an important role in a fictional Christian romance.

4.3

Ἡνίκα δὲ τὰ θηρία[1] ἐπόμπευεν,[2] προσέδησαν αὐτὴν λεαίνῃ πικρᾷ,[3] καὶ ἡ βασίλισσα Τρύφαινα ἐπηκολούθει αὐτῇ. ἡ δὲ λέαινα ἐπάνω καθεζομένης Θέκλης περιέλειχεν αὐτῆς τοὺς πόδας,[4] καὶ πᾶς ὁ ὄχλος ἐξίστατο·[5] ἡ δὲ αἰτία τῆς ἐπιγραφῆς[6] αὐτῆς ἦν αὕτη, Ἱερόσυλος.[7] αἱ δὲ γυναῖκες μετὰ τῶν τέκνων[8] ἔκραζον ἄνωθεν λέγουσαι Ὦ θεέ, ἀνοσία κρίσις γίνεται ἐν τῇ πόλει ταύτῃ.[9] Καὶ ἀπὸ τῆς πομπῆς πάλιν ἔλαβεν[10] αὐτὴν ἡ Τρύφαινα· ἡ γὰρ θυγάτηρ αὐτῆς Φαλκονίλλα ἡ τεθνεῶσα, καὶ κατ᾽ ὄναρ[11] εἶπεν αὐτῇ Μῆτερ, τὴν ξένην τὴν ἔρημον ὀνόματι[12] Θέκλαν ἕξεις εἰς τὸν ἐμὸν τόπον, ἵνα εὔξηται ὑπὲρ ἐμοῦ καὶ μετατεθῶ[13] εἰς τὸν τῶν δικαίων τόπον.

Translation

But at the time when the animals were being paraded out in a procession, they bound her to a fierce lioness, and Queen Tryphaena was following after her. But the lioness, whom Thecla was sitting upon, was licking her feet, and all the crowd was amazed. But the accusation of her inscription was this: Guilty of Sacrilege. But the women with their children, cried out from above saying "O God, a profane judgment has come into this city." And Tryphaena took her again from the procession. For her daughter Falconilla, who was dead, said to her in a dream, "Mother, the deserted stranger, named Thecla, you will take in my place, in order that she might pray on my behalf and I might be translated into the place of righteousness."

4.3.1 Textual Notes

[1] Fighting with wild beasts is centerpiece for the *APTh*, as well as the *AP* in general. In particular, the "beast fighting" takes place in Ephesus (as

told within the Hamburg papyrus) and in the *Acts of Thecla*. For the use θηρίον, τό and other derivatives from the θηρί- root (such as θηριομάχος or θηριομαχέω), see *APTh* 45 (2x) (from Codex *A*, *B*, and *C*); 4.2 (2x), 3, 4 (2x), 5, 6, 7, 9 (2x); 10 (3x), 11, 12 (3x), 13, 17; 9.14 (2x), 15 (2x), 16, 17, 19 (2x), 23, 25 (3x), and 28. This scene with Thecla in the arena with the wild beasts is what *1 Clem 6.2* and Ignatius, *To the Romans* 5.2 have in mind in their references.

[2] On the parade, see G. Ville, *La gladiature en Occident des origine à la mort de Domitien* (Rome: Ecole française de Rome, 1981), 364f.; S. R. F. Price, *Rituals and Power: The Roman Imperial Cult in Asia Minor* (Cambridge and New York: Cambridge UP, 1984), 110; Bremmer, "Magic, Martyrdom, and Women's Liberation," 53, footnote 59.

[3] For a suggested translation, see recommendation of BDAG, 813, following *NTApoc* 2:244.

[4] There is a possible connection between this passage and *AP* 3.18.

[5] Once again, the maiden Thecla is miraculously preserved through difficult tests. See *3.22.1 Textual Notes*, note 7.

[6] Cf. Mark 15:26 (Hills, "The Acts of the Apostles in the *Acts of Paul*," 36–37 gives this connection between Mark 15 and *AP* an "A" rating). See MacDonald, "Apocryphal and Canonical Narratives," 62. He argues for understanding the Apocryphal Acts within the framework of passion narratives. This is Thecla's (second) passion. See *AP* 3.22 and 10.4.6. The term ἐπιγραφή, meaning "description," carries a "legal sense" or legal description of a crime written on a placard (see Van den Hoek and Herrmann, "Thecla the Beast Fighter," 223–24).

[7] Literally, Thecla is a "temple robber" (LSJ, 822), but following the translation by Wilson of Schneemelcher, *NTApoc* 2:244, "Guilty of Sacrilege." There seems to be a deep disagreement as to who is acting appropriately in the presence of the gods, for the women and Tryphaena are accusing the governor (and Alexander) of an ἀνοσία κρίσις (profane judgment), while Thecla is being accused of profane *behavior*. As to the specific nature of Thecla's sacriligeous behavior, Jensen (*Thekla – die Apostelin: Ein apokrypher Text neu entdeckt: Übersetzt und kommentiert* [Freiburg, Basel, and Wien: Herder, 1995] 34) is helpful in making the connection to Jesus who was found guilty because of "seiner Kritik am Tempelkult." On the other hand her dismissal of the court charge as not applicable to Thecla (and thus representing "offensichtlich verschiedene Traditionen") overlooks the connections between the *APTh* and the ancient novel. The relationship between what is holy/profane and just/unjust are very closely related, as the Ethiopian King, Hydaspes struggles with whether or not he must offer up Charicleia to the gods. See especially chapter ten of Heliodorus, *Aeth.* Part of this is due to the uniform role of the governor/king/judge, who often meets out justice in the presence of the *daemon*

of Caesar or the equivalent thereof, thus the justice of the court represents the judgment of Caesar, who represents the justice of the gods. In the case of the *APTh*, the reader will soon be able to answer the question whether or not Alexander/Governor or Tryphaena is able to accurately determine what is profane, since God will intervene into this situation and determine that the judgment of the court is profane (4.8–11).

[8] See *3.11.1 Textual Notes*, note 6. The crying out of the women plays an important role in Antioch. See 4.2, here, 7, 8 (2x), 9, 10, and 13.

[9] Cf. the crowd crying out in *AP* 9.25–26.

[10] ἔλαβεν instead of λαμβάνει (Schmidt, *Acta Pauli*, 46.)

[11] See *4.1.2 General Comment*.

[12] ὀνόματι added upon the evidence of Cop[1].

[13] The meaning is somewhat unclear concerning the result that Falconilla desires. See Acts 7:16; Herm., *Vis.* 3.7.6; Heb 11:5; *1 Clem.* 9.3 (BDAG, 642). It appears that two things can be ascertained from the vision of Tryphaena. One, Thecla is deemed as worthy (via a divine vision) to be able to be a mediator between the human and the divine (in particular for Falconilla). This is an affirmation of Thecla's approval by God, in lieu of her present circumstances. Two, Falconilla desires to be in a place of justice, and somehow Thecla is able to assist in this *translation* from her present location to another. Unfortunately, very little is said concerning metaphysics by the author of the *AP*, so it is difficult to ascertain what sort of *translation* is envisioned, other than a very general image.

4.3.2 General Comment

As a procession of animals comes out, Thecla is immediately bound to a lioness. It is unclear whether or not this was intended to bring about the demise of Thecla right away or if Thecla is somehow bound to the lioness in such a way as to inhibit the lioness from hurting her yet. This may be the case due to the anticlimactic way in which 4.3 begins by talking about Thecla attached to the lioness, even before we are introduced to the inscription posted over Thecla (See Kyle, *Sport and Spectacle in the Ancient World*, 327–29). The future of Thecla and the events in Antioch from this point forward will continually foreshadow a better future, and a constant revealing and unveiling of the female apostle, "Thecla, servant of God." The lioness licks the feet of Thecla honoring her, not unsimilar to the talking lion who pays obeisance to Paul in the Ephesian episode (*AP* 9).

An inscription is placed over Thecla's head indicating that she (like the Christ) has profaned and shamed the temple cult. In the case of Christ, he called for a destruction of the temple. Is Thecla guilty of such a crime? Thecla has attempted to assume authority within the Christian movement that Paul has deemed inappropriate, but unfortunately for Thecla, her God-driven ambition is not to be realized within the ranks of the Christian movement alone, but applies to the elemental construction of the cosmos, and she immediately rejects the social hierarchy imposed upon her in Iconium, and even as an alien in Antioch she rejects the social advances of Alexander. This is nothing short of attempting to overthrow the social system (which is not to be dissected and differentiated from the spiritual, i.e. the temple *cultus* from an enlightened Cartesian perspective that separates body and soul, i.e. social and spiritual) and must be dealt with in the severest of methods: public death in the arena. Keeping with the ancient novel, the question is whether or not Thecla is truly sacrilegious and profane or whether there has been a reordering of the cosmos in favor of Thecla's actions (see note 6 above). The "yes" answer will continue to unfold.

4.4

῞Οτε δέ ἀπὸ τῆς πομπῆς[1] ἐλάμβανεν αὐτήν, ἅμα μὲν ἐπένθει ὅτι ἔμελλεν εἰς τὴν αὔριον θηριομαχεῖν,[2] ἅμα δὲ[3] καὶ στέργουσα[4] τὴν θυγατέρα αὐτῆς Φαλκονίλλα εἶπεν Τέκνον μου Θέκλα, δεῦρο πρόσευξαι ὑπὲρ τοῦ τέκνου μου, ἵνα ζήσεται·[5] τοῦτο γὰρ εἶδον ἐν ὕπνοις[6] δεύτερον ἤδη. ἡ δὲ θέκλα μὴ μελλήσασα ἐπῆρεν τὴν φωνὴν αὐτῆς καὶ εἶπεν ῾Ο θεὸς τῶν οὐρανῶν, ὁ υἱὸς τοῦ ὑψίστου,[7] δὸς αὐτῇ κατὰ τὸ θέλημα αὐτῆς, ἵνα ἡ θυγάτηρ αὐτῆς Φαλκονίλλα ζήσεται εἰς τοὺς αἰῶνας. καὶ ἀκούσασα ταῦτα[8] Θέκλης ἐπένθει ἡ Τρύφαινα[9] θεωροῦσα[10] τοιοῦτον κάλλος[11] εἰς θηρία βαλλόμενον.[12]

Translation

And when Tryphaena had received her from the procession, she was mourning because Thecla was about to fight the wild beasts in the morning, but at the same time loving her daughter Falconilla and said, "My child, Thecla, Come pray on behalf of my child, in order that she may live. For this I saw twice in a dream." But Thecla, without delay, lifted up her voice and said, "O God of the heavens, the son of the Most High, give to her according to her wish, in order that her daughter Falconilla might live forever." And having heard these things of Thecla, Tryphaena mourned seeing such a beautiful one being cast to the beasts.

4.4.1 Textual Notes

[1] See *AP* 4.3.

[2] See *4.3.1 Textual Notes*, note 1.

[3] ἅμα μὲν ... ἅμα δὲ – see 4.2; in reference to Alexander. Here the balancing of polarization in Tryphaena (mourning for Thecla/loving her dearly) is contrasted with that of Alexander (love/shame). This construc-

tion is also found in 3.10 in reference to Thamyris expressing his mixed emotions for Thecla as he feared her leaving him. This is typical of the ancient novel. See Heliodorus, *Aeth.* 7.18.2; Xenophon, *Ephesiaca* 5.4.7.

[4] This describes the love shared as in the love shared between parents and children. This is not homoerotic (LSJ, 1639). The term στέργω is absent in the New Testament and only here in *AP* (στοργή is in 3.19). Also ἐμπόνως ὡς which followed after στέργουσα has been cut from the text based on the omission found in *C F, H,* and Cop[1] (ⲚⲀⲈ ⲀⲚ ⲚⲈⲤⲘⲀⲈⲒⲈ ⲚⲦⲈⳠⲰⲈⲈⲢⲈ ⲪⲀⲖⲕⲰⲚⲒⲀⲀⲀ).

[5] εἰς τοὺς αἰῶνας is not in Cop[1], *A, B, F, H,* Latin A, B$_{ab}$, Syr., and Arm. texts. See Thecla's prayer a few lines down in 4.4, "...ἵνα ἡ θυγάτηρ αὐτῆς Φαλκονίλλα ζήσεται εἰς τοὺς αἰῶνας."

[6] In 4.3, the text says that Tryphaena had a vision/dream (ὄναρ), but here it is refered to as a ὕπνοις (sleep/dream). ὕπνος is also found in 4.10; 4.18, *APTh* 44; 9.19. This last example (9.19) includes a vision that comes in wakefulness as Paul prays for deliverance from a prison situation.

[7] Ὁ θεός τῶν οὐρανῶν, ὁ υἱὸς τοῦ ὑψίστου – see Cop[1], Latin versions (Schmidt, *Acta Pauli*, 46; Gebhardt, *Passio*, CI–CII). See *AP* 3.6 and see also *3.6.1 Textual Notes*, note 5; see especially Luke 6.35. This is a designation that goes back to the Hebrew Bible term אל עליון translated in the Septuagint as ὕψιστος. This term equates Jesus with the "Most High" God, namely Yahweh, the Father, the Creator of the Universe. This term is uncommon in the early Christianity outside of Gnostic circles; see *ATh* 39; 45; 49; 78; 150; *Martyrium Andreae* prius 14; Ignatius, the prescript to *Rom.* in reference to πατρὸς ὑψίστου καὶ ᾿Ιησοῦ Ξριστοῦ ("ὕψιστος," *TDNT* 8:614–20). See also Luke 1:32, 35, 76, 78; 2:14; 10:15, 19:38; 24:49; Acts 2:33; 5:31; 7:48; 13:17; 16:17.

[8] Changed from ταῦτα εἰπούσης to ἀκούσασα ταῦτα. See Schmidt, *Acta Pauli*, 47.

[9] On ἐπένθει ἡ Τρύφαινα see the first sentence of 4.4, ἅμα μὲν ἐπένθει ὅτι ἔμελλεν εἰς τὴν αὔριον θηριομαχεῖν. See also *4.5.1 Textual Notes*, note 6.

[10] Replace ἐπέχουσα (manuscript *A, C* and with Tischendorf and *AAA,* 257) with θεωροῦσα (with *F, H,* Cop[1] (ⲈⲤⲞⲰⳠⲦ'), and Schmidt, *Acta Pauli*, 47).

[11] Here the tragedy of "beauty and the beast" is carried out as the beauty, Thecla is cast to the beasts. This is reiterated in *AP* 3.25 and verbatim in 4.9, αἱ γυναῖκες καὶ πᾶς ὁ ὄχλος ἔκλαυσαν...ὅτι τοιοῦτον κάλλος φῶκαι ἔμελλον ἐσθίειν; see *4.9.1 Textual Notes*, note 10;.

[12] The structure of *AP* 4.4 is a chiasm. See *4.4.2 General Comment*. Obviously this will resurrect several text critical issues about this text, namely, there is some disagreement over whether δευτερον should be located where I have placed it above or before the name of Thecla. Also, εἰς τοὺς αἰῶνας appears after ζήσεται in two places according to several texts,

but appears only once after ζήσεται in only the second location according to Schmidt and Rordorf (against *AAA*). If the text is originally chiastic, it appears to make better sense that δεύτερον has been misplaced by latter scribal editing with the thought that visions "twice" told makes little sense, thus δεύτερον was relocated in order to identify Thecla as a second daughter (in agreement with 4.5). Also, a scribe could have accidentally recorded εἰς τοὺς αἰῶνας twice, while εἰς τοὺς αἰῶνας only appearing once is the more difficult reading.

4.4.2 General Comment

Upon the opening line of *AP* 4.4, Queen Tryphaena is taking Thecla out of the parade apparently in hopes of temporarily protecting Thecla from the wild beasts on the morrow. The most notable feature of this paragraph is that the chapter represents a chiastic structure. Notice closely:

A. Tryphaena receives Thecla, protecting her from the beasts
  B. Tryphaena mourns and loves her daughter (Thecla?)
   C. Tryphaena requests Thecla pray that Falconilla might live
    D. and D'. Tryphaena sees Falconilla in dream (twice)
   C'. Thecla prays on behalf of Tryphaena that Falconilla might live
  B'. Tryphaena mourns her daughter (Thecla?)
A'. Tryphaena releases Thecla, seeing her cast to the beasts.

The thrust of the structure is the vision that presents Tryphaena's daughter to her. D. is represented by stating τοῦτο γὰρ εἶδον ἐν ὕπνοις ... ἤδη. D'. is then represented by inserting that twice within the dream Tryphaena sees these things ὕπνοις δεύτερον ἤδη.

Regarding the content of 4.4, there does not appear to be any real attempt by Tryphaena to preserve Thecla from the oncoming events, but rather 4.4 seems to represent a literary device to demonstrate Tryphaena's concern, not necessarily for Thecla, but Thecla as a divine mediator to bring her daughter, Falconilla, eternal life. Tryphaena needs Thecla, because her daughter told her that Thecla had to mediate the situation to provide eternal life for Falconilla. This digression from the events of Thecla provides a brief window into the patroness who will continue to play a role in the coming chapters, as her visionary experiences clearly indicate that there is something "divine" within Thecla, but that is yet to be revealed. At this point, we are left helpless, after embracing the help of temporary refuge, and now witnessing passively (βαλλόμενον, a passive participle) Thecla being thrown to the beasts.

4.5

Καὶ ὅτε ὄρθρος[1] ἐγένετο, ἦλθεν Ἀλέξανδρος παραλαβεῖν αὐτήν, αὐτὸς γὰρ ἐδίδου τὰ κυνήγια,[2] λέγων πρὸς τὴν τρύφαιναν[3] Ὁ ἡγεμὼν κάθηται καὶ ὁ ὄχλος θορυβεῖ ἡμᾶς· δὸς ἀπαγάγω[4] τὴν θηριομάχον. ἡ δὲ Τρύφαινα, ἡ βασίλισσα,[5] ἀνέκραξεν[6] τὸν ἀλέξανδρον[7] ὥστε φυγεῖν αὐτὸν[8] λέγουσα· Φαλκονίλλης δεύτερον πένθος[9] ἐπὶ τὴν οἰκίαν μου γίνεται, καὶ οὐδεὶς ὁ βοηθήσων·[10] οὔτε τέκνα, ἀπέθανον γάρ,[11] οὔτε συγγενής,[12] χήρα γάρ εἰμι.[13] ὁ θεὸς Θέκλης τοῦ τέκνου μου, βοήθησον Θέκλη.[14]

Translation

And when morning was dawning, Alexander went to take her, for he was funding the games, saying to Tryphaena, "The Governor is sitting and the crowd is shouting for us. Give her (to me so that) I might carry off the beastfighter." But Tryphaena the queen cried out against Alexander so that he fled, and she said, "A second mourning of Falconilla has come upon my house, and there is no one helping; neither children, for they have died, not kinsperson, for I am a widow. The God of Thecla, my child, help (thou) Thecla".

4.5.1 Textual Notes

[1] See *3.15.1 Textual Notes*, note 4.

[2] ἐδίδου τὰ κυνήγια – literally "he was giving the hunt," but contextually, in light of the knowledge that he was providing for the games (*AP* 4.2) as the *munerarius* (See *4.2.1 Textual Notes*, note 4).

[3] λέγων πρὸς τὴν τρύφαιναν – based upon the Cop[1frag], and supported also by manuscripts *F* and *H*. Rordorf has "dit à Tryphaine" (*ÉAC*, 1138). The 1909 fragment that Schmidt published (discovered through the joint efforts of W. E. Crum), recovered the portion of the *AP* 4.5 through the last line of 4.8 conveniently filling in the missing section of Cop[1].

[4] ἀπαγάγω from the aorist active sunjunctive of ἀπάγω. See LSJ, 174, "2. law-term, *bring before a magistrate and accuse* (cf. ἀπαγωγή III)."

[5] ἡ βασίλισσα – supported Cop[1frag] and other Latin witnesses.

[6] See 3.20; 4.1, 2, and here. See *3.20.1 Textual Notes*, note 12.

[7] τὸν ἀλέξανδρον – supported by Cop[1frag], *F*, and *H*.

[8] Literally, "so as to flee him."

[9] See 3.10, 4.4 (2x), 8; 9.27 and *4.4.1 Textual Notes*, note 9.

[10] On βοηθέω, see *3.24.1 Textual Notes,* note 8.

[11] This is in reference to Falconilla (*AP* 4.3–4).

[12] See also *AP* 4.11.

[13] See Ramsay, *The Church in the Roman Empire*, 389. Ramsay argues that Tryphaena's claim to have no relatives is an exaggeration made in grief. This may be the case, but unlikely. It is not probable that Tryphaena's expression of grief would have anything to do with descendents, especially in terms of preservation of wealth or status. First, she was independently wealthy. Second, any fears of protection and care would be alleviated due to having sons. If she lost her daughter, there would have been no loss of status or protection, but rather a deep expression of sorrow would likely have been expressed in other words or other ways. While a connection to the historical Tryphaena of Pontus is possibly still intended by the author of the *AP*, the historicity and accuracy of detail is in doubt, being of secondary importance to the novel.

[14] On Tryphaena, the "widow's" prayer, see also Luke 2:37; 18:3; Acts 6:1; 9:39, 41; 1 Tim 5:3–16. The contrast of 1 Timothy and Luke-Acts is astounding in regard to the perspective of considering a "useful" role for widows. For possible connections, compare the examples groups of women/widows in Luke-Acts mentioned above to those in *AP* 4.8–9. See also Turid Karlsen Seim, *The Double Message: Patterns of Gender in Luke and Acts* (Nashville: Abingdon, 1994), 249–58.

4.5.2 General Comment

Upon the morning, following the mourning of Tryphaena, Alexander arrives, hoping to meet the deadline and expectations as a *munerarius*, hoping to please a waiting Governor and a shouting crowd. Clearly, Alexander is concerned more with the appeasement of a crowd than the perceived justice of shaming a rebellious girl. As he attempts to reclaim her, Tryphaena reacts violently crying out, and forcing Alexander to flee her house after demanding to have Thecla. The question of Tryphaena being a widow is inconsistent with historical evidence of the Tryphaena who was from Pontus. This offers support, not necessarily against the intentions of the author of the *AP* to make reference to the historical figure, but for the supposition of Davies (et. al.), who suggests that Tryphaena (and Thecla) are giving voice to women and virgins, so that it can be suggested that "Son Sitz im Leben est un mouvement d'émancipation feminine." (Rordorf, "Tradition et composition," 283; See also Davies, "Widows and the Apocryphal Acts," *The Revolt*, 70–94; Davies, "The Social World of the Apocryphal Acts." [Ph.D. diss., Temple University, 1978] 104–05; MacDonald, *The Legend*, 75–76). As Tryphaena sees no hope of deliverance, she is then led down a similar path as Thecla (and soon many others in Antioch) that concludes that God alone can save Thecla (and hence hope of eternal life for Falconilla).

4.6

Καὶ πέμπει ὁ ἡγεμὼν στρατιώτας ἵνα ἀχθῇ.[1] ἡ δὲ Τρύφαινα οὐκ ἀπέστη,[2] ἀλλὰ αὐτὴ λαβομένη τῆς χειρὸς αὐτῆς ἀνήγαγεν[3] λέγουσα Τὴν μὲν θυγατέρα μου Φαλκονίλλαν ἀπήγαγον εἰς τὸ μνημεῖον· σὲ δέ, Θέκλα, εἰς θηριομαχίαν[4] ἀπάγω.[5] καὶ ἔκλαυσεν Θέκλα πικρῶς[6] καὶ ἐστέναξεν πρὸς κύριον, λέγουσα Κύριε ὁ θεὸς[7] ᾧ ἐγὼ πιστεύω, ἐφ᾽ ὃν ἐγὼ κατέφυγα, ὁ ῥυσάμενός με ἐκ πυρός,[8] ἀπόδος μισθὸν Τρυφαίνῃ[9] τῇ εἰς τὴν δούλην[10] σου συμπαθησάσῃ, καὶ ὅτι με ἁγνὴν[11] ἐτήρησεν.

Translation

And the governor sent soldiers, so that they might take her. But Tryphaena did not shrink back, but having taken her hand, she led her up, saying "My daughter Falconilla has departed into the tomb; but you, Thecla, must go to fight the beasts." And Thecla was calling out bitterly and mourned to the Lord, saying, "Lord, God, in whom I believe, to whom I flee for refuge, the one who rescued me out of fire, reward Tryphaena, the one who has sympathized with your slave, and who has kept me pure.

4.6.1 Textual Notes

[1] Alexander sends reinforcements to take Thecla by force after having failed previously in 4.5.

[2] A form of ἀφίστημι is also found in 3.8, where Thecla cannot remove herself from the window, when listening to Paul. Here the form is passive, indicating a slightly different translation (LSJ, 291). Also, notice the repetition of the various verbs with the root ἄγω and the repetition of α-sounds. ἀπέστη, ἀλλά, αὐτή, …αὐτῆς, ἀνήγαγεν, …ἀπήγαγον …θηριομαχίαν ἀπάγω.

[3] Presumably handed her up/over to Alexander. Compare this to *AP* 4.16, λαβομένηος ὁ Παῦλος τῆς χειρὸς αὐτῆς; See note 4 below.

[4] See *4.3.1 Textual Notes*, note 1.

[5] Notice that Falconilla has been handed over (ἀπήγαγον) to the tomb; Thecla is handed over (ἀπάγω) to the beasts. This comparison of Thecla and Falconilla, with an emphasis upon life/eternal life (4.4 especially) reinforces the theological themes and the connections between purity and continence that lead to resurrection and eternal life. This thought is continued by extension to Falconilla, whom Tryphaena would like to see Thecla bring back.

If one continues this to completion, Paul receives Thecla by the hand (λαβομένηος ὁ Παῦλος τῆς χειρὸς αὐτῆς), in the same way she is received here by Tryphaena (αὐτὴ λαβομένη τῆς χειρὸς αὐτῆς) initially when she is finally able to teach those in the house of Hermias (4.16) mirroring

3.5, when Paul entered into the house of Onesiphorus to teach. The layering of images with deep theological significance is unmistakable.

[6] See 3.11; 4.1; 9.15; see also *3.11.1 Textual Notes*, note 2.

[7] This prayer is certainly directed toward the "Lord God," Jesus. See also 4.4, "God in the heavens, son of the most high."

[8] Here Jesus Christ, called the "Lord God," is credited with being the source of "rescue/salvation." In particular, a God who saves out of fire (See *AP* 3.22).

[9] See *4.14.1 Textual Notes*, note 4.

[10] See *4.1.1 Textual Notes*, note 11, and *4.1.2 General Comment*.

[11] See 4.2; See *3.6.2 General Comment*; and *3.12.1 Textual Notes*, note 5.

4.6.2 General Comment

In continuing to read the *APTh,* one cannot help but notice the multiple comparisons of various themes and individuals in the text. For example:

1. Thecla/Falconilla
2. Patron Alexander/Patroness Tryphaena
3. Thecla and life/ Falconilla and death
4. Acceptance and commission of Thecla as a teacher by Tryphaena / rejection and lack of commission of Thecla as a teacher by Paul

Numerous questions emerge based on these points. First, what is the significance of the death of Falconilla? Second, is it possible that Alexander is the suggested former lover of Falconilla in that she is the second child of Tryphaena, and she has become such a pivotal point of contention between two patrons of Antioch, who are escalating tensions between one another with Thecla in the midst, who is offering life eternal? It is possible that the connection between Thecla and Tryphaena will symbolize their unity in that they will both die and be born again during the trial with the beasts. Only after rebirth, Tryphaena seems to be the patroness of Thecla, but spiritually (and apologetically from the perspective of making a case for Thecline apostolic authority) Paul is the patron of Thecla. More will be said concerning this in the Notes and Comments of 4.16–17.

As the moment (where Thecla is to be thrown to the beasts) intensifies, we see Thecla offering up a prayer asking for the Lord Jesus to reward Tryphaena, who has helped "her servant" (τὴν δούλην σου). This appears to be somewhat of a title indicating the role that Thecla is assuming; see note 9 above. Thecla's prayer is motivated out of the basis that Tryphaena has assisted Thecla in preserving her virginity overnight, and thus preserving Thecla's possibility for eternal life. For after all, those who are not truly virgins cannot endure the tests placed upon them. This is also a common theme in the ancient novel (See Parthenius, *The Story of Pallene* 5–6; Achilles Tatius, *Leuc. Clit.* 8.3; 8.6; Heliodorus, *Aeth.* 10.7; 8.9.9–16; See *3.22.2 General Comment*).

4.7

Θόρυβος[1] οὖν ἐγένετό τε καὶ πάταγος τῶν θηρίων καὶ βοὴ τοῦ δήμου καὶ τῶν γυναικῶν[2] ὁμοῦ καθεσθεισῶν,[3] τῶν μὲν λεγόντων Τὴν ἱερόσυλον[4] εἰσάγαγε· τῶν δὲ λεγουσῶν ᾿Αρθήτω[5] ἡ πόλις ἐπὶ τῇ ἀνομίᾳ[6] ταύτῃ· αἶρε πάσας ἡμᾶς, ἀνθύπατε· πικρὸν[7] θέαμα, κακὴ κρίσις.[8]

Translation

Therefore there was an uproar from both the rumbling of the beasts and shouting of the people and of the the women who were sitting at the same place. Now some were saying, "Bring in the 'Sacrilegious One,'" while others were saying, "May the city be wiped out concerning this unlawful act. Wipe us all out, Proconsul. A bitter spectacle, evil judgment!"

4.7.1 Textual Notes

[1] See Callimachus, *Aetia (in P. Oxy 2079)*, 2079.3; "*noise, esp. the confused noise of a crowded assembly*...of animals (LSJ, 803–04); Aristophanes, *Lys.* 328–29. See also *AP* 4.5 (in reference to the crowd); see also 9.14 and 9.15. Interestingly in 9.14, the crowd is θόρυβος, causing the governor Hieronymus to throw Paul to the beasts, but 9.15 is similar to 4.7, in that the θόρυβος foreshadows the spectacle. See also *Mart. Pol.* 8.3.

[2] See *3.11.1 Textual Notes*, note 6; see also *4.3 Textual Notes,* note 7.

[3] Thecla has apparently entered into the theatre (τὸ θέατρον). This is the second instance of Thecla entering into trial in the theater (Coleman, "Fatal Charades," 51–52). See 3.20, 21 and also in the *Ephesian Episode*, 9.14. A significant difference between the two occasions is that Thecla enters into the trial in Antioch with massive support among the δῆμος, especially among the woman (γυναικες here, See note 2).

[4] This designation is referring back to the slogan that has been placed with (?) her. See also *4.3 Textual Notes,* note 5. It is unclear on what material the inscription and accusation would have been made, much less where it would have been placed. Placing it near her seems to be merely a borrowing from the Gospel accounts of Jesus, who had the inscription placed on his cross (John 19:19).

[5] ᾿Αρθήτω is the aorist imperative of ἀείρω (LSJ, 27), meaning *raise up, lift*, in this case *to destroy*.

[6] Notice that the response of the crowd *against* the judgment of the governor is the opposite response of Theocleia in *AP* 3.20. *AP* 9.17 (14.4 also) seems to be somewhat of a dialogue on 4.7, with regard to Paul addressing the sentiment of the crowd and what he seems to believe is also the result desired by God on the unrighteous acts of humans. See also 13.5 (2x), 10.2.8; Manuscript *G* (2x). Lawnessness is consistently connected to the destruction of the world.

[7] See *AP* 3.6!

[8] See *AP* 4.2.

4.7.2 General Comment

As Thecla enters into the theater, the events appear very similar in many respects to the episode that takes place with Paul in Ephesis (*AP* 9). There are several similarities in events and language between these two cases where the heroine and the hero have trials with lions respectively. In both cases, the lioness, and then the lion turn out to be advocates instead of adversaries to Thecla, and then Paul. In the first case the lioness protects Thecla, and in the second case, Paul has a conversation with the lion, which Paul had baptized on an earlier occasion. Nonetheless, Thecla enters into a theater that is embracing the situation in a very mixed way. It appears that the anticipation and excitement of the theater may be an unwelcome event according to the mass of the people. The split crowd is crying for both the destruction of Thecla and the destruction of the city for an unjust decision. The apocalyptic overtones in the chants of the crowd, who are in support of Thecla, seem to suggest that the question of theodicy has been raised, and it is undecided whether or not a trial, *via* public execution and spectacle for the crowd is warranted. If it is not, then the crowd calls for divine intervention with language used throughout the remainder of the *AP* in an apocalyptic sense (see *Textual Notes*, note 6). This issue is somewhat acute considering that the legal justification for a public spectacle within the theater is dependent upon the nature of the crime and the demand of the *demos* for such trial (Coleman, "Fatal Charades," 54–55, 57–58). This consensus seems to be lacking here. As the *APTh* have continued, Thecla's social approval has gone from good standing to complete social death to a continual rise and restitution of her role and shame in society. This will be completely tested in the coming chapters.

4.8

'Η δὲ Θέκλα ἐκ χειρὸς Τρυφαίνης ληφθεῖσα[1] ἐξεδύθη καὶ ἔλαβεν διαζώστραν[2] καὶ ἐβλήθη εἰς τὸ στάδιον.[3] καὶ λέοντες καὶ ἄρκοι[4] ἐβλήθησαν ἐπ' αὐτήν. καὶ

πικρὰ λέαινα⁵ προσδραμοῦσα εἰς τοὺς πόδας αὐτῆς ἀνεκλίθη·⁶ ὁ δὲ ὄχλος τῶν
γυναικῶν ἐβόησεν μέγα.⁷ καὶ ἔδραμεν ἐπ' αὐτὴν ἄρκος· ἡ δὲ λέαινα δραμοῦσα
ὑπήντησεν καὶ διέρρηξεν τὴν ἄρκον. καὶ πάλιν λέων δεδιδαγμένος⁸ ἐπ'
ἀνθρώπους ὃς ἦν Ἀλεξάνδρου⁹ ἔδραμεν ἐπ' αὐτήν· καὶ ἡ λέαινα συμπλέξασα τῷ
λέοντι συνανηρέθη.¹⁰ μειζόνως δὲ ἐπένθησαν αἱ γυναῖκες,¹¹ ἐπειδὴ καὶ ἡ βοηθὸς
αὐτῇ λέαινα ἀπέθανεν.¹²

Translation

But Thecla, who had been taken out of the hands of Tryphaena, was
stripped and she received underpants and was cast into the stadium. And
lions and bears were cast upon her, and a ferocious lion, running toward
her lay down at her feet. But the crowd of women cried out greatly. And a
bear ran upon her; but the lioness, while running, came and tore the bear
apart. And again a lion which had been trained (to fight) against humans,
which belonged to Alexander, was running upon her. And the lioness having engaged the lion was destroyed with it. But the women mourned even
more, since even her assistant, the lioness had died.

4.8.1 Textual Notes

¹ ἐκ χειρὸς Τρυφαίνης ληφθεῖσα – genitive absolute.

² This is probably intended to be quasi-erotic (unlike *AP* 3.22 and Acts
16:22 which do not emphasize nakedness as found here in 4.8–12). For a
comparison in other ancient (Christian) novels, see *AJ* 70–74. For other
examples of erotic displays and exhibitions within the amphitheater or
theater, see K. M. Coleman, "Launching into History: Aquatic Displays in
the Early Empire," *The Journal of Roman Studies* 83 (1993): 64–65. See
also Martial, *Spec.* 26; John Chrysostom, *Hom. Matt.* 7.6; and Catullus
64.14–18. See also Jan N. Bremmer, "III. Magic, martyrdom and women's
liberation in the Acts of Paul and Thecla," *Apocryphal Acts of Paul and
Thecla*, 53; and *Passio Perpetuae 20.2*. In addition, Thecla's being given
διαζώστραν as a present form of bodily protection (hardly protective in this
case) will soon be contrasted with the fact that God will engulf her and
protect her with fire (καὶ ἦν περὶ αὐτὴν νεφέλη πυρός, *AP* 4.9; *4.9.1 Textual
Notes*, note 13; see Plutarch, *Brut.* 31, where the city is metaphorically
"engulfed" in flames [LSJ, 394]).

³ τὸ στάδιον – "i.e. in the amphitheatre." (LSJ, 1631). See *CIG* 4377.

⁴ The beasts (θηρίον, τό) are further specified. See *4.3.1 Textual Notes*,
note 1. In addition to the bears and lions (plural), a lioness had already
been mentioned in *AP* 4.3.

⁵ See *AP* 4.3; *4.3.1 Textual Notes*, note 2.

⁶ ἀνακλίνω is the same verb used when one is reclining at table, the typical posture for meals in the symposium. See Luke 12:37; Mark 6:39; Plu-

tarch, *Mor.* 157D; 704D; "συμπόσιον, τό," (BDAG, 959). Here the lioness is reclining at Thecla's feet. It is uncertain whether or not this is the same lioness. The text does not specify (πικρὰ λέαινα has no article). This is similar to Daniel 6:18–23. However, sitting at Thecla's feet is a demonstration of the Thecla discipling the lioness. Compare 3.18 (Thecla before Paul), 9.17 (Artemilla before Paul), 9.23 (Lion before Paul; ὁ λέων...ἦλθε δρομέως καὶ ἀνεκλίθη παρὰ τὰ σκέλη τοῦ Παύλου ὡς ἀμνὸς...).

⁷ See *3.11.1 Textual Notes*, note 6; see also *4.3 Textual Notes,* note 7. Concerning the role of these women and issues of women's liberation, see Jan N. Bremmer, "Magic, martyrdom and women's liberation," 36–59, see especially 51. See also Bremmer, "Women in the *Apocryphal Acts of John,*" *The Apocryphal Acts of John,* (Jan N. Bremmer, ed.; Kampen: Kok Pharos, 1995), 37–56; and D. Potter, "Martyrdom as Spectacle," *Theater and Society in the Classical World* (ed. R. Scodel; Ann Arbor: University of Michigan, 1993), 53–88. See also Davies, *Revolt of the Widows,* 60–61.

⁸ δεδιδαγμένος – This is the perfect passive participle, nominative masculine singular of διδάσκω.

⁹ The text is making it very clear that Alexander, the *munerarius,* is financially responsible for this event and the lions that are being sent against her. The proconsul is not being blamed for these events, but rather Alexander. See also See 4.2 (*4.2.1 Textual Notes,* note 4), 5 (*4.5.1 Textual Notes,* note 2).

¹⁰ συναινηρέθη – this is the second aorist passive indicative of συναναιρέω. The text is suggesting that the lioness counter attacks the lion that has been set against Thecla, and both die together in the struggle, thus preserving Thecla.

¹¹ μειζόνως δὲ ἐπένθησαν αἱ γυναῖκες – see 4.4 (2x), 4.5, especially *4.5.1 Textual Notes,* note 6. See also note 7 above concerning the role of the women in this public spectacle.

¹² It appears that the lioness is playing the role of a steward/assistant to a soldier in battle. See Herodotus 5.77; 6.100; *POxy* 1469.10 (See LSJ, 320).

4.8.2 General Comment

As the rosy fingers of dawn reach over the world in Antioch, Thecla is taken from Tryphaena for *damnati ad bestias* (See Coleman, "Fatal Charades," 44–73; Bremmer, "Magic, martyrdom and women's liberation," 36–59, see especially 53). She is immediately humiliated and stripped of all clothing except for an undergarment given to her and then cast into the stadium. The details of the event suggest that Alexander is specifically bringing together this public spectacle of the destruction of Thecla. This is historically problematic for several reasons. First, it is unlikely that a spectacle would be called together so quickly for the sole purpose of the execution of one "criminal." Executions, especially of this scale would have taken extensive planning, and included many animals and unimportant criminals. Secondly, it is doubtful that the killing of Thecla would have been the climax of the spectacle. This is reinforced by Coleman who states that "There is some evidence that those who were *damnati ad bestias* were dispatched in the arena during the midday pause between the morning's *venations* and the afternoon's *munera*. This pause seems to have been observed regularly from the time of Claudius onwards (Suet[onius]. *Claud.* 34.2):" ("Fatal Charades," 55).

Apparently, once again, the historicity of this event is not the matter under consideration. There are several other theological issues that are under consideration here. First, it is clear that this execution is primarily due to the work of the patron and *munerarius* Alexander who is attempting to defame and humiliate Thecla, and then execute her in a degrading and harsh way. But as the lions and bears are released, it is Thecla's helper (ἡ βοηθὸς αὐτῇ), the lioness, who specifically wards off Alexander's lion (λέων δεδιδαγμένος ἐπ᾽ ἀνθρώπους ὃς ἦν Ἀλεξάνδρου). At this point, the women are beginning to wager an even greater voice (specifically mentioned in 4.8 twice) in the rejection of the spectacle that is taking place, yet by the end of 4.8 the outcome is not yet decided. This is demonstrated by the result that neither Thecla's lioness or Alexander's lion is successful in winning the engagement, but rather both die in the confrontation.

4.9

Τότε εἰσβάλλουσιν πολλὰ θηρία,[1] ἑστώσης[2] αὐτῆς καὶ ἐκτετακυίας τὰς χεῖρας καὶ προσευχομένης.[3] ὡς δὲ ἐτέλεσεν τὴν προσευχήν, ἐστράφη καὶ εἶδεν ὄρυγμα μέγα πλῆρες ὕδατος,[4] καὶ εἶπεν Νῦν καιρὸς λούσασθαί με. καὶ ἔβαλεν ἑαυτὴν εἰς τὸ ὕδωρ λέγουσα Ἐν τῷ ὀνόματι Ἰησοῦ Χριστοῦ[5] ὑστέρᾳ ἡμέρᾳ[6] βαπτίζομαι[7]. Καὶ ἰδοῦσαι αἱ γυναῖκες καὶ πᾶς ὁ ὄχλος ἔκλαυσαν λέγοντες[8] Μὴ βάλῃς ἑαυτὴν εἰς τὸ ὕδωρ, ὥστε καὶ τὸν ἡγεμόνα δακρῦσαι,[9] ὅτι τοιοῦτον κάλλος[10] φῶκαι[11] ἔμελλον ἐσθίειν. ἡ μὲν οὖν ἔβαλεν ἑαυτὴν εἰς τὸ ὕδωρ ἐν τῷ ὀνόματι Ἰησοῦ Χριστοῦ·[12] αἱ δὲ φῶκαι πυρὸς ἀστραπῆς φέγγος ἰδοῦσαι νεκραὶ ἐπέπλευσαν. καὶ ἦν περὶ αὐτὴν νεφέλη πυρός,[13] ὥστε μήτε τὰ θηρία ἅπτεσθαι αὐτῆς, μήτε θεωρεῖσθαι αὐτὴν γυμνήν.[14]

Translation

Then they sent in many wild beasts, while she stood and extended her hands and was praying. But as she was completing the prayer, she turned and saw a great ditch full of water, and said "Now is time for me to wash myself." And she cast herself into the water, saying, "In the name of Jesus Christ I baptize myself for the last day." And looking on, the women and all the crowd cried out saying "Do not cast yourself into the water," so that even the governor was weeping, because seals were about to eat her. But Thecla therefore cast herself into the water in the name of Jesus Christ. But the seals looking upon a light of fiery lightning floated up as corpses. And there was a cloud of fire around her, so that neither the beasts could touch her, nor could they see her naked.

4.9.1 Textual Notes

[1] See for more discussion on the θηρία, see *4.3.1 Textual Notes*, note 1.

[2] Cop[1] begins again here as a fragmented text. The text broke off at the conclusion to *AP* 4.4 (See Schmidt, *Acta Pauli*, 47, 16*) and begins here following ἑστώσης.

[3] This description of Thecla standing, raising her hands, and praying, appears to be the same as the archaeological evidence of that found in the catacombs of the "praying orantes." For several examples from the catacomb of St. Callistus in Rome, see Antonio Baruffa, *The Catacombs of St. Callixtus: History, Archaeology, Faith*, (trans. William Purdy; Vatican City: Libreria Editrice Vaticana, 2000), 37, 81, 84, 110. The implications of this are not that Thecla is lost in prayer alone, but rather that her soul is in a state of bliss and contentment, as if she is already dead, and oblivious of the events surrounding her. See also figures 7–11 in Stephen J. Davis, *The Cult of Saint Thecla: A Tradition of Women's Piety in Late Antiquity* (Oxford: Oxford UP, 2001), 215–219, where the praying Orans, Thecla, became a prominent Christian symbol in later centuries.

[4] It is unclear whether or not the ditch (*trench or moat*, LSJ, 1257) full of water was always there within the amphitheater, or whether it miraculously appears. Part of the problem is that Thecla does not state what events took place within her prayerful state. Apparently something became clear within the prayer, and it almost seems that Thecla turns and realizes that there is now water near her. On the other hand, looking further ahead in 4.9 one realizes that there were seals within the water, suggesting that Thecla simply has some type of vision or message from God making the decision for baptism clear. See also Dunn, "The *Acts of Paul*," 66–67; Barrier, "Tertullian and the Acts of Paul or Thecla?". Regarding Aquatic displays, see K. M. Coleman, "Launching into History," 48–74.

[5] Ἐν τῷ ὀνόματι Ἰησοῦ Χριστοῦ – "In the name of Jesus Christ" also found in Herm, *Vis.* 3.7.3; Origen, *Comm. Rom.* 5.8. Contrast βαπτίζοντες αὐτοὺς εἰς τὸ ὄνομα τοῦ πατρὸς καὶ τοῦ υἱοῦ καὶ τοῦ ἁγίου πνεύματος (Matt 28:19; Acts 2:38, 3:6, 8:12, 10:48, 15:26, 16:18; without Χριστοῦ Acts 4:18, 8:16, 9:27, 19:5, 13, 17, 21:13, 26:9; *Did.* 7.1).

[6] A possible relationship exists between 1 Tim 4:1 and this text in the
APTh. ὑστέρᾳ ἡμέρᾳ – 1 Tim 4:1; See "ὕστερος, α ον," BDAG, 1044, 2.b.a;
i.e. Judgment Day. This is supported by Cop[1] (ⲅⲁⲉ – Crum, *Coptic Dictionary*, 635).

[7] This is self-baptism. See Dunn, "The *Acts of Paul*," 66, footnote 46
and the reference to Lampe, "βαπτίζω," *Patristic Greek Lexicon*, (Oxford:
Clarendon Press, 1961), 283, II.C.2.c.ii [correction from Dunn's identification as II.B.ii.], which states that the "use of med. Indicates self-baptism in
case of Thecla . . . but this case recognized as exceptional and highly irregular." Lampe lists one other source, namely Basil of Seleucia (now believed to be Pseudo-Basil [see Scott Fitzgerald Johnson, *The Life and
Miracles of Thekla: A Literary Study,* (Cambridge: Harvard UP, 2006), 6–
7; and Dagron, *Vie et Miracles de Sainte Thècle*,13–15,]), *Life and Miracles of Thecla*, 1. Thecla's self-baptism is definitely a unique situation (See
also *NTApoc* 2:221). Dunn's arguments on linguistic grounds for hesitancy
to translate βαπτίζομαι in the middle voice are strong, based on a lack of
specificity in the *APTh* and based upon the rarity of the use of the middle
over the passive. However, the fact that the text twice says that she cast
herself (βάλης ἑαυτήν...ἔβαλεν ἑαυτήν) into the water clearly indicates that
Thecla immersed herself in the water. Even if one insisted upon a passive
translation of the verb here, the text still indicates that Thecla threw herself
into the water unassisted. To close the matter, Thecla states also that she
will "wash herself" (λούσασθαί) clearly in the middle voice. The context
surrounding βαπτίζομαι is decisive for determining the voice here.

[8] Cop[1] fragmented page 23 breaks off here.

[9] The text further indicated the one who should be held responsible for
the spectacle involving Thecla. Namely this is Alexander, and not the governor, who is now crying for Thecla. See *4.8.2 General Comment*.

[10] See τοιοῦτον κάλλος also in 4.4 as Tryphaena mourned over "such a
beautiful one" being thrown to the beasts. Κάλλος also describes Artemilla
in 9.17, who is a convert to Paul in Ephesus. See also, *4.4.1 Textual Notes*,
note 11 below.

[11] See Calpurnius Siculus, 7.65–66 (discussion found in Coleman,
"Launching into History," 48–74); Peter Robert Lamont Brown argues that
these are sharks in *The Body and Society: Men, Women, and Sexual Renunciation in Early Christianity* (New York: Columbia UP, 1988), 158;
For seals, see Bruno Lavagnini, "S. Tecla nella vasca delle foche e gli
spettacoli in acqua," *Byzantion* 33 (1963) 185–90. Bremmer, "Magic, Martyrdom, and Women's Liberation," 54, decides on seals (see note 64 also);
For more on "ferocious" seals see Ingvild Sælid Gilhus, *Animals, Gods,
and Humans: Changing Attitues to Animals in Greek, Roman, and Early
Christian Ideas* (New York: Routledge, 2006), 192–5; Janet Elizabeth
Spittler, "Wild Kingdom: Animals in the Apocryphal Acts of the Apostles"

(Ph.D. diss., The University of Chicago, 2007), 225–54, especially 253–4 on seals; and Horst Scheider, "Thekla und die Robben," *VC* 55.1 (2001): 45–57.

[12] ἡ μὲν οὖν ἔβαλεν ἑαυτὴν εἰς τὸ ὕδωρ ἐν τῷ ὀνόματι Ἰησοῦ Χριστοῦ carries two meanings. On the one hand, Thecla casts herself into the water, but at a deeper level, this is written in such a way to clearly indicate that Thecla is baptizing herself (against Dunn, "The *Acts of Paul*," 64). This answers the question of passive or middle deponent of βαπτίζομαι, in favor of the middle voice. See note 7 above. See also Tertullian, *Bapt.* 17 (similar to *Didascalia* 15) for a response to this text by Tertullian who takes issue with Thecla's baptizing (See notes by Evans, *Tertullian's Homily on Baptism*, 100–01). See Barrier, "Tertullian and the Acts of Paul or Thecla?", that argues that Tertullian is concerned that the *APTh* shows Paul endorsing Thecla's self-baptism, which is a divine commission from God to "Go and teach the Word of God." (4.16) and this is endorsed by Paul in the text.

[13] The cloud hides her nakedness (See Didascalia 16). This appears to be the divine intervention of God using OT imagery. See Exodus 13:21 and Ezekiel 1:4. An important distinction from the LXX texts and the *AP* is that in the *AP* you have a νεφέλη πυρός, but in the LXX Exodus it is a *pillar/column* of cloud by day and a pillar of fire by night (στῦλος τῆς νεφέλης ἡμέρας καὶ ὁ στῦλος τοῦ πυρὸς νυκτός). It is possible that the *AP* is drawing a connection between this text and Acts 2:3 and the Holy Spirit coming upon the apostles with γλῶσσαι ὡσεὶ πυρὸς being present.

[14] See Hippolytus, *Trad. Ap.* 22, where such great care is taken to preserve and protect the newly baptized individual, who was believed to be under immediate threat by the Devil. Thecla is being protected in the same way here.

4.9.2 General Comment

This chapter focuses in upon the baptism of Thecla. The chapter begins with Thecla who is naked standing in the posture of the praying orans before her baptism and wild beasts are ready to attack her. The chapter ends with Thecla's nakedness hidden by God after her baptism and the wild beasts are either dead or cannot see her. The ceremonial rite of baptism is adhered to in this text in a way that is similar to didactic texts that address the process of baptism (see note 14 in *3.25.1 Textual Notes*). First, those who are being initiated into Christ will devote themselves to prayer. Then they will step into the water, naked, and the presbyter will baptize them in the name of Jesus Christ (Tertullian, *Bapt.* 17 and Hippolytus, *Trad. ap.* 21), then they will be covered and protected, and given a seal through the application of an ointment or water to complete the sealing of the Holy

Spirit. Twice within this chapter Thecla declares "In the name of Jesus Christ I cast myself into the water." The key feature missing in these baptisms is the presbyter. It appears that Thecla foregoes the necessity of the presbyter, and yet paradoxically God sends several divine signs to suggest that this has been sanctioned by God. It is not God who does the baptizing, but rather after Thecla baptizes herself God provides several evidences that God does approve of these events. The implications of this self-baptism are far reaching. It is near to the close of the *Acts of Paul and Thecla* that these potentialities are explored (see note 11 above). Thecla has been sealed in Christ without the (previously thought) necessary apostolic sanctioning, but rather is directly selected by God. This is no different than the calling of Paul and the other apostles (Acts 2 – tongues of fire, see note 12 above). The implications of this are that Thecla has the authority by God to teach and in 4.16, Paul can do nothing but sanction what God has already sanctioned (Acts 10:44–48). At this point, it finally becomes clear that this story that began in Iconium has steadily been climaxing as the apostle Paul has faded, while Thecla's role and development as an apostle of God has continued to increase eventuating in the baptism of Thecla and the seal finally being granted. The climactic story will not end yet, but will continue to develop further in the remaining chapters.

Outside of the theological framework one will notice that the historical representation of Thecla's theatrical event lacks some detail. First, it would have been unlikely that Thecla's death could have brought the population of Antioch together just to see her fight against the beasts, as well as an aquatic exhibition. This would have been very costly. In addition, Thecla's death by animals would have been an anticlimactic death during an intermission between the real spectacles (See *4.8.2 General Comment*). The aquatic display, absent at first, almost miraculously appears and Thecla is prepared to jump in, in spite of the imminent threat of death by the seals. The reinactement of the mythological themes lacks detail in this account. There may be none, but it is unlikely that there would not have been some historical or mythological "narrative" being presented within such an expensive and costly *munerarii* and the *naumachia* that follows.

4.10

Αἱ δὲ γυναῖκες[1] ἄλλων θηρίων[2] βαλλομένων φοβερωτέρων ὠλόλυξαν,[3] καὶ αἱ μὲν ἔβαλλον φύλλον,[4] αἱ δὲ νάρδον, αἱ δὲ ἄμωμον, αἱ δὲ κασίαν,[5] ὡς εἶναι πλῆθος μύρων.[6] πάντα δὲ τὰ βληθέντα θηρία ὥσπερ ὕπνῳ κατασχεθέντα οὐχ ἥψαντο αὐτῆς·[7] ὡς τὸν Ἀλέξανδρον εἰπεῖν τῷ ἡγεμόνι Ταύρους[8] ἔχω λίαν φοβερούς, ἐκείνοις προσδήσωμεν τὴν αὐτήν.[9] καὶ στυγνάσας ἐπέτρεψεν[10] λέγων Ποίει ὃ θέλεις. Καὶ ἔδησαν αὐτὴν[11] ἐκ τῶν ποδῶν μέσον τῶν ταύρων, καὶ ὑπὸ τὰ ἀναγκαῖα[12] αὐτῶν πεπυρωμένα σίδηρα ὑπέθηκαν, ἵνα πλείονα ταραχθέντες ἀποκτείνωσιν[13] αὐτήν. οἱ μὲν οὖν ἥλλοντο· ἡ δὲ περικαιομένη φλὸξ[14] διέκαυσεν τοὺς κάλους, καὶ ἦν ὡς οὐ δεδεμένη.

Translation

But while even more fearful wild beasts were being sent out, the women cried out with a loud voice, and they cast herbs and spices, nard, cassius, amomum, so that there was an abundance of ointments. And all the wild beasts, which had been sent out, did not touch her just as if they had been withheld by a sleep. So Alexander said to the governor, "I have very fearful bulls, We should bind her to these." And dejectedly he permitted it, saying, "Do what you wish." And he bound her from the feet to the midst of the two bulls and he placed a flaming hot iron under their genitals, in order that by being stirred up more they might kill her. Therefore, they leapt up, but the flame inflaming itself burned through the good ropes, and it was as if she had not been bound.

4.10.1 Textual Notes

[1] See *4.3.1 Textual Notes*, note 8. This is similar to the death of Perpetua and Felicita, and the crowd cannot persuade the rulers (*Passio Perpet. Et Felic.* 20.2).

[2] See *4.3.1 Textual Notes*, note 1 for more discussion on the θηρία.

[3] ὠλόλυξαν, aorist activie indicative from ὀλολύζω (Lat. *Ululātiōn-, ululātio*; Eng. Ululate [verb] or ululation [noun]) meaning *cry out with a loud voice*; this is a bacchic, frenzied crying and wailing, probably reaching a point near pandemonium in the arena. In Euripides, *Bacch.* 689, a herdsman messenger brings a report to Penthius, king of the land of Thebes concerning the bacchant women (including his mother) he saw in the fields at day break and he states ἡ σὴ δὲ μήτηρ ὠλόλυξεν ἐν μέσαις σταθεῖσα Βάκχαις ἐξ ὕπνου κινεῖν δέμας...; "...later, mostly of women *crying* to the gods..."; ("ὀλολύζω," LSJ, 1217); see also Isaiah 16:7 and Amos 8:3 (LXX); Jas 5:1.

[4] This could be *leaves, plants, foliage, herbs*, or petals. Schneemelcher (*NTApoc* 2:245), and Elliott (*ANT* 370) following Schmidt (Blätter [this is not based on Cop[1], which is too fragmented]) has petals, but Rordorf suggests a better translation of *aromates* (*ÉAC*, 1140) indicating that these are ointments and oils following the baptismal rites.

[5] ἄμωμον and κασίαν switched according to the evidence of Cop[1].

[6] This is a continuation of the baptismal story of Thecla. Here it is not the presbyter who anoints Thecla with ointments, but rather it is women! See *4.9.2 General Comment* above. See especially *Apostolic Constitutions* 7.22; quoting from *ANF* 7, "But thou shalt beforehand anoint the person with the holy oil, and afterward baptize him with the water, and in the con-

clusion shalt seal him with the anointment (χαὶ τελευταῖον σφραγίσεις μύρῳ)."

[7] The reason for the sleep coming over the wild beasts is not explained, although I might add that the implications of this sleep (ὕπνος) are either that God sent a visionary sleep (4.4) or death (4.18), such as Thecla's final *sleep*.

[8] See *ÉAC*, 1140, note IV,10, "*Taureaux*: c'est peut-être une influence du mythe d'Hippolyte." See L. Radermacher, *Hippolytos und Thekla: Studien zur Geschichte von Legende und Kultus* (Sitzungsberichte der Kaiserlichen Akademie der Wissenschaften in Wien; Philosophisch-historische Klasse 182; Vienne: Buchhändler der Kaiserlicke Academie der Wissenschaften, 1916). See section III, "The Evidence for Fatal Charades," in Coleman, "Fatal Charades," 60–66, especially 64–66. The use of bulls is found in tortures and eventual death that made use of both practices of bestiality and tying people to bulls. Davies, *The Revolt of the Widows*, 106 is too presumptious to suggest that the authorship of the *APTh* is more likely to be a female "resentful to men" and transfixed upon "sexual sadism," As the evidence suggests sexual sadism and other tortures were standard practice within the theaters and amphitheaters as a means for mythological stagings that were the vehicle for the death of prisoners, slaves, gladiators, and Christian martyrs, and therefore it would not have been an uncommon matter to have written about Thecla's harsh tortures in this way. For an example see Apuleius, *Metam.* 10.28–34. In the *Golden Ass* (Metamorphoses), Lucian, as a donkey, is going to be required to have sexual relations with a woman who has been condemned to die by wild beasts in the theater. The text suggests that the wild beasts would have been released upon the woman and Lucian, while they are in the act. Also, their act would follow upon the mythological reenactment when Paris selects Venus as the most beautiful one over Pallas Athena and Juno (See also Fergus Millar, "The World of the Golden Ass," 63–75.). See also *1 Clem* 6.1 (and notes by Bart Ehrman, ed. And trans., "First Clement," *Apostolic Fathers* (LCL 24; Harvard: Harvard UP, 2003) 1:44–45, n. 16; Compare Suetonius, *Nero* 11–12. In the case of Thecla, this is most likely the mythological recreation of Dirce and the bull (*1 Clem* 6.1). See also Eleanor W. Leach, "The Punishment of Dirce: A Newly Discovered Painting in the Casa di Giulio Polibio and its Significance within the Visual Tradition," *MDAI* 93 (1986): 157–82, color plates 1–2.; David L. Balch, "Zeus, Vengeful Protector of the Political and Domestic Order: Frescoes in Dining Rooms N and P of the House of the Vettii in Pompeii, Mark 13.12–13, and 1 Clement 6.2," *Picturing the New Testament: Studies in Ancient Visual Images* (Ed. Annette Weissenrieder, Friederike Wendt, and Petra von Gemünden; WUNT 2.193; Tübingen: Mohr Siebeck, 2005), 67–95, plates 1–9, especially discussion on page 88.

[9] Replace θηριομάχον with αὐτὴν based on Cop[1]. See Schmidt, *Acta Pauli*, 48.

[10] After ἐπέτρεψεν cut out ὁ ἡγεμὼν from the evidence of *E* and Cop[1].

[11] The text implies that Thecla is tied, by Alexander himself, to the bulls, being between them, so as to rip her apart by her feet.

[12] τὰ ἀναγκαῖα – "genitals," see "ἀναγκαῖος, α, ον," BDAG, 60. 1 Cor 12:22; *1 Clem* 37.5; Diodorus of Sicily 1.34; *POxy* 56.6; 1068.16; Philo, *Prob.* 76; Athenagoras 22.4, etc.

[13] Alexander's intentions are to have Thecla ripped apart and killed through the burning of the male genitalia of the bulls.

[14] ἡ δὲ περικαιομένη φλόξ – there is some difficulty in determining whether or not the reading should be περικαιομένη (*A*, *B*, *m*, *s*, Tischendorf) or περικειμένη (*C* and *E*). The more difficult reading is the former, which is also the preferred reading of *AAA*, 262. If it is a flame that surrounds Thecla, then the release of Thecla appears more miraculous with a flame surrounding her. This also implies that the *cloud of fire* still surrounds Thecla. This correction can easily be explained as a scribal correction to a more difficult text that does not appear to flow well. Schneemelcher (*NTApoc* 2:245) and Rordorf (*ÉAC*, 1140) support the latter reading. In the former reading περικαιομένη is a present middle deponent participle, nominative feminine singular of περικαίω.

4.10.2 General Comment

Davies, *Revolt of the Widows*, 106, states it best, "This passage is a graphic portrayal of sexual sadism. A beautiful naked woman with her legs ripped apart by bulls enraged to a frenzy by the application of hot irons to their sexual organs-such an image could come from a disturbed mind." Sadly enough, this is not an exceptional situation, and the "disturbed mind" is an anachronistic assessment that is not borne out in the testimony and other sources from antiquity. Here Alexander finally takes the death and shame brought upon him into his own hands, taking the legal reigns from a passive proconsul and attempts to pay back Thecla for her dishonoring him by denying his sexual advances (4.1). Initially Alexander tried to bind her and failed, but now he can bind her. Initially Alexander made sexual advances on her, but now he is able to inflame the genitalia of the bulls with the result of the destruction of Thecla's legs being pulled apart (this is exactly what he was denied in 4.1).

In this "fatal charade" in the theater, where the wild beasts are set against her, Thecla has just received the seal of baptism and God sends signs to demonstrate his blessing of her self-baptism. This is immediately followed by Thecla's ritualistic anointing with ointments at the beginning of 4.10. After she is anointed, then the trials of the adversary begin instantly, but as the baptism proves true, Thecla is preserved from these threats, and the the key virtue of sexual purity is maintained (See *3.6.2 General Comment*; and *3.12.1 Textual Notes*, note 5). The text is able to blend adequately the themes of the ancient novel, early Christian rites and theology with an engaging historically based episode of mythological re-enactments in the theater with the result of the death of Thecla, a criminal and scourge to Antiochene society (as deemed by Alexander).

4.11

'Η δὲ Τρύφαινα[1] ἐξέψυξεν ἑστῶσα παρὰ τὴν ἀρήναν ἐπὶ τοὺς ἄβακας,[2] ὥστε τὰς θεραπαινίδας[3] εἰπεῖν 'Απέθανεν ἡ βασίλισσα Τρύφαινα. καὶ ἐπέσχεν ὁ ἡγεμών,[4] καὶ πᾶσα ἡ πόλις ἐπτύρη·καὶ ὁ 'Αλέξανδρος[5] πεσὼν εἰς τοὺς πόδας τοῦ ἡγεμόνος εἶπεν· 'Ελέησον κἀμὲ καὶ τὴν πόλιν, καὶ ἀπόλυσον[6] τὴν θηριομάχον,[7] μὴ καὶ ἡ πόλις συναπόληται. ταῦτα γὰρ ἐὰν ἀκούσῃ ὁ Καῖσαρ,[8] τάχα ἀπολέσει σὺν ἡμῖν καὶ τὴν πόλιν, ὅτι ἡ συγγενὴς[9] αὐτοῦ Τρύφαινα ἡ βασίλισσα[10] ἀπέθανεν παρὰ τοὺς ἄβακας.[2]

Translation

But Tryphaena lost consciousness, while standing alongside the arena upon the sideboard of the theater, so that the female slaves said, "Queen Tryphaena is dead." And the governor stopped, and the whole city was frightened. And Alexander falling at the feet of the governor said "Have mercy on me and the city, and release the beastfighter, lest the city be destroyed with her. For if the Caesar should hear of these things, quickly he will destroy us and the city together, because his kinsperson, Tryphaena the Queen, has died by the sideboard of the arena."

4.11.1 Textual Notes

[1] For a discussion on Tryphaena, see *4.2.1 Textual Notes*, note 11.

[2] Rordorf (*ÉAC*, 1140) translates this as "vers les premières places" with a footnote IV,11 that states "ces places étaient recouvertes de marbre ou de bois." It appears that the *abacus* or *sideboard* was a technical name for a marble/wood slab that was next to or part of the theater ("ἄβαξ," LSJ, 1).

[3] See *4.1.1 Textual Notes*, note 11, concerning a discussion Thecla as a *handmaid of God*.

[4] The potential death of Tryphaena even stills the governor as the madness of Alexander has been raging unchecked.

[5] See *4.1.1 Textual Notes*, note 1. See also Acts 19:33 (2x); 1 Tim 1:20; and 2 Tim 4:14.

[6] This is *release* in the sense of *acquit*. Alexander would like to dismiss the case based on the possible repercussions that could come from the death of a family member of Caesar.

[7] It is possible that θηριομάχον could have been absent from the original text, but there is no conclusive evidence. See *4.11.1 Textual Notes*, note 9. See also *4.3.1 Textual Notes* note 1, for further discussion and information on θηριομάχον. A reference to "the feminine θηριομάχος is unprecedented" (Van den Hoek and Herrmann, "Thecla the Beast Fighter," 225).

[8] These words are somewhat prophetic for what will take place in the martyrdom of Paul. Nero's knowledge of the death of his beloved slave, Patroclus, leads to the mass persecution of Christians in Rome and the eventual execution of Paul (*AP* 14.2–5).

[9] For further discussion of the possible connection of Tryphaena to Caesar, see *4.2.1 Textual Notes*, note 11.

[10] Τρύφαινα ἡ βασίλισσα is probably a later addition. See Gebhardt, *Passio*, CIV.

4.11.2 General Comment

As soon as Alexander's plans for the sadistic death of Thecla fail in 4.10, the chapter begins with the collapse of queen Tryphaena into unconsciousness. This brings about a response from a group of women other than those who have consistently called out for the salvation of Thecla. This time it is the slaves/handmaids of Tryphaena who quickly evaluate the situation incorrectly by proclaiming that Tryphaena is dead. This announcement seems to bring the whole city to a sudden halt. The shift and transition of the Antiochene texts balances upon the fulcrum sentence in three parts: (1) Tryphaena is dead, (2) The governor stops (centerpoint), and (3) the city is frightened. The death of this queen could bring about the complete collapse and destruction of the city of Antioch if Caesar hears of these events. This news brings about a repentant response from Alexander, who is now more concerned for his life, rather than Thecla's death. As the "leading man of the city," Alexander must consider first how he must mitigate this situation.

The scene of these events is presented in a very dramatic way in terms of the scale of its size and scope. First of all, there are dead lions and lionesses, sleeping wild beasts (leopards, bears, lions, tigers?) scattered throughout the theater, and a pit of water filled with dead animals, namely seals. In addition to this there is Thecla, who has been the source of a show of fire and lightning, then a cloud of fire hiding her naked body, and now Thecla, with the remains of cords that bound her burned away, remains standing within the theater, most likely wet from her immersion into the water and naked again with the fiery cloud having receded (see *3.12.1 Tex-*

tual Notes, note 2). In addition to this, there are angry bulls about, and a crowd full of spectators shouting disapproval of the entire situation. This overwhelming image of the theater is suddenly brought to a grinding halt upon the announcement of the possible death of Queen Tryphaena. It is almost as if time freezes as the situation now centers on the death of the queen.

4.12

Καὶ ἐκάλεσεν ὁ ἡγεμὼν τὴν Θέκλαν ἐκ μέσου τῶν θηρίων καὶ εἶπεν αὐτῇ Τίς εἶ σύ;[1] καὶ τίνα τὰ περὶ σέ,[2] ὅτι οὐδὲ ἓν τῶν θηρίων ἥψατό σου;[3] ἡ δὲ εἶπεν Ἐγὼ μέν εἰμι θεοῦ τοῦ ζῶντος δούλη.[4] τὰ δὲ περὶ ἐμέ, εἰς ὃν εὐδόκησεν ὁ θεὸς υἱὸν αὐτοῦ ἐπίστευσα· δι' ὃν οὐδὲ ἓν τῶν θηρίων ἥψατό[5] μου.[6] οὗτος γὰρ μόνος σωτηρίας ὅρος[7] καὶ ζωῆς αἰωνίου[8] ὑπόστασίς[9] ἐστιν· χειμαζομένοις γὰρ γίνεται καταφυγή,[10] θλιβομένοις ἄνεσις,[11] ἀπηλπισμένοις[12] σκέπη, καὶ ἁπαξαπλῶς ὃς ἐὰν μὴ πιστεύσῃ εἰς αὐτόν, οὐ ζήσεται ἀλλὰ ἀποθανεῖται εἰς τοὺς αἰῶνας.[13]

Translation

And the governor called Thecla out of the midst of the wild beasts and said to her, "Who are you and what is it about you, that none of the beasts touched you?" But Thecla said, "I am a slave of the living God. But the things concerning me, I have placed my trust in the one whom God blessed, namely his son; on account of which not one of the beasts touched me. For this is the only way of salvation and the substance of deathless life. For to the one being stormed-tossed he is a place of refuge, a loosening to the one being oppressed, a shelter to the one who is in despair, and in general, whoever should not believe in him, shall not live but will die forever.

4.12.1 Textual Notes

[1] Achilles Tatius, *Leuc. Clit.* 6.21–22; 8.6–8; Parthenius, *The Story of Pallene* 5–6;

[2] This can be translated as either "and what are the things surrounding you" or "what is it about you?" I do not agree with Bovon who suggests that there is a "thème de la barrière protectrice" ("La Vie des Apôtres: Traditions Bibliques et Narrations Apocryphes," *Les Actes Apocryphes des Apotres*, 154). See Schneemelcher, *NTApoc* 2.267, note 52; Bovon, *Lukas in neuer Sicht: gesammelte Aufsätze* (Biblisch-theologische Studien 8; Neukirchen-Vluyn: Neukirchener Verlag, 1985), 244, note 56. Wilson is translating Schneemelcher into English (while Schneemelcher is following Bovon's German translation) when he states, "τίνα τὰ περὶ σέ [*AAA* 1:263]

– 'what is it about thee?' is probably better to be rendered 'what surrounds you?'. The motif of the protective enfolding deserves closer examination." This is an English translation of a German translation of Bovon's article originally in French. See Bovon, "La Vie des Apôtres: Traditions Bibliques et Narrations Apocryphes," especially note 56 on page 154, where Bovon is conjuring up the image of the protective surrounding that he suggests is around Thecla. He also cites Job 1:10 and Mark 12:1. This evidence is not conclusive. The connections to both Job and Mark are tenuous and unlikely. Bovon's assertion may be based upon faulty textual evidence in 4.10 (see *4.10.1 Textual Notes,* note 14 concerning περικειμένη). Textually the support for a "hedge" is poor. Secondly, this makes little sense in the context. For instance, upon Thecla baptizing herself, she is surrounded by a pillar of fire to keep the wild beasts from touching her and to cover her nakedness (4.9). Then in 4.10, Alexander approaches her to tie her to the bulls. If the fire had remained, then Alexander would not have been able to approach her. Instead, one should understand the apocalyptic fire as a demonstration of God's approval of Thecla. In addition, if a fire were still surrounding Thecla when she approached the governor, then why would he have suggested for her to have garments brought to her (4.13). Thecla's response further supports that the *cloud of fire* was a temporary enclosure, when she refers to it in past tense Ἡ δὲ εἶπεν Ὁ ἐνδύσας με γυμνὴν ἐν τοῖς θηρίοις, οὗτος ἐν ἡμέρᾳ κρίσεως ἐνδύσει με σωτηρίαν.. Notice that ἐνδύσας is an aorist active participle referring to a past time when God had clothed her from her nakedness (4.9).

[3] See 4.9–10. See also 2 Tim 4:17.

[4] See *4.1.1 Textual Notes*, note 11 on the expression τὴν τοῦ θεοῦ δούλην. See Rordorf, *ÉAC*, 1140, note IV,12: "*La servante du Dieu vivant:* voir Lc 1,38. Thècle pronounce sa confession de foi; voir sa prière en IV,17."

[5] See 3.22; 4.9, 10, here (2x); Heliodorus, *Aeth.* 10.

[6] The governor asks Thecla two questions: (1) who are you, and (2) what is it about you that the beasts do not touch you? Thecla answers both. First she says that she is a servant of God, believing in Jesus as the son of God. Secondly, she states that Jesus, the son of God, is the sole salvation that protected her from these events.

[7] See Bovon, "La Vie des Apôtres," 154, note 56, preferring the reading of ὁδός against *AAA*, but with Vouaux, *Actes de Paul*, 218, note 3. See Acts 16:17. It appears from the context (in agreement with Rordorf, *ÉAC*, 1141) that the reading should remain ὄρος with *AAA*. Three reasons can be suggested. (1) ὄρος provides the less common reading, due to the fact that a scribe would have been tempted to change this to ὁδός which would be the more obvious wording (Acts 16:17). (2) ὄρος preserves a more consistent reading that deals with the *landmark/boundary* of salvation and the *substance/framework* of eternal life. (3) The most decisive evidence would

have to be a lack in gender agreement between ὁδός (feminine) and οὗτος (masculine). On the other hand, οὗτος which would require a masculine subject is consistent with ὄρος.

[8] Changed to αἰωνίου based on Cop[1]. On the reading of *AAA*, ἀθανάτου, see 1 Tim 6:16.

[9] ὑπόστασίς – it is difficult to decide how to translate this noun, which carries a very rich meaning philosophically. See Lampe, *Patristic Greek Lexicon*, 1454–61, especially I.A and III.A. See also "ὑπόστασίς, ἡ," BDAG, 1040–41. This word also carries a rich meaning especially within the Christian wisdom tradition. See Plutarch, *Mor.* 894b; Wis 16:21; Philo, *Aet.* 88, 92; etc.

[10] This is an image from the Hebrew Bible/LXX. See Exod 17:15; 4 Kgdms 22:3; Ps 9:9, 17:18, 45:1, etc. See also *Jos. Asen.* 13.1.

[11] There is a possible connection between *Jos. Asen.* 12.10–11. Aseneth fearing to tell her father because she is being *oppressed*, says

Lord, rescue me from his hands, and from his mouth deliver me, lest he carry me off like a lion, and tear me up and throw me into the flame of the fire, and the fire will wrap me up in darkness and throw me out into the deep of the sea and the big sea monster who (exists) since eternity will swallow me, and I will be destroyed for ever (and) ever…rescue me, Lord…because my father and my mother disowned me…and guard me a virgin (who is) abandoned and an orphan…"

These are the same events that transpired in the life of Thecla, and yet, contrary to what Aseneth expects, the Lord does deliver Thecla. 2 Tim 4:17 also connects with this passage; see also LXX Ps 21.21–22, 90.13.

[12] See Isa 29:19.

[13] See 4.4 (2x).

4.12.2 General Comment

Now that the pendulum has swung in a different direction than that which began in 4.1–2 (see *4.11.2 General Comment*), Thecla is beginning to be able to explain and teach her message to the governor of Antioch and those in the theater who have been standing by. Several key factors are synergizing by this point in the text. First, it should be very transparent that the theme of the untouched virgin from the ancient novel is dominating the text (see note 1). True to the other examples in the ancient novel, when tested Thecla comes through trials untouched, proving her innocence and virginity. But one cannot stop here. Second, it is clear that the author of the *Acts of Paul and Thecla* is bringing to a climax the theological agenda associated with women and authority in the early church. It has been clearly demonstrated in the textual notes and comments surrounding 4.9–10 that Thecla has just gone through the baptismal rite (without the bishop present) as comparisons with other early Christian didactic texts indicate (see

4.9.2 General Comment). Then in 4.10–11, Thecla is tested immediately following her baptism and anointing and succeeds. Then finally in 4.12, Thecla is able to preach her first sermon as a baptized, sealed believer, having been commissioned by God, essentially as a female apostle. This verification is demonstrated later in 4.16, taking much the same shape as Galatians 1–2, where Paul seeks verification from the other apostles and James the Lord's brother.

One might also note the similarities between Joseph and Aseneth 12.10–11 and the *Acts of Paul and Thecla* at several points:

1. Aseneth and Thecla describe God as one who rescues.
2. Thecla is delivered from a lion, while Aseneth fears the lion.
3. Thecla was thrown into flames, while Aseneth fears the flame of the fire.
4. Thecla was wrapped by a flame (provided by God) and Aseneth fears being wrapped up by a flame of darkness.
5. Thecla threw herself into the water, while Aseneth fears being cast into the sea.
6. The water is Thecla's salvation (like Jonah) and brings eternal life, while Aseneth fears that the eternity in the sea will be eternal death.
7. Thecla has been disowned by her mother, while Aseneth fears being disowned.
8. Thecla and Aseneth seek a "guarding" as they are virgins and both have been abandoned like orphans. Not even Paul defends Thecla in Antioch.

Now that God has brought deliverance and commission to Thecla she is able to begin, and does so immediately (such as Paul is said to have done in Acts 9:20), and only later seeks confirmation. It is very clear by this point that the agenda is to demonstrate and sanction the apostolic work of the female Thecla, in opposition to those who are arguing for the silencing of women (such as Tertullian in *Bapt.* 17).

4.13

Καὶ ταῦτα ἀκούσας[1] ὁ ἡγεμὼν ἐκέλευσεν ἐνεχθῆναι ἱμάτια καὶ εἶπεν· Ἔνδυσαι τὰ ἱμάτια.[2] Ἡ δὲ εἶπεν Ὁ ἐνδύσας με γυμνὴν ἐν τοῖς θηρίοις, οὗτος ἐν ἡμέρᾳ κρίσεως[3] ἐνδύσει με σωτηρίαν. Καὶ λαβοῦσα τὰ ἱμάτια ἐνεδύσατο. καὶ ἐξέπεμψεν εὐθέως ὁ ἡγεμὼν ἄκτον[4] λέγων Θέκλαν τὴν τοῦ θεοῦ δούλην[5] τὴν θεοσεβῆ ἀπολύω ὑμῖν. Αἱ δὲ γυναῖκες πᾶσαι[6] ἔκραξαν φωνῇ μεγάλῃ καὶ ὡς ἐξ ἑνὸς στόματος ἔδωκαν αἶνον τῷ θεῷ λέγουσαι Εἷς θεὸς ὁ Θέκλαν σώσας,[7] ὥστε ἀπὸ τῆς φωνῆς σεισθῆναι τὴν πόλιν,

Translation

After having heard these things, the governor called to have garments
brought in and said, "Put the garments on for yourself." But Thecla said,
"The one who has clothed my nakedness while with the wild beasts, this
one will clothe me with salvation on the Day of Judgment." And receiving
the garments, she put them on. And the governor sent out a policy immediately saying, "Thecla, the slave of God, the Godfearer, I release to you."
But all the women cried out in a great voice and as out of one voice they
gave thanks to God saying, "One is God who has saved Thecla," so that
the whole city was shaken by the sound.

4.13.1 Textual Notes

[1] It appears that the end result within this story of the governor is not his
conversion (conversion is never the end result in the canonical Acts of the
Apostles), but rather his support and confirmation of Thecla's innocence.

[2] The issue of Thecla's nakeness has been an underlying theme throughout the Antioch episode. Thecla is made to strip off her clothing in
Iconium upon the event of her *crematio* (3.22). This is counterbalanced by
Paul taking off his garment to end a fast and prayer for Thecla (3.23), then
again in the theater in Antioch, Thecla is stripped of her clothing. One
might notice that the second time around, she is given underpants (see
4.9.1 Textual Notes, note 2), and it appears that a contrast of what is "surrounding" or "engulfing" Thecla is being emphasized, while at the same
time baptismal preparation is what the author of the *AP* has in mind this
time (4.8). Upon the completion of her diving into the water/baptism, she
is immediately engulfed by the presence of God with a cloud of fire (4.9).
So upon standing before the governor now, Thecla affirms that she is
clothed in the garments that are necessary for salvation from God. The
paradoxical situation is that Thecla is standing naked before all, yet is able
to proclaim that she is pure and clothed, and her deliverance through fire,
lions, and seals is the testimony. See also *4.9.1 Textual Notes*, note 13 and
14.

[3] See *4.9.1 Textual Notes*, note 6 and Thecla's speech on salvation connected to Jesus in 4.12.

[4] This is from the Latin, *actio,* meaning "proposal...policy." See definition 2 in P. G. W. Glare, *Oxford Latin Dictionary* (Oxford: Clarendon
Press, 1982), 30. Thecla leaves with her shame and dignity (See Acts
16.35–39).

[5] See *4.1.1 Textual Notes*, note 11 on the expression τὴν τοῦ θεοῦ δούλην.
See also comments under *4.12.1 Textual Notes*, note 6.

[6] See also *3.11.1 Textual Notes*, note 6; and *4.3.1 Textual Notes*, note 8.

[7] Change πᾶσαν τὴν πόλιν to τὴν πόλιν following Schmidt's reconstruction of Cop[1] (Schmidt, *Acta Pauli*, 18*). It appears that πᾶσαν τὴν πόλιν (ϩⲱⲥⲧⲉ ⲁⲧⲣⲉ ⲧⲡⲟⲗⲓⲥ [ⲧⲏⲣⲟⲩ]) would not have fit within the lines of the manuscript. Rordorf also translates this passage as "«Il n'y a qu'un seul Dieu, celui qui a sauvé Thècle», de sorte que la ville fut ébranlée par cette clameur." (Rordorf, *ÉAC*, 1141).

4.13.2 General Comment

Having heard the proclamation and *kerygma* as delivered by Thecla, the governor can make no other pronouncement, but to send out a policy, an act and declaration proclaiming the innocence of Thecla. One oversight of the governor is his continued lack of understanding of how Thecla's God covers one in salvation. He sees Thecla naked and in need of clothing, but Thecla sees herself as clothed in God and having no need of the governor's clothing. This reorientation of Thecla's "body" and "person" serves to contrast the nakedness and eroticization of Thecla, while at the same time Thecla stands before the governor as pure, chaste, and a virgin. Vorster argues for no less than a revisioning "of the social hierarchies during the second century CE." (Vorster, "Construction of Culture," 117). In relation to the themes of the ancient novel, Thecla has passed the litmus test.

The voice of the women that began cacophonously in 4.2 has finally become organized into one voice. Their *one voice* in harmony can now blend to make the unified proclamation of the *one God*. Their voice, testifiying to the salvation, is overpowering and it shakes the city. At this point, one needs to take note that Paul is absent, and has been absent from the entire trial and situation of Antioch, since 4.1 (see note *4.1.1 Textual Notes*, note 6). While realizing that this is not the abandonment of Thecla by Paul (following the ancient novel), Paul's absence also serves to show that Thecla's calling and commission by God was not by the hands of humans (Gal 1:1, 12, 15–23), especially not from Paul, but from God himself. In fact, Paul had already left Antioch, but had gone on to Myra (4.15), further separating the apostolic commission of Thecla from Paul. The reason for showing Paul's resistance in 3.25 is not to exhibit Paul in a bad light, but to further separate Thecla's commission from Paul (see *3.25.1 Textual Notes*, note 14 and *3.25.2 General Comment*).

4.14

καὶ τὴν Τρύφαιναν εὐαγγελισθεῖσαν[1] ἀπαντῆσαι τῇ θέκλῃ[2] μετὰ ὄχλου καὶ περιπλακῆναι αὐτῇ[3] καὶ εἰπεῖν Νῦν πιστεύω ὅτι νεκροὶ ἐγείρονται·[4] νῦν πιστεύω ὅτι τὸ τέκνον μου ζῇ·[5] δεῦρο τέκνον μου[6] ἔσω εἰς τὸν οἶκόν μου,[7] καὶ τὰ ἐμὰ πάντα σοὶ καταγράψω.⁸ ἡ δὲ εἰσῆλθεν μετ᾽ αὐτῆς καὶ ἀνεπαύσατο εἰς τὸν οἶκον αὐτῆς ἡμέρας ὀκτώ, ⁹ κατηχήσασα¹⁰ αὐτὴν τὸν λόγον,¹¹ ὥστε πιστεῦσαι τῷ θεῷ¹² καὶ τῶν παιδισκῶν¹³ τὰς πλείονας, καὶ μεγάλην εἶναι χαρὰν ἐν τῷ οἴκῳ.¹⁴

Translation

And when the good news had been told to Tryphaena, she was meeting Thecla with a crowd and being embraced by her and said, "Now I believe that the dead are raised. Now I believe that my child lives. Come inside my child, into my house, and I will transfer all of my property to you. Therefore Thecla entered with her and refreshed herself in her house for eight days, teaching her the word, so that she believed in God and also many of the slaves, and great was the joy in her house.

4.14.1 Textual Notes

[1] This is probably not only intended in the general sense of "good news" about Thecla's deliverance, but this further demonstrates the *gospel-like* character of this document. Thecla's "resurrection" from the dead provides this post-resurrection confession of faith by queen Tryphaena. See *AP* 3.17; MacDonald, "Apocryphal and Canonical Narratives," 61–63; Richard I. Pervo, "14 Early Christian Fiction," *Greek Fiction: The Greek Novel in Context* (ed. J. R. Morgan and Richard Stoneman; London and New York: Routledge, 1994) 244; and *3.6.2 General Comment*.

[2] The text according to *AAA*, 265, is ἀπαντῆσαι μετὰ ὄχλου καὶ περιπλακῆναι τῇ θέκλῃ καὶ εἰπεῖν. The text has been edited based upon Cop¹: ⲁⲥⲉⲓ ⲁⲃⲁⲗ᾽ ⲁⲧⲱⲙⲛ̄ⲧ ⲁⲑⲉⲕⲗⲁ ⲙⲛ̄ ⲡⲙⲏⲩϣⲉ· ⲁⲩⲱ ⲁⲥϩⲱⲗϭ ⲁϩⲟⲩⲛ ⲁⲣⲁⲥ ⲉⲥⲭⲟⲩ ⲙ̄ⲙⲁⲥ ⲇⲉ...(Schmidt, *Acta Pauli*, 18*).

[3] The resurrection of the dead is an important theme of the *AP*. On the dead being raised, compare *AP* 3.8; 4.14; 9.23; 10.4.6; 10.5.26, 27, 31, 32; 13.2; 13.8; 14.4, 5; and also Matt 26:64; 28:7; Mark 16:14; and John 21.14. See Bremmer, "Magic, Martyrdom, and Women's Liberation," 55; Pieter J. Lalleman, "VIII. The Resurrection in the Acts of Paul," *The Apocryphal Acts of Paul and Thecla*, 126–41.

[4] See Lalleman, "The Resurrection," 133; Tryphaena believes that her daughter Falconilla lives (eternally) now, after Thecla prayed for her (*AP* 4.6), and Tryphaena now has evidence that God can miraculously raise up someone from the "dead."

[5] τέκνον μου and εἰς τὸν οἶκόν μου added to text based upon Cop¹, *A*, *B*,C *E* for τέκνον μου and *F*, *G*, Latin *C_{ab}*, *C_c*, etc.

[6] The development of a patron-client relationship is the most likely explanation of what is going on in the text, although specific patronage ter-

minology is missing (Misset-Van de Weg, "Answers," 156–62). In addition to a patron-client relationship under development, the reoroientation and conversion of Tryphaena to Christ is evident, and Tryphaena quickly develops her Christian role in economic enablement and begins funding the ministry of Thecla. The acceptance of Thecla as a bodily manifestation of Falconilla is somewhat possible also, but only in a spiritual sense. See Misset-Van de Weg, "A Wealthy Woman Named Tryphaena: Patroness of Thecka of Iconium," 32–35.

[7] From ἡ μὲν οὖν θέκλα to ἡ δὲ following Cop[1], C F, and G.

[8] See *3.13.1 Textual Notes*, note 1.

[9] There is some difficulty in knowing whether or not this is supposed to be ὀκτώ (supported by *AAA* and Rordorf) or δέκα (Schmidt with support of Cop[1]). See Schmidt's comments under footnote 26.10, *Acta Pauli*, 50.

[10] Thecla begins to teach. See *4.9.1 Textual Notes*, note 4.

[11] Omit τοῦ θεοῦ, in agreement with Cop[1], A, B, G, d, s, and Tischendorf.

[12] Add τῷ θεῷ following Cop[1].

[13] Could be men or women. See *3.10.1 Textual Notes*, note 9; *3.11.1 Textual Notes*, note 6; and *3.11.2 General Comment*; *3.22.1 Textual Notes*, note 1 for further discussion.

[14] See *3.2.1 Textual Notes*, note 1; *3.5.1 Textual Notes*, note 2; and *4.16.1 Textual Notes*, note 2.

4.14.2 General Comment

One is quickly reminded of the connections of the *AP* and the Gospels (See note 1 above). Here, one is able to experience the *resurrection* of Thecla from the beasts, and Queen Tryphaena hears the *gospel* of Thecla, as reported to the governor (4.13). Tryphaena greets and embraces Thecla along with the crowd that are standing by, and she invites Thecla to come home with her. This follows after Tryphaena's confession that she truly believes that her daughter Falconilla lives (See note 4 above). This is not a testimony where Tryphaena is mistaking Thecla for her daughter Falconilla, but yet the spiritual resurrection (and bodily?) resurrection of Thecla is evidence enough for Tryphaena that her daughter can now live. Tryphaena immediately offers all of her possessions to Thecla after making her confession. First of all, this is evidence of a complete conversion of Tryphaena to Christ through Thecla. Notice the similarities to the complete devotion that Thecla showed to Paul in 3.18–22, as now witnessed in Tryphaena's devotion. This appears to be the offer of a patroness to a client, offering full support of Thecla's apostolic teaching ministry. It cannot be forgotten that Thecla has also had an experience with Jesus in 3.21 (See *3.21.1 Textual Notes*, note 10). Upon hearing this, Thecla does go to the house of Tryphaena and begins her ministry. The immediate response is the acceptance of the Word, not only by Tryphaena, but also a host of slaves and the people in her house (foreshadowed and interpreted by similar responses in 3.5 and 20). This text seems to suggest the gathering and meeting of a house church in the home of Tryphaena, in which Thecla is the evangelist that has established and is encouraging this church (see also Osiek, Mac-Donald, and Tulloch, *A Woman's Place*, 241–42; Misset-Van de Weg, "A wealthy woman named Tryphaena," 32–33.).

4.15

Ἡ δὲ Θέκλα Παῦλον[1] ἐζήτει αὐτὸν περιπέμπουσα πανταχοῦ·[2] καὶ ἐμηνύθη αὐτῇ ἐν Μύροις[3] εἶναι αὐτόν. καὶ λαβοῦσα νεανίσκους[4] καὶ παιδίσκας,[5] ἀναζωσαμένη καὶ ῥάψασα τὸν χιτῶνα εἰς ἐπενδύτην σχήματι ἀνδρικῷ[6] ἀπῆλθεν ἐν Μύροις, καὶ εὗρεν Παῦλον λαλοῦντα τὸν λόγον τοῦ θεοῦ[7] καὶ ἐπέστη αὐτῷ. ὁ δὲ ἐθαμβήθη βλέπων αὐτὴν καὶ τὸν ὄχλον[8] τὸν μετ᾽ αὐτῆς, λογισάμενος μή τις αὐτῇ πειρασμὸς πάρεστιν ἕτερος.[9] ἡ δὲ συνιδοῦσα[10] εἶπεν αὐτῷ Ἔλαβον τὸ λουτρόν,[11] Παῦλε· ὁ γὰρ σοὶ συνεργήσας εἰς τὸ εὐαγγέλιον[12] κἀμοὶ συνήργησεν εἰς τὸ λούσασθαι.[13]

Translation

But Thecla was seeking after Paul and was sending people around in every direction. And it was made known to her that he was in Myra, and taking young men and women, having girded her loins and stitched together a garment into a masculinely fashioned robe and she went to Myra and found Paul speaking the Word of God and she went to him. But he was astonished to see her and the crowd that was with her, considering whether some other temptation might be upon her. But having become aware of his thinking, she said to him, "I took the bath, Paul; For the one who worked with you in the Gospel has even worked for me in the washing.

4.15.1 Textual Notes

[1] ἐπεπόθει καὶ has been rejected based upon Cop[1] and C.

[2] Here the depiction of Thecla has changed radically from her initial situation immediately after she decided to renounce her social status and marriage in Iconium. Now the apostle/Jesus figure is sending out her own male and female servants (presumably Tryphaena's servants who are now at Thecla's disposal) and in hopes of reuniting with Paul.

[3] Myra is further support and evidence that the likelihood of Antioch being the Antioch in Pisidia. See also *3.26.1 Textual Notes*, note 5; *4.13.2 General Comment*.

⁴ See 9.20, 21; Mark 14:51. This is the first time that the text articulates the gender of these young men. See note 5 below. See Vouaux, *Actes de Paul*, 223, note 2*, "La présence de l'apôtre à Myre et le voyage entrepris à pied par Thècle et son escorte prouvent qu'il s'agit bien d'Antioche de Pisidie; et certes, la course est déjà bien longue d'une ville à l'autre."

⁵ It appears that Thecla has drawn young disciples that are both male and female. This would have aroused Tertullian (*Bapt.* 17) and possibly others, where this clearly indicates that Thecla had converted many, and is now exerting influence over both young men and women. See *3.10.1 Textual Notes*, note 9; *3.11.1 Textual Notes*, note 6; and *3.11.2 General Comment*; *3.22.1 Textual Notes*, note 1 for further discussion.

⁶ See 3.25; see also Vouaux, *Actes de Paul*, 223, note 3*; J. Anson, "The Female Transvestite in Early Monasticism: the Origin and Development of a Motif," *Viator* 5 (1974): 1–32; Evelyne Patlagean, "L'histoire de la femme déguisée en moine et l'évolution de la sainteté feminine à Byzance," *Studi Medievali* III.17 (1976): 597–623; reproduced in *Structure sociale, famille, chrétienté à Byzance: IVe–Xie siècle* (London: Variorum Reprints, 1981, 1964), chapter 11 and Addenda, 2; J. C. B. Petropoulos, "Transvestite Virgin with a Cause. The Acta Pauli and Theclae and Late Antique Proto-'Feminism'," *Greece and Gender* (eds. Brit Berggreen and Nanno Marinatos; Bergen: Norwegian Institute at Athens, 1995), 125–39. Bremmer, "Magic, Martyrdom, and Women's Liberation," 55, regards Petropoulos' article as "less helpful."

⁷ On teaching the *word of God*, see *AP* 3.5, 7 (2x) for Paul, and 4.14 for Thecla. See also *AP* 12.1; 13.4, 7 (2x); 14.1 (2x), 3, 4. See also Acts 13:5.

⁸ Thecla has developed and maintained a following.

⁹ See 3.25; See *3.25.1 Textual Notes*, note 17 on Thecla's temptations.

¹⁰ See Acts 12.12; *AP* 14.1 – Paul "perceives in the Spirit" that ὁ πονηρός would tempt them.

¹¹ Within Tit 3:5 and Eph 5:26, τὸ λουτρόν is in reference to baptism. The Ephesian account synthesizes the concepts of bathing and spiritual cleansing by the λόγος.

¹² See Gal 2.8 (!) for a strong parallel between Paul and Peter, now being applied to Paul and Thecla. Regarding εὐαγγέλιον, see *4.14.1 Textual Notes*, note 1. See also *AP* 4.1, 17; 10.6.34. See also Gerhard Friedrich, "εὐαγγέλιον," *TDNT* 2:729–36. εὐαγγέλιον is still being used in an oracular sense, where the "basic meaning is that εὐαγγέλιον is the preached word." (735). The usage in 4.1 (*4.1.1 Textual Notes*, note 8), which is not original to the document, falls outside of the parameters of "preached word." See note 13 below also.

¹³ See 4.9, Νῦν καιρὸς λούσασθαί με (Now is the time for me to wash myself). Paul's conversion does not specify any form of baptism, yet both Thecla and Paul have an encounter with God the Father by means of a spe-

cific εὐαγγέλιον (see also *AP* 9.5; ⲚⲦⲀϥⲢ ⲉⲨⲀⲅⲅⲉⲗⲓⲍⲉ ⲚⲎⲈⲒ ⲘⲠⲉϥϢⲎⲢⲉ; the suffixed Pronoun Ⲣ in ⲚⲦⲀϥⲢ refers back to ⲠⲉⲒⲰⲦ; see Kasser and Luisier, "Le Papyrus Bodmer XLI," 316; István Czachesz, *Commission Narratives: A Comparison Study of the Canonical and Apocryphal Acts* (Studies on Early Christian Apocrypha 8; Peeters: Leuven, 2007), 89–91.

4.15.2 General Comment

Several factors are noteworthy in this very interesting chapter. First, this is the anticlimactic point in the text where Thecla, having already established herself as an evangelist, apostle, and prophet of God with the title *handmaid of God* (δούλη τοῦ θεοῦ), is now going to find her mentor. Thecla has established her validity as a teacher and servant of God without his aid. This is not anti-Pauline polemics, but rather serves to demonstrate Thecla's independence from Paul in her commission and to emphasize her direct connection to God. As has been previously noted in the comments of *AP* 3 and 4, a strong relationship existed between Paul and Thecla, but God had other plans for Thecla than to follow Paul alone (3.18; 24–25). As Thecla seeks to find Paul, she now travels, not alone as she left Iconium for Antioch (3.26), but rather with the social and legal blessing of the proconsul of Antioch, a host of followers, a patroness funding the ministry, and the seal of God provided under miraculous circumstances. Thecla begins by attempting to change her clothing by making an overcoat/robe that will present Thecla in the garb of a man, as she travels (Artemilla feels compelled to alter her clothing before Paul, in order to hide her beauty among other possibilities, see *AP* 9.17). She girds her loins (probably for travel), but then dons the masculine clothing. Once she travels to Myra and finds Paul, Paul is hesitant to greet her, knowing what happened last time, that Thecla was persistent in changing her appearance and following him. It is obvious that a female apostle, by this point, was not an acceptable role for a woman in the church. The figure of Thecla is an attempt to tell the story of a woman within the Pauline/Acts tradition, which, by all appearances, tries to authenticate an alternative story and theological perspective of of Paul's ministry as opposed to the accounting recorded in the Pastorals.

In this brief encounter of Paul and Thecla, Paul is blinded in astonishment by Thecla and this great crowd. This is contrasted by Thecla's ability to see quite clearly (at a deeper level than mere visual recognition) that she is there for providential reasons. Thecla then approaches Paul and proclaims that she has received the bath, i.e. baptism, and then goes on to explain that God has been inwardly working within (συνεργάζομαι) both of their lives in the same way (see note 13 above). This solemnizes Thecla's proclamation and explanation of her authenticity as a teacher and apostle of God (see *3.21.1 Textual Notes*, note 10; *4.12.2 General Comment* for a comparison to Paul's justification of apostolicity). The question is how will Paul react, when he recovers from his astonishment?

4.16

Καὶ λαβόμενος[1] ὁ Παῦλος τῆς χειρὸς αὐτῆς ἀπήγαγεν αὐτὴν εἰς τὸν οἶκον[2] Ἑρμείου καὶ πάντα ἀκούει παρ' αὐτῆς, ὥστε ἐπὶ πολὺ θαυμάσαι τὸν Παῦλον,[3] καὶ τοὺς ἀκούοντας στηριχθῆναι καὶ προσεύξασθαι[4] ὑπὲρ τῆς Τρυφαίνης. καὶ ἀναστᾶσα Θέκλα εἶπεν τῷ Παύλῳ[5] Πορεύομαι εἰς Ἰκόνιον.[6] Ὁ δὲ Παῦλος εἶπεν Ὕπαγε καὶ δίδασκε τὸν λόγον τοῦ θεοῦ.[7] ἡ μὲν οὖν Τρύφαινα ἱματισμὸν[8] καὶ χρυσὸν ἔπεμψεν αὐτῇ,[9] ὥστε καταλιπεῖν τῷ Παύλῳ πολλὰ[10] εἰς διακονίαν τῶν πτωχῶν.[11]

Translation

And Paul, having taken her by the hand led her into the house of Hermias and he heard everything from her, so that Paul marveled much, and the ones who had heard were strengthened and prayed concerning Tryphaena, and Thecla, having risen up, said to Paul, "I am going into Iconium." And Paul said, "Go and teach the word of God." Therefore, Tryphaena sent an abundance of clothing and gold with her, in order to leave at the disposal of Paul in the service of the poor.

4.16.1 Textual Notes

[1] Paul accepts Thecla at this critical moment, as he did immediately after Iconium in 3.26 (καὶ οὕτως λαβόμενος τὴν Θέκλαν). This acceptance is often misunderstand, because of Paul's actions and statements that follow in 4.1. See *4.1.1 Textual Notes*, note 6.

[2] The activity of the church is always presented within the home, and is only brought into the civic arena and civic spaces under compulsion. Within the *AP* one finds the centering on the οἶκος in 3.4 (2x), 5, 7 (2x), 10, 13, 15 [also found in *APTh* 45]; 4.14 (2x), 16, 17 (2x); 10.4.10; 12.1; and 13.4. See *3.2.1 Textual Notes*, note 1; *3.5.1 Textual Notes*, note 2.

[3] Thecla reports everything to Paul, and once again Paul responds in amazement (4.15).

[4] It is evident that Thecla preaches to the church here in Myra on account of the group that heard her testimony of God's working in her (4.15, ὁ γὰρ σοὶ συνεργήσας εἰς τὸ εὐαγγέλιον κἀμοὶ συνήργησεν εἰς τὸ λούσασθαι). It appears that prayers are then offered up concerning the new house church in the home of Tryphaena (4.14).

[5] τῷ Παύλῳ has been removed by Schmidt (*Acta Pauli*, 51, footnote 27.12) based on the lack of evidence in Cop[1] (This line in Cop[1] has been reconstructed due to the fact that most of the line is missing, but based on Schmidt's reconstruction of τῷ Παύλῳ there is no room for this addition), but *AAA* (267) and Rordorf (*ÉAC*, 1142) have kept it with manuscripts *A*, *B*, *L*, and against *C E*, *F*, *G*, *H*, Cop[1].

[6] Thecla is going to go back to her homeplace as a witness to the power of God. One might notice that she *informs* Paul, and does not necessarily *ask* Paul. Confirmation and approval by Paul is very important at this point, although unlikely to be denied after hearing how God worked with her (cf. Acts 11:15–18; Gal 2:1–10. Paul never sought approval [Gal 2], but yet wanted to see the reaction to his testimony).

[7] See Stegemann and Stegemann, *Jesus Movement*, 402–07, especially 403 and 474, n. 67 for an explanation of the connection between *AP* 3–4 and the early Christian discussion of the subordination of women in the early Church. Paul gives approval to Thecla as having been immersed and to teach. See *3.25.2 General Comment*.

[8] See Luke 7:25; Plutarch, *Alexander* 39.

[9] Tryphaena as patroness; see *4.14.1 Textual Notes*, note 6 and *4.14.2 General Comment*.

[10] Insert πολλὰ based on Cop[1] (ογαϣн), *A*, *B*, and Tischendorf, exerpt πολὺν from Τρύφαινα πολὺν ἱματισμὸν (*AAA*, 267 based upon the same textual support).

[11] This text appears to model both Acts 11:29 (τῶν δὲ μαθητῶν καθὼς εὐπορεῖτό τις ὥρισαν ἕκαστος αὐτῶν εἰς διακονίαν πέμψαι τοῖς κατοικοῦσιν ἐν τῇ Ἰουδαίᾳ ἀδελφοῖς·) and Galatians 2, and especially 2:10 (μόνον τῶν πτωχῶν ἵνα μνημονεύωμεν, ὃ καὶ ἐσπούδασα αὐτὸ τοῦτο ποιῆσαι). The two verbal touchstones are εἰς διακονίαν and τῶν πτωχῶν coming from both Acts and Galatians.

4.16.2 General Comment

This text appears to model the experiences of Paul and the early church by combining two issues into one. Galatians 2 combines the need for reconciliation between Paul and the Jerusalem leaders of the church to be witnessed with the "blessing" of the ministry of Paul, while at the same time addressing the problem of poverty and hunger in Judaea, of which Paul becomes an emissary. Acts 11:29 elaborates upon the problem of why poverty and hunger had grown so greatly in Palestine. *AP* 4.16 seems to combine these same two elements in the "blessing" of Thecla by Paul. Here, one of the emerging elements that Christendom plays within attitudes toward poverty in the Roman Empire (possibly "conjunctural poverty") is that poverty is something that should be remedied. This perspective demonstrates a shift in which poverty is not the result of vices, but rather demonstrates a structural shift in the Empire to view poverty as a problem, and the financial relief of poverty viewed as a virtue. Here this perspective is reinforced and endorsed by the author of the *AP*, in the gift left for Paul intended to bring relief to the poor, who are disenfranchised for whatever reason (see Robin Osborne, "Introduction: Roman Poverty in Context," *Poverty in the Roman World*, [ed. Margaret Atkins and Robin Osborne; Cambridge: Cambridge UP, 2006], 1–20.).

Thecla now has extensive financial resources which she contributes to the ministry of the poor in which Paul is working. I do not think that the author of the *AP* is attempting to reconcile *AP* to the story of Acts, but I do think that the tradition that Paul gathered funds for the poor must have been known to the author of the *AP* and he likewise incorporates this mission into the text. Therefore Thecla contributes after giving her testimony. Then she tells Paul her intentions and Paul endorses this decision. One other aspect that is worth noting is that Thecla does not ask for approval, but rather informs Paul of her plans, while at the same time seeking to be able to exchange information.

The theme of the "two lovers" has continued, yet developed in a very interesting ways. As Paul brings Thecla in, leading her by the hand, it becomes clear that Thecla's desire was not truly for Paul, but the Lord. While her longing for Paul leads her from Iconium to Antioch in order to be with and remain with Paul, her second quest from Antioch to Myra leads her to Paul again not to stay, but to say goodbye, thus concluding the relationship between the two "lovers," finally made clear as lovers of their Lord (cf. Chariton, *Callirhoe* 8.5).

In addition to the continuation of these themes, a second cycle of social space shift is completed. First, the *APTh* begins with the οἶκος of Onesiphorus (3.5–11), then moves into the civic arena with the first trial of Paul and Thecla (3.16–22). Then the text moves back to the domestic space again with the οἶκος of Onesiphorus (3.23–26). Then, in chapter four (4.1–12), the text moves back into the civic space with the trial of Thecla in Antioch. Upon the completion of the trial, the text shifts back to the οἶκος with the house of Tryphaena (4.14), and finally here in Myra with the οἶκος of Hermias.

4.17

Αὐτὴ δὲ ἀπῆλθεν[1] εἰς Ἰκόνιον. καὶ εἰσῆλθεν[2] εἰς τὸν Ὀνησιφόρου οἶκον,[3] καὶ ἔπεσεν εἰς τὸ ἔδαφος[4] ὅπου Παῦλος καθεζόμενος ἐδίδασκεν τὰ λόγια τοῦ θεοῦ,[5] καὶ πάλιν[6] ἔκλαιεν[7] λέγουσα

Ὁ θεός ἡμῶν καὶ τοῦ οἴκου τούτου,⁸ ὅπου μοι τὸ φῶς ἔλαμψεν,⁹ Χριστέ¹⁰ ὁ
υἱὸς τοῦ θεοῦ,¹¹
    ὁ ἐμοὶ
        βοηθὸς ἐν φυλακῇ,
        βοηθὸς ἐπὶ ἡγεμόνων,
        βοηθὸς ἐν πυρί,
        βοηθὸς ἐν θηρίοις,¹²
αὐτὸς εἶ θεός,
    καὶ
σοὶ ἡ δόξα εἰς τοὺς αἰῶνας, ἀμήν.¹³

Translation

But she departed to Iconium and she entered into the house of Onesiphorus, and she fell on the floor where Paul had sat and taught the words of
God, and wailed saying:

O, our God even of this house, where the light was revealed to me,
Christ, son of God,

    O, My helper in prison,
        My helper before governors,
        My helper in the fire,
        My helper before the wild beasts,
He is God,
    and
the glory is yours forever, amen.

4.17.1 Textual Notes

[1] See *3.19.1 Textual Notes*, note 5 for other references for ἀπῆλθεν.

[2] εἰσῆλθεν as supported by Cop¹ (ᴀᴄʙⱳᴋ), *C E, I, K, L,* and *M.*

[3] On Αὐτὴ δὲ ἀπῆλθεν εἰς Ἰκόνιον. Καὶ εἰσέρχεται εἰς τὸν Ὀνησιφόρου οἶκον
– This is similar to Paul's entrance into Iconium in 3.1 and 3.5. On
Ὀνησιφόρου and οἶκον see *3.2.1 Textual Notes*, note 1 and *3.5.1 Textual
Notes*, note 2 and *3.5.2 General Comment.*

[4] Compare 9.17 (only other time ἔδαφος is literarally mentioned); see
also 3.7, 8, 10, 18. See *4.8.1 Textual Notes*, note 6 on the discipling of others by "sitting at their feet." The key to this language may be found in Acts
22:7, where the text states of Paul, "ἔπεσά τε εἰς τὸ ἔδαφος καὶ ἤκουσα φωνῆς
λεγούσης μοι..." While the connection between Acts and the *AP* may not be
absolutely proven with this phrase here (Hills, "The Acts of the Apostles,"
43 gives the connection a "B" rating), this seems to be very convincing as
evidence of a strong awareness by the author of the *AP* of the stories found
in Acts. If the author does not have a copy of Acts, then he or she has definitely seen one at some point or heard the stories from it. The only criti-

cism of this would be the objection of Schmidt (*Acta Pauli*, 51, note 27.20) of the accuracy of the original text reading ἔδαφος based on the Coptic text that has the word ⲡⲙⲁ. Schmidt suggests τόπος instead of ἔδαφος, although there are no Greek texts to support such a reading. In *ÉAC*, 1142, Rordorf follows the reading of ἔδαφος (*se jeta à terre à l'endroit*). After all, ⲡⲙⲁ can be translated very diversely ranging from *place* to *temple* to *dwelling place* (Crum, *Coptic Dictionary*, 153).

⁵ This is referring back to *AP* 3.5–7 and the conversion of Thecla. On the τὰ λόγια (plural here, 3.1 and 3.6 [see *3.6.1 Textual Notes*, note 2]) τοῦ θεοῦ, see 4.14, 15, 16, etc. (*4.15.1 Textual Notes* note 7). Preaching the "Word of God" is a key concept in the *AP*. Although the preaching of τὰ λόγια τοῦ θεοῦ is not an uncommon subject for the *AP*, there seems to be some question as to whether it is the original wording of this text. See Schmidt, *Acta Pauli*, 51. It is not found in Cop¹, as well as a number of Greek manuscripts.

⁶ Add πάλιν based on the evidence of Cop¹.

⁷ The usage of κλαίω suggests the mixed feelings of Thecla who revisits this sight out of sorrow as she cries out over the past events mixed with praise and thanks to God.

⁸ Thecla remembers how God worked on her in the house of Onesiphorus (*AP* 3.5–8).

⁹ This should be Χριστέ instead of Χριστέ Ἰησοῦ with Cop¹ and Latin Cₐ. See Schmidt, *Acta Pauli*, 51 and Rordorf, *ÉAC*, 1142.

¹⁰ Thecla does not refer to her "conversion" as *the light shined upon me* in any other place in the *AP*. This is language familiar in the canonical NT. See Matt 15:15–16; Luke 17:24; Acts 12:7; 2 Cor 4:6 (2x).

¹¹ Compare *AP*, Χριστέ Ἰησοῦ ὁ υἱὸς τοῦ θεοῦ to Matthew 16:16, "σὺ εἶ ὁ χριστὸς ὁ υἱὸς τοῦ θεοῦ τοῦ ζῶντος.

¹² A recapulation of all of the trials, in which God has been a helper to lead Thecla through prison (3.18), before two proconsuls in Antioch and Iconium (3.20 and 4.1–2 and 12), in a fire (3.22), and before beasts in Antioch (4.8–10).

¹³ With the conclusion to Thecla's comments, it becomes apparent that she has been offering up a prayer in rememberance of Christ, and somewhat mixed with praise of Paul (remember *AP* 3.21).

4.17.2 General Comment

The text has finally come full circle, with Thecla now entering Iconium as the teacher, while Paul is still in Myra, where we continue to follow him later in *AP* 5. Thecla enters into the house of Onesiphorus (as Paul had done) and immediately finds the location where Paul had taught. The vacancy of the location further suggests that the church was meeting in an adjoining workshop (see *3.5.2 General Comment*). Thecla finally throws herself onto the ground where Paul had taught, as she had desired to do the first time around, but could not because she was so transfixed and intently gazing upon Paul (ἀτενίζουσα, 3.7–8). As Thecla throws herself down, she then breaks out into a sorrow-filled prayer of thanksgiving for the deliverance of God through Christ beginning with her conversion to the message of Paul in 3.5–6. She hits several of the high points of God's protection and deliverance through the two cities filled with fires, prisons, proconsuls, and wild beasts. This summary of saving events ends with a doxology and a final amen.

4.18

Καὶ εὖρεν τὸν Θάμυριν[1] τεθνεῶτα,[2] τὴν δὲ μητέρα ζῶσαν· καὶ προσκαλεσαμένη τὴν μητέρα αὐτῆς[3] λέγει αὐτῇ· Θεοκλεία μῆτερ, δύνασαι πιστεῦσαι ὅτι ζῇ κύριος ἐν οὐρανοῖς;[4] εἴτε γὰρ χρήματα[5] ποθεῖς, δώσει σοι κύριος δι᾽ ἐμοῦ· εἴτε τὸ τέκνον, ἰδού, παρέστηκά[6] σοι. καὶ ταῦτα διαμαρτυραμένη[7] ἀπῆλθεν[8] εἰς Σε-λεύκειαν,[9] καὶ πολλοὺς[10] φωτίσασα τῷ λόγῳ τοῦ θεοῦ[11] μετὰ καλοῦ ὕπνου[12] ἐκοιμήθη.

Translation

And she found Thamyris had died, but her mother was living; and having summoned her mother, she said to her, "Theocleia, mother, Are you able to believe that the Lord lives in heaven? For whether you desire treasures, the Lord will give to you through me, or you desire a child, behold, I stand before you. When she had presented these things as testimony, she departed into Seleucia, and having brought to light many by the Word of God she lay down with a good sleep.

4.18.1 Textual Notes

[1] On Thamyris, see 3.7. This is Thecla's betrothed in Iconium. The circumstances of his death are not known or reported. The text does not specify how much time has elapsed, since Thecla left Iconium, but it is unlikely to have been an extensive amount of time. A period of a few months or within a few years is probably intended. This is partly due to the fact that Paul is still in Myra upon the completion of the *APTh*, when the *AP* continues in chapter five. In ch. 45 of the *APTh*, Thecla is on the pyre in Iconium at age 17, and then before the wild beasts in Antioch at age 18.

[2] τεθνεῶτα is the perfect active participle, accusative mascline singular of θνήσκω.

³ Cop¹ is very fragmentary for page 28 of the Heidelberg Papyrus that breaks off here.

⁴ See Matthew 11:25.

⁵ Thecla offers her mother a way to restore her wealth (lost due to lack of a wedding between Thecla and Thamyris), her honor, and a new Christianized social status. See comments by Vorster, "Construction of Culture," 108; and comments in *3.10.1 Textual Notes*, note 6. However, no response from Theocleia is recorded.

⁶ This is the "complexive aorist" (See Smyth, *Greek Grammar*, 430–31, §1927).

⁷ Acts 20:24 states, "ὡς τελειῶσαι τὸν δρόμον μου καὶ τὴν διακονίαν ἣν ἔλαβον παρὰ τοῦ κυρόυ Ἰησοῦ, διαμαρτύρασθαι τὸ εὐαγγέλιον τῆς χάριτος τοῦ θεοῦ" where Paul speaks of his desire to complete his ministry and testify to the Gospel. This is what Thecla is doing with her mother. διαμαρτύρομαι appears in Acts nine times; See also 1 Tim 5:21; 2 Tim 1:14 and 4:1. The quasi-dialogue of the *AP* with the Pastorals (?) continues here, where Thecla, "ordained" by God (and blessed by Paul), goes and instructs/warns her mother. This could be a somewhat humorous play on the concept of 1 Tim 5:21, which warns not to ordain anyone too quickly, in order to remain pure (ἁγνὸν, see *3.6.2 General Comment*) in verse 22. Also 2 Tim 4:1 warns (διαμαρτύρομαι) Timothy, Paul's anointed companion, to "preach the word," which is exactly what Thecla is doing, both teaching and warning her mother. See "διαμαρτύρομαι," *TDNT*, 4:510–12.

⁸ See *3.19.1 Textual Notes*, note 5 for other references for ἀπῆλθεν.

⁹ Σελεύκειαν – This is probably Seleucia of Cilicia Trachea. If the Antioch of 3.26 is not Pisidian Antioch, then it is possible that Thecla has gone from Syrian Antioch to Seleucia Pieria. This option is less likely (see *3.1.1 Textual Notes*, note1). See also Vouaux, *Actes de Paul*, 229, note 2*, "il n'y a pas de raison de ne pas penser à la Séleucie de Cilicie, où l'on honorait la sainte d'un culte ancien." There is very little material culture of Thecla in and around Syrian Antioch, but quite the contrary in Cilician Antioch. See also Davis, *The Cult of Saint Thecla*, 36–80 and Johnson, *The Life and Miracles of Thekla: A Literary Study*, 169–71, etc.

¹⁰ Cop¹ begins again here and seamlessly proceeds from *AP* 4.18 to the scene in Myra. In fact, upon the conclusion of 4.18, the text transitions with a two line introduction with a border similar to the beginning of the *APTh* section.

¹¹ See *4.17.1 Textual Notes*, note 5.

¹² On the abrupt conclusion to the story of Thecla, see Vouaux, *Actes de Paul*, 229–230, note 3*. It appears that one explanation given is that a speedy end to Paul and Thamyris is inconsequential as part of the *AP*, but is expanded further as the *APTh* began to circulate as a separate text and

thus demanded more detail. See also *AP* 4.4, 10; *4.4.1 Textual Notes*, note 6 and *4.10.1 Textual Notes*, note 7. Thecla's "sleep" is death.

4.18.2 General Comment

This chapter is almost like a postscript, in which the conclusion to the life of Thecla is quickly accounted for as Thecla goes home, finds her betrothed dead due to unknown reasons, and then makes an appeal to her mother. The figure of Thecla's new patroness, Tryphaena, cannot help but be contrasted to her mother, whom she is attempting to convert to Christ (See *4.14.1 Textual Notes*, note 6 and Misset-Van de Weg, "Answers to the Plight," 156–62). The success of Thecla's preaching to her mother is not reported. The most probable point to Thecla teaching her mother is not the conversion of her mother, but to demonstrate that Thecla is now committed to teaching the λόγος τοῦ θεοῦ, an idea, namely a woman teaching, that is heretical to Tertullian and others. This is reinforced by the fact that Thecla offers a message that included the social reclamation of Theocleia, where the necessity of marriage and sexual relations is not instrumental. Also, the attention of the conversion of a woman (Theocleia) seems to have higher priority to the author than just the conversion of anyone, thus emphasizing the theme of the role of women within the text.

Upon completing her mission to Iconium, Thecla then quickly moves to Seleucia, where it is reported that she had a *good sleep* indicating a good death after converting many there. This brings the *APTh* to a conclusion as the text of the *AP* will then continue with Paul in Myra as indicated in 4.15.

*Note on the APTh 44, 45, and Recension G (Codex G)

AAA's text of the *AP* includes chapters 44 and 45 (this assumes that one does not break the *APTh* into two chapters [chs. 3–4], but rather the numeration continues from 3.1–43 instead of 3.1–26 and 4.1–18) that are found in codices *A*, *B*,C but not in manuscript *G*, which includes a variant ending to the *Acts of Paul and Thecla*, entitled Codex Barocciano (Codex *G* in *AAA*). Johann Ernest Grabe first edited codex Barocciano in 1698 in *Spicilegium SS. Patrum ut et Hæreticorum*, (2nd ed.; Oxoniæ: E Theatro Sheldoniano, 1700), 116–19. *AAA* reproduced Grabe's text, and is here reproduced from the greek manuscript. Following Rordorf, *ÉAC*, 1142, Lipsius, *AAA*, 270–72 Vouaux, *Actes de Paul*, 230–38, and Schmidt, *Acta Pauli*, 52 (Cop[1] preserves none of these three endings) that none of these endings is original to the *AP*, but I have maintained them in the tradition of Lipsius. Therefore I reproduce here chapters 44, 45, and Codex *G* according to Grabe and Lipsius. See Elliott's *ANT*, 372–4, for a translation into English.

Acts of Paul and Thecla 44

Τινὲς δὲ τῆς πόλεως Ἕλληνες ὄντες τὴν θρησκείαν, ἰατροὶ δὲ τὴν τέχνην, ἀπέστειλαν πρὸς αὐτὴν ἄνδρας νεωτέρους σοβαροὺς ἐπὶ τὸ φθεῖραι αὐτήν· ἔλεγον γὰρ ὅτι τῇ Ἀρτέμιδι δουλεύει παρθένος οὖσα, καὶ ἐκ τούτου ἰσχύει πρὸς τὰς ἰάσεις. προνοίᾳ δὲ θεοῦ εἰσῆλθεν ἐν τῇ πέτρᾳ ζῶσα, καὶ τὴν γῆν ὑπέβη. καὶ ἀπῆλθεν ἐν τῇ Ῥώμῃ θεάσασθαι τὸν Παῦλον, καὶ εὗρεν αὐτὸν κοιμηθέντα. μείνασα δὲ ἐκεῖ χρόνον οὐ πολύν, μετὰ καλοῦ ὕπνου ἐκοιμήθη· καὶ θάπτεται ὡς ἀπὸ δύο ἢ τριῶν σταδίων τοῦ μνήματος τοῦ διδασκάλου Παύλου.

Acts of Paul and Thecla 45

Ἐβλήθη μὲν οὖν εἰς τὸ πῦρ χρόνων οὖσα ἑπτὰ καὶ δέκα, καὶ εἰς Σελεύκειαν, καὶ πολλοὺς φωτίσασα τῷ λόγῳ τοῦ θεοῦ μετὰ καλοῦ ὕπνου ἐκοιμήθη.

Codex Barocciano (Codex G or Codex Grabii)

Καὶ νεφέλη φωτεινὴ ὡδήγει αὐτήν. καὶ εἰσελθοῦσα ἐν Σελευκίᾳ ἐξῆλθεν ἔξω τῆς πόλεως ἀπὸ ἑνὸς σταδίου· καὶ ἐκείνους δὲ ἐδεδοίκει, ὅτι τὰ εἴδωλα ἐθεράπευον. καὶ ὁδηγὸς γέγονεν αὐτῆς ἐν τῷ ὄρει τῷ λεγομένῳ Καλαμῶνος ἤτοι Ῥοδεῶνος· καὶ εὑροῦσα ἐκεῖ σπήλαιον εἰσῆλθεν αὐτῷ. καὶ ἦν ἐκεῖ ἐπὶ ἔτη ἱκανά, καὶ πολλοὺς καὶ χαλεποὺς πειρασμοὺς ὑπέστη ὑπὸ τοῦ διαβόλου, καὶ ὑπήνεγκεν γενναίως βοηθουμένη ὑπὸ τοῦ Χριστοῦ. Μαθοῦσαι δέ τινες τῶν εὐγενίδων γυναικῶν περὶ τῆς παρθένου Θέκλης, ἀπίησαν πρὸς αὐτὴν καὶ ἐμάνθανον τὰ λόγια τοῦ θεοῦ· καὶ πολλαὶ ἐξ αὐτῶν ἀπετάξαντο τῷ βίῳ καὶ συνήσκουν αὐτῇ. καὶ φήμη ἀγαθὴ ἤχθη πανταχοῦ περὶ αὐτῆς, καὶ ἰάσεις ἐγίνοντο ὑπ' αὐτῆς. γνοῦσα οὖν πᾶσα ἡ πόλις καὶ ἡ περίχωρος, ἔφερον τοὺς ἀρρώστους αὐτῶν ἐν τῷ ὄρει, καὶ πρινὴ τῇ θύρᾳ προσεγγίσωσι, θᾶττον ἀπηλλάττοντο, οἵῳ δήποτε κατείχοντο νοσήματι, καὶ τὰ πνεύματα τὰ ἀκάθαρτα κράζοντα ἐξήρχοντο· καὶ πάντες κατελάμβανον τὰ ἴδια αὐτῶν ὑγιῆ, δοξάζοντες τὸν θεὸν δόντα τοιαύτην χάριν τῇ παρθένῳ Θέκλῃ. οἱ ἰατροὶ οὖν τῆς πόλεως Σελευκίων ἐξουδενώθησαν, τὴν ἐμπορείαν ἀπολέσαντες, καὶ οὐδεὶς λοιπὸν προσεῖχεν αὐτοῖς· καὶ φθόνου καὶ ζήλου πλησθέντες ἐμηχανοῦντο κατὰ τῆς τοῦ Χριστοῦ δούλης τὸ τί αὐτῇ ποιήσωσιν. Ὑποβάλλει οὖν αὐτοῖς ὁ διάβολος λογισμὸν πονηρόν. καὶ μιᾷ τῶν ἡμερῶν συναχθέντες καὶ συνέδριον ποιήσαντες συμβουλεύονται πρὸς ἀλλήλους λέγοντες Αὕτη ἡ παρθένος ἱερὰ τυγχάνει τῆς μεγάλης θεᾶς Ἀρτέμιδος· καὶ εἴ τι ἂν αἰτήσει αὐτήν, ἀκούει αὐτῆς ὡς παρθένου οὔσης, καὶ φιλοῦσιν αὐτὴν πάντες οἱ θεοί. δεῦτε οὖν λάβωμεν ἄνδρας ἀτάκτους καὶ μεθύσωμεν αὐτοὺς οἶνον πολὺν καὶ δώσωμεν αὐτοῖς χρυσίον πολὺ καὶ εἴπωμεν αὐτοῖς Εἰ δυνηθῆτε φθεῖραι καὶ μιᾶναι αὐτήν, διδοῦμεν ὑμῖν καὶ ἄλλα χρήματα. Ἔλεγον οὖν πρὸς αὐτοὺς οἱ ἰατροὶ ὅτι Ἐὰν ἰσχύσουσιν αὐτὴν μιᾶναι, οὐκ ἀκούσουσιν αὐτῆς οἱ θεοὶ οὔτε Ἄρτεμις ἐπὶ τῶν ἀσθενούντων. ἐποίησαν οὖν οὕτως. καὶ ἀπελθόντες οἱ πονηροὶ ἄνδρες ἐπὶ τὸ ὄρος, καὶ ἐπιστάντες ὡς λέοντες τῷ σπηλαίῳ ἐπάταξαν τὴν θύραν· ἤνοιξεν δὲ ἡ ἁγία μάρτυς Θέκλα, θαρροῦσα ᾧ ἐπίστευσεν θεῷ· προέγνω γὰρ τὸν δόλον αὐτῶν. καὶ λέγει πρὸς αὐτοὺς Τί θέλετε, τέκνα; Οἱ δὲ εἶπον Τίς ἐστιν ἐνταῦθα λεγομένη Θέκλα; Ἡ δὲ εἶπεν Τί αὐτὴν θέλετε; Λέγουσιν αὐτῇ ἐκεῖνοι Συγκαθευδῆσαι αὐτῇ θέλομεν. Λέγει αὐτοῖς ἡ μακαρία Θέκλα Ἐγὼ ταπεινὴ γραῦς εἰμί, δούλη δὲ τοῦ κυρίου μου Ἰησοῦ Χριστοῦ· καὶ κᾶν τί ποτε δρᾶσαι θέλετε ἄτοπον εἰς ἐμέ, οὐ δύνασθε. Λέγουσιν αὐτῇ ἐκεῖνοι Οὐκ ἔστιν δυνατὸν μὴ πρᾶξαι εἰς σὲ ἃ θέλομεν. Καὶ ταῦτα εἰπόντες ἐκράτησαν αὐτὴν ἰσχυρῶς, καὶ ἐβούλοντο καθυβρίσαι αὐτήν. ἡ δὲ λέγει αὐτοῖς μετ᾽ ἐπιεικείας Ἀναμείνατε, τέκνα, ἵνα ἴδητε τὴν δόξαν κυρίου. Καὶ κρατουμένη ὑπ᾽ αὐτῶν ἀνέβλεψεν εἰς τὸν οὐρανὸν καὶ εἶπεν Ὁ θεὸς ὁ φοβερὸς καὶ ἀνείκαστος καὶ ἔνδοξος τοῖς ὑπεναντίοις, ὁ ῥυσάμενός με ἐκ πυρός, ὁ μὴ παραδώσας με Θάμυρι, ὁ μὴ παραδώσας με Ἀλεξάνδρῳ, ὁ ῥυσάμενός με ἐκ θηρίων, ὁ διασώσας με ἐν τῷ βυθῷ, ὁ πανταχοῦ συνεργήσας μοι καὶ δοξάσας τὸ ὄνομά σου ἐν ἐμοί, καὶ τανῦν ῥῦσαί με ἐκ τῶν ἀνόμων ἀνθρώπων τούτων, καὶ μὴ ἐάσῃς με ἐνυβρίσαι τὴν παρθενίαν μου, ἣν διὰ τὸ ὄνομά σου ἐφύλαξα μέχρι τοῦ νῦν, ὅτι σὲ φιλῶ καὶ σὲ ποθῶ καὶ σοὶ προσκυνῶ τῷ πατρὶ καὶ τῷ υἱῷ καὶ τῷ πνεύματι ἁγίῳ εἰς τοὺς αἰῶνας, ἀμήν. Καὶ ἐγένετο φωνὴ ἐκ τοῦ οὐρανοῦ λέγουσα Μὴ φοβηθῇς Θέκλα, δούλη μου ἀληθινή, μετὰ σοῦ γὰρ εἰμί· ἀπόβλεψον καὶ ἴδε ὅπου ἠνέωκται ἔμπροσθέν σου, ἐκεῖ γὰρ οἶκος αἰώνιος ἔσται σοι, κἀκεῖ τὴν ἐπίσκεψιν δέχῃ. Καὶ προσχοῦσα ἡ μακαρία Θέκλα ἴδεν τὴν πέτραν ἀνεῳχθεῖσαν ὅσον χωρεῖ ἄνθρωπον εἰσιέναι, καὶ κατὰ τὸ λεχθὲν αὐτῇ ἐποίησεν, καὶ ἀποφυγοῦσα γενναίως τοὺς ἀνόμους εἰσῆλθεν εἰς τὴν πέτραν· καὶ συνεκλείσθη εὐθὺς ἡ πέτρα, ὥστε μήτε ἁρμὸν φαίνεσθαι. ἐκεῖνοι δὲ θεωροῦντες τὸ παράδοξον θαῦμα ὥσπερ ἐν ἐκστάσει ἐγίνοντο, καὶ οὐκ ἴσχυσαν ἐπισχεῖν τὴν τοῦ θεοῦ δούλην, ἀλλ᾽ ἢ μόνον τοῦ μαφορίου αὐτῆς ἐπελάβοντο καὶ μέρος τι ἠδυνήθησαν ἀποσπάσαι· κἀκεῖνο κατὰ συγχώρησιν θεοῦ πρὸς πίστιν τῶν ὁρώντων τὸν σεβάσμιον τόπον, καὶ εἰς εὐλογίαν ταῖς μετὰ ταῦτα γενεαῖς, τοῖς πιστεύουσιν εἰς τὸν κύριον ἡμῶν Ἰησοῦν Χριστὸν ἐκ καρδίας καθαρᾶς. Ἔπαθεν οὖν ἡ τοῦ θεοῦ πρωτομάρτυς καὶ ἀπόστολος καὶ παρθένος Θέκλα ἡ ἀπὸ τοῦ Ἰκονίου ἐτῶν δέκα ὀκτώ· μετὰ δὲ τῆς ὁδοιπορίας καὶ τῆς περιόδου καὶ τῆς ἀσκήσεως τῆς ἐν τῷ ὄρει ἔζησεν ἔτη ἄλλα ἑβδομήκοντα καὶ δύο· ὅτε δὲ προσελάβετο αὐτὴν ὁ κύριος, ἦν ἐτῶν ἐνενήκοντα, καὶ οὕτως ἡ τελείωσις αὐτῆς γίνεται. γίνεται δὲ ἡ ὁσία μνήμη αὐτῆς μηνὶ Σεπτεμβρίῳ εἰκάδι τετάρτῃ, εἰς δόξαν τοῦ πατρὸς καὶ τοῦ υἱοῦ καὶ τοῦ ἁγίου πνεύματος νῦν καὶ ἀεὶ καὶ εἰς τοὺς αἰῶνας τῶν αἰώνων, ἀμήν.

Bibliography

Primary Sources

Achelis, Hans von. *Die Canones Hippolyti. Texte und Untersuchungen zur Geschichte der altchristlichen Literatur* 6.4. Leipzig: J.C. Hinrichs, 1891.

Achilles Tatius, *Leucippe and Clitophon*. Trans. S. Gaselee. London: William Heinemann, 1917.

Apuleius. *The Golden Ass* or *The Metamorphoses of Lucius Apuleius*. Trans. W. Adlington. LCL 44. Cambridge: Harvard UP, 1965.

Aristotle, "On Marvelous Things." Pages 237–328 in *Aristotle: Minor Works*. Translated by W. S. Hett. LCL 307. Cambridge, Harvard UP, 1963.

(Pseudo) Athanasius. *Synopsis Scripturae Sacrae*. Edited by Jacques Paul Migne in *Patrologiae cursus completus (series Graeca) (MPG)* 28. Paris: Migne, 1857–1866.

Bidez, J. *L'empereur Julien. Oeuvres completes*. Vol. 1.2. 2d ed. Paris: Les Belles Lettres, 1960.

Blanc, Cécile. *Origène. Commentaire sur saint Jean*. 3 vols. SC 120, 157, 222. Paris: Éditions du Cerf, 1966, 1970, 1975.

Bouriant, Urban. "Fragments de texte grec du livre d'Énoch det de quelqeus écrits attributes à saint Pierre," Pages 137–42 in *Mémoires publiés par les members de la mission archéologique française au Caire 9.1*. Paris: Le Caire, 1892.

Burchard, C., ed. "Joseph and Aseneth." Pages 177–247 in *The Old Testament Pseudepigrapha*. Ed. James H. Charlesworth. Vol. 2. New York: Doubleday, 1985.

Cadbury, H. J., and Kirsopp Lake, *Part 1: The Acts of the Apostles*. Edited by F. J. Foakes Jackson and Kirsopp Lake, Vol. 1 of *The beginnings of Christianity*. Grand Rapids: Baker, 1920–33, 1979.

Chariton. *Callirhoe*. Edited and Translated by G. P. Goold. LCL 481. Cambridge: Harvard UP, 1995.

Conybeare, Frederick Cornwallis, ed. *The Apology and Acts of Apollonius and other Monuments of Early Christianity*. 49–88. London: Swan Sonnenschein; New York: MacMillan, 1894.

–. *The Armenian Apology and the Acts of Apollonius and Other Monuments of Early Christianity*. 2d ed with an Appendix. London: Swan Sonnenschein; New York: MacMillan. 1896.

Edmonds, John Maxwell. *Elegy and Iambus: being the remains of all the Greek elegiac and iambic poets from Callinus to Crates, excepting the choliambic writers, with the Anacreontea*. 2 vols. London: W. Heinemann, 1931.

Ehrman, Bart D., ed. and trans. *The Apostolic Fathers*. LCL 25. 2 vols. Cambridge, Mass. And London: Harvard UP, 2003.

Euripides, *Bacchae*. Translated by David Kovacs. LCL 495. Cambridge: Harvard UP, 2003.

Eusebius. *Ecclesiastical History.* Loeb Classical Library. Cambridge, Mass.: Harvard UP, 1926–32.

Funk, F. X., and K. Bihlmeyer, eds. *Die Apostolischen Väter I.* Edited by W. Schneemelcher. Sammlung ausgewählter kirchen- und dogmengeschichtlicher Quellenschriften 2.1. 2d ed. Tübingen: J. C. B. Mohr (Paul Siebeck), 1956.

Goodspeed, Edgar Johnson. *Die ältesten Apologeten.* Göttingen: Vandenhoeck & Ruprecht, 1915.

Görgemanns, H. and H. Karpp. "De Principiis," Pages 462–560, 668–764 in *Origenes vier Büchern von den Prinzipien.* Darmstadt: Wissenschaftliche Buchgesellschaft, 1976.

Heliodorus. *An Ethiopian Romance.* Translated by Moses Hadas. Philadelphia: U of Penn P, 1957.

Horner, G. *The Coptic Version of the New Testament in the Southern Dialect, Otherwise Called Sahidic or Thebaic.* Oxford: Clarendon Press, 1911–24.

Kraft, Robert A., ed. *The Testament of Job,* SBLTT 5, Pseudepigrapha Series 4. Atlanta: Scholars Press, 1974.

Lefèvre, Maurice. *Hippolyte: Commentaire sur Daniel.* SC 14. Paris: Éditions du Cerf, 1947.

Leloir, Louis. "Martyre de Paul." Pages 77–86 in *Écrits Apocryphes sur les apôtres: Traduction de l'édition Arménienne de Venise. I. Pierre, Paul, André, Jacques, Jean.* Turnhout: Brepols, 1986.

Lewis, Agnes Smith, trans. *Acta Mythologica Apostolorum: transcribed from an Arabic MS in the convent of deyr-Es-Suriani, Egypt, and from MSS in the Convent of St. Catherine, on Mount Sinai.* London: C. J. Clay and Sons, 1904.

Lewis, Agnes Smith and F. Crawford Burkitt. Pages 190–205 in *Select Narratives of Holy Women: Select narratives of holy women, from the Syro-Antiochene or Sinai palimpsest as written above the old Syriac Gospels.* Studia Sinaitica 9. London: C. J. Clay and Sons, 1900.

Lightfoot, Joseph Barber. *The Apostolic Fathers.* 2d ed. London: MacMillan and Co., 1889.

Lipsius, Richard Adelbert. *Die apokryphen Apostelgeschichten und Apostellegenden.* Braunschweig: C. A. Schwetschke und Sohn, 1887.

Lipsius, Richard Adelbert, and Maximillian Bonnet. *Acta apostolorum apocrypha.* Leipzig: Hermann Mendelssohn, 1891–1903; Repr. Hildesheim: G. Olms Verlagsbuchhandlung, 1959.

Longus. *Daphnis and Chloe.* Edited by J. M. Edmonds. Translated by George Thornley. LCL 69. Cambridge: Harvard UP, 1916.

Lucian. "The Passing of Peregrinus" in *Lucian.* Edited by A. M. Harmon. LCL 302. Cambridge: Harvard, 1936.

Nautin, Pierre. *Origène. Homélies sur Jérémie.* vol. 1. SC 232. Paris: Éditions du Cerf, 1976.

Parthenius, *The Story of Pallene.* Translated by S. Gaselee. LCL 69. Cambridge: Harvard UP, 1916.

Philostratus. *The Life of Apollonius of Tyana.* Edited by Christopher P. Jones. 2 vols. Loeb Classical Library 16. Cambridge, Ma.: Harvard UP, 2005.

Photius. *Bibliothèque.* Edited by René Henry. 8 vols. Paris: Société d'édition Les Belles lettres, 1959–1977.

Tertullian. *Tertulliani Opera: Pars I.* Edited by J. G. Ph. Borleffs. CCSL. Turnholti: Typographi Brepols Editores Pontificii, 1954).

–. *Tertullian's Homily on Baptism.* Edited and Translated by Ernest Evans. London: SPCK, 1964.

Theodore of Mopsuestia. *Epistolas B. Pauli Commentarii.* Edited by H. B. Swete. Cambridge: University Press, 1880–82.

Varro, Marcus Terentius. *Cato and Varro: On Agriculture.* Edited and Translated by William David Hopper. Revised by Harrison Boyd Ash. LCL 283. Cambridge: Harvard UP, 1934.

Witte, Bernd. *Die Schrift des Origenes "Über das Passa."* Arbeiten zum spätantiken und koptischen Ägypten 4. Altenberge: Oros, 1993.

Secondary Sources

Accademia ercolanese di archeologia (Naples, Italy), Ottavio Antonio Baiardi, and Pasquale Carcani. *Le Pitture Antiche d'Ercolano E Contorni Incise con Qualche Spiegazione.* Le Antichità di Ercolano Esposte. In Napoli: Nella Regia stamperia, 1757–92.

Adamik, Tamás. "The Image of Simon Magus in the Christian Tradition." Pages 52–54 in *The Apocryphal Acts of Peter: Magic, Miracles, and Gnosticism.* Edited by Jan N. Bremmer. Leuven: Peeters, 1998.

Albrecht, Ruth. *Das Leben der heiligen Makrina auf dem Hintergrund der Thekla- Traditionen: Studien zu den Ursprüngen des weiblichen Mönchtums im 4. Jahrhundert in Kleinasien.* Gottingen: Vandenhoeck & Ruprecht, 1986.

–. "Thekla." Page 298 in *Der Neue Pauly. Enzyklopädie der Antike.* Edited by Hubert Cancik and Helmuth Schneider. Alterum Vol 12/1, Tam-Vel. Stuttgart and Weimar: J. B. Metzler, 2000.

Altendorf, Hans-Dietrich. "Orthodoxie et hérésie: réflexions provisoires." *Cahiers de la Revue de théologie et de philosophie* 17 (1993): 125–40.

Amiot, F. *La Bible apocryphe: Évangiles apocryphes.* Textes pour l'histoire sacrée, Edited by H. Daniel-Rops. Paris, 1983.

Anson, John. "The Female Transvestite in Early Monasticism: The Origin and Development of a Motif." *Viator: Medieval and Renaissance Studies* 5 (1974): 1–32.

Appel, Andrea. "Möglichkeiten und Grenzen für ein Amt der Frau in frühchristlichen Gemeinden am Beispiel der Pastoralbriefe und der Thekla-Akten," in *Frauen in der Geschichte,* vol. 7. Edited by Werner Affeldt and Annette Kuhn, 244–56. Düsseldorf: Pädagogischer Verlag Schwann, 1986.

Aubin, Melissa. "Reversing Romance? The *Acts of Thecla* and the Ancient Novel." *Ancient Fiction and Early Christian Narrative.* Edited by Ronald F. Hock, J. Bradley Chance, and Judith Perkins. Atlanta: Scholars Press, 1998), 257–72.

Aubineau, Michel. "Compléments au dossier de sainte Thécle." *Analecta Bollandiana* 93 (1975): 356–62.

–. "Le panéyrique de Thècle, attribué à Jean Chrysostome *(BHG* 1720): la fin retrouvée d'un texte motile." *Analecta Bollandiana* 93 (1975): 349–62.

Babcock, William S. *Paul and the Legacies of Paul.* Dallas: Southern Methodist University Press, 1990.

Balch, David L. *Roman Domestic Art and Early House Churches.* (Tübingen: Mohr, forthcoming 2008).

–."Zeus, Vengeful Protector of the Political and Domestic Order: Frescoes in Dining Rooms N and P of the House of the Vettii in Pompeii, Mark 13.12–13, and 1 Clement 6.2." Pages 67–95 in *Picturing the New Testament: Studies in Ancient Visual Images.* Edited by Annette Weissenrieder, Friederike Wendt, and Petra von Gemünden. WUNT 2.193. Tübingen: Mohr Siebeck, 2005.

Balch, David L. and Carolyn Osiek, eds. *Early Christian Families in Context: An Interdisciplinary Dialogue.* Grand Rapids: Eerdmans, 2003.

Baldasarre, Ida, ed. *Pompei: Pitture e Mosaici.* 10 vols. Roma: Instituto della Enciclopedia Italiana, 1994.

Bammel, C. P. Review of *Marcion: On the Restitution of Christianity. An Essay on the Development of Radical Paulinist Theology in the Second Century,* by R. J. Hoffmann. *Journal of Theological Studies* 39 (1988): 227–32.

Bardy, G. "Apocryphes à tendance encratite." *Dictionnaire de Spiritualité.*1 (1937): 752–65.

Barns, J. W. B. "Appendix II." Pages 570–78 in *The Apocryphal New Testament.* Edited by Montague Rhodes James. 2d ed. Oxford: Clarendon, 1953.

–. "Pauline Controversies in the Post-Pauline Period." *New Testament Studies* 21 (1974–75): 229–45.

Barrier, Jeremy W. "Tertullian and the Acts of Paul or Thecla? Readership of the Ancient Novel and the Invocation of Thecline and Pauline Authority." Paper presented at the annual meeting of the SBL. Washington, D. C., November 20, 2006.

Bassler, Jouette M. "The Widows' Tale: A Fresh Look at 1 Tim 5:3–16." *Journal of Biblical Literature* 103 (1984): 23–41.

Bauckham, R. J. "The *Acts of Paul* as a Sequel to Acts." Pages 105–52 in *The Book of Acts in Its Ancient Literary Setting,* Edited by B. W. Winter and A. D. Clarke. Grand Rapids: Eerdmans; Carlisle: Paternoster Press, 1993.

Bauer, Walter. *Orthodoxy and Heresy in Earliest Christianity.* London/Philadelphia: SCM/Fortress Press, 1971.

–. *A Greek-English Lexicon of the New Testament and Other Early Christian Literature.* Trans. W. F. Arndt, F. W. Gingrich, and F. Danker. 3d ed. Chicago: University of Chicago Press, 1979.

Baumstark, Anton. Review of ΠΡΑΞΕΙΣ ΠΑΥΛΟΥ. *Acta Pauli. Nach dem Papyrus der Hamburger Staats und Universitäts-Bibliothek.* Edited by Carl Schmidt in collaboration with Wilhelm Schubart. Glückstadt and Hamburg: J. J. Augustin, 1936. *Oriens Christianus* 34 (1937): 122–26.

–. *Die Petrus- und Paulusacten in der litterarischen Ueberlieferung der syrischen Kirche.* Leipzig: Otto Harrassowitz, 1902.

Beard, Mary, Alan K. Bowman et al. *Literacy in the Roman World.* Journal of Roman Archaeology Supplementary Series Number 3. Ann Arbor, MI: Department of Classical Studies, University of Michigan, 1991.

Bedjan, Paul. *Acta Martyrum et Sanctorum.* Paris: Via Dicta De Sèvres; Leipzig: Otto Harrassowitz, 1890.

Bell, H. I. Review of ΠΡΑΞΕΙΣ ΠΑΥΛΟΥ. *Acta Pauli. Nach dem Papyrus der Hamburger Staats- und Universitäts-Bibliothek..* Edited by Carl Schmidt in collaboration with Wilhelm Schubart. Glückstadt and Hamburg: J. J. Augustin, 1936. *Journal of Theological Studies* 38 (1937): 189–91.

Biblia Patristica: Index des citations et allusions bibliques dans la littérature patristique. Paris: Editions du Centre National de la Recherche Scientifique, 1975–91.

Blumenthal, M. *Formen und Motive in den apokryphen Apostelgeschichten.* Texte und Untersuchungen zur Geschichte der altchristlichen Literatur 48.1. Leipzig: J. C. Hinrichs, 1933.

Boer, Martinus C. de. "Images of Paul in the Post-Apostolic Period." *Catholic Biblical Quarterly* 42 (1980): 359–80.

Boese, H. "Über eine bisher unbekannte Handschrift des Briefwechsels zwischen Paulus und den Korinthern." *Zeitschrift für die neutestamentliche Wissenschaft* 44 (1952–53): 66–76.

Botterweck, G. Johannes and Helmer Ringgren. *Theological Dictionary of the Old Testament.* Trans. John T. Willis. 15 vols. Grand Rapids: Eerdmans, 1974–.

Boughton, L. C. "From Pious Legend to Feminist Fantasy: Distinguishing Hagiographical License from Apostolic Practice in the *Acts of Paul/Acts of Thecla*." *Journal of Religion* 71 (1991): 362–83.

Bovon, François. "A New Citation of the *Acts of Paul* in Origen," Pages 267–70 in *Studies in Early Christianity*. Edited by Jörg Frey. Wissenschaftliche Untersuchungen zum Neuen Testament 161. Tübingen: J. C. B. Mohr (Paul Siebeck), 2003.

–. *Lukas in neuer Sicht: gesammelte Aufsätze*. Biblisch-theologische Studien 8; Neukirchen-Vluyn: Neukirchener Verlag, 1985.

–. "Une nouvelle citation des *Actes de Paul* chez Origène." *Apocrypha* 5 (1994): 113–17.

–. "Vers une nouvelle edition de la literature apocryphe chrétienne. La *Series Apocryphorum* du *Corpus Christianorum*," *Augustinianum* 33 (1983): 373–78.

Bovon, François, Ann Graham Brock, and Christopher R. Matthews. *The Apocryphal Acts of the Apostles: Harvard Divinity School Studies*. Cambridge: Harvard UP, 1999.

Bovon, François, Michel van Esbroeck, Richard Goulet, Eric Junod, Jean-Daniel Kaestli, Françoise Morard, Gérard Poupon, Jean-Marc Prieur, and Yves Tissot. *Les Actes apocryphes des Apôtres. Christianisme et monde païen*. Publication de la faculté de théologie de l'Université de Genève. Geneva: Labor et Fides, 1981

Bovon, François, and Pierre Geoltrain, eds. *Écrits apocryphes chrétiens*. Bibliothèque de la Pléiade, Index by J. Voicu. Saint Herblain: Gallimard, 1997.

Bowie, Ewen. "The Readership of Greek Novels in the Ancient World." Pages 435–59 in *The Novel in the Ancient World*. Edited by Gareth L. Schmeling. rev. ed. Leiden: Brill, 2003.

Bratke, Eduard. "Ein zweiter lateinischer Text des apokryphen Briefwechsels zwischen dem Apostel Paulus und den Korinthern." *Theologische Literaturzeitung* 17 (1892): 585–88.

Bremmer, Jan, N., ed. *The Apocryphal Acts of Paul and Thecla*. Kampen: Kok Pharos, 1996.

–. "Aspects of the *Acts of Peter*: Women, Magic, Place, and Date." Pages 1–20 in *The Apocryphal Acts of Peter: Magic, Miracles, and Gnosticism*. Edited by Jan N. Bremmer. Leuven: Peeters, 1998.

–. "Women in the *Apocryphal Acts of John*." Pages 37–56 in *The Apocryphal Acts of John*. Edited by Jan N. Bremmer. Kampen: Kok Pharos, 1995.

Brooten, Bernadette J. "Early Christian Women in their Cultural Context: Issues of Method in Historical Reconstruction." Pages 65–91 in *Feminist Perspectives on Biblical Scholarship*. Edited by Adela Yarbro Collins. Chico, Ca.: Scholars Press, 1985.

Brock, Ann Graham. "Genre of the *Acts of Paul*." *Apocrypha* 5 (1994): 119–36.

–. "Political Authority and Cultural Accomodation: Social Diversity in the *Acts of Paul* and the *Acts of Peter*." Pages 145–70 in *The Apocryphal Acts of the Apostles: Harvard Divinity School Studies*. Edited by François Bovon, Ann Graham Brock, and Christopher R. Matthews. Cambridge: Harvard UP, 1999.

Brown, Peter. *The Body and Society: Men, Women, and Sexual Renunciation in Early Christianity*. New York: Columbia UP, 1988.

Brown, Raymond E. *The Gospel according to John I–XII: A New Translation with Introduction and Commentary*. Anchor Bible 29. New York: Doubleday, 1966.

Bruyne, D. de, "Nouveau fragments des Actes de Pierre, de Paul, de Jean, d'André, et de l'Apocalypse d'Élie." *Revue Bénédictine* 25 (1908): 149–60.

–. "Un nouveau manuscrit de la Troisième Lettre de Saint Paul aux Corinthiens." *Revue Bénédictine* 25 (1908): 431–34.

–. "Un quatrième manuscrit latin de la Correspondance apocryphe de S. Paul avec les Corinthiens." *Revue Bénédictine* 45 (1933): 189–95.

Budge, E. A. Wallis. Pages 43–8, 527–685 in *The Contendings of the Apostles being The Histories of the Lives and Martyrdoms and Deaths of the twelve Apostles and Evangelists" The Ethiopic Texts Now First Edited from Manuscripts in the British Museum*. Vol. 2. London: Henry Frowde, 1901.

Burrus, Virginia. "Chastity as Autonomy: Women in the Stories of the Apocryphal Acts." Pages 101–17 in *Semeia 38: The Apocryphal Acts of the Apostles*. Atlanta: Scholars Press, 1986.

–. *Chastity as Autonomy. Women in the Stories of Apocryphal Acts*. Queenston, Ont.: Mellen, 1987.

Calef, Susan A. "Thecla 'Tried and True' and the Inversion of Romance," Pages 163–85 in *A Feminist Companion to the New Testament Apocrypha*. Edited by Amy-Jill Levine with Maria Mayo Robbins. Feminist Companion to the New Testament and Early Christian Writings, 11. Cleveland: The Pilgrim Press, 2006.

Carlé, Birte. *Thekla: en kvindeskikkelse i tidlig kristen fortællekunst*. Copenhagen: Delta, 1980.

Carolis, Ernesto De. *God and Heroes in Pompeii*. Trans. by Lori-Ann Touchette. Rome: "L'erma" di Bretscheider, 2001.

Carrière, A., and S. Berger. "La Correspondance apocryphe de saint Paul et des Corinthiens." *Revue de Théologie et de Philosophie* 24 (1891): 333–51.

–. *La Correspondance apocryphe de Saint Paul et des Corinthiens: ancienne version Latine et traduction du texte Arménien*. Paris: Librairie Fiscbacher, 1891.

Cartlidge, David R. and J. Keith Elliott. "5 Paul, Thecla, and Peter." Pages 134–71 in *Art and the Christian Apocrypha*. London and New York: Routledge, 2001.

–. "Thecla," *BR* 20.6 (2004): 33.

Chadwick, Henry. "Enkrateia," Pages 5:343–65 in *RAC*. Stuttgart: Hiersemann, 1962.

Ciarallo, Annamaria. *Gardens of Pompeii*. Trans. by Lori-Ann Touchette. Rome: "L'erma" di Bretscheider, 2001.

Clemen, Carl. "Miszellen zu den Paulusakten." *Zeitschrift für die neutestamentliche Wissenschaft* 5 (1904): 228–47.

Cole, Susan Guettel. "Could Greek Women Read and Write?" Pages 219–45 in *Reflections of Women in Antiquity*. Edited by Helene P. Foley. New York: Gordon and Breach Science Publishers, 1981.

Coleman, K. M. "Fatal Charades: Roman Executions Staged As Mythological Enactments." *Journal of Roman Studies* 80 (1990): 44–73.

–. "Launching into History: Aquatic Displays in the Early Empire." *Journal of Roman Studies* 83 (1993): 48–74.

Conzelmann, Hans. *Acts of the Apostles*. Edited by Eldon Jap Epp with Christopher R. Matthews. Translated by James Limburg, A. Thomas Kraabel, and Donald H. Juel. Hermeneia. Philadelphia: Fortress, 1987.

Corssen, Peter. "Die Urgestalt der Paulusakten." *Zeitschrift für die neutestamentliche Wissenschaft* 4 (1903): 22–47.

–. Review of *Acta Pauli aus der Heidelberger koptischen Papyrushandschrift Nr. 1*. Leipzig: J. C. Heinrichs, 1905. Reprint, Hildesheim: Georg Olms, 1965. *Göttingische gelehrte Anzeigen* 156 (1904): 702ff.

–. "Der Schluss der Paulusakten." *Zeitschrift für die neutestamentliche Wissenschaft* 6 (1905): 317–38.

Crum, W. E. "New Coptic Manuscripts in the John Rylands Library." *Bulletin of the John Rylands University Library of Manchester* 5 (1918–20): 501.

–. *Coptic Dictionary*. Oxford: Clarendon Press, 1939.

Dagron, Gilbert in collaboration with Marie Dupré La Tour. *Vie et miracles de sainte Thècle: texte grec, traduction et commentaire.* Subsidia Hagiographica 62. Brussels: Societe des Bollandistes, 1978.

Dassmann, Ernst. *Der Stachel im Fleisch: Paulus in der frühchristlichen Literatur bis Irenäus.* Münster: Aschendorff, 1979.

Davies, Stevan L. *The Revolt of the Widows: The Social World of the Apocryphal Acts.* London: Feffer & Simons. 1980.

–. "The Social World of the Apocryphal Acts." Ph.D. diss., Temple University, 1978.

–. "Women, Tertullian and the *Acts of Paul.*" Pages 139–43 in *Semeia 38: The Apocryphal Acts of the Apostles.* Atlanta: Scholars Press, 1986.

Davis, Stephen J. *The Cult of St. Thecla: A Tradition of Women's Piety in Late Antiquity.* Oxford: Oxford, 2001.

Deeleman, C. F. M., "Acta Pauli." *Theological Studies* 26 (1908): 1–44.

–. "Acta Pauli et Theclae." *Theological Studies* 26 (1908): 273–301.

–. "De apocriefe briefwisseling tusschen Paulus en de Cointhiërs." *Theological Studies* 27 (1909): 37–56.

Devos, P. "Actes de Thomas et Actes de Paul." *Analecta Bollandiana* 69 (1951): 119–30.

Dobschütz, Ernst von. *Die Thessalonicher-Briefe.* Meyer's Kommentar. Göttinger: Vandenhoek and Ruprecht, 1909.

Dowden, Ken. "The Roman Audience of the *Golden Ass.*" Pages 260–70 in *The Novel in the Ancient World.* Edited by Gareth L. Schmeling, rev. ed. Leiden: Brill, 2003.

Drijvers, H. J. W. "Der getaufte Löwe und die Theologie der Acta Pauli." Pages 181–89 in *Carl-Schmidt-Kolloquium an der Martin-Luther-Universität 1988.* Edited by Peter Nagel. Kongress und Tagungsberichte der Martin-Luther-Universität, Halle-Wittenberg, Halle: Abt. Wissenschaftspublizistik der Martin-Luther-Universität, 1990.

Dundes, Alan, ed. *The Study of Folklore.* Englewood Cliffs: Prentice-Hall, 1965.

Dunn, James D. G. *Unity and Diversity in the New Testament: An Inquiry into the Character of Earliest Christianity.* 2d ed. London: SCM Press, 1990.

–. *The Partings of the Ways: Between Christianity and Judaism and Their Significance for the Character of Christianity.* London: SCM Press, 1991.

Dunn, Peter W. "The *Acts of Paul* and the Pauline Legacy in the Second Century." Ph.D. diss., University of Cambridge, 1996.

–. "Women's Liberation, the *Acts of Paul,* and Other Apocryphal Acts of the Apostles: A Review of Some Recent Interpreters." *Apocrypha* 4 (1993): 245–61.

Ebner, Martin. *Aus Liebe zu Paulus? Die Akten Thekla neu aufgerollt.* Stuttgart: Verlag Katholisches Biblelwerk, 2005.

Eck, W. "Senatorische Familien der Kaiserzeit in der Provinz Sizilien," *Zeitschrift für Papyrologie und Epigraphik* 113 (1996): 109–28.

Eggers, Brigitte. "Women and Marriage in the Greek Novels: The Boundaries of Romance." Pages 260–79 in *The Novel in the Ancient World.* Edited by Gareth L. Schmeling. rev. ed. Leiden: Brill, 2003.

Ehrman, Bart D. *Lost Christianities: The Battles for Scripture and the Faiths We Never Knew.* Rev. ed. Oxford: Oxford UP, 2005.

–. *Lost Scriptures: Books That Did Not Make It Into the New Testament.* Oxford: Oxford UP, 2003.

Elanskaya, A. I. "*Passio Pauli* in the Coptic Ms. GMII I.Ib.686." Pages 19–37 in *Mélanges Antoine Guillaumont: contributions à l'étude des christianismes orientaux: avec une bibliographie du dédicataire.* Cahiers d'orientalisme 20. Genève: Patrick Cramer, 1988.

Elliot, J. K. *The Apocryphal New Testament: A Collection of Apocryphal Christian Literature in an English Translation.* Oxford: Clarendon Press, 1993.
–. "The Apocryphal Acts." *Expository Times* 105 (1993–94): 71–77.
–. Review of *Écrits apocryphes chrétiens.* Bibliothèque de la Pléiade, eds. François Bovon and Pierre Geoltrain, Index by J. Voicu. Saint Herblain: Gallimard, 1997. *NovT* 40.3 (1998): 300–06.
Ellis, E. Earle. "The Pastorals and Paul." *Expository Times* 104 (1992–93): 45–47.
Erbetta, Mario. *Atti e leggende: versione e commento.* Gli apocrifi del Nuovo Testamento, 2d ed. Vol. 2. Mariotti: Torini, 1978.
–. *Lettere e apocalissi: versione e commento.* Gli apocrifi del Nuovo Testamento. Vol. 3. Mariotti: Torini, 1969.
Evans, Elizabeth Cornelia. "The Study of Physiognomy in the Second Century A.D." *Transactions and Proceedings of the American Philological Association* 72 (1941): 96–108.
–. *Physiognomics in the Ancient World.* Transactions of the American Philosophical Society 59.5. Philadelphia: American Philosophical Society, 1969.
Fabricius, Johann Albert. *Codex Apocryphus Novi Tesamenti.* Hamburg: B. Schiller, 1703.
–. *Codex Apocryphus Novi Tesamenti: Collectus, castigatus, testimoniisque, censuris & animadversionibus illustratus à Johanne Alberto Fabricio.* 2d ed. 3 vols. Hamburg: B. Schiller & Joh. Christoph. Kisneri, 1719–43.
Festugière, A. J. "Les énigmes de Ste Thècle." *Comptes rendus* (1968): 52–63.
Findlay, Adam Fyfe. *Byways in Early Christian Literature: Studies in the Uncanonical Gospels and Acts.* Edinburgh: T. & T. Clark, 1923.
Finney, Paul Corby. *The Invisible God: The Earliest Christians on Art.* New York and Oxford: Oxford, 1994.
Fitzmyer, Joseph. *Dead Sea Scrolls and Christian Origins.* Grand Rapids: Eerdmans, 2000.
Gallagher, Eugene, "Conversion and Salvation in the Apocryphal Acts of the Apostles." *The Second Century* 8 (1991): 13–29.
Gamble, Harry Y. *Books and Readers in the Early Church: A History of Early Christian Texts.* New Haven and London: Yale UP, 1995.
García, A López. "P. Lit. Palau Rib. 18: *Martyrium Pauli* 1.18–22." *Zeitschrift für Papyrologie und Epigraphik* 110 (1996): 132.
Garnsey, P. "Why penalties become harsher: the Roman case, late Republic to fourth century Empire," *Natural Law Forum* 13 (1968): 141–62.
Gasque, W. Ward. "Iconium." Pages 357–58 in the *Anchor Bible Dictionary.* Edited by David Noel Freedman *et al.* vol. 3. Doubleday: New York, 1992.
Gebhardt, Oscar von, ed. *Passio S. Theclae virginis: Die lateinischen Übersetzungen der Acta Pauli et Theclae nebst Fragmenten, Auszügen und Beilagen. Texte und Untersuchungen zur Geschichte der altchristlichen Literatur* 7 (Neuen Folge). Leipzig: J. C. Hinrichs, 1902.
Geerard, Mauritii, ed. "Acta Pauli." Pages 117–26 in *Clavis Apocryphum Novi Testamenti.* Corpus Christianorum. Turnhout: Brepols, 1992.
Gilhus, Ingvild Sælid. *Animals, Gods, and Humans: Changing Attitues to Animals in Greek, Roman, and Early Christian Ideas.* New York: Routledge, 2006.
Goodspeed, Edgar Johnson. "The Book of Thekla." *American Journal of Semitic Languages and Literatures* 17 (1901): 65–95.
–. "The Epistle of Pelagia." *American Journal of Semitic Languages and Literatures* 20 (1904): 95–105.

–. *The Book of Thekla*. University of Chicago Historical and Linguistic Studies in Literature related to the New Testament, i. Ethiopic Texts. Chicago: University of Chicago Press, 1901.

Grabe, Johann Ernest. *Spicilegium SS. Patrum ut et Hæreticorum: Seculi post Christum natum I. II. & III. quorum vel integra monumenta, vel fragmenta, partim ex aliorum patrum libris jam impressis collegit, & cum codicibus manuscriptis contulit, partim ex MSS. nunc pr mum edidit, ac singula tam præfatione, quàm notis subjunctis illustravit : tomus I. sive seculum I.* 2d ed. Oxoniæ: E Theatro Sheldoniano, 1700.

Grant, Robert M. "The Description of Paul in the Acts of Paul and Thecla." *Vigiliae christianae* 36 (1982): 1–4.

Grenfell, Bernard P., and Arthur S. Hunt, eds. and trans. "VI. Acts of Paul and Thecla." Pages 9–10 in *The Oxyrhynchus Papyri Part 1*. London: Egypt Exploration Fund, 1898.

–. "1602. Homily to Monks." Pages 23–25 in *The Oxyrhynchus Papyri Part 13*. London: Egypt Exploration Fund, 1919.

Gronewald, M. "Einige Fackelmann-Papyri." *Zeitschrift für Papyrologie und Epigraphik* 28 (1978): 274–75.

Gryson, Roger. *The Ministry of Women in the Early Church*. Trans. Jean Laprote and Mary Louise Hall. Collegeville: Liturgical Press, 1976.

Guidi, Ignazio. "Frammenti copti."*Atti della Reale Accademia dei Lincei. Rendiconti.* 4 (1887): 65–67.

–. "Gli atti apocrifi degli Apostoli nei test copti, arabi ed etiopici." *Giornale della Società Asiatica Italiana* 2 (1888): 36–7.

Guthrie, Donald. "Acts and Epistles in Apocryphal Writings." Pages 328–45 in *Apostolic History and the Gospel: Biblical and Historical Essays Presented to F. F. Bruce on His 60th Birthday*. Edited by W. Ward Gasque and Ralph P. Martin. Grand Rapids, Mich.: Eerdmans, 1970.

Gutschmid, Alfred von. "Die Königsnamen in den apokryphen Apostelgeschichten. Ein Beitrag zur Kenntnis des geschichtlichen Romans." *Rheinisches Museum für Philologie* 19 (1864): 161–83.

Guzzo, Pier Giovanni. *Pompeii: Tales from an Eruption*. Milan: Mondadori Electra, 2007.

Gwynn, J. "Thecla." Pages 882–96 in vol. 4 of *Dictionary of Christian Biography, Literature, Sects and Doctrines: being a continuation of "The dictionary of the Bible"*. Edited by William George Smith and Henry Wace. London: J. Murray, 1877–87.

Haenchen, Ernst. *The Acts of the Apostles: A Commentary*. Trans. Bernard Noble, Gerald Shinn, and R. McL. Wilson. Philadelphia: Westminster Press, 1971.

Hägg, Tomas. *The Novel in Antiquity*. Berkeley and Los Angeles: U of Cal P, 1983.

Halkin, François. *Auctarium Bibliothecae hagiographicae graecae*. Bruxelles: Société des Bollandistes, 1969.

–. *BHG*. 3 vols. 3d ed. Bruxelles: Société des Bollandistes, 1957.

–. "La légende crétoise de saint Tite." *Analecta Bollandiana* 79 (1961): 241–56.

Hamman, A. "'Sitz im Leben' des actes apocryphes du Nouveau Testament." StPatr. *Texte und Untersuchungen zur Geschichte der altchristlichen Literatur* 93, Vol. 8. Berlin: Academie-Verlag., 1962).

Hanson, Anthony Tyrell. *Studies in the Pastoral Epistles*. London: SPCK, 1968.

Hanson, R. P. C. *Tradition in the Early Church*. London: SCM Press; Philadelphia: Westminster Press, 1962.

Harnack, Adolf von, ed. "Der Korintherbrief." Pages 6–23 in *Apocrypha IV: Die apokryphen Briefe des Paulus an die Laodicener und Korinther*. Berlin: De Gruyter, 1931.

–. *Brod und Wasser: die eucharistischen Elemente bei Justin.* Edited by Oscar von Gebhardt and Adolf Harnack. *Texte und Untersuchungen zur Geschichte der altchristlichen Literatur* 7. Leipzig: J. C. Hinrichs, 1891

–. *Drei wenig beachtete Cyprianische Schriften und die 'Acta Pauli.'* *Texte und Untersuchungen zur Geschichte der altchristlichen Literatur* 4.3b. Leipzig: J. C. Hinrichs, 1899.

–. "Paulus, Apostel, angeblicher Brief an die Korinther als Antwort auf ein angebliches Schreiben der Korinther an ihn." Pages 37–39 in *Geschichte der altchristlichen Literatur bis Eusebius.* Leipzig: J. C. Hinrichs, 1893.

–. "V. Zu den Paulusakten," Pages 100–06 in *Die Pfaff'schen Irenäus-fragmente als fälschungen Pfaffs nachgewiesen. Miszellen zu den Apostolischen Vätern, den Acta Pauli, Apelles, dem Muratorischen Fragment, den pseudocyprianischen Schriften und Claudianus Marmertus.* Leipzig: J. C. Hinrichs, 1900.

–. "Untersuchungen über den apokryphen Briefwechsel der Korinther mit dem Apostel Paulus." *Sitzungsberichte der preussischen Akademie der Wissenschaften* 1 (1905): 3–35.

–. *Marcion: Das Evangelium vom Fremden Gott.* Leipzig: J. C. Hinrichs, 1924.

–. *Marcion: The Gospel of the Alien God.* trans. John E. Steely and Lyle D. Bierma. Durham, N.C.: Labyrinth, 1990.

Harris, William V. *Ancient Literacy.* Cambridge: Harvard UP, 1989.

Heimgartner, Martin "Paulusakten." Pages 441–42 in vol. 9 of *DNP.* Edited by Hubert Cancik and Helmuth Schneider. Stuttgart and Weimar: J. B. Metzler, 2000.

Hills, Julian V. "The Acts of the Apostles in the *Acts of Paul,*" Pages 1–47 in *SBL Seminar Papers, 1994.* Edited by E. H. Lovering, Jr. Atlanta: Scholars Press, 1994.

Hodske, Jürgen. *Mythologische Bildthemen in den Häusern Pompejis: Die Bedeutung der zentralen Mythenbilder für die Bewohner Pompejis.* Stendaler Winckelmann-Forschungen 6. Ruhpolding: Verlag Franz Philipp Rutzen, 2007.

Hoffmann, R. J. *Marcion: On the Restitution of Christianity. An Essay on the Development of Radical Paulinist Theology in the Second Century.* Chico: Scholars Press, 1984.

Holzberg, Niklas. *The Ancient Novel: An Introduction.* London; New York: Routledge, 1995.

Holzhey, Carl. *Die Thekla-Akten. Ihre Verbreitung und Beurteilung in der Kirche.* Veröffentlichungen aus dem Kirchenhistorischen Seminar München 2.7. Munich: E. Stahl, 1905.

Hone, William. *Apocryphal New Testament: being all the gospels, epistles, and other pieces now extant, attributed in the first four centuries to Jesus Christ, His Apostles and their companions and not included in the New Testament by its compilers. Translated from the original tongues, and now first collected into one volume, with prefaces and tables, and various notes and references.* London: W. Hone, 1820.

Horn, Cornelia B. "Suffering Children, Parental Authority and the Quest for Liberation?: A Tale of Three Girls in the *Acts of Paul (and Thecla).*" Pages 118–45 in *A Feminist Companion to the New Testament Apocrypha.* Edited by Amy-Jill Levine with Maria Mayo Robbins. Feminist Companion to the New Testament and Early Christian Writings, 11. Cleveland: The Pilgrim Press, 2006.

Howe, E. Margaret. "Interpretations of Paul in *The Acts of Paul and Thecla,*" Pages 33–39 in *Pauline Studies. Essays Presented to Professor F. F. Bruce on His 70th Birthday.* Exeter and Devon: Paternoster, 1980.

Jackson, Howard M. *The Lion Becomes Man. The Gnostic Leontomorphic Creator and the Platonic Tradition.* Society of Biblical Literature Dissertation Series 81. Atlanta, Ga.: Scholars Press, 1985.

Jacques, Xavier. "Les deux fragments conservés des Actes d'André et Paul. Cod. Borg Copt. 109, fasc. 132," *Or* 38 (1969): 187–213.

James, Montague Rhodes. *Apocrypha Anecdota: A Collection of Thirteen Apocryphal Books and Fragments.* Texts and Studies 2.3. Cambridge: University Press, 1893.

–. "A Note on the *Acta Pauli.*" *Journal of Theological Studies* 6 (1905): 244–46.

–. "The Acts of Titus and the Acts of Paul." *Journal of Theological Studies* 6 (1905): 549–56.

–. *The Apocryphal New Testament.* Oxford: Clarendon, 1924.

–. Review of *Les Actes de Paul et ses lettres Apocryphes:* Introduction, textes, traduction et commentaire, par Léon Vouaux, agrégé de l'Université , professeur au college de la Malgrange. In 'Les Apocryphes du N. T. publiés sous la direction de J. Bourguet et E. Amann'. (Letouzey, Paris, 1913). *Journal of Theological Studies* 14 (1913): 604–06.

–. Review of *The Contendings of the Apostles, being the Histories of the Lives and Martyrdoms and Deaths of the Twelve Apostles and Evangelists; the Ethiopic texts now first edited from MSS in the British Museum, with an English translation. By E. A. Wallis Budge. Vol. II: the English Translation. Journal of Theological Studies* 3 (1902): 286–91.

Jashemski, Wilhelmina Mary Feemster. *The Gardens of Pompeii: Herculaneum and the Villas Destroyed by Vesuvius.* New Rochelle, N.Y.: Caratzas Bros., 1979–93.

Jensen, Anne. *God's Self-confident Daughters: Early Christianity and the Liberation of Women.* Kampen: Kok Pharos, 1996.

–. "Thekla, Vergessene Verkündingerin." Pages 173–79 in *Zwischen Ohnmacht und Befreiung: Biblische Frauengestalten.* Edited by Karin Walter. Freiburg, Basel, and Wien: Herder, 1988.

–. *Thekla – die Apostelin: Ein apokrypher Text neu entdeckt: Übersetzt und kommentiert.* Freiburg, Basel, and Wien: Herder, 1995.

Jensen, Anne in collaboration with Livia Neureiter. *Femmes des premiers siècles chrétiens.* Trans. Gérard Poupon. Bern and New York: P. Lang, 2002.

–. *Frauen im frühen Christentum.* Bern and New York: P. Lang, 2002.

Jensen, Robin M. "Baptismal Rites and Architecture." Pages 117–44 in *Late Ancient Christianity.* Edited by Virginia Burrus. A People's History of Christianity. Minneapolis: Augsburg Fortress, 2005.

Johnson, Scott Fitzgerald. *The Life and Miracles of Thekla: A Literary Study.* Cambridge: Harvard, 2006.

Jones, F. Stanley. "Principal Orientations on the Relations Between the Apocryphal Acts (*Acts of Paul* and *Acts of John; Acts of Peter* and *Acts of John*)," Pages 485–505 in *SBL Seminar Papers, 1993.* Edited by E. H. Lovering, Jr. Atlanta: Scholars Press, 1993.

Jones, Jeremiah. *A New and Full Method of Settling the Canonical Authority of the New Testament to which is subjoined a Vindication of the Former part of St. Matthew's Gospel, from Mr. Whiston's Charge of Dislocations.* 3 vols. Oxford: Clarendon Press, 1798.

Junod, Éric. "Actes Apocryphes et Hérésie: Le Judement de Photius." Pages 11–24 in *Les Actes apocryphes des Apôtres. Christianisme et monde païen.* Edited by François Bovon, et. al. Publication de la faculté de théologie de l'Université de Genève. Geneva: Labor et Fides, 1981.

–. "Apocryphal Literature, B. Christian." Pages 844–46 in Antiquity vol. 1 of *New Pauly: Brill's Encyclopedia of the Ancient World.* Edited by Hubert Cancik and Helmuth Schneider, English Translation Edited by Christine F. Salazar and assistant by David E. Orton. Leiden and Boston: Brill, 2002.

–. "Créations romanesques et traditions ecclésiastiques dans les Actes apocryphes des Apôtres. L'alternative fiction romanesque-vérité historique: une impasse," *Augustinianum* 23 (1983): 271–85.

–. "Origène, Eusèbe et la tradition sur la répartition des champs de mission des apôtres (Eusèbe, HE III,1,1–3)." Pages 233–48 in *Les Actes apocryphes des Apôtres. Christianisme et monde païen.*Edited by François Bovon, *et al.* Publication de la faculté de théologie de l'Université de Genève. Geneva Labor et Fides, 1981.

Junod, Eric, and Jean-Daniel Kaestli. *L'histoire des Actes Apocryphes des Apôtres du IIIe au IXe siecle: le cas des Actes de Jean.* Cahiers de la Revue de Theologie et de Philosophie 7. Geneva: Imprimerie La Concorde, 1982.

–. *Acta Iohannis.* Corpus Christianorum, Series Apocryphum 1–2. Turnhout: Brepolis, 1983.

Kaestli, Jean-Daniel. "Les principales orientations de la recherche sur les Actes apocryphes des Apôtres." Pages 49–61 in *Les Actes apocryphes des Apôtres. Christianisme et monde païen.* François Bovon, *et al.* Publication de la faculté de théologie de l'Université de Genève. Geneva: Labor et Fides, 1981.

–. "Le rôle des textes bibliques dans la genèse et Ie développment des légendes apocryphes: le cas du sort final de l'apôtre Jean." *Augustinianum* 23 (1983): 271–85.

–. "Les Actes Apocryphes et la reconstitution de l'histoire des femmes dans le christianisme ancien." *FoiVie* 28 (1989): 71–79.

–. "Fiction littéraire et réalité sociale: que peut-on savoir de la place des femmes dans le milieu de production des Actes apocryphes des Apôtres?" *Apocrypha* 1 (1990): 279–302.

Kasser, Rodolphe. "Acta Pauli 1959." *Revue d'histoire et de philosophie religieuses* 40 (1960): 45–57.

Kasser, Rodolphe and Philippe Luisier. "Le Bodmer XLI en Édition Princeps l'Épisode d'Èphèse des *Acta Pauli* en Copte et en Traduction." *Le Muséon* 117 (2004): 281–384.

Kerenyi, Karl. *Der Antike Roman: Einführung und Textauswahl.* Darmstadt: Wissenschaftliche Buchgesellschaft, 1971.

–. *Die griechische-orientalische Romanliteratur in religionsgeschichter Beleuchtung.* Tübingen: J. C. B. Mohr (Paul Siebeck), 1927; Repr. Darmstadt: Wissenschaftliche Buchgesellschaft, 1962.

Kittel, G., and G. Friedrich, eds. *TDNT.* Translated by G. W. Bromiley. 10 vols. Grand Rapids: Eerdmans, 1964–1976.

Kilpatrick, G. D. "The *Acta Pauli:* A New Fragment." *Journal of Theological Studies* 47 (1946): 196–9.

Klauk, Hans-Josef. "Die Paulusakten." Pages 61–92 in *Apokryphe Apostelakten: Eine Einführung.* Stuttgart: Katholisches bibelwerk, 2005.

–. *Hausgemeinde und Hauskirche im frühen Christentum.* SBS 103. Stuttgart: Katholisches Bibelwerk, 1981.

Klijn, A. F. J. "The Apocryphal Correspondence Between Paul and the Corinthians." *Vigiliae christianae* 17 (1963): 2–23.

Koch, Guntram. *Early Christian Art and Architecture: An Introduction.* London: SCM Press, 1996.

Kraemer, Ross S. "The Conversions of Women to Ascetic Forms of Christianity." *Signs: Journal of Women in Culture and Society* 6.2 (1980): 298–307.

Krüger, G. "Noch einmal der getaufte Löwe." *Zeitschrift für die neutestamentliche Wissenschaft* 5 (1904): 261–63.

Kurfess, A. "Zu dem Hamburger Papyrus der *Praxeis Paulou.*" *Zeitschrift für die neutestamentliche Wissenschaft* 38 (1939): 164–70.

Lake, Kirsopp. "Appendix 1." Pages 236–40 in *The Earlier Epistles of St. Paul: Their Motive and Origin.* London: Rivingtons, 1911.

Lampe, G. W. H. ed. *A Patristic Greek Lexicon.* Oxford: Clarendon Press, 1961.

Lampe, Peter. "The Eucharist: Identifying with Christ on the Cross." *Interpretation* 48.1 (1994): 36–49.

Lavagnini, Bruno. "S. Tecla nella vasca delle foche e glo spettacoli in acqua." *Byzantion* 33 (1963): 185–90.

Leach, Eleanor Winsor. "The Punishment of Dirce: A Newly Discovered Painting in the Casa di Giulio Polibio and its Significance within the Visual Tradition." *Mitteilungen des Deutschen archäologischen Instituts. Römische Abteilung* 93 (1986): 157–82

–. *The Social Life of Painting in Ancient Rome and on the Bay of Naples.* Cambridge: Cambridge UP, 2004.

Lindemann, Andreas. *Paulus im ältesten Christentum. Das Bild des Apostels und die Rezeption der paulinischen Theologie in der frühchristlichen Literatur bis Marcion.* Beiträge zur historischen Theologie 58. Tübingen: J. C. B. Mohr (Paul Siebeck), 1979.

Lohse, Eduard. *Colossians and Philemon.* Edited by Helmut Koester. Trans. William R. Poehlmann and Robert J. Karris. Hermeneia. Philadelphia: Fortress, 1971.

Luttikhuizen, Gerard. "Simon Magus as a narrative Figure in the Acts of Peter," Pages 39–51 in *The Apocryphal Acts of Peter: Magic, Miracles, and Gnosticism.* Edited by Jan N. Bremmer. Leuven: Peeters, 1998.

MacDonald, Dennis Ronald. "The *Acts of Paul* and The *Acts of John:* Which Came First?" Pages 506–10 in *SBL Seminar Papers, 1993.* Atlanta: Scholars Press, 1993.

–. "The *Acts of Paul* and The *Acts of Peter:* Which Came First?" Pages 214–24 in *SBL Seminar Papers, 1992.* Atlanta: Scholars Press, 1992.

–. "Apocryphal and Canonical Narratives about Paul." Pages 55–70 in *Paul and the Legacies of Paul.* Edited by William S. Babcock. Dallas: Southern Methodist UP, 1990.

–. "A Conjectural Emendation of 1 Cor 15:31–32; or the Case of the Misplaced Lion Fight." *Harvard Theological Review* 73 (1980): 265–76.

–, ed. *Semeia 38: The Apocryphal Acts of the Apostles.* Atlanta: Scholars Press, 1986.

–. *The Legend and the Apostle: The Battle for Paul in Story and Canon.* Philadelphia, PA: Westminster, 1983.

–. "The Role of Women in the Production of the Apocryphal Acts of the Apostles." *Iliff Review* 40 (1984): 21–38.

–. "Which Came First? Intertextual Relationships Among the Apocryphal Acts of the Apostles." Pages 11–18 in *Semeia 80: The Apocryphal Acts of the Apostles in Intertextual Perspectives.* Atlanta: Scholars Press, 1997.

MacDonald, Dennis Ronald and A. D. Scrimgeour. "Pseudo-Chrysostom's Panegyric to Thecla: The Heroine of the *Acts of Paul* in Homily and Art." Pages 151–59 in *Semeia 38: The Apocryphal Acts of the Apostles.* Atlanta: Scholars Press, 1986.

Mackay, Thomas W. "Observations on P. Bodmer X (Apocryphal Correspondence between Paul and the Corinthian Saints)," Pages 119–28 in vol. 3 of *Papyrologica Bruxellensia 18: Actes du XVe Congrès International de Papyrologie.* Bruxelles: Fondation Egyptologique Reine Elisabeth, 1979.

–. "Content and Style in Two Pseudo-Pauline Epistles (3 Corinthians and the Epistle to the Laodiceans)." Pages 215–40 in *Apocryphal Writings and Latter-Day Saints.* Salt Lake City: Brigham Young University, 1986.

–. "Response." Pages 145–49 in *Semeia 38: The Apocryphal Acts of the Apostles.* Atlanta: Scholars Press, 1986.

Malan, Solomn Caesar. Pages 11–15 in *The Conflicts of the Holy Apostles: An Apocryphal Book of the Early Eastern Church*. London: D. Nutt, 1871.

Malherbe, A. J. "A Physical Description of Paul." *Harvard Theological Review* 79 (1986): 170–75.

Malina, Bruce J. *The New Testament World: Insights from Cultural Anthropology*. 3d ed. Philadelphia: Westminster John Knox Press, 2001.

Malina, Bruce J. and Jerome H. Neyrey. *Portraits of Paul: An Archaeology of Ancient Personality*. Louisville: Westminster/John Knox Press, 1996.

Mombritius, Boninus (or Bonino Mombrizio), *Sanctuarium seu Vitae sanctorum*. Milan, 1476 or 1477.

Matthews, Christopher R. "Articulate Animals: A Multivalent Motif in the Apocryphal Acts of the Apostles." Pages 205–32 in *The Apocryphal Acts of the Apostles: Harvard Divinity School Studies*. Edited by François Bovon, Ann Graham Brock, and Christopher R. Matthews. Cambridge: Harvard UP, 1999.

Matthews, Shelly. "Thinking of Thecla: Issues in Feminist Historiography," *Journal of Feminist Studies in Religion* 17 (2001): 39-55.

McHardy, W. D. "A Papyrus Fragment of the *Acta Pauli*." *Expository Times* 58 (1947): 279.

Metzger, Bruce M. "St. Paul and the Baptized Lion." *Princeton Seminary Bulletin* 39 (1945): 11–21.

–. *A Textual Commentary on the Greek New Testament*. 2d ed. Stuttgart: United Bible Societies, 1971.

Michaelis, Wilhelm. "Paulus-Akten." Pages 268–317 in *Die Apokryphen Schriften zum Neuen Testament*. Bremen: Schünemann, 1956.

Migliarini, Margherita. *Alle origini del Duomo. La basilica e il culto di Santa Tecla*. Milano: NED, 1990.

Migne, Jacques Paul. Pages 961–88 in vol. 2 of *Dictionnaire des Apocryphes: ou, Collection de tous les livres apocryphes relatifs à l'Ancien et au Nouveau Testament*. Troisième et dernière encyclopédie théologique 23 and 24. 1856. Repr., Turnhout: Typographi Brepols, 1989.

Millar, Fergus. "Condemnation to hard labour in the Roman Empire, from the Julio-Claudians to Constantine." *Papers of the British School of Rome* 52 (1984): 124–47.

–. "The World of the Golden Ass." *Journal of Religious Studies* 71 (1981): 63–75.

Misser, S. *El Libro de Santa Tecla, con una monografia sobre su nueva parroguia en Barcelona y con una documentación gráica de 164 grabados*. Barcelona: Parroquia de Santa Tecla, 1977.

Misset-van de Weg, Magna. "Answers to the Plights of an Ascetic Woman Named Thecla." Pages 146–62 in *A Feminist Companion to the New Testament Apocrypha*. Edited by Amy-Jill Levine with Maria Mayo Robbins. Cleveland: Pilgrim's Press, 2006.

–. "A Wealthy Woman Named Tryphaen : Patroness of Thecla of Iconium." Pages 16–35 in *The Apocryphal Acts of Paul and Thecla*. Edited by Jan N. Bremmer. Kampen: Kok Pharos, 1996.

Moda, Aldo. "Per una Biographia Paolina: La Lettura di Clemente, il Canon Muratoriana, la Letteratura Apocrifa," pages 289–315 in *Testimonium Christi: Scritti in Onore di Jacques Dupont*. Edited by Jacques Dupont. Brescia: Paideia, 1985.

Moraldi, Luigi. Pages 1061–1130 in vol. 2 of *Apocrifi del Nuovo Testamento*. Turin: Unione Typigrafico-editrice torinese, 1971.

Musurillo, H., ed. and trans. *The Acts of the Christian Martyrs*. Oxford: Oxford UP, 1972.

Nau, F. "La version syriaque des martyres de S. Pierre, S. Paul et S. Luc." *Revue de l'Orient chrétien* 3 (1898): 39–57.

Nauerth, Claudia. "Nachlese von Thekla-Darstellungen." Pages 14–18 in *Studien zur spätantiken und frühchristlichen Kunst und Kultur des Orients.* Edited by Guntram Koch. Wiesbaden: Otto Harrassowitz, 1982.

Nauerth, Claudia, and Rüdiger Warns. *Thekla, ihre Bilder in der frühchristlichen Kunst.* Göttinger Orient-forschungen II, Studien zur spätantiken und frühchristlichen Kunst 3. Wiesbaden: Otto Harrassowitz, 1981.

Niederwimmer, Kurt. *The Didache: A Commentary.* Edited by Harold W. Attridge. Translated by Linda M. Maloney. Hermeneia. Minneapolis: Fortress Press, 1998.

Nock, A. D. Pages 308–30 in vol. 3 of *Essays on Religion in the Ancient World.* Edited by Zeph Steward. Cambridge: Harvard, 1972.

Ohm Wright, Ruth. "The Ambiguity of Interpretation: Paul and Thekla in Ephesos." Paper presented at the annual meeting of the SBL. Washington, D. C., November 20, 2006, 1–11.

Olrik, Axel. "Epic Laws of Folk Narrative," in *The Study of Folklore.* Edited by Alan Dundes, 131–41. Englewood Cliffs: Prentice-Hall, 1965.

Osborne, Robin. "Introduction: Roman Poverty in Context." Pages 1–20 in *Poverty in the Roman World.* Edited by Margaret Atkins and Robin Osborne. Cambridge: Cambridge UP, 2006.

Osiek, Carolyn. *The Shepherd of Hermas.* Edited by Helmut Koester. Hermeneia. Minneapolis: Fortress, 1999.

Osiek, Carolyn and David L. Balch. *Families in the New Testament World: Households and House Churches.* Philadelphia: Westminster John Knox Press, 1997.

Parrott, Douglas M. trans. Introduction to "Eugnostos the Blessed (III,*3* and V,1) and The Sophia of Jesus Christ (III,*4* and BG 8502,*3*)." Pages 220–21 in *The Nag Hammadi Library* Edited by James M. Robinson, rev. ed. New York: Harper Collins, 1978, 1990.

Parsons, Mikeal C. *Body and Character in Luke and Acts: The Subversion of Physiognomy in Early Christianity.* Grand Rapids: Baker, 2006.

Patlagean, Evelyne. "L'histoire de la femme déguisée en moine et l'évolution de la sainteté feminine à Byzance." *Studi Medievali* III.17 (1976): 597–623; Repr. in chapter 11 and Addenda 2 in *Structure sociale, famille, chrétienté à Byzance: IVe–XIe siècle.* London: Variorum Reprints, 1981.

Pervo, Richard I. "Early Christian Fiction." Pages 239–54 in *Greek Fiction. The Greek Novel in Context.* Editded by J. R. Morgan and R Stoneman. London and New York: Routledge, 1994.

–. "A Hard Act to Follow: The Acts of Paul and the Canonical Acts." *Journal of Higher Criticism* 2 (1995): 3–32.

–. *Profit with Delight:* The *Literary Genre of Acts of the Apostles.* Philadelphia: Fortress Press, 1987.

Peterson, Erik. "Die Acta Xanthippe et Polyxenae und die Paulusakten." *Analecta Bollandiana* 65 (1947): 57–60.

–. "Einige Bemerkungen zum Hamburger Papyrusfragment der *Acta Pauli.*" *Vigiliae christianae* 3 (1949): 142–62.

Petropoulos, J. C. B. "Transvestite Virgin with a Cause. The Acta Pauli and Theclae and Late Antique Proto-'Feminism'." Pages 125–39 in *Greece and Gender.* Edited by Brit Berggreen and Nanno Marinatos. Bergen: Norwegian Institute at Athens, 1995.

Pick, Bernhard. "Acts of Paul." Pages 1–49 in *The Apocryphal Acts of Paul, Peter, John, Andrew, and Thomas.* Chicago: The Open Court Publishing Co., 1909.

Pillinger, Renate. "Recente scoperta di antiche pitture ad Efeso." *Eteria* 4.18 (1999): 64.

–. "Neu entdeckte antike Malereien in Ephesus. Eine Darstellung des Apostels Paulus." *Welt und Umwelt der Bibel* 15.1 (2000): 282.

–. "Neue Entdeckungen in der sogenannten Paulusgrotte von Ephesos." *Mitteilungen zur Christlichen Archäologie* 6 (2000): 16–29.

–. "Wandmalereien und Graffiti als neue Zeugnisse der Paulusverehrung in Ephesus." Pages 213–226 in *Mit den Augustinianumen des Herzens sehen. Der Epheserbrief als Leitfaden für Spiritualität und Kirche*. Edited by M. Theobald. Würzburg: Echter, 2000.

–. "Paolo e Tecla ad Efeso. Nuove scoperte nella grotta (chiesa rupestre) sul Bülbülda," Pages 213–37 in *Atti del VIII Simposio di Efeso su S. Giovanni apostolo*. Edited by Luigi Padovese. Roma: Istituto francescano di spiritualità and Pontificio ateneo antoniano, 2001.

–. Interview for RAI and Radio Vatikan concerning the so-called Paulusgrotte in Ephesus. December 12, 2001.

–. Interview through Ruth Ohm for BBC-London concerning the so-called Paulusgrotte in Ephesus. December 19, 2001.

–. "Paolo e Tecla a Efeso." *Eteria* 7.31 (2002): 26–37.

–. "Discovery of St. Paul's Grotto in Ephesus. Some Recent Archaeological Findings." *The Pauline Cooperator* 3.2 (2002): 20.

–. "Das frühbyzantinische Ephesos. Ergebnisse der aktuellen Forschungsprojekte. Die sogenannte Paulusgrotte." Pages 158–63 and Plates 20–25 in *Neue Forschungen zur Religionsgeschichte Kleinasiens: Elmar Schwertheim zum 60. Geburtstag gewidmet*. Edited by Elmar Schwertheim, Gudrun Heedemann, and Engelbert Winter. Asia Minor Studien 49. Bonn: Habelt, 2003.

–. "Neues zur sog. Paulusgrotte in Ephesos." *Mitteilungen der Arbeitsgemeinschaft Christliche Archäologie* 21 (2005): 5f.

–. Vielschichtige Neuigkeiten in der so genannten Paulusgrotte von Ephesos (dritter vorläufiger Bericht, zu den Jahren 2003 und 2004). *Mitteilungen zur Christlichen Archäologie* 11 (2005): 56–62.

Pillinger, Renate and E. Eseroğlu. "Efes'te 2000 yıllık bir mağara." *Rehber Dünyasi* 37 (2005): 67.

Pillinger, Renate, L. Bratasz, G. Fulgoni, F. Ghizzoni, S. Gianoli, S. Salvatori, K. Sterflinger, and J. Weber. "Die Wandmalereien in der so genannten Paulusgrotte von Ephesos: Studien zur Ausführungstechnik und Erhaltungsproblematik, Restaurierung und Konservierung." *Anzeiger der philosophisch-historischen Klasse der Österreichischen Akademie der Wissenschaften, Wien* 143.1 (2008): 71–116.

Pink, K. "Die Pseudo-paulinischen Briefe." *Biblica* 6 (1925): 68–78.

Plümacher, Eckhard. "Apokryphe Apostelakten." Pages 11–70. PW. München: Alfred Druckenmüller, 1978.

Potter, D. "Martyrdom as Spectacle." Pages 53–88 in *Theater and Society in the Classical World*. Edited by R. Scodel. Ann Arbor: University of Michigan, 1993.

Poupon, Gerard. "L'accusation de magie dans les Actes apocryphes." Pages 71–93 in *Les Actes apocryphes des Apôtres. Christianisme et monde païen*. Edited by François Bovon, *et al.* Publication de la faculté de théologie de l'Université de Genève. Geneva: Labor et Fides, 1981.

–. "Les Actes de Pierre' et leur remaniement," Pages 4463–83 in vo. 25.6 of *Aufstieg und Niedergang der Römischen Welt*. Edited by Wolfgang Haase. Berlin and New York: De Gruyter, 1988.

Price, S. R. F. *Rituals and Power: The Roman Imperial Cult in Asia Minor*. Cambridge and New York: Cambridge UP, 1984.

Quasten, Johannes. *Patrology*. Westminster: Newman; Utrecht, Brussels: Spectrum, 1950.

Rademacher, L. *Hippolytos und Thekla: Studien zur Geschichte von Legende und Kultus.* Sitzungsberichte der Kaiserlichen Akademie der Wissenschaften in Wien: Philoso-phisch-historische Klasse 182; Vienna: Buchhändler der Kaiserlichen Akademie der Wissenschaften, 1916.

Ramsay, William M. *The Church in the Roman Empire Before A.D. 170.* New York and London: G. P. Putnam's Sons, 1893.

Reardon, Bryan P. "The Greek Novel." *Phoenix* 23 (1969): 291–309.

Rebell, Walter. *Neutestamentliche Apokryphen und Apostolische Väter.* München: Chr. Kaiser Verlag, 1992.

Reinach, Salomon. "Thekla." *Annales du Musee Guimet* 35 (1910): 103–40.

–. Pages 229–51 in *Cultes, Mythes et Religions IV.* Paris: Ernest Leroux, 1912.

Rey, A. *Étude sur les Acta Pauli et Theclae et la légende de Thecla.* Paris: Jouve, 1890.

Rinck, Wilhelm F. *Das Sendschreiben der Korinther an den Apostel Paulus und das dritte Sendschreiben Pauli an die Korinther, in armenischer Übersetzung erhalten, nun verdeutscht und mit einer Einleitung über die Ächtheit begleitet.* Heidelberg: Winter, 1823.

Rist, M. "III Corinthians as a Pseudepigraphic Refutation of Marcionism." *Iliff Review* 26 (1969): 49–58.

Roberts, Colin H. "A Fragment of an Uncanonical Gospel." *Journal of Theological Studies* 47 (1946): 56–7.

–. "The Acta Pauli: A New Fragment." *Journal of Theological Studies* 47 (1946) 196–99.

–. "The Acts of Paul and Thecla." Pages 26–28 in *The Antinoopolis Papyri Part 1.* London: Egypt Exploration Society, 1950.

Robinson, James M., ed. *The Nag Hammadi Library.* Leiden: Brill, 1988.

Robinson, Thomas A. *The Bauer Thesis Examined: The Geography of Heresy in the Early Christian Church.* Lewiston and Queenston: The Edwin Mellen Press, 1988.

Rohde, Erwin. *Der griechische Roman und seine Vorläufer.* 2d ed. Leipzig: Breitkopf and Hartel, 1900.

Rohde, J. "Pastoralbriefe und Acta Pauli." *Studia evangelica* 103 (1968): 303–10.

Rolffs, Ernst. "Paulusakten." Pages 358–95 in *Handbuch zu den Neutestamentlichen Apokryphen in Verbindung mit Fachgelehrten.* Edited by Edgar Hennecke. Tübingen: J. C. B. Mohr (Paul Siebeck), 1904.

–. "Das Problem der Paulusakten." in *Harnack-Ehrung.* Leipzig: J. C. Hinrichs, 1921.

–. "Paulusakten." Pages 357–82 in *Neutestamentliche Apokryphen in Verbindung mit Fachgelehrten in deutscher Übersetzung und mit Einleitungen.* Edited by Edgar Hen-necke.Tübingen and Leipzig: J. C. B. Mohr (Paul Siebeck), 1904.

–. "Paulusakten," Pages 192–212 in *Neutestamentliche Apokryphen in Verbindung mit Fachgelehrten in deutscher Übersetzung und mit Einleitungen.* Edited by Edgar Hen-necke. 2d ed. Tübingen: J. C. B. Mohr (Paul Siebeck), 1924.

Rordorf, Willy. "Die neronische Christenverfolgung im Spiegel der apokryphen Paulus-akten." Pages 368–74 in *Lex Orandi – Lex Credendi: Gesammelte Aufsätze zum 60. Geburtstag.* Paradosis 36. Freiburg: Universitätsverlag Freiburg in der Schweiz, 1993.

–. "Sainte Thècle dans la tradition hagiographique occidentale." Pages 435–43 in *Lex Orandi – Lex Credendi: Gesammelte Aufsätze zum 60. Geburtstag.* Paradosis 36. Freiburg: Universitätsverlag Freiburg in der Schweiz, 1993.

–. "La prière de Sainte Thècle pour une défunte paienne et son importance œcuménique." Pages 445–55 in *Lex Orandi – Lex Credendi: Gesammelte Aufsätze zum 60. Geburts-tag.* Paradosis 36. Freiburg: Universitätsverlag Freiburg in der Schweiz, 1993.

–. *Liturgie, foi et vie des premiers Chrétiens.* Théologie Historique 75. Paris: Beauchesne, 1986.

–. "The Relation between the *Acts of Peter* and the *Acts of Paul*: State of the Question." Pages 178–91 in *The Apocryphal Acts of Peter: Magic, Miracles, and Gnosticism* Edited by Jan N. Bremmer. Leuven: Peeters, 1998.

–. "Tradition and Composition in the *Acts of Thecla*." Pages 43–52 in *Semeia 38: The Apocryphal Acts of the Apostles*. Atlanta: Scholars Press, 1986.

–. "Tradition et composition dans les *Actes de Thècle*: Etat de la question." *TZ* 41 (1985): 272–83.

–. "Nochmals: Paulusakten und Pastoralbriefe." Pages 466–74 in *Lex Orandi – Lex Credendi: Gesammelte Aufsätze zum 60. Geburtstag*. Paradosis 36. Freiburg: Universitätsverlag Freiburg in der Schweiz, 1993.

–. "In welchem Verhältnis stehen die apokryphen Paulusakten zur kanonischen Apostelgeschichte und zu den Pastoralbriefen?" Pages 449–65 in *Lex Orandi – Lex Credendi: Gesammelte Aufsätze zum 60. Geburtstag*. Paradosis 36. Freiburg: Universitätsverlag Freiburg in der Schweiz, 1993.

–. "Les Actes de Paul sur papyrus: problèmes liés aux P. Michigan inv. 1317 et 3788." Pages 453–60 in vol. 2 of *Proceedings of the XVIII International Congress of Papyrology: Athens, 25–31 May 1986*. Edited by Vasileios G. Mandelaras. Athens: Greek Papyrological Society, 1988.

–. "Quelques jalons pour une interprétation symbolique des *Actes de Paul*." Pages 251–65 in *Early Christian Voices: In Texts, Traditions, and Symbols*. Edited by David H. Warren, Ann Graham Brock, and David W. Pao. Leiden: Brill, 2003.

–. "Was wissen wir über Plan und Absicht der Paulusakten?" Pags 485–96 in *Lex Orandi – Lex Credendi: Gesammelte Aufsätze zum 60. Geburtstag*. Paradosis 36. Freiburg: Universitätsverlag Freiburg in der Schweiz, 1993.

–. "Tertullien et les *Actes de Paul*." Pages 475–84 in *Lex Orandi – Lex Credendi: Gesammelte Aufsätze zum 60. Geburtstag*. Paradosis 36. Freiburg: Universitätsverlag Freiburg in der Schweiz, 1993.

–. "Terra Incognita. Recent Research on Christian Apocryphal Literature, especially on some Acts of the Apostles." Pages 432–48 in *Lex Orandi – Lex Credendi: Gesammelte Aufsätze zum 60. Geburtstag*. Paradosis 36. Freiburg: Universitätsverlag Freiburg in der Schweiz, 1993.

–. "Hérésie et orthodoxie selon la Correspondance apocryphe entre les Corinthiens et l'apôtre Paul." Pages 389–431 in *Lex Orandi – Lex Credendi: Gesammelte Aufsätze zum 60. Geburtstag*. Paradosis 36. Freiburg: Universitätsverlag Freiburg in der Schweiz, 1993.

–. *Lex Orandi – Lex Credendi: Gesammelte Aufsätze zum 60. Geburtstag*. Paradosis 36. Freiburg: Universitätsverlag Freiburg in der Schweiz, 1993.

–. "Bedeutung und Grenze der altkirchlichen ökumenischen Glaubensbekenntnisse (Apostolikum und Nicaeno-Constantinopolitanum)." *Theologische Zeitschrift* 51 (1995): 50–64.

–. "Paul's Conversion in the Canonical Acts and the *Acts of Paul*." Paper presented at the XIIth International Congress on Patristic Studies. Trans. Peter W. Dunn. Oxford, 1995.

Rordorf, Willy, in collaboration with Pierre Cherix and Rudophe Kasser. "Actes de Paul." Pages 1115–77 in vol. 1 of *Écrits apocryphes chrétiens*. Edited by François Bovon and Pierre Geoltrain with an Index by J. Voicu. Bibliothèque de la Pléiade. Saint Herblain: Gallimard, 1997.

Sanders, H. A. "A Fragment of the *Acta Pauli* in the Michigan Collection." *Harvard Theological Review* 31 (1938): 70–90.

–. "Three Theological Fragments." *Harvard Theological Review* 36 (1943): 165–67.

Santos Otero, Aurelio de. Pages 43–51 in *Die handschriftliche Uberlieferung der altslavischen Apokryphen.* PTS. Berlin and New York: de Gruyter, 1978.

Schaff, Philip, and Henry Wace, eds. *Nicene and Post-Nicene Fathers: Second Series.* 1890. Repr., Peabody, Ma..: Hendrickson Publishers, 1993.

Scheider, Horst. "Thekla und die Robben," *Vigiliae christianae* 55.1 (2001): 45–57.

Schlau, Carl. *Die Acten des Paulus und die ältere Thekla-Legende: Ein Beitrag zur christlichen Literaturgeschichte.* Leipzig: J. C. Hinrichs, 1877.

Schmeling, Gareth L. "Myths of Person and Place: The Search for a Model for the Ancient Greek Novel." Pages 425–43 in *The Ancient Novel and Beyond.* Edited by Stelios Panayotakis, Maaike Zimmerman, and Wytse Keulen. Leiden: Brill, 2003.

–. *The Novel in the Ancient World.* Rev. ed. Leiden: Brill, 2003.

Schmidt, Carl. "Acta Pauli." *Forschungen und Fortschritte* 28 (1936): 352–4.

–. *Acta Pauli aus der Heidelberger koptischen Papyrushandschrift.* Leipzig: J. C. Hinrichs, 1904.

–. *Acta Pauli aus der Heidelberger koptischen Papyrushandschrift Nr. 1: Tafelband.* Leipzig: J. C. Hinrichs, 1904.

–. *Acta Pauli aus der Heidelberger koptischen Papyrushandschrift: Zusätze zur ersten Ausgabe* Leipzig: J. C. Hinrichs, 1905.

–. "Ein Berliner Fragment der alten Πράξεις Παύλου." *Sitzungsberichte der preussischen Akademie der Wissenschaften* (19 Feb. 1931): 37–40.

–. *Kanonische und Apokryphe Evangelien und Apostelgeschichten.* Heinrich Majer, 1944.

–. "Neue Funde zu den alten Πράξεις Παύλου." *Sitzungsberichte der preussischen Akademie der Wissenschaften* (28 Feb. 1929): 176–83.

–. "Ein neues Fragment der Heidelberger Acta Pauli." *Sitzungsberichte der preussischen Akademie der Wissenschaften* (4 Feb. 1909): 216–20.

Schmidt, Carl, and Wilhelm Schubart. *ΠΡΑΞΕΙΣ ΠΑΥΛΟΥ: Acta Pauli nach dem Papyrus der Hamburger Staats und Universitäts-Bibliothek.* Glückstadt and Hamburg: J. J. Augustin, 1936.

Schneemelcher, Wilhelm. "Der getaufte Löwe in den Acta Pauli." Pages 223–49 in *Gesammelte Aufsätze zum Neuen Testament und zur Patristik.* Edited by W. Bienert and K. Schäferdiek. Thessaloniki: Patriarchal Institute for Patristic Studies, 1974.

–. "Paulus in der griechischen Kirche des zweiten Jahrhunderts." Pages 154–81 in *Gesammelte Aufsätze zum Neuen Testament und zur Patristik.* Edited by W. Bienert and K. Schäferdiek. Thessaloniki: Patriarchal Institute for Patristic Studies, 1974.

–. "Die Apostelgeschichte des Lukas und die Acta Pauli." Pages 204–22 in *Gesammelte Aufsätze zum Neuen Testament und zur Patristik.* Edited by W. Bienert and K. Schäferdiek. Thessaloniki: Patriarchal Institute for Patristic Studies, 1974.

–. "Die Acta Pauli-Neue Funde und neue Aufgaben." Pages 182–203 in *Gesammelte Aufsätze zum Neuen Testament und zur Patristik.* Edited by W. Bienert and K. Schäferdiek. Thessaloniki: Patriarchal Institute for Patristic Studies, 1974.

–. *Gesammelte Aufsätze zum Neuen Testament und zur Patristik.* Edited by W. Bienert and K. Schäferdiek. Thessaloniki: Patriarchal Institute for Patristic Studies, 1974.

–. "The Acts of Paul." Pages 322–90 in vol. 2 of *New Testament Apocrypha.* Edited by Edgar Hennecke, Wilhelm Schneemelcher, and Robert McLachlan Wilson. Trans. by Robert McLachlan Wilson. Philadelphia: Westminster Press. 1963–6.

–. "The Acts of Paul," Pages 213–70 in vol. 2 of *New Testament Apocrypha.* Edited by Edgar Hennecke, Wilhelm Schneemelcher, and Robert McLachlan Wilson. Trans. by R. McL. Wilson. Rev. ed. James Clarke & Co.: Cambridge; Philadelphia: Westminster/John Knox Press, 1992.

Schneelmelcher, Wilhelm and Rudolphe Kasser, eds. "Paulusacten." Pages 221–70 in vol. 2 of *Neutestamentliche Apokryphen in Verbindung mit Fachgelehrten in deutscher Übersetzung und mit Einleitungen.* Edited by Edgar Hennecke and Wilhelm Schneelmelcher, 3d ed. Tübingen: J. C. B. Mohr (Paul Siebeck), 1959–64.

–. "Paulusacten," Pages 193–243 in vol. 2 of *Neutestamentliche Apokryphen in Verbindung mit Fachgelehrten in deutscher Übersetzung und mit Einleitungen.*Edited by Edgar Hennecke and Wilhelm Schneelmelcher. 5th ed. Tübingen: J. C. B. Mohr (Paul Siebeck), 1987.

Schüssler Fiorenza, Elisabeth. "Apocalyptic and Gnosis in the Book of Revelation and Paul." *Journal of Biblical Literature* 92 (1973): 565–81.

Seim, Turid Karlsen. *The Double Message: Patterns of Gender in Luke and Acts.* Nashville: Abingdon, 1994.

Sellew, Philip. "Paul, Acts Of." Pages 202–03 in vol. 5 of the *Anchor Bible Dictionary.* New York and London: Doubleday. 1992.

Smith, Dennis E. *From Symposium to Eucharist: The Banquet in the Early Christian World.* Minneapolis: Fortress, 2003.

Smyth, Herbert Weir, *Greek Grammar.* Revised by Gordon M. Messing. Cambridge: Harvard UP, 1920.

Söder, Rosa. *Die apokryphen Apostelgeschichten und die romanhafte Literatur der Antike.* Würzburger Studien zur Altertumswissenschaft 3. Stuttgart: W. Kohlhammer, 1932.

Souter, Alexander. "Acta Pauli, etc. in Tertullian." *Journal of Theological Studies* 25 (1924): 292.

Spittler, Janet Elizabeth. "Wild Kingdom: Animals in the Apocryphal Acts of the Apostles." Ph.D. diss., The University of Chicago, 2007.

Spittler, R. P. "Testament of Job." *The Old Testament Pseudepigrapha.* Edited by James H. Charlesworth. 2 vols. New York: Doubleday, 1983.

Stegemann, Ekkehard W. and Wolfgang Stegemann. *The Jesus Movement: A Social History of the First Century.* Translated by O. C. Dean Jr. Minneapolis: Fortress Press, 1999.

Stephens, Susan A. "87. Fragment of *Acta Pauli?*" Pages 3–7 in *Yale Papyri in the Beinecke Rare Book and Manuscript Library II.* American Studies in Papyrology 24. Chico, Calif.: Scholars Press, 1985.

–. "Who Read Ancient Novels?" in Pages 405–17 in *The Novel in the Ancient World.* Edited by Gareth L. Schmeling. Rev. ed. Leiden: Brill, 2003.

Stoops, Robert F. Jr. "Apostolic Apocrypha: Where Do We Stand with Schneemelcher's Fifth Edition?" Pages 634–41 in *SBL Seminar Papers, 1993.* Atlanta: Scholars Press, 1993.

–. "Peter, Paul, and Priority in the Apocryphal Acts." Pages 225–33 in *SBL Seminar Papers, 1992.* Atlanta: Scholars Press, 1992.

Stowers, Stanley K. "Comment: What Does *Unpauline* Mean?" Pages 70–77 in *Paul and the Legacies of Paul.* Edited by William S. Babcock. Dallas: Southern Methodist University Press, 1990.

Streete, Gail P. C. "Buying the Stairway to Heaven: Perpetua and Thecla as Early Christian Heroines." Pages 186–205 in *A Feminist Companion to the New Testament Apocrypha.* Edited by Amy-Jill Levine with Maria Mayo Robbins. Feminist Companion to the New Testament and Early Christian Writings, 11. Cleveland: The Pilgrim Press, 2006.

Tajra, Harry W. *The Martyrdom of St. Paul: Historical and Judicial Context, Traditions and Legends.* Wissenschaftliche Untersuchungen zum Neuen Testament 2.67. Tübingen: J. C. B. Mohr (Paul Siebeck), 1994.

Testuz, M. *Papyrus Bodmer X–XI. X: Correspondance apocryphe des Corinthiens et de l'apôtre Paul. XI: Onzième Odes Salomon. XII: Fragment d'un Hymne liturgique.* Cologny and Genève: Bibliotheca Bodmeriana, 1959.

Thomas, Christine M. "Word and Deed: The *Acts of Peter* and Orality." *Apocrypha* 3 (1992): 125–64.

Thompson, J. David. *A Critical Concordance to the New Testament Acts: Acts of Paul.* Edited by Watson E. Mills and David Noel Freedman. The Computer Bible 44.1–2. Lewiston: Edwin Mellen, 2001.

Tischendorf, Constantin von and Theodor Zahn. *Acta Joannis.* Erlangen: Deichert, 1880.

Tissot, Yves. "Encratisme et Actes Apocryphes." Pags 109–19 in *Les Actes apocryphes des Apôtres. Christianisme et monde païen.* Edited by François Bovon, *et. al.* Publication de la faculté de théologie de l'Université de Gènève. Geneva: Labor et Fides, 1981.

–. "L'encratisme des Actes de Thomas." Pages 4415–30 in vol. 25.6 of *Aufstieg und Niedergang der Römischen Welt.* Edited by Wolfgang Haase. Berlin and New York: De Gruyter, 1988.

Valantasis, Richard "The Question of Early Christian Identity: Three Strategies Exploring a Third *Genos.*" Pages 60–76 in *A Feminist Companion to the New Testament Apocrypha.* Edited by Amy-Jill Levine with Maria Mayo Robbins. Feminist Companion to the New Testament and Early Christian Writings, 11. Cleveland: The Pilgrim Press, 2006.

Vetter, P. "Der apokryphe dritte Korintherbrief neu übersetzt und nach seiner Entstehung untersucht." *Theologische Quartalschrift* 72 (1890): 610–39.

–. *Der apokryphe dritte Korintherbrief.* Tübingen: Universitätsfestschrift, 1894.

–. "Eine rabbinische Quelle des apokryphen dritten Korintherbriefes." *Theologische Quartalschrift* 4 (1895): 622–33.

Vielhauer, Ph. *Geschichte der urchristlichen Literatur. Einleitung in das Neue Testament, die Apokryphen und die Apostolischen Väter.* Berlin: De Gruyter, 1975.

Ville, G. *La gladiature en Occident des origins à la mort de Domitien.* Rome: Ecole française de Rome, 1981.

Vogt, A. "Panégyrique de St. Pierre; Panégyrique de St. Paul. Deux discours inédits de Nicétas de Paphlagonie, disciple de Photius." *Orientalia Christiana* 23 (1931): 5–97.

Von Dobschutz, E. "Der Roman in der altchristlichen Literatur." *Deutsche Rundschau* 111 (1902): 87–106.

Von Lemm, O. "Koptische apokryphe Apostelacten." *Mélanges Asiatiques* 10 (1892): 354–81.

Vorster, Johannes N. "Construction of Culture Through the Construction of Person: The Construction of Thecla in the *Acts of Thecla*," Pages 98–117 in *A Feminist Companion to the New Testament Apocrypha.* Edited by Amy-Jill Levine with Maria Mayo Robbins. Feminist Companion to the New Testament and Early Christian Writings, 11. Cleveland: The Pilgrim Press, 2006.

Vouaux, Léon. *Les Actes de Paul et ses lettres Apocryphes: Introduction, textes, traduction et commentaire.* Les Apocryphes du Nouveau Testament. Paris: Librairie Letouzey et Ané, 1913.

–. *Les Actes de Pierre: Introduction, textes, traduction et commentaire.* Paris: Librairie Letouzey et Ané, 1922.

Wake, William, William Hone and Jeremiah Jones. *The lost books of the Bible: being all the Gospels, Epistles, and other pieces now extant attributed in the first four centuries to Jesus Christ, His Apostles and their companions, not included by its compilers, in the Authorized New Testament, and the recently discovered Syriac mss. of Pilate's letters to Tiberius, etc.* New York: Alpha Publishing Co., 1926.

Walcot, Peter. "On Widows and Their Reputation in Antiquity." *Symbolae Osloenses* 66 (1991): 526.

Walker, Alexander, trans. *Apocryphal Gospels, Acts, and Revelation.* Edited by Alexander Roberts and James Donaldson. Ante-Nicene Christian Library 16. Edinburgh: T. & T. Clark, 1870.

Warns, Rüdiger. "Weitere Darstellungen der heiligen Thekla," Pages 75–131 in. *Studien zur frühchristlichen Kunst II.* Edited by Guntram Koch. Studien zur spätantiken und frühchristlichen Kunst und Kultur des Orients. Wiesbaden: Otto Harrassowitz, 1986.

Warren David H. "The Greek Language of the Apocryphal Acts of the Apostles: A Study of Style." Pages 101–24 in *The Apocryphal Acts of the Apostles: Harvard Divinity School Studies.* Edited by François Bovon, Ann Graham Brock, and Christopher R. Matthews. Cambridge: Harvard UP, 1999.

Wiles, Maurice F. *The Divine Apostle: The Interpretation of St Paul's Epistles in the Early Church.* Cambridge: The University Press, 1967.

Wilson, Robert McLachlan. "Apokryphen II." Pages 316–62 in vol. 3 of *Theologische Realenzyklopädie.* Edited by Gerhard Krause and Gerhard Müller. Berlin and New York: Walter de Gruyter, 1978.

Wright, William. *Apocryphal Acts of the Apostles: Edited from Syriac Manuscripts in the British Museum and Other Libraries.* 1871. Repr., Amsterdam: Philo Press, 1968.

Wudel (Lipsett), Barbara Diane. "Seductions of Self-Control: Narrative Transformations in Hermas, Thecla, and Aseneth." Ph.D. diss., University of North Carolina, 2005.

Young, Prances. *The Theology of the Pastoral Letters.* New Testament Theology. Cambridge: Cambridge University Press, 1994.

Zahn, Theodor. "Der apokryphe Briefwechsel zwischen Paulus und den Korinthern." Pages 595–611 in vol. 2 of *Geschichte des neutestamentlichen Kanons.* Erlangen and Leipzig: A. Deichert, 1890. Repr., Hildesheim and New York: Georg Olms, 1975.

–. *Göttingische Gelehrte Anzeigen* (1877): 1307.

Zanker, Paul. *Pompeii: Public and Private Life.* Trans. Deborah Lucas Schneider. Cambridge, Mass.: Harvard, 1998.

Index

Ancient Authors

Apostolic Fathers

Old Testament, Apocrypha/Deuterocanon, and Pseudepigrapha

New Testament

1 John		*Revelation*	
5:20–21	38, 111	3:4	99
		14:4	99
		19:7	119

New Testament Apocrypha and Early Christian Literature

Acts of John		3.12	42, 77, 78, 80, 92, 93,
18	105		97, 98, 108, 109, 116
48	105	3.13	67, 69, 90, 100, 102,
70–74	158		104, 109, 116, 122, 141,
			181
Acts of Paul		3.14	37, 38, 69, 77, 93, 97,
3	136, 180		98, 109, 112
3–4	180, 188	3.14–16	75
3.1	18, 37, 39, 68, 77, 90,	3.15	69, 70, 104, 105, 106,
	99, 104, 105, 109, 116,		107, 108, 111, 114, 116,
	122, 184, 185		141, 181
3.1–2	44	3.15–16	106
3.2	31, 70, 74, 131	3.16	69, 77, 97, 98, 109, 116,
3.2–3	51		122, 144
3.2–5	18	3.16–22	183
3.3	25, 72, 76, 105, 116,	3.17	39, 69, 99, 104, 105,
	122		108, 109, 114, 125
3.4	70, 77, 84, 100, 105,	3.18	106, 115, 116, 119, 122,
	119, 181		147, 159, 180, 184, 185
3.5	30, 39, 70, 79, 84, 92,	3.18–19	8
	99, 111, 122, 130, 133,	3.18–22	177
	154, 178, 179, 181, 184	3.19	102, 113, 116, 122, 123,
3.5–6	33, 36, 43, 44, 54, 80,		128, 141, 150
	82, 84, 99, 104, 112,	3.20	89, 95, 106, 107, 108,
	124, 125		109, 110, 119, 120, 123,
3.5–7	185		124, 125, 130, 133, 144,
3.5–11	183		152, 156, 178, 185
3.6	30, 83, 92, 97, 100, 109,	3.20–21	95, 98
	150, 157, 185	3.21	89, 116, 117, 119, 122,
3.6–10	95		123, 125, 156, 177, 185
3.7	18, 70, 78, 83, 92, 97,	3.21–22	8, 9
	98, 109, 115, 179, 181,	3.21–23	115
	184, 186	3.22	8, 33, 97, 105, 109, 122,
3.7–10	51		124, 128, 130, 134, 147,
3.7–8	94, 186		155, 158, 171, 174, 185
3.8	8, 97, 102, 109, 141,	3.22–26	141
	154, 176, 184	3.23	70, 127, 137, 174
3.9	39, 67, 89, 90, 92, 97,	3.23–26	72, 183
	98, 109	3.24	31, 79. 130, 133, 134
3.10	89, 144, 149, 152, 181,	3.24–25	180
	184	3.25	70, 87, 119, 132, 134,
3.11	97, 98, 109, 116, 154		135, 137, 141, 150, 175,

Qumran

Modern Authors

Subject and Key Terms

Wissenschaftliche Untersuchungen zum Neuen Testament

Alphabetical Index of the First and Second Series

Bennema, Cornelis: The Power of Saving Wisdom. 2002. *Vol. II/148.*

Bergman, Jan: see *Kieffer, René*

Bergmeier, Roland: Das Gesetz im Römerbrief und andere Studien zum Neuen Testament. 2000. *Vol. 121.*

Bernett, Monika: Der Kaiserkult in Judäa unter den Herodiern und Römern. 2007. *Vol. 203.*

Betz, Otto: Jesus, der Messias Israels. 1987. *Vol. 42.*

– Jesus, der Herr der Kirche. 1990. *Vol. 52.*

Beyschlag, Karlmann: Simon Magus und die christliche Gnosis. 1974. *Vol. 16.*

Bieringer, Reimund: see *Koester, Craig.*

Bittner, Wolfgang J.: Jesu Zeichen im Johannesevangelium. 1987. *Vol. II/26.*

Bjerkelund, Carl J.: Tauta Egeneto. 1987. *Vol. 40.*

Blackburn, Barry Lee: Theios Aner and the Markan Miracle Traditions. 1991. *Vol. II/40.*

Blanton IV, Thomas R.: Constructing a New Covenant. 2007. *Vol. II/233.*

Bock, Darrell L.: Blasphemy and Exaltation in Judaism and the Final Examination of Jesus. 1998. *Vol. II/106.*

Bockmuehl, Markus N.A.: Revelation and Mystery in Ancient Judaism and Pauline Christianity. 1990. *Vol. II/36.*

Bøe, Sverre: Gog and Magog. 2001. *Vol. II/135.*

Böhlig, Alexander: Gnosis und Synkretismus. Vol. 1 1989. *Vol. 47* – Vol. 2 1989. *Vol. 48.*

Böhm, Martina: Samarien und die Samaritai bei Lukas. 1999. *Vol. II/111.*

Böttrich, Christfried: Weltweisheit – Menschheitsethik – Urkult. 1992. *Vol. II/50.*

– and *Herzer, Jens* (Ed.): Josephus und das Neue Testament. 2007. *Vol. 209.*

Bolyki, János: Jesu Tischgemeinschaften. 1997. *Vol. II/96.*

Bosman, Philip: Conscience in Philo and Paul. 2003. *Vol. II/166.*

Bovon, François: New Testament and Christian Apocrypha. 2009. *Vol. 237.*

– Studies in Early Christianity. 2003. *Vol. 161.*

Brändl, Martin: Der Agon bei Paulus. 2006. *Vol. II/222.*

Breytenbach, Cilliers: see *Frey, Jörg.*

Brocke, Christoph vom: Thessaloniki – Stadt des Kassander und Gemeinde des Paulus. 2001. *Vol. II/125.*

Brunson, Andrew: Psalm 118 in the Gospel of John. 2003. *Vol. II/158.*

Büchli, Jörg: Der Poimandres – ein paganisiertes Evangelium. 1987. *Vol. II/27.*

Bühner, Jan A.: Der Gesandte und sein Weg im 4. Evangelium. 1977. *Vol. II/2.*

Burchard, Christoph: Untersuchungen zu Joseph und Aseneth. 1965. *Vol. 8.*

– Studien zur Theologie, Sprache und Umwelt des Neuen Testaments. Ed. by D. Sänger. 1998. *Vol. 107.*

Burnett, Richard: Karl Barth's Theological Exegesis. 2001. *Vol. II/145.*

Byron, John: Slavery Metaphors in Early Judaism and Pauline Christianity. 2003. *Vol. II/162.*

Byrskog, Samuel: Story as History – History as Story. 2000. *Vol. 123.*

Cancik, Hubert (Ed.): Markus-Philologie. 1984. *Vol. 33.*

Capes, David B.: Old Testament Yaweh Texts in Paul's Christology. 1992. *Vol. II/47.*

Caragounis, Chrys C.: The Development of Greek and the New Testament. 2004. *Vol. 167.*

– The Son of Man. 1986. *Vol. 38.*

– see *Fridrichsen, Anton.*

Carleton Paget, James: The Epistle of Barnabas. 1994. *Vol. II/64.*

Carson, D.A., O'Brien, Peter T. and *Mark Seifrid* (Ed.): Justification and Variegated Nomism.
Vol. 1: The Complexities of Second Temple Judaism. 2001. *Vol. II/140.*
Vol. 2: The Paradoxes of Paul. 2004. *Vol. II/181.*

Chae, Young Sam: Jesus as the Eschatological Davidic Shepherd. 2006. *Vol. II/216.*

Chapman, David W.: Ancient Jewish and Christian Perceptions of Crucifixion. 2008. *Vol. II/244.*

Chester, Andrew: Messiah and Exaltation. 2007. *Vol. 207.*

Chibici-Revneanu, Nicole: Die Herrlichkeit des Verherrlichten. 2007. *Vol. II/231.*

Ciampa, Roy E.: The Presence and Function of Scripture in Galatians 1 and 2. 1998. *Vol. II/102.*

Classen, Carl Joachim: Rhetorical Criticsm of the New Testament. 2000. *Vol. 128.*

Colpe, Carsten: Griechen – Byzantiner – Semiten – Muslime. 2008. *Vol. 221.*

– Iranier – Aramäer – Hebräer – Hellenen. 2003. *Vol. 154.*

Coppins, Wayne: The Interpretation of Freedom in the Letters of Paul. 2009. *Vol. II/261.*

Crump, David: Jesus the Intercessor. 1992. *Vol. II/49.*

Dahl, Nils Alstrup: Studies in Ephesians. 2000. *Vol. 131.*

Daise, Michael A.: Feasts in John. 2007. *Vol. II/229.*

Deines, Roland: Die Gerechtigkeit der Tora im Reich des Messias. 2004. *Vol. 177.*

– Jüdische Steingefäße und pharisäische Frömmigkeit. 1993. *Vol. II/52.*

– Die Pharisäer. 1997. *Vol. 101.*

Deines, Roland and *Karl-Wilhelm Niebuhr*
(Ed.): Philo und das Neue Testament. 2004.
Vol. 172.

Dennis, John A.: Jesus' Death and the Gathering
of True Israel. 2006. *Vol. 217.*

Dettwiler, Andreas and *Jean Zumstein* (Ed.):
Kreuzestheologie im Neuen Testament.
2002. *Vol. 151.*

Dickson, John P.: Mission-Commitment in
Ancient Judaism and in the Pauline Communities. 2003. *Vol. II/159.*

Dietzfelbinger, Christian: Der Abschied des
Kommenden. 1997. *Vol. 95.*

Dimitrov, Ivan Z., James D.G. Dunn, Ulrich Luz
and *Karl-Wilhelm Niebuhr* (Ed.): Das Alte
Testament als christliche Bibel in orthodoxer
und westlicher Sicht. 2004. *Vol. 174.*

Dobbeler, Axel von: Glaube als Teilhabe. 1987.
Vol. II/22.

Docherty, Susan E.: The Use of the Old Testament in Hebrews. 2009. *Vol. II/260.*

Downs, David J.: The Offering of the Gentiles.
2008. *Vol. II/248.*

Dryden, J. de Waal: Theology and Ethics in
1 Peter. 2006. *Vol. II/209.*

Dübbers, Michael: Christologie und Existenz
im Kolosserbrief. 2005. *Vol. II/191.*

Dunn, James D.G.: The New Perspective on
Paul. 2005. *Vol. 185.*

Dunn , James D.G. (Ed.): Jews and Christians.
1992. *Vol. 66.*

– Paul and the Mosaic Law. 1996. *Vol. 89.*

– see *Dimitrov, Ivan Z.*

–, *Hans Klein, Ulrich Luz,* and *Vasile Mihoc*
(Ed.): Auslegung der Bibel in orthodoxer
und westlicher Perspektive. 2000. *Vol. 130.*

Ebel, Eva: Die Attraktivität früher christlicher
Gemeinden. 2004. *Vol. II/178.*

Ebertz, Michael N.: Das Charisma des Gekreu-
zigten. 1987. *Vol. 45.*

Eckstein, Hans-Joachim: Der Begriff Syneide-
sis bei Paulus. 1983. *Vol. II/10.*

– Verheißung und Gesetz. 1996. *Vol. 86.*

Ego, Beate: Im Himmel wie auf Erden. 1989.
Vol. II/34.

Ego, Beate, Armin Lange and *Peter Pilhofer*
(Ed.): Gemeinde ohne Tempel – Community
without Temple. 1999. *Vol. 118.*

– and *Helmut Merkel* (Ed.): Religiöses Lernen
in der biblischen, frühjüdischen und frühchristlichen Überlieferung. 2005. *Vol. 180.*

Eisen, Ute E.: see *Paulsen, Henning.*

Elledge, C.D.: Life after Death in Early Judaism. 2006. *Vol. II/208.*

Ellis, E. Earle: Prophecy and Hermeneutic in
Early Christianity. 1978. *Vol. 18.*

– The Old Testament in Early Christianity.
1991. *Vol. 54.*

Elmer, Ian J.: Paul, Jerusalem and the Judaisers.
2009. *Vol. II/258.*

Endo, Masanobu: Creation and Christology.
2002. *Vol. 149.*

Ennulat, Andreas: Die 'Minor Agreements'.
1994. *Vol. II/62.*

Ensor, Peter W.: Jesus and His 'Works'. 1996.
Vol. II/85.

Eskola, Timo: Messiah and the Throne. 2001.
Vol. II/142.

– Theodicy and Predestination in Pauline Soteriology. 1998. *Vol. II/100.*

Fatehi, Mehrdad: The Spirit's Relation to the
Risen Lord in Paul. 2000. *Vol. II/128.*

Feldmeier, Reinhard: Die Krisis des Gottessoh-
nes. 1987. *Vol. II/21.*

– Die Christen als Fremde. 1992. *Vol. 64.*

Feldmeier, Reinhard and *Ulrich Heckel* (Ed.):
Die Heiden. 1994. *Vol. 70.*

Fletcher-Louis, Crispin H.T.: Luke-Acts: Angels, Christology and Soteriology. 1997.
Vol. II/94.

Förster, Niclas: Marcus Magus. 1999. *Vol. 114.*

Forbes, Christopher Brian: Prophecy and In-
spired Speech in Early Christianity and its
Hellenistic Environment. 1995. *Vol. II/75.*

Fornberg, Tord: see *Fridrichsen, Anton.*

Fossum, Jarl E.: The Name of God and the Angel of the Lord. 1985. *Vol. 36.*

Foster, Paul: Community, Law and Mission in
Matthew's Gospel. *Vol. II/177.*

Fotopoulos, John: Food Offered to Idols in Roman Corinth. 2003. *Vol. II/151.*

Frenschkowski, Marco: Offenbarung und Epi-
phanie. Vol. 1 1995. *Vol. II/79* – Vol. 2 1997.
Vol. II/80.

Frey, Jörg: Eugen Drewermann und die biblische Exegese. 1995. *Vol. II/71.*

– Die johanneische Eschatologie. Vol. I. 1997.
Vol. 96. – Vol. II. 1998. *Vol. 110.* – Vol. III.
2000. *Vol. 117.*

Frey, Jörg and *Cilliers Breytenbach* (Ed.): Auf-
gabe und Durchführung einer Theologie des
Neuen Testaments. 2007. *Vol. 205.*

– and *Udo Schnelle* (Ed.): Kontexte des Jo-
hannesevangeliums. 2004. *Vol. 175.*

– and *Jens Schröter* (Ed.): Deutungen des
Todes Jesu im Neuen Testament. 2005.
Vol. 181.

–, *Jan G. van der Watt,* and *Ruben Zimmermann* (Ed.): Imagery in the Gospel of John.
2006. *Vol. 200.*

Freyne, Sean: Galilee and Gospel. 2000.
Vol. 125.

Fridrichsen, Anton: Exegetical Writings. Edited by C.C. Caragounis and T. Fornberg. 1994. *Vol. 76.*

Gadenz, Pablo T.: Called from the Jews and from the Gentiles. 2009. *Vol. II/267.*

Gäbel, Georg: Die Kulttheologie des Hebräerbriefes. 2006. *Vol. II/212.*

Gäckle, Volker: Die Starken und die Schwachen in Korinth und in Rom. 2005. *Vol. 200.*

Garlington, Don B.: 'The Obedience of Faith'. 1991. *Vol. II/38.*

– Faith, Obedience, and Perseverance. 1994. *Vol. 79.*

Garnet, Paul: Salvation and Atonement in the Qumran Scrolls. 1977. *Vol. II/3.*

Gemünden, Petra von (Ed.): see *Weissenrieder, Annette.*

Gese, Michael: Das Vermächtnis des Apostels. 1997. *Vol. II/99.*

Gheorghita, Radu: The Role of the Septuagint in Hebrews. 2003. *Vol. II/160.*

Gordley, Matthew E.: The Colossian Hymn in Context. 2007. *Vol. II/228.*

Gräbe, Petrus J.: The Power of God in Paul's Letters. 2000, ²2008. *Vol. II/123.*

Gräßer, Erich: Der Alte Bund im Neuen. 1985. *Vol. 35.*

– Forschungen zur Apostelgeschichte. 2001. *Vol. 137.*

Grappe, Christian (Ed.): Le Repas de Dieu / Das Mahl Gottes. 2004. *Vol. 169.*

Gray, Timothy C.: The Temple in the Gospel of Mark. 2008. *Vol. II/242.*

Green, Joel B.: The Death of Jesus. 1988. *Vol. II/33.*

Gregg, Brian Han: The Historical Jesus and the Final Judgment Sayings in Q. 2005. *Vol. II/207.*

Gregory, Andrew: The Reception of Luke and Acts in the Period before Irenaeus. 2003. *Vol. II/169.*

Grindheim, Sigurd: The Crux of Election. 2005. *Vol. II/202.*

Gundry, Robert H.: The Old is Better. 2005. *Vol. 178.*

Gundry Volf, Judith M.: Paul and Perseverance. 1990. *Vol. II/37.*

Häußer, Detlef: Christusbekenntnis und Jesusüberlieferung bei Paulus. 2006. *Vol. 210.*

Hafemann, Scott J.: Suffering and the Spirit. 1986. *Vol. II/19.*

– Paul, Moses, and the History of Israel. 1995. *Vol. 81.*

Hahn, Ferdinand: Studien zum Neuen Testament.

Vol. I: Grundsatzfragen, Jesusforschung, Evangelien. 2006. *Vol. 191.*

Vol. II: Bekenntnisbildung und Theologie in urchristlicher Zeit. 2006. *Vol. 192.*

Hahn, Johannes (Ed.): Zerstörungen des Jerusalemer Tempels. 2002. *Vol. 147.*

Hamid-Khani, Saeed: Relevation and Concealment of Christ. 2000. *Vol. II/120.*

Hannah, Darrel D.: Michael and Christ. 1999. *Vol. II/109.*

Hardin, Justin K.: Galatians and the Imperial Cult? 2007. *Vol. II /237.*

Harrison; James R.: Paul's Language of Grace in Its Graeco-Roman Context. 2003. *Vol. II/172.*

Hartman, Lars: Text-Centered New Testament Studies. Ed. von D. Hellholm. 1997. *Vol. 102.*

Hartog, Paul: Polycarp and the New Testament. 2001. *Vol. II/134.*

Heckel, Theo K.: Der Innere Mensch. 1993. *Vol. II/53.*

– Vom Evangelium des Markus zum viergestaltigen Evangelium. 1999. *Vol. 120.*

Heckel, Ulrich: Kraft in Schwachheit. 1993. *Vol. II/56.*

– Der Segen im Neuen Testament. 2002. *Vol. 150.*

– see *Feldmeier, Reinhard.*

– see *Hengel, Martin.*

Heiligenthal, Roman: Werke als Zeichen. 1983. *Vol. II/9.*

Heliso, Desta: Pistis and the Righteous One. 2007. *Vol. II/235.*

Hellholm, D.: see *Hartman, Lars.*

Hemer, Colin J.: The Book of Acts in the Setting of Hellenistic History. 1989. *Vol. 49.*

Hengel, Martin: Jesus und die Evangelien. Kleine Schriften V. 2007. *Vol. 211.*

– Die johanneische Frage. 1993. *Vol. 67.*

– Judaica et Hellenistica. Kleine Schriften I. 1996. *Vol. 90.*

– Judaica, Hellenistica et Christiana. Kleine Schriften II. 1999. *Vol. 109.*

– Judentum und Hellenismus. 1969, ³1988. *Vol. 10.*

– Paulus und Jakobus. Kleine Schriften III. 2002. *Vol. 141.*

– Studien zur Christologie. Kleine Schriften IV. 2006. *Vol. 201.*

– Studien zum Urchristentum. Kleine Schriften VI. 2008. *Vol. 234.*

– and *Anna Maria Schwemer:* Paulus zwischen Damaskus und Antiochien. 1998. *Vol. 108.*

– Der messianische Anspruch Jesu und die Anfänge der Christologie. 2001. *Vol. 138.*

– Die vier Evangelien und das eine Evangelium von Jesus Christus. 2008. *Vol. 224.*

Hengel, Martin and *Ulrich Heckel* (Ed.): Paulus und das antike Judentum. 1991. *Vol. 58.*

– and *Hermut Löhr* (Ed.): Schriftauslegung im antiken Judentum und im Urchristentum. 1994. *Vol. 73.*

– and *Anna Maria Schwemer* (Ed.): Königsherrschaft Gottes und himmlischer Kult. 1991. *Vol. 55.*

– Die Septuaginta. 1994. *Vol. 72.*

–, *Siegfried Mittmann* and *Anna Maria Schwemer* (Ed.): La Cité de Dieu / Die Stadt Gottes. 2000. *Vol. 129.*

Hentschel, Anni: Diakonia im Neuen Testament. 2007. *Vol. 226.*

Hernández Jr., Juan: Scribal Habits and Theological Influence in the Apocalypse. 2006. *Vol. II/218.*

Herrenbrück, Fritz: Jesus und die Zöllner. 1990. *Vol. II/41.*

Herzer, Jens: Paulus oder Petrus? 1998. *Vol. 103.*

– see *Böttrich, Christfried.*

Hill, Charles E.: From the Lost Teaching of Polycarp. 2005. *Vol. 186.*

Hoegen-Rohls, Christina: Der nachösterliche Johannes. 1996. *Vol. II/84.*

Hoffmann, Matthias Reinhard: The Destroyer and the Lamb. 2005. *Vol. II/203.*

Hofius, Otfried: Katapausis. 1970. *Vol. 11.*

– Der Vorhang vor dem Thron Gottes. 1972. *Vol. 14.*

– Der Christushymnus Philipper 2,6–11. 1976, ²1991. *Vol. 17.*

– Paulusstudien. 1989, ²1994. *Vol. 51.*

– Neutestamentliche Studien. 2000. *Vol. 132.*

– Paulusstudien II. 2002. *Vol. 143.*

– Exegetische Studien. 2008. *Vol. 223.*

– and *Hans-Christian Kammler:* Johannesstudien. 1996. *Vol. 88.*

Holloway, Paul A.: Coping with Prejudice. 2009. *Vol. 244.*

Holmberg, Bengt (Ed.): Exploring Early Christian Identity. 2008. *Vol. 226.*

– and *Mikael Winninge* (Ed.): Identity Formation in the New Testament. 2008. *Vol. 227.*

Holtz, Traugott: Geschichte und Theologie des Urchristentums. 1991. *Vol. 57.*

Hommel, Hildebrecht: Sebasmata. Vol. 1 1983. *Vol. 31.* Vol. 2 1984. *Vol. 32.*

Horbury, William: Herodian Judaism and New Testament Study. 2006. *Vol. 193.*

Horn, Friedrich Wilhelm and *Ruben Zimmermann* (Ed.): Jenseits von Indikativ und Imperativ. Vol. 1. 2009. *Vol. 238.*

Horst, Pieter W. van der: Jews and Christians in Their Graeco-Roman Context. 2006. *Vol. 196.*

Hvalvik, Reidar: The Struggle for Scripture and Covenant. 1996. *Vol. II/82.*

Jauhiainen, Marko: The Use of Zechariah in Revelation. 2005. *Vol. II/199.*

Jensen, Morten H.: Herod Antipas in Galilee. 2006. *Vol. II/215.*

Johns, Loren L.: The Lamb Christology of the Apocalypse of John. 2003. *Vol. II/167.*

Jossa, Giorgio: Jews or Christians? 2006. *Vol. 202.*

Joubert, Stephan: Paul as Benefactor. 2000. *Vol. II/124.*

Judge, E. A.: The First Christians in the Roman World. 2008. *Vol. 229.*

Jungbauer, Harry: „Ehre Vater und Mutter". 2002. *Vol. II/146.*

Kähler, Christoph: Jesu Gleichnisse als Poesie und Therapie. 1995. *Vol. 78.*

Kamlah, Ehrhard: Die Form der katalogischen Paränese im Neuen Testament. 1964. *Vol. 7.*

Kammler, Hans-Christian: Christologie und Eschatologie. 2000. *Vol. 126.*

– Kreuz und Weisheit. 2003. *Vol. 159.*

– see *Hofius, Otfried.*

Karakolis, Christos: see *Alexeev, Anatoly A.*

Karrer, Martin und *Wolfgang Kraus* (Ed.): Die Septuaginta – Texte, Kontexte, Lebenswelten. 2008. *Vol. 219.*

Kelhoffer, James A.: The Diet of John the Baptist. 2005. *Vol. 176.*

– Miracle and Mission. 1999. *Vol. II/112.*

Kelley, Nicole: Knowledge and Religious Authority in the Pseudo-Clementines. 2006. *Vol. II/213.*

Kennedy, Joel: The Recapitulation of Israel. 2008. *Vol. II/257.*

Kieffer, René and *Jan Bergman* (Ed.): La Main de Dieu / Die Hand Gottes. 1997. *Vol. 94.*

Kierspel, Lars: The Jews and the World in the Fourth Gospel. 2006. *Vol. 220.*

Kim, Seyoon: The Origin of Paul's Gospel. 1981, ²1984. *Vol. II/4.*

– Paul and the New Perspective. 2002. *Vol. 140.*

– "The 'Son of Man'" as the Son of God. 1983. *Vol. 30.*

Klauck, Hans-Josef: Religion und Gesellschaft im frühen Christentum. 2003. *Vol. 152.*

Klein, Hans: see *Dunn, James D.G.*

Kleinknecht, Karl Th.: Der leidende Gerechtfertigte. 1984, ²1988. *Vol. II/13.*

Klinghardt, Matthias: Gesetz und Volk Gottes. 1988. *Vol. II/32.*

Kloppenborg, John S.: The Tenants in the Vineyard. 2006. *Vol. 195.*

Koch, Michael: Drachenkampf und Sonnenfrau. 2004. *Vol. II/184.*

Koch, Stefan: Rechtliche Regelung von Konflikten im frühen Christentum. 2004. *Vol. II/174.*

Köhler, Wolf-Dietrich: Rezeption des Matthäusevangeliums in der Zeit vor Irenäus. 1987. *Vol. II/24.*

Köhn, Andreas: Der Neutestamentler Ernst Lohmeyer. 2004. *Vol. II/180.*

Koester, Craig and *Reimund Bieringer* (Ed.): The Resurrection of Jesus in the Gospel of John. 2008. *Vol. 222.*

Konradt, Matthias: Israel, Kirche und die Völker im Matthäusevangelium. 2007. *Vol. 215.*

Kooten, George H. van: Cosmic Christology in Paul and the Pauline School. 2003. *Vol. II/171.*

– Paul's Anthropology in Context. 2008. *Vol. 232.*

Korn, Manfred: Die Geschichte Jesu in veränderter Zeit. 1993. *Vol. II/51.*

Koskenniemi, Erkki: Apollonios von Tyana in der neutestamentlichen Exegese. 1994. *Vol. II/61.*

– The Old Testament Miracle-Workers in Early Judaism. 2005. *Vol. II/206.*

Kraus, Thomas J.: Sprache, Stil und historischer Ort des zweiten Petrusbriefes. 2001. *Vol. II/136.*

Kraus, Wolfgang: Das Volk Gottes. 1996. *Vol. 85.*

– see *Karrer, Martin.*

– see *Walter, Nikolaus.*

– and *Karl-Wilhelm Niebuhr* (Ed.): Frühjudentum und Neues Testament im Horizont Biblischer Theologie. 2003. *Vol. 162.*

Krauter, Stefan: Studien zu Röm 13,1-7. 2009. *Vol. 243.*

Kreplin, Matthias: Das Selbstverständnis Jesu. 2001. *Vol. II/141.*

Kuhn, Karl G.: Achtzehngebet und Vaterunser und der Reim. 1950. *Vol. 1.*

Kvalbein, Hans: see *Ådna, Jostein.*

Kwon, Yon-Gyong: Eschatology in Galatians. 2004. *Vol. II/183.*

Laansma, Jon: I Will Give You Rest. 1997. *Vol. II/98.*

Labahn, Michael: Offenbarung in Zeichen und Wort. 2000. *Vol. II/117.*

Lambers-Petry, Doris: see *Tomson, Peter J.*

Lange, Armin: see *Ego, Beate.*

Lampe, Peter: Die stadtrömischen Christen in den ersten beiden Jahrhunderten. 1987, ²1989. *Vol. II/18.*

Landmesser, Christof: Wahrheit als Grundbegriff neutestamentlicher Wissenschaft. 1999. *Vol. 113.*

– Jüngerberufung und Zuwendung zu Gott. 2000. *Vol. 133.*

Lau, Andrew: Manifest in Flesh. 1996. *Vol. II/86.*

Lawrence, Louise: An Ethnography of the Gospel of Matthew. 2003. *Vol. II/165.*

Lee, Aquila H.I.: From Messiah to Preexistent Son. 2005. *Vol. II/192.*

Lee, Pilchan: The New Jerusalem in the Book of Relevation. 2000. *Vol. II/129.*

Lee, Simon S.: Jesus' Transfiguration and the Believers' Transformation. 2009. *Vol. II/265.*

Lichtenberger, Hermann: Das Ich Adams und das Ich der Menschheit. 2004. *Vol. 164.*

– see *Avemarie, Friedrich.*

Lierman, John: The New Testament Moses. 2004. *Vol. II/173.*

– (Ed.): Challenging Perspectives on the Gospel of John. 2006. *Vol. II/219.*

Lieu, Samuel N.C.: Manichaeism in the Later Roman Empire and Medieval China. ²1992. *Vol. 63.*

Lindemann, Andreas: Die Evangelien und die Apostelgeschichte. 2009. *Vol. 241.*

Lindgård, Fredrik: Paul's Line of Thought in 2 Corinthians 4:16–5:10. 2004. *Vol. II/189.*

Loader, William R.G.: Jesus' Attitude Towards the Law. 1997. *Vol. II/97.*

Löhr, Gebhard: Verherrlichung Gottes durch Philosophie. 1997. *Vol. 97.*

Löhr, Hermut: Studien zum frühchristlichen und frühjüdischen Gebet. 2003. *Vol. 160.*

– see *Hengel, Martin.*

Löhr, Winrich Alfried: Basilides und seine Schule. 1995. *Vol. 83.*

Lorenzen, Stefanie: Das paulinische Eikon-Konzept. 2008. *Vol. II/250.*

Luomanen, Petri: Entering the Kingdom of Heaven. 1998. *Vol. II/101.*

Luz, Ulrich: see *Alexeev, Anatoly A.*

– see *Dunn, James D.G.*

Mackay, Ian D.: John's Raltionship with Mark. 2004. *Vol. II/182.*

Mackie, Scott D.: Eschatology and Exhortation in the Epistle to the Hebrews. 2006. *Vol. II/223.*

Magda, Ksenija: Paul's Territoriality and Mission Strategy. 2009. *Vol. II/266.*

Maier, Gerhard: Mensch und freier Wille. 1971. *Vol. 12.*

– Die Johannesoffenbarung und die Kirche. 1981. *Vol. 25.*

Markschies, Christoph: Valentinus Gnosticus? 1992. *Vol. 65.*

Marshall, Jonathan: Jesus, Patrons, and Benefactors. 2009. *Vol. II/259.*

Marshall, Peter: Enmity in Corinth: Social Conventions in Paul's Relations with the Corinthians. 1987. *Vol. II/23.*

Martin, Dale B.: see *Zangenberg, Jürgen.*

Mayer, Annemarie: Sprache der Einheit im Epheserbrief und in der Ökumene. 2002. *Vol. II/150.*

Mayordomo, Moisés: Argumentiert Paulus logisch? 2005. *Vol. 188.*

McDonough, Sean M.: YHWH at Patmos: Rev. 1:4 in its Hellenistic and Early Jewish Setting. 1999. *Vol. II/107.*

McDowell, Markus: Prayers of Jewish Women. 2006. *Vol. II/211.*

McGlynn, Moyna: Divine Judgement and Divine Benevolence in the Book of Wisdom. 2001. *Vol. II/139.*

Meade, David G.: Pseudonymity and Canon. 1986. *Vol. 39.*

Meadors, Edward P.: Jesus the Messianic Herald of Salvation. 1995. *Vol. II/72.*

Meißner, Stefan: Die Heimholung des Ketzers. 1996. *Vol. II/87.*

Mell, Ulrich: Die „anderen" Winzer. 1994. *Vol. 77.*

– see *Sänger, Dieter.*

Mengel, Berthold: Studien zum Philipperbrief. 1982. *Vol. II/8.*

Merkel, Helmut: Die Widersprüche zwischen den Evangelien. 1971. *Vol. 13.*

– see *Ego, Beate.*

Merklein, Helmut: Studien zu Jesus und Paulus. Vol. 1 1987. *Vol. 43.* – Vol. 2 1998. *Vol. 105.*

Metzdorf, Christina: Die Tempelaktion Jesu. 2003. *Vol. II/168.*

Metzler, Karin: Der griechische Begriff des Verzeihens. 1991. *Vol. II/44.*

Metzner, Rainer: Die Rezeption des Matthäusevangeliums im 1. Petrusbrief. 1995. *Vol. II/74.*

– Das Verständnis der Sünde im Johannesevangelium. 2000. *Vol. 122.*

Mihoc, Vasile: see *Dunn, James D.G..*

Mineshige, Kiyoshi: Besitzverzicht und Almosen bei Lukas. 2003. *Vol. II/163.*

Mittmann, Siegfried: see *Hengel, Martin.*

Mittmann-Richert, Ulrike: Magnifikat und Benediktus. 1996. *Vol. II/90.*

– Der Sühnetod des Gottesknechts. 2008. *Vol. 220.*

Miura, Yuzuru: David in Luke-Acts. 2007. *Vol. II/232.*

Mournet, Terence C.: Oral Tradition and Literary Dependency. 2005. *Vol. II/195.*

Mußner, Franz: Jesus von Nazareth im Umfeld Israels und der Urkirche. Ed. von M. Theobald. 1998. *Vol. 111.*

Mutschler, Bernhard: Das Corpus Johanneum bei Irenäus von Lyon. 2005. *Vol. 189.*

Nguyen, V. Henry T.: Christian Identity in Corinth. 2008. *Vol. II/243.*

Niebuhr, Karl-Wilhelm: Gesetz und Paränese. 1987. *Vol. II/28.*

– Heidenapostel aus Israel. 1992. *Vol. 62.*

– see *Deines, Roland*

– see *Dimitrov, Ivan Z.*

– see *Kraus, Wolfgang*

Nielsen, Anders E.: "Until it is Fullfilled". 2000. *Vol. II/126.*

Nielsen, Jesper Tang: Die kognitive Dimension des Kreuzes. 2009. *Vol. II/263.*

Nissen, Andreas: Gott und der Nächste im antiken Judentum. 1974. *Vol. 15.*

Noack, Christian: Gottesbewußtsein. 2000. *Vol. II/116.*

Noormann, Rolf: Irenäus als Paulusinterpret. 1994. *Vol. II/66.*

Novakovic, Lidija: Messiah, the Healer of the Sick. 2003. *Vol. II/170.*

Obermann, Andreas: Die christologische Erfüllung der Schrift im Johannesevangelium. 1996. *Vol. II/83.*

Öhler, Markus: Barnabas. 2003. *Vol. 156.*

– see *Becker, Michael.*

Okure, Teresa: The Johannine Approach to Mission. 1988. *Vol. II/31.*

Onuki, Takashi: Heil und Erlösung. 2004. *Vol. 165.*

Oropeza, B. J.: Paul and Apostasy. 2000. *Vol. II/115.*

Ostmeyer, Karl-Heinrich: Kommunikation mit Gott und Christus. 2006. *Vol. 197.*

– Taufe und Typos. 2000. *Vol. II/118.*

Paulsen, Henning: Studien zur Literatur und Geschichte des frühen Christentums. Ed. von Ute E. Eisen. 1997. *Vol. 99.*

Pao, David W.: Acts and the Isaianic New Exodus. 2000. *Vol. II/130.*

Park, Eung Chun: The Mission Discourse in Matthew's Interpretation. 1995. *Vol. II/81.*

Park, Joseph S.: Conceptions of Afterlife in Jewish Insriptions. 2000. *Vol. II/121.*

Pate, C. Marvin: The Reverse of the Curse. 2000. *Vol. II/114.*

Pearce, Sarah J.K.: The Land of the Body. 2007. *Vol. 208.*

Peres, Imre: Griechische Grabinschriften und neutestamentliche Eschatologie. 2003. *Vol. 157.*

Perry, Peter S.: The Rhetoric of Digressions. 2009. *Vol. II/268.*

Philip, Finny: The Origins of Pauline Pneumatology. 2005. *Vol. II/194.*

Philonenko, Marc (Ed.): Le Trône de Dieu. 1993. *Vol. 69.*

Pilhofer, Peter: Presbyteron Kreitton. 1990. *Vol. II/39.*

– Philippi. Vol. 1 1995. *Vol. 87.* – Vol. 2 2000. *Vol. 119.*

Siegert, Folker: Drei hellenistisch-jüdische Predigten. Teil I 1980. *Vol. 20* – Teil II 1992. *Vol. 61.*
– Nag-Hammadi-Register. 1982. *Vol. 26.*
– Argumentation bei Paulus. 1985. *Vol. 34.*
– Philon von Alexandrien. 1988. *Vol. 46.*
Simon, Marcel: Le christianisme antique et son contexte religieux I/II. 1981. *Vol. 23.*
Smit, Peter-Ben: Fellowship and Food in the Kingdom. 2008. *Vol. II/234.*
Snodgrass, Klyne: The Parable of the Wicked Tenants. 1983. *Vol. 27.*
Söding, Thomas: Das Wort vom Kreuz. 1997. *Vol. 93.*
– see *Thüsing, Wilhelm.*
Sommer, Urs: Die Passionsgeschichte des Markusevangeliums. 1993. *Vol. II/58.*
Sorensen, Eric: Possession and Exorcism in the New Testament and Early Christianity. 2002. *Vol. II/157.*
Souček, Josef B.: see *Pokorný, Petr.*
Southall, David J.: Rediscovering Righteousness in Romans. 2008. *Vol. 240.*
Spangenberg, Volker: Herrlichkeit des Neuen Bundes. 1993. *Vol. II/55.*
Spanje, T.E. van: Inconsistency in Paul? 1999. *Vol. II/110.*
Speyer, Wolfgang: Frühes Christentum im antiken Strahlungsfeld. Vol. I: 1989. *Vol. 50.*
– Vol. II: 1999. *Vol. 116.*
– Vol. III: 2007. *Vol. 213.*
Spittler, Janet E.: Animals in the Apocryphal Acts of the Apostles. 2008. *Vol. II/247.*
Sprinkle, Preston: Law and Life. 2008. *Vol. II/241.*
Stadelmann, Helge: Ben Sira als Schriftgelehrter. 1980. *Vol. II/6.*
Stein, Hans Joachim: Frühchristliche Mahlfeiern. 2008. *Vol. II/255.*
Stenschke, Christoph W.: Luke's Portrait of Gentiles Prior to Their Coming to Faith. *Vol. II/108.*
Sterck-Degueldre, Jean-Pierre: Eine Frau namens Lydia. 2004. *Vol. II/176.*
Stettler, Christian: Der Kolosserhymnus. 2000. *Vol. II/131.*
Stettler, Hanna: Die Christologie der Pastoralbriefe. 1998. *Vol. II/105.*
Stökl Ben Ezra, Daniel: The Impact of Yom Kippur on Early Christianity. 2003. *Vol. 163.*
Strobel, August: Die Stunde der Wahrheit. 1980. *Vol. 21.*
Stroumsa, Guy G.: Barbarian Philosophy. 1999. *Vol. 112.*
Stuckenbruck, Loren T.: Angel Veneration and Christology. 1995. *Vol. II/70.*

–, *Stephen C. Barton* and *Benjamin G. Wold* (Ed.): Memory in the Bible and Antiquity. 2007. *Vol. 212.*
Stuhlmacher, Peter (Ed.): Das Evangelium und die Evangelien. 1983. *Vol. 28.*
– Biblische Theologie und Evangelium. 2002. *Vol. 146.*
Sung, Chong-Hyon: Vergebung der Sünden. 1993. *Vol. II/57.*
Tajra, Harry W.: The Trial of St. Paul. 1989. *Vol. II/35.*
– The Martyrdom of St.Paul. 1994. *Vol. II/67.*
Tellbe, Mikael: Christ-Believers in Ephesus. 2009. *Vol. 242.*
Theißen, Gerd: Studien zur Soziologie des Urchristentums. 1979, ³1989. *Vol. 19.*
Theobald, Michael: Studien zum Römerbrief. 2001. *Vol. 136.*
Theobald, Michael: see *Mußner, Franz.*
Thornton, Claus-Jürgen: Der Zeuge des Zeugen. 1991. *Vol. 56.*
Thüsing, Wilhelm: Studien zur neutestamentlichen Theologie. Ed. von Thomas Söding. 1995. *Vol. 82.*
Thurén, Lauri: Derhethorizing Paul. 2000. *Vol. 124.*
Thyen, Hartwig: Studien zum Corpus Iohanneum. 2007. *Vol. 214.*
Tibbs, Clint: Religious Experience of the Pneuma. 2007. *Vol. II/230.*
Toit, David S. du: Theios Anthropos. 1997. *Vol. II/91.*
Tolmie, D. Francois: Persuading the Galatians. 2005. *Vol. II/190.*
Tomson, Peter J. and *Doris Lambers-Petry* (Ed.): The Image of the Judaeo-Christians in Ancient Jewish and Christian Literature. 2003. *Vol. 158.*
Toney, Carl N.: Paul's Inclusive Ethic. 2008. *Vol. II/252.*
Trebilco, Paul: The Early Christians in Ephesus from Paul to Ignatius. 2004. *Vol. 166.*
Treloar, Geoffrey R.: Lightfoot the Historian. 1998. *Vol. II/103.*
Tsuji, Manabu: Glaube zwischen Vollkommenheit und Verweltlichung. 1997. *Vol. II/93.*
Twelftree, Graham H.: Jesus the Exorcist. 1993. *Vol. II/54.*
Ulrichs, Karl Friedrich: Christusglaube. 2007. *Vol. II/227.*
Urban, Christina: Das Menschenbild nach dem Johannesevangelium. 2001. *Vol. II/137.*
Vahrenhorst, Martin: Kultische Sprache in den Paulusbriefen. 2008. *Vol. 230.*
Vegge, Ivar: 2 Corinthians – a Letter about Reconciliation. 2008. *Vol. II/239.*
Visotzky, Burton L.: Fathers of the World. 1995. *Vol. 80.*

Vollenweider, Samuel: Horizonte neutestament-
licher Christologie. 2002. *Vol. 144.*
Vos, Johan S.: Die Kunst der Argumentation bei
Paulus. 2002. *Vol. 149.*
Waaler, Erik: The *Shema* and The First Com-
mandment in First Corinthians. 2008.
Vol. II/253.
Wagener, Ulrike: Die Ordnung des „Hauses
Gottes". 1994. *Vol. II/65.*
Wahlen, Clinton: Jesus and the Impurity of
Spirits in the Synoptic Gospels. 2004.
Vol. II/185.
Walker, Donald D.: Paul's Offer of Leniency (2
Cor 10:1). 2002. *Vol. II/152.*
Walter, Nikolaus: Praeparatio Evangelica. Ed.
von Wolfgang Kraus und Florian Wilk.
1997. *Vol. 98.*
Wander, Bernd: Gottesfürchtige und Sympathi-
santen. 1998. *Vol. 104.*
Wasserman, Emma: The Death of the Soul in
Romans 7. 2008. *Vol. 256.*
Waters, Guy: The End of Deuteronomy in the
Epistles of Paul. 2006. *Vol. 221.*
Watt, Jan G. van der: see *Frey, Jörg*
Watts, Rikki: Isaiah's New Exodus and Mark.
1997. *Vol. II/88.*
Wedderburn, A.J.M.: Baptism and Resurrection.
1987. *Vol. 44.*
Wegner, Uwe: Der Hauptmann von Kafarnaum.
1985. *Vol. II/14.*
Weiß, Hans-Friedrich: Frühes Christentum und
Gnosis. 2008. *Vol. 225.*
Weissenrieder, Annette: Images of Illness in the
Gospel of Luke. 2003. Vol. II/164.
–, Friederike Wendt and *Petra von Gemünden*
(Ed.): Picturing the New Testament. 2005.
Vol. II/193.
Welck, Christian: Erzählte ‚Zeichen'. 1994.
Vol. II/69.
Wendt, Friederike (Ed.): see *Weissenrieder,
Annette.*
Wiarda, Timothy: Peter in the Gospels. 2000.
Vol. II/127.
Wifstrand, Albert: Epochs and Styles. 2005.
Vol. 179.
Wilk, Florian: see *Walter, Nikolaus.*
Williams, Catrin H.: I am He. 2000. *Vol. II/113.*

Wilson, Todd A.: The Curse of the Law and the
Crisis in Galatia. 2007. *Vol. II/225.*
Wilson, Walter T.: Love without Pretense. 1991.
Vol. II/46.
Winn, Adam: The Purpose of Mark's Gospel.
2008. *Vol. II/245.*
Winninge, Mikael: see *Holmberg, Bengt.*
Wischmeyer, Oda: Von Ben Sira zu Paulus.
2004. *Vol. 173.*
Wisdom, Jeffrey: Blessing for the Nations and
the Curse of the Law. 2001. *Vol. II/133.*
Witmer, Stephen E.: Divine Instruction in Early
Christianity. 2008. *Vol. II/246.*
Wold, Benjamin G.: Women, Men, and Angels.
2005. *Vol. II/2001.*
Wolter, Michael: Theologie und Ethos im frühen
Christentum. 2009. *Vol. 236.*
– see *Stuckenbruck, Loren T.*
Wright, Archie T.: The Origin of Evil Spirits.
2005. *Vol. II/198.*
Wucherpfennig, Ansgar: Heracleon Philologus.
2002. *Vol. 142.*
Yates, John W.: The Spirit and Creation in Paul.
2008. *Vol. II/251.*
Yeung, Maureen: Faith in Jesus and Paul. 2002.
Vol. II/147.
Zangenberg, Jürgen, Harold W. Attridge and
Dale B. Martin (Ed.): Religion, Ethnicity
and Identity in Ancient Galilee. 2007.
Vol. 210.
Zimmermann, Alfred E.: Die urchristlichen Leh-
rer. 1984, ²1988. *Vol. II/12.*
Zimmermann, Johannes: Messianische Texte
aus Qumran. 1998. *Vol. II/104.*
Zimmermann, Ruben: Christologie der Bilder
im Johannesevangelium. 2004. *Vol. 171.*
– Geschlechtermetaphorik und Gottesverhält-
nis. 2001. *Vol. II/122.*
– (Ed.): Hermeneutik der Gleichnisse Jesu.
2008. *Vol. 231.*
– see *Frey, Jörg.*
– see *Horn, Friedrich Wilhelm.*
Zugmann, Michael: „Hellenisten" in der Apostelgeschichte. 2009. *Vol. II/264.*
Zumstein, Jean: see *Dettwiler, Andreas*
Zwiep, Arie W.: Judas and the Choice of Matthias. 2004. *Vol. II/187.*

For a complete catalogue please write to the publisher
Mohr Siebeck • P.O. Box 2030 • D–72010 Tübingen/Germany
Up-to-date information on the internet at www.mohr.de